PLATO'S MORAL REALISM

Plato's moral realism rests on the Idea of the Good, the unhypothetical first principle of all. It is this, as Plato says, that makes just things useful and beneficial. That Plato makes the first principle of all the Idea of the Good sets his approach apart from that of virtually every other philosopher. This fact has been occluded by later Christian Platonists, who tried to identify the Good with the God of scripture. But for Plato, theology, though important, is subordinate to metaphysics. For this reason, ethics is independent of theology and attached to metaphysics. This book challenges many contemporary accounts of Plato's ethics that start with the so-called Socratic paradoxes and attempt to construct a psychology of action or moral psychology that makes these paradoxes defensible. Rather, Lloyd P. Gerson argues that Plato at least never thought that moral realism was defensible outside of a metaphysical framework.

LLOYD P. GERSON is Professor of Philosophy at the University of Toronto. He is the author and co-author of 25 books on ancient philosophy, including monographs, edited volumes, and translations, and has published around 250 articles and reviews.

PLATO'S MORAL REALISM

LLOYD P. GERSON
University of Toronto

Shaftesbury Road, Cambridge CB2 8EA, United Kingdom

One Liberty Plaza, 20th Floor, New York, NY 10006, USA

477 Williamstown Road, Port Melbourne, VIC 3207, Australia

314–321, 3rd Floor, Plot 3, Splendor Forum, Jasola District Centre, New Delhi – 110025, India

103 Penang Road, #05–06/07, Visioncrest Commercial, Singapore 238467

Cambridge University Press is part of Cambridge University Press & Assessment, a department of the University of Cambridge.

We share the University's mission to contribute to society through the pursuit of education, learning and research at the highest international levels of excellence.

www.cambridge.org
Information on this title: www.cambridge.org/9781009329941

DOI: 10.1017/9781009329934

© Lloyd P. Gerson 2023

This publication is in copyright. Subject to statutory exception and to the provisions of relevant collective licensing agreements, no reproduction of any part may take place without the written permission of Cambridge University Press & Assessment.

First published 2023
First paperback edition 2025

A catalogue record for this publication is available from the British Library

Library of Congress Cataloging-in-Publication data
NAMES: Gerson, Lloyd P., author.
TITLE: Plato's moral realism / Lloyd P. Gerson, University of Toronto.
OTHER TITLES: Moral realism
DESCRIPTION: Cambridge, United Kingdom ; New York, NY, USA : Cambridge University Press, 2023. | Includes bibliographical references and index.
IDENTIFIERS: LCCN 2022056959 | ISBN 9781009329989 (Hardback) | ISBN 9781009329941 (Paperback) | ISBN 9781009329934 (ebook)
SUBJECTS: LCSH: Moral realism. | Ethics. | Metaphysics. | Plato – Ethics.
CLASSIFICATION: LCC BJ1500.M67 G47 2023 | DDC 171/.2–dc23/eng/20230307
LC record available at https://lccn.loc.gov/2022056959

ISBN 978-1-009-32998-9 Hardback
ISBN 978-1-009-32994-1 Paperback

Cambridge University Press & Assessment has no responsibility for the persistence or accuracy of URLs for external or third-party internet websites referred to in this publication and does not guarantee that any content on such websites is, or will remain, accurate or appropriate.

To
Eli
James
Vivian
Amelia
Colette
Léon

Contents

Acknowledgments		*page* viii
1	Introduction: Platonism and Moral Realism	1
2	The Idea of the Good	29
3	Virtue, Knowledge, and the Good	75
4	Socratic versus Platonic Ethics?	116
5	Moral Responsibility	147
6	*Philebus* and *Statesman*	171
7	Morality, Religion, and Politics	190
8	Concluding Remarks	223
Bibliography		228
Index Locorum		250
General Index		260

Acknowledgments

This book was written mainly during the time of the worldwide pandemic, which made travel difficult or impossible. Inevitably, the airing of research results that I would normally aim for in lectures and in conference appearances was curtailed. Nevertheless, it is a pleasure for me to thank colleagues and friends who have, sometimes under trying circumstances, cheerfully offered advice on and criticism of earlier drafts of this book. In particular, I would like to thank Hugh Benson, Justin Broakes, Rafael Ferber, and Melissa Lane, who read portions of the book and made many astute comments and suggestions. I do not think for a moment that any of these scholars would agree with much of what I have written, but I would like to believe that as a result of reading my work they are at least slightly more inclined to see Plato's ethics in a systematic light. I want to single out Anthony Price, who read the entire manuscript with a critical, though sympathetic eye, and who saved me from many errors. Probably, Anthony will mildly regret not having been able to save me from many more. I would also like to thank two anonymous readers for Cambridge University Press, who made helpful suggestions both structural and substantive. Most readers of this book will know how time-consuming such work can be when done properly. This work was completed with the generous assistance of the Social Sciences and Humanities Research Council of Canada (SSHRC). The indexes were expertly prepared by Rachel O'Keefe.

CHAPTER I

Introduction
Platonism and Moral Realism

1.1 The Metaphysical Foundation of Ethics

Plato tells us in *Republic* that the Idea of the Good is the "unhypothetical first principle of all."[1] He also says that it is the Good that makes just things and other useful things actually become useful (χρήσιμα) or beneficial (ὠφέλιμα).[2] Further, he says that the knowledge of this Good is the means to human happiness and the explanation (αἰτία) for everything right and beautiful (ὀρθῶν τε καὶ καλῶν).[3] Finally, he says that no one can act wisely (ἐμφρόνως), either in private or in public, without seeing the Good.[4] It seems reasonable to suggest that an innocent or unbiased perusal of these

---

[1] See *Rep.* 6.510B6–7, 511B5–6; 7.533C8–D4, 534B8–10. See my 2020, 120–127, for a fuller discussion of the "unhypothetical first principle of all" and why it is most plausibly identified with the Idea of the Good. See 122, n. 11, for some discussion of the relatively rare view of some scholars that this is not the case. Most recently, Broadie 2021, 34–39, has added her voice to those who identify the two. The words ἀνυπόθετον ("unhypothetical") and ἀρχή ("first principle") have both an ontological and an epistemological connotation. Within a scientific explanatory framework, where explanations for various phenomena are "hypothesized," to reach an unhypothetical first principle is to achieve explanatory adequacy. As I shall argue below, for Plato the denial of such an explanatory stopping-point amounts to the denial of the possibility of genuine explanation altogether. The Good for Plato is not philosophical filigree. What is most noteworthy and perhaps surprising is that for Plato the terminus of scientific explanation is a patently axiological principle. That is, for Plato normativity is not an excrescence on the scientific enterprise but an integral part of it.

[2] *Rep.* 6.505A2–4, 7.517C1, echoing 2.379B11. At the end of Bk. 1, 354A–B, Socrates bullies Thrasymachus into accepting his claim that a just person is happy and an unjust unhappy. He adds that being unjust is therefore never more profitable (λυσιτελέστερον) than being just. Socrates concludes that since he does not know what justice is, he is actually in no position to know its properties, including whether being just is more or less beneficial than being unjust. Clearly, after the definition of justice in Bk. 4, the Idea of the Good is introduced to answer the question about the profitability or usefulness of justice. Cf. *Alc.* I 113D1–8, where Alcibiades insists that the just and the beneficial are not identical; it is a real question whether or not something just benefits us. The conclusion of Socrates' argument, 116D3, that the just is beneficial depends on showing that just things are good and because they are good, they are beneficial. It seems that the Idea of the Good serves to provide the metaphysical foundation for Socrates' conclusion.

[3] *Rep.* 7.517C1. Cf. *Tht.* 186A9: καλὸν καὶ αἰσχρὸν καὶ ἀγαθὸν καὶ κακόν (noble and shameful and good and bad), a loose gathering of basic normative terms. Thanks to Justin Broakes for pointing out this passage.

[4] *Rep.* 7.517C3–4.

passages and many others should lead one to conclude that a study of Plato's ethics ought to try to take account of the Idea of the Good. Of course, "good" is a key term used in all accounts of Plato's ethics. But the Idea of the Good is manifestly more than a word or a concept; it is, as Plato says, both the starting-point of everything and the goal at which everything aims. And in calling it "the Idea of the Good," he is saying more than that there is a first principle of all, something too remote or unattainable to bother with when trying to understand how to live or how to interact with other human beings. Rather, in calling the first principle of all "the Idea of the Good," Plato seems clearly to be setting his ethics within a radically original metaphysical framework.

Anyone who finds this claim obvious should be astonished, or at least deeply puzzled, to discover that most contemporary scholarship on Plato's ethics studiously avoids any suggestion that Plato believes that there is a metaphysical foundation for his ethics.[5] This is a charge that is all too easy to substantiate, and I shall do so in the following pages. But for the moment, I simply want to point out the apparent discordance between the presence of a metaphysical principle found in *Republic* and named "the Idea of the Good" and an approach to Plato's ethics that eschews or ignores any appeal to metaphysics altogether.

There are at least three possible explanations for this discordance. First, Aristotle presents us with a perspicuous example of how ethics can be detached from metaphysics, namely, the distinction between practical and theoretical science.[6] The principles of the former are distinct from those of

---

[5] I shall here set aside the idiosyncratic view of Martin Heidegger to the effect that the Idea of the Good has nothing to do with Plato's ethics. See El Murr 2019, 30–31. Shorey 1903, 9–26, recognizes the importance of the Idea of the Good, but he thinks it has no *ontological importance* (my emphasis). It is, he says, 16, a "regulative conception," not "a practical possibility," evidently assuming that these are exclusive alternatives. Cf. Shorey 1895, 23; Trabattoni 2000; 2022, 86, n. 3. Davidson 1993, 192–193, thinks that "[in] the late dialogues, [Plato] found more and more reasons to be dissatisfied with his earlier doctrine about the forms, and no aspect of this dissatisfaction is more evident than the abandonment of any close connection between the forms and value." Davidson is followed by Rowe 2005 and many others. By contrast, Erler 2007, 430–431, in his magisterial survey of Plato's philosophy on Plato, takes it as obvious. Cooper 1999, 142–149, acknowledges the centrality of metaphysics in Plato's moral realism, and even its ultimately mathematical dimension. In his relatively brief remarks, however, he makes several claims that cannot, I think, be substantiated in the text. He says, 143, that the Good is a good thing, and, 145, that "a just person is a devotee of *the* Good, not *his own* good; and these are very different things." As we shall see, the Good cannot be a good thing and it is essential to Plato's moral realism that *the* Good and *one's own* good are identical.

[6] The idea that Aristotle's ethics can be detached from his metaphysics has been disputed by, among others, Höffe 1996; Horn 2016; Baker 2017; Herzberg 2017. Herzberg argues that Aristotle's ethics is rooted in metaphysics in the sense that the life of the Unmoved Mover is the primary analogate of the meaning of "good." See for example, Aristotle, *Meta.* Λ 7, 1072a27–b3. Even if this is true, Aristotle

1.1 The Metaphysical Foundation of Ethics

the latter, even if the latter science in some sense embraces the former owing to its complete generality. It is no doubt tempting to retroject Aristotle's definitional clarity into an account of Plato's ethics, particularly if Plato's metaphysics is thought to be obscure or bizarrely implausible.[7]

This explanation leads us to the second. How in the world can a superordinate Good, that which is "beyond essence (ἐπέκεινα τῆς οὐσίας),"[8] have any relevance whatsoever to the existential dilemmas and urgent real-life problems that we find so marvelously canvassed in, say, *Gorgias* and *Protagoras* and, indeed, even in *Republic* itself?[9] Is it not precisely because the Idea of the Good is not or does not itself have an essence that it is irrelevant to answering the deep personal questions that Socrates and his interlocutors are habitually wrestling with? So, the second explanation for the absence of attention to the Idea of the Good in studies of Plato's ethics is found in the difficulty – many would say impossibility – of integrating the Idea of the Good into an account of Plato's ethics, including or even especially what he has to say about what is good (and bad or evil) in human life and human action.[10]

A third reason for the diffidence of most scholars to Plato's metaphysics when discussing his ethics rests upon an assumption that the core of Plato's ethics is, in fact, Socratic, and that Socratic ethics is rather clearly innocent of all metaphysical doctrine. Unquestionably, the work of Gregory Vlastos has had a major impact in this regard in the latter half of the twentieth century.[11] The followers of Vlastos are divided according to whether they

---

has at the same time laid out a schema for the independence of ethical science, a schema embraced by those who disdain metaphysics altogether in trying to formulate or defend what has become known as "virtue ethics." In fact, for Aristotle, if the Unmoved Mover did not exist, metaphysics would not be possible even though practical science would presumably continue to be possible. Kant, for example, presents us with another way to detach moral absoluteness from metaphysics. See for example, Korsgaard 1983.

[7] It is possible that the division of philosophy into three (ethics, logic, and physics) by Xenocrates, the "head" of the Academy after Speusippus, has some role to play here, too. See Dillon 2003, 136–150. Cicero, *Acad.* I 19, and Sextus Empiricus, *M.* VII 16, apparently rely on this division, which is employed by Alcinous, *Didaskalikos*, and others. Note that in Xenocrates' division, only logic could conceivably attain to the universality that Plato seeks in his foundation for ethics.

[8] See *Rep.* 6.509B9–10.

[9] Along these lines, many antimoral realists have argued that it is only possible to justify morality from *inside* morality. See for example, Hayward 2019. The initial plausibility of this view indicates why we should pay careful attention to Plato's assumption that metaphysics and axiology must converge in an absolutely first principle of all that is the Good itself. See Annas 1997, 147, "Plato holds not only that facts and values are not radically different kinds of thing, known in different ways, but that values are fundamental to explaining facts."

[10] Penner 2007a indirectly makes this point by his (in my view) unsupportable reduction of the superordinate Good to the "Form of Advantage," that is, to personal happiness.

[11] See Vlastos esp. 1973; 1991; 1994.

see Plato as adding nothing worthwhile to Socratic ethics and those who see him as adding quite a bit, but nothing of a metaphysical import.[12] My own view is diametrically opposed to that of Vlastos and others. There is no distinctive Socratic philosophy in the dialogues and Plato's metaphysics underlies everything he says about ethics even in the so-called early dialogues.[13] In the fourth chapter, I shall present the case for rejecting any meaningful distinction between "Socratic" ethics and Platonic ethics and for maintaining that the identical metaphysical principles underlie both.

My aim in the present work is to try to situate Plato's ethics firmly within the metaphysical framework seemingly demanded by the text. But as I shall also try to show, there are multiple indications in the text that the Idea of the Good is not, as it were, an utterly contentless or merely formal principle of normativity.[14] There is, in fact, quite a lot that can be said about the Good that illuminates and supports the ethical claims made in the dialogues. Indeed, without the integration of the first principle of all into the ethics, the claims that are made in the dialogues are, as I shall argue, plainly unsupportable. That is, they amount to nothing more than rhetoric, prejudice, and pious hope. Plato believes that these claims are supportable because he never considered ethics as autonomous. This is in sharp contrast to most modern scholars, who take these claims to be possibly supportable *only* if they are autonomous, that is, detached from metaphysics. I shall not here contend that a deracinated Platonic ethics has no attractions. Obviously, what has come to be called by some Plato scholars "prudentialism" is not a crazy position to defend.[15] Old saws like

---

[12] Former: Penner, Rowe, Brickhouse and Smith, Rudebusch, Benson. Latter: Irwin 2007; Trabbatoni 2020.

[13] See Rist 2012; Gerson 2014a; 2020.

[14] See Cross and Woozley 1964, 260, who say about the Idea of the Good, "it is very difficult indeed to form any clear idea of what was in Plato's mind." See Eklund 2017, ch. 6, who argues that normative concepts describe properties that are themselves not normative. Therefore, there is no normativity in the world, only in our thoughts and concepts. Plato's firm rejection of this view is an application of his general argument in *Parm*. 132B3–C11 against the claim that Forms are concepts. Normativity is rooted in the Idea of the Good, just as the concept of circularity is rooted in the Form of Circularity.

[15] Penner 2007a calls it "pure prudentialism." By this he means that there is no moral dimension to this theory. See also 2005, 186, where he calls it "psychological egoism." White 1985 calls it "rational prudence." Irwin 1995, 53, calls it "eudaimonism." He defines it thus: "(1) In all our rational actions we pursue our own happiness. (2) We pursue happiness only for its own sake, never for the sake of anything else. (3) Whatever else we rationally pursue, we pursue it for the sake of happiness." Also, Stemmer 1988, 554; Taylor 1998, 50; Annas 1999, ch. 2; Berman 2003; Annas 2015; Timmermann 2019, 140. Shorey 1895, 213–214, firmly rejects prudentialism, arguing that Plato thought that there was a necessary connection between virtue and happiness. But Shorey is committed to the view that there is no ontological foundation for this, certainly not the Idea of the Good. Sidgwick 1907 [1874],

"always keep your promises," "better safe than sorry," "look before you leap," "virtue is its own reward," and "waste not, want not" are old saws for a perfectly understandable reason. They are sound guides to action, especially for those who need practical heuristics. But the prudentialism that generates these saws could never attain to the exceptionless or unconditional universality of ethics as articulated by Plato. For Plato, just as there is a metaphysical basis for the exceptionless universality of mathematics, so, too, is there one for ethics.[16]

Although I shall be contrasting my interpretation of Plato's ethics with many others throughout this book, it will perhaps be useful to explain upfront what I take to be the core idea that separates my account from others. Many interpreters and even proponents of Platonic ethics wish to stress the objectivity of Plato's ethical claims. This objectivity – contrasted with subjectivity – consists in the fact that a subject S is not an infallible judge of what is good for S. This is the case even if S's view of what is good for S is not irrelevant to whether it is or not. What is good for S is objective if and only if there is no necessary entailment from "S thinks that g is good for himself" to "g is good for him." I certainly do not wish to argue that Plato denies this.[17] After all, even S may, not infrequently, come to see that what he thought was good for himself is in fact not so. Of course, it should be added that if S comes to see this, it is still the case that "S thinks that g is good (or bad) for himself" does not entail that "g is good (or bad) for himself." Objectivity should not be touted as a bit of Platonic triumphalism. For objectivity is cheaply bought, just as cheaply bought as the doubtlessly justified assertion of objectivity in the determination of, say, physical health.[18]

Objectivity, however, may fall short of universality since what is objectively good for S may not be, for all we know, objectively good for R.[19]

---

has, it seems to me, had an enormous effect in the English-speaking world in his prudentialist reading of Plato.

[16] See Murdoch 1970, 29, 42, on Good as a "concrete universal" which captures the virtuality of the Good in relation to the entire array of Forms, as we shall see in the next chapter. See Burnyeat 2000, 19–22, who takes the metaphysical primacy of the Good as obvious and in need of no argument.

[17] See Vogt 2017, ch. 4, on "Measure Realism," an understanding of "good-for" that tries to accommodate the truth in Protagorean relativism. But Vogt holds that Measure Realism is primarily relative to the human species, not to any individual human being. In that, the question of universality remains open, for what might be good for one or many might at the same time be bad for someone else.

[18] Putnam 2005, 77–78, argues for ethics which contains "objectivity without ontology" or "objectivity without objects." It is not clear how his objectivity goes beyond relativism. Indeed, his "conceptual relativism" seems very much in line with his de facto ethical relativism.

[19] See Barney 2010b, 56, who glimpses the distinction between objectivity and universality when she concedes that the objectivity of the good does not defeat the self-seeking person. But universality requires the introduction of metaphysics, which Barney does not countenance.

A mere hope or assumption that objectivity can be elided with universality is, I maintain, the indefensible burden shared by all those who reject a metaphysical foundation for Plato's ethics. The pious belief that one can never profit from wrongdoing is logically available only to one who sees this as resting on that metaphysical foundation. Prudentialists, who draw the plausibility of their view from the unjustifiable elision of objectivity and universality, want to insist that the wicked can never prosper. They can never prosper even if they believe, wrongly, that they can do so. Plato surely believes this, too. What, though, makes the prudentialists so confident that this is in fact the case? As we shall see, the answer that is usually given is that it is something like a law of nature that there is no profit in wrongdoing. Laws of nature, however, as they pertain to changeable or mutable things, are not exceptionless. One could hardly suppose otherwise, given a Platonic account of the sensible world. It is, though, the mantra of the tyrant that *he* is the exception, perhaps the sole exception to, say, the laws of a decent society.[20] Even if he does run afoul of these laws, and even if he is punished according to these laws, he might well continue to maintain that the benefits he derived from his tyranny outweighed the subsequent risk of downfall. There may well be objectivity here, but there is no universality. We should not dismiss out of hand the defiant cry of the tyrant brought low that, despite everything, it was all worth it.

Universality requires that it is not possible that "g is good for S" if S having or doing g is bad for R.[21] This is, as we shall see, a very substantial

---

[20] See Nill 1985, ch. 3, who shows that Antiphon clearly recognized the practical limitations of prudentialism, since it does indeed sometimes occur that self-regarding behavior is harmful to oneself. In the 1956 novel, *The Last Hurrah*, by Edwin O'Connor, the corrupt politician Frank Skeffington is on his deathbed, lapsing into and out of unconsciousness. His parish priest, who has been called in to administer the last rites, says to the family, "I bet if he had it to do all over again, he would have lived a different life." Just then, Skeffington opens an eye and growls, "the hell I would." What does the "prudentialist" Socrates say to a Frank Skeffington?

[21] Prichard, in his now famous inaugural lecture in 1928, "Duty and Interest," argued that Platonic ethics does not actually rise to the level of morality because for Plato the Good is inseparable from one's own good. According to Prichard 2003 [1928], 26–27, Plato provides no argument for the view that morality can be independent of one's own interests and even counter to them. In effect, he denies that Plato can establish the universality of his ethical claims. As he goes on to say, 29, "We are therefore forced to allow that in order to maintain that for an action to be right [or good], it must be advantageous, we have to maintain that advantageousness is what renders an action right [or good]. But this is obviously something that no one is going to maintain if he considers it seriously." Prichard has no conception of how the Idea of the Good might provide the requisite universality nor, indeed, how one's own personal interest might coincide with the interests of everyone else. There is undoubtedly a political aspect underlying the contention that morality and self-interest often do conflict, even if they do not always conflict. I shall return to this in ch. 7. Mabbott 1971, indirectly replying to Prichard, argues that Plato is not a utilitarian, though it is not clear what Mabbott thinks is the correct interpretation of Plato's view. Annas 2008 rebuts the charge that virtue

requirement.²² For example, it appears to rule out any version of utilitarianism that allows that if g is good for S as well as being good for everyone else, with one exception, then g ought to be pursued. The Platonic principle cannot compromise universality as must perforce be done when one countenances actions that are "good for most if not for all" or "for the common good, with but a few 'minor' exceptions."

If we focus on exceptionless universality, we can see that Plato's moral theory does not comport with any form of utilitarianism which focuses on a net sum of good results (however conceived), allowing that the good of some might be sacrificed for the good of the whole. If the utilitarian abandons generality or "for-the-most-part" for true universality, then as I understand this position, he or she has abandoned utilitarianism. And if the universal value is just the good, then I fail to see how it differs from Plato's theory unless it can be shown that that theory can be maintained without a transcendent Good.

Of course, exceptionless universality still requires a nuanced understanding of "must" and "should." After all, the absolutist prohibition on wrongdoing expressed by Socrates in *Crito* is not an assertion of a physical impossibility. This prohibition, just like a positive law, is always accompanied by a sanction. So, "one must never do wrong" is elliptical for "one must never do wrong, and if one does wrong, then compensation must be paid to the one who suffered the wrong." It is a nice question – a metaphysical question, as a matter of fact – as to whether universality requires that the compensation not paid in this life will necessarily be paid in the next and if not, whether universality in ethics can still be defended.²³

One might raise the following objection. There is in fact a distinction without a difference between what is objectively good for A and an instance of the universal Good as it pertains to A. In that case, universality does not

---

ethics is egoistic. Insofar as Plato's ethics can be categorized as "virtue ethics," her rebuttal would apply to Plato.

²² Suppose that S's acting virtuously provokes R to act viciously. I owe this example to Anthony Price in personal correspondence. If this were possible, it would seem not to be the case that the good brought about by S is also good for R. I think Plato is committed to saying that it is not possible that the instantiation of a good by S could be both good and bad for R. So, R's acting viciously cannot possibly be caused by S acting virtuously, even if S's virtuous behavior may be said to be the occasion for R reacting viciously. If, say, A's heroic behavior makes B kill herself in shame and in despair of ever being able to duplicate such behavior, it is surely not A's fault. Nor would it change the fact that it is good for B that A behaves that way.

²³ The absoluteness of Plato's moral realism should be distinguished from a Kantian categorical imperative, since the latter, unlike the former, is consciously detached from personal interest. See Chapter 4, Section 4.4. Thus, rejection of a categorical imperative is not necessarily a rejection of Platonic absolutism. See Joyce 2001, 176–177, who takes the rejection of the cogency of a categorical imperative to imply the shipwreck of all moral discourse.

add anything to objectivity; in fact, universality can be reduced to mere generality. The correct reply to this objection is this. If an instance of the universal Good as it pertains to A is not distinct from what is objectively good for A, then it is possible that what is objectively good for A or B or C is radically equivocal. That is, what may be good for the tyrant may be not good for his victims and vice versa. Universality is required to ensure that this is not so. But since the Good does not have a defined nature, universality does not entail univocity in predication. The Good can be variously instantiated or manifested. But in each case, what is good is universally good. This could hardly be the case if the Good had a substantial nature. If it did, it would be child's play to generate counterexamples showing that participation in the substantive nature said to be good for A is in fact not good for B on this or another occasion.

For universality, a supernatural law is required, supernatural in the sense that this law is rooted in the immutable and eternal intelligible world.[24] It is my contention that Plato believes in universality, not merely objectivity, and that he sees clearly that universality requires a metaphysical foundation. That is what the superordinate Idea of the Good provides. It is the task of this book to show exactly how this works.

1.2 How Should We Classify Plato's Ethics?

The modern lack of interest in the metaphysical foundation of Plato's ethics is reflected in something like diffidence in classifying the type of ethical theory that Platonism proposes. Although one could make a case that there are elements of consequentialism and of deontology in Plato's ethics, neither of these categories even begins to get at the strongly metaphysical foundation. Most typically, surveys of Plato's ethics in collections on Plato or ancient ethics begin with the rather loosely defined so-called Socratic paradoxes and then go on to try to construct a moral psychology that makes these paradoxes plausible or defensible.[25]

---

[24] See Rist 2002, 28, "Plato's fundamental thesis is that there is a transcendental aspect to morality or morality is somehow man-made."

[25] See, for example, O'Brien 1967, 16, "The basic ethical doctrines of Plato ... are paradoxes." See also Kraut 1992, wherein the treatment of Plato's ethics is dispersed over four papers with the titles, "Socrates and the Early Dialogues," "Platonic Love," "The Defense of Justice in Plato's *Republic*," and "Disintegration and Restoration: Pleasure and Pain in Plato's *Philebus*." Taylor 1998, 76, understands Plato's ethics as an attempt to ground morality in "an adequate theory of human nature." Although Taylor, 67, does in passing mention the Idea of the Good, what he takes to be the objective foundation of morality for Plato is the coincidence of individual and *social* good. How this amazing coincidence occurs Taylor does not say. In Fine 2011, we do find a separate chapter on

1.2 *How Should We Classify Plato's Ethics?*

Sometimes, the vague term "intellectualism" is used to express what is taken to be a focus of the ethics, namely, that the attainment of virtue is somehow related to knowledge, although the metaphysical implications of the possibility of such knowledge are usually passed over in silence.[26] One gets the impression that the word "knowledge" in these accounts is taken to be unproblematic and to be more or less equivalent to the standard modern analysis of knowledge as justified true belief.

Clearly enough, we should begin by classifying Plato's ethics as a form of moral realism, generally the philosophical position that holds that normative or prescriptive propositions have real truth-makers in the world.[27]

Plato's ethics (Annas), set apart from a chapter on Socrates' ethics and moral psychology (Devereux). Annas' chapter does explicitly focus on Plato's "ethical theory," which she argues, 269, is "structured by a broad eudaimonistic assumption." Annas adds, "The main lines of Plato's ethics are thus best followed by doing the following: looking at his theoretical answer to the question about virtue and happiness, then examining the way he discusses virtue, and then exploring his positions on pleasure." Annas, 284, does conclude her chapter by briefly mentioning the "metaphysical background" of Plato's ethics. She says, "As with the political background, there is a sense in which [the metaphysics] does not make a profound difference to the ethical ideas that have already been developed in other contexts." In Bobonich 2017, Plato's ethics is parceled out in three chapters: "Virtue and Happiness in Plato (Devereux), "Plato's Ethical Psychology" (Kamtekar), and "Plato on Love and Friendship" (Sheffield). In Crisp 2013, White, 25, acknowledges the centrality of the concept of goodness in Plato's ethics, but he does not take there to be any metaphysical issues surrounding this concept. Rather, he takes Plato's moral theory generally to be an account of human psychology intended to support "Socratic" ethics. So, too, Warren 2017. In Hardy and Rudebusch 2014, the section on Plato contains seven papers, six of which focus on various features of "Socratic" ethics, while the one paper on Plato, although it mentions the Idea of the Good in passing, focuses on the structure of the Divided Line. Irwin 1977; 1995; 2007, follows the well-trodden path of ignoring the metaphysical foundations altogether. Among other puzzling omissions, Irwin makes no mention of the famous passage at *Tht.* 176B1–2 where Socrates exhorts his interlocutor to "assimilation to god (ὁμοίωσις θεῷ)." Throughout antiquity this exhortation was taken to be the principal emblem of Platonic ethics much as one might say that "the Golden Rule" is an emblem of Christian ethics. Socrates adds that the way this assimilation occurs is by becoming "just and pious with wisdom (δίκαιον καὶ ὅσιον μετὰ φρονήσεως)." As we shall see, the words "with wisdom" indicate the indispensable role of philosophy in Plato's ethics, where "philosophy" is explicitly rooted in knowledge of the unhypothetical first principle of all. Penner 2011 argues that the simple belief/desire psychology of action is the key to Socratic ethics as opposed to Platonic ethics. The Idea of the Good has no part to play in Socratic ethics and enters Platonic ethics only as a sort of excrescence on Socratic ethics. By way of contrast, see Boys-Stones 2014 for some illuminating observations on how the so-called Middle Platonists assumed the metaphysical foundation of Platonic ethics in their opposition to Stoicism.

[26] On the so-called Socratic intellectualism see O'Brien 1967, esp. ch. 3; Irwin 1977, 76–96; Penner, 1991; 1996; 1997; 2005, 175–186; Brickhouse and Smith 1994; 2000; 2010; Kahn 1996, 224–233; Nehemas 1999; Šegvić 2000; Rowe 2007; Evans 2010; Hardy 2014; Monteils-Laeng 2014, 29–38; Blackson 2015; Callard 2017; Butler 2019.

[27] The opposite of moral realism – moral antirealism – is conveniently divisible into (a) subjectivism or constructivism, holding that moral claims have meaning but no objective foundations; (b) non-cognitivism, which denies that claims in morality are either true or false or, alternatively, that there is no such thing as moral knowledge; and (c) moral error theory, which holds that claims in morality are uniformly false, though still containing some meaning, usually pragmatic in nature.

An informal list of the sorts of topics that the Platonic moral realist is concerned with is found, for example, in *Gorgias*:

> Is it the case that the orator is in the position with regard to what is just and unjust, shameful and noble, good and evil as he is with respect to what is healthy and the subjects of the other crafts?[28]

Broadly speaking, "just and unjust," "shameful and noble," "good and evil" are the terms that appear in the propositions that will belong to the fabric of Plato's moral realism. Also to be noted here is the assumption that because the propositions in which these terms appear do indeed have truth-makers in the world, it is plausible that there is a craft concerned with determining whether or not a give moral proposition is true or false, a craft that is analogous to that of healthcare. In this dialogue, Socrates goes on to show Gorgias that rhetoric is not that craft.

Graham Oddie developed a useful schema of grades of moral realism, ranging from weak to extremely strong according to the answers to five questions: (1) Does the moral theory claim propositional content? (2) Does the moral theory claim that objective presuppositions of the truth of propositions are met? (3) Does the moral theory claim that these objective presuppositions are mind-independent? (4) Does the moral theory claim that these are irreducible to nonmoral truths or facts? (5) Are the objective presuppositions causally networked?[29] The theory that answers all questions in the affirmative is called by Oddie "robust realism." Oddie's schema sharply distinguishes Plato's robust moral realism from other types of realism, especially naturalism and idealism, the first of which answers "no" to the question about irreducibility and the second of which answers "no" to the question about mind-independence. This schema, however, does not clearly distinguish Plato's theory from a theologically based type of moral realism according to which moral truths are equivalent, say, to divine commands or are reflective somehow of a personal God.[30] So, I am

---

[28] *Gorg.* 459C8–D3: ἆρα τυγχάνει περὶ τὸ δίκαιον καὶ τὸ ἄδικον καὶ τὸ αἰσχρὸν καὶ τὸ καλὸν καὶ ἀγαθὸν καὶ κακὸν οὕτως ἔχων ὁ ῥητορικὸς ὡς περὶ τὸ ὑγιεινὸν καὶ περὶ τὰ ἄλλα ὧν αἱ ἄλλαι τέχναι;.

[29] See Oddie 2005, 22ff. Timmermann 2019, 94–99, provides another similar sketch of forms of moral realism, contrasting these with various antirealist accounts. M. Smith 2004 classifies moral realism as either nonnaturalistic or naturalistic, and under the former heading, externalist or internalist, and under the latter heading, relativistic or nonrelativistic. Whether there can be a coherent naturalistic moral realism is a question that I address in the next section. A somewhat different taxonomy is provided by Railton 2003, 4–5.

[30] See, for example, Adams 1999; Rea 2006; Brenner 2018 for versions of such theories.

1.2 How Should We Classify Plato's Ethics?

content to classify Plato's theory as robust realism with the proviso that his realism be distinguished from moral theology.[31]

Plato's distinctive robust moral realism is the subject of this book. I doubt that any of those mentioned above who write on Plato's ethics would deny that, broadly speaking, Plato embraces robust moral realism.[32] Where the dispute lies, and what motivates this book, is my claim that the robust moral realism rests upon a systematic metaphysical basis.[33] I suppose that many will find the word "systematic" more chafing than the word "metaphysics," although as I have already briefly mentioned, there are some who find the use of the term for Platonic ethics pejorative, at least insofar as Platonic ethics is supposed to be continuous with Socratic ethics. Thus, if Plato introduced a metaphysical framework for Socratic ethics, so much the worse for Plato. My use of the term "systematic" is guided mainly by what Plato says about the unhypothetical first principle of all. The manifestly unifying or comprehensive role of such a principle is sufficient

---

[31] The exhortation to "assimilation to god" as in footnote 25 above does not, as we shall see, contradict this claim. The god to which we are bidden to assimilate does not prescribe or invent norms. Norms flow from the first principle of all which is superior to the gods. See Catana 2019, 153–157, who has a revealing discussion of how some eighteenth–century historians of philosophy opposed "Platonic virtue ethics." By this Catana is referring to the ideal of assimilation to god and the gradations of virtue in *Phaedo* and *Republic*. The opposition came from Protestant scholars who saw the Platonic account of virtue as antithetical to Christian doctrine. Usually the term "virtue ethics" is applied to Aristotle's work and not to Plato's. "Platonic virtue ethics," though definitely including both of the above features, is misleading if it suggests that virtue is a first principle for Plato, even a first normative principle. Chappell 2014, ch. 12, defends what he calls "Platonistic Virtue Ethics" (PVE) which is Aristotelian virtue ethics but for the addition of a Form of the Good. This view, which is inspired by Iris Murdoch, has much to recommend it, although I think that Chappell's concept of the Good is not quite Plato's. Chappell, 295, defines PVE thus: "Good agency in the truest and fullest sense presupposes the contemplation of the Form of the Good."

[32] I am conscious of Elizabeth Anscombe's remark 1958, 1, that the term "moral," so much used in modern philosophy, does not really fit as a descriptive term for Aristotle. I think that Anscombe's concern is very much to the point for Plato as well. Her remark is especially apt in reference to what we are used to calling "moral responsibility." See below Chapter 5, Section 5.1. Nevertheless, I use the term "moral" here and throughout the book, along with the synonymous term "ethical" to indicate primarily the adjective in "moral realism." That is, Plato is a realist about propositional claims in which a certain class of terms, including "good," "bad," "right," and "wrong," irreducibly appear. But since for Plato the ultimate truth-maker for these claims is a metaphysical principle, "morality" for him does not quite have the distinctive subject matter that Anscombe says is missing in Aristotle and, I add, is missing in Plato. See Stemmer 1988, 549, who makes the important point that the distinction between things that are instrumentally good and things that are "good in themselves" does not imply the existence of a moral good.

[33] See for example, Enoch 2011, 5, who argues vigorously for "robust" moral realism, disclaiming any interest in metaphysics. As I shall argue, this position, famously held by G. E. Moore, amounts to an untenable *tertium quid* between metaphysical realism and the reductionism of moral properties to natural properties.

to indicate a system.³⁴ We must add here that the unification is primarily explanatory. That is, the system must be adduced to provide adequate explanations for all phenomena – including especially moral phenomena. By "moral phenomena" I mean the appearance that actions and psychical states can be said to be good or bad, right or wrong, and so on, where these predicates are irreducible to "naturalistic" categories. It hardly seems necessary to justify the claim that Plato believes that the explanation for the truth of "x is F" where "F" indicates a moral predicate, is to be found in the intelligible world. This is the core of Plato's entire explanatory framework.³⁵ The contentious point is that the terminus is not a Form of Good co-ordinate with all the others, but rather a superordinate Idea of the Good which, as Aristotle tells us, Plato identified with the One.

It will perhaps be thought by some that the positing of an unhypothetical first principle of all is not sufficient to make Plato's philosophy systematic. There are two other texts from *Republic*, however, which serve to counter the force of this objection. First, Plato says that the Good, like the sun, is "overflowing (ἐπίρρυτον)."³⁶ Because the Good is "above essence," it does not flow in one direction rather than another or in one amount rather than another or up to some limit or other. It is eternally doing what it does, or rather, what it is, as that which exceeds everything else in power. Accordingly, there could be nothing that is not affected by the Good's overflowing. If, *per impossibile*, there were something that was impervious to the operation of the Good, then that would indicate a defect or limitation in the Good, an incapacity to "reach down" to that thing. Because the Good exceeds the limitations imposed by essence, it cannot in fact have any limitations. As we shall see, a crucial qualification of this

---

³⁴ See Theophrastus, *Meta.* 6b11–16: Πλάτων μὲν οὖν ἐν τῷ ἀνάγειν εἰς τὰς ἀρχὰς δόξειεν ἂν ἅπτεσθαι τῶν ἄλλων εἰς τὰς ἰδέας ἀνάπτων, ταύτας δ' εἰς τοὺς ἀριθμούς, ἐκ δὲ τούτων εἰς τὰς ἀρχάς, εἶτα κατὰ τὴν γένεσιν μέχρι τῶν εἰρημένων· οἱ δὲ τῶν ἀρχῶν μόνον (Plato, then, referring things to the principles, would seem to grasp things other than Ideas and connect them to the Ideas, and these with Numbers, and from these to the principles, then proceeding via generation down to the things mentioned. Others grasp the principles alone). Theophrastus could well have drawn this sketch of the Platonic system from *Republic* alone, though he no doubt had Aristotle's testimony as well.

³⁵ See my 2020, ch. 3. Sartre 1989, assumes that "the good" does not exist and therefore "everything is permitted." This is the starting-point for existentialism. Sartre, however, seems to assume that "the good" would just be God. He does not consider the Platonic alternative. Sedley 2019, 49–50, argues that *Timaeus* represents a comprehensive expression of Plato's systematic philosophy – "a global system" – variously represented piecemeal in earlier dialogues. He adds that this system has a "strong Pythagorean colouring," a fact whose relevance to the present work will be discussed below in Chapter 2, Section 2.5.

³⁶ See *Rep.* 6.508B6–7. Although the word ἐπίρρυτον is fairly rare, its meaning is not, I think, obscure. The Good is eternally active, it is unlimited in its activity, and that activity is the transmission of its own (unlimited) nature to whatever is apt for receiving it in any way.

1.2 How Should We Classify Plato's Ethics?

claim is that things participate in the Good only according to and to the extent that their own nature allows. It is not a limitation in the Good that it cannot, say, transmit the goodness of intellection to a plant. Thus, the heart of the system dynamically pervades the entire articulated and variegated system. The other text is central in Plato's entire philosophy, and we shall return to it several times,

> Is it not clear that while many people would choose things that appear to be just and beautiful, even if they were not, and would still act and seek to possess them and acquire beliefs on this basis, no one would think it sufficient to possess things that seem to be good; rather, that they seek things that are really good, and everyone disdains mere seeming in this case? – Indeed – Then, what every soul pursues and on account of which it does everything it divines to be something. But it is puzzled and it is not able to grasp sufficiently what it is nor attain the stable confidence in it that it has about other things, and because of this it misses out on what is beneficial in these other things.[37]

We have already seen that things are right and beautiful because of the Good. Everyone desires the Good which not only makes things really good but is also the cause of their being.[38] Presumably, its "overflowing" activity is constitutive of this causality. We should not reject out of hand the claim that that which is outside of time can have a causal relation to that which is in time. For Plato, eternity is intimately present to the world of becoming at every moment since the being of this world is continuously constituted by participation in the intelligible world. Eternity is not alien to the world of becoming; it is inextricable from its ever-changing compromised being.

The claim that all desire the real good rests upon several major assumptions. The first of these is that such a good exists.[39] Even one who denied

---

[37] *Rep.* 6.505D5–E5: οὐ φανερόν, ὡς δίκαια μὲν καὶ καλὰ πολλοὶ ἂν ἕλοιντο τὰ δοκοῦντα, κἂν <εἰ> μὴ εἴη, ὅμως ταῦτα πράττειν καὶ κεκτῆσθαι καὶ δοκεῖν, ἀγαθὰ δὲ οὐδενὶ ἔτι ἀρκεῖ τὰ δοκοῦντα κτᾶσθαι, ἀλλὰ τὰ ὄντα ζητοῦσιν, τὴν δὲ δόξαν ἐνταῦθα ἤδη πᾶς ἀτιμάζει; – Καὶ μάλα, ἔφη – Ὃ δὴ διώκει μὲν ἅπασα ψυχὴ καὶ τούτου ἕνεκα πάντα πράττει, ἀπομαντευομένη τι εἶναι, ἀποροῦσα δὲ καὶ οὐκ ἔχουσα λαβεῖν ἱκανῶς τί ποτ' ἐστὶν οὐδὲ πίστει χρήσασθαι μονίμῳ οἵᾳ καὶ περὶ τἆλλα, διὰ τοῦτο δὲ ἀποτυγχάνει καὶ τῶν ἄλλων εἴ τι ὄφελος ἦν ... Cf. *Phil.* 20D7–10.

[38] See *Rep.* 7.516C1–2: ἐκείνων ὧν σφεῖς ἑώρων τρόπον τινὰ πάντων αἴτιος (The Idea of the Good is in a certain sense the cause of all things that they [the philosopher and the prisoners in the cave] used to see).

[39] It is the Good (singular) that makes things good (plural). The locution εἶναί τι ("to be something") is always used by Plato to indicate something real or extra mental, certainly not as Shorey 1933, 230–231, and others suppose, a "regulative conception." That every soul – not only the souls of philosophers – "divines" the Good to be something is a strong indication of Plato's moral realism, not only of its metaphysical focus but also of its universal relevance. Thus, I think Barney 1998, 78, n. 5, is mistaken in saying, "Plato is far more concerned to establish moral elitism than moral realism." She overlooks this passage in claiming that Plato does not accept the consequence of the analogy of the Good and the sun, namely, that these are available to all. Nevertheless, it is right to insist that philosophers seek an intimacy with the Good that most people cannot hope to attain.

the reality of the Idea of the Good, or denied the reality of the intelligible world altogether and went on to argue that the real good is equivalent to any and all apparent goods, would be endorsing the real good as the goal of all. Second, Plato's claim about the nature of desire is set within the framework of an account or, better, analysis of human action. Insofar as action originates in desire of some sort, all action is then aimed at the real good even if it turns out that what appears to be the real good is in fact not so. As we shall see, it follows from this that even the incontinent or acratic, who acts counter to her belief that something is really good or bad, nevertheless acts to achieve the real good. How this is even possible is of course immensely complicated and contentious. But as we shall see, the real good will be an essential component of the explanation of the possibility. Third, since there is no entailment from the fact that something appears to be good to the conclusion that it is the real good, and given that we only want the latter, considerable effort will need to be expended by Plato into strategies for securely connecting the two. The strategies cannot fruitlessly focus on the collection of more and more affective and conative "data." That is why Plato's moral realism cannot but be intellectualist in *some* sense. How can we come to understand or know when what appears to be good is in fact so and when it is not? There does not seem to be a solution in adding more appearances.

The first principle is also the goal *because* it is first. But this is so only if the first principle is the Good, that is, only if axiology and ontology coincide at their apex.[40] Suppose that this is not the case, that axiology is dependent on ontology in some way. In that case, there would be no reason to suppose anything other than an "open" universe or linear progression in which the good for each thing is sought in separation from the first principle of all. This is apparently what Speusippus thought in dissenting from Plato.[41] Plato's view in *Republic* seems unambiguous. The first principle of all overflows in its goodness and therefore, all things, desiring

---

[40] See Leslie 1979, who calls this view "extreme axiarchism." In 2019, 70, he characterizes the first principle as "creative value." I take it that "creative value" is equivalent to the "overflowing" of the Good. Also Burnyeat 2000; Rescher 2010, ch. 3. Rowe 2005, by contrast, argues for "the abandonment [by Plato] of any close connection between the forms and value." So, too, indirectly, Enoch 2021, who defends moral realism by arguing for a distinction between metaphysical and normative or moral grounding.

[41] See Aristotle, *Meta.* Λ 7, 1072b30–34. It seems to me not unlikely that Plato's early Pythagorean inclinations led him to posit the One and the Indefinite Dyad as first principles even before he came to identify the One as the Good. The view of Speusippus may reflect a separation between One and Good that Plato once held. But this is speculation and does not pertain to my main thesis. See Krämer 2014, 241–270, for a detailed argument that the doctrine of principles was the core of Plato's philosophy from the earliest period of his writings.

their own good, desire it or perhaps more accurately, manifestations of it. There is certainly a nice systematic unity to this architecture. But why suppose that it is true? Why reject linearity in favor of circularity? I can only give the briefest of answers to this question here. Much of the rest of this book will be taken up with what I hope is a more extensive and penetrating response.

What connects the Good as beginning and the Good as end is the principle of integrative unity. This is most evident in *Republic*, where the best city and the best person are assumed to be integrated unities. The virtuous person "becomes one out of many."[42] But even before *Republic*, in dialogues such as *Protagoras* and *Gorgias*, Plato introduces the craft of measurement as a normative criterion. Things are good to the extent that they achieve proportionality according to kind, that is, an integrative unity. I use the word "integrative" to indicate the dynamic path between endowment and achievement represented by the Greek term φύσις. Achieving an integrative unity according to kind is achieving what one's nature is meant to achieve.[43] It may well have been the case that Plato, under Pythagorean influence, identified the first principle of all as the One and posited a co-ordinate Form of the Good along with other Forms to indicate what it was that all goals had in common. Whether it was at the instigation of Aristotle's arguments or those of other members of the Academy, Plato came to see both that "good" was not a univocal predicate and that, nevertheless, "good" had to be rooted in that which had a unique and universal superordinate status. The reason for this is that in seeking any good, where "good" named a genus of perfections, it was always open to raising the radically pertinent question: Is this good for me?

---

[42] See *Rep*. 4.443E1: ἕνα γενόμενον ἐκ πολλῶν; cf. 8.554D9-10; *Phdr*. 230A3-6. Also, *Tim*. 31B8–C4, 32B3–C4 on cosmological integrative unity. See especially 32A5–7, where the integration of the elements of the world's body is a dynamic process ("having become identical with each other [τὰ αὐτὰ γενόμενα ἀλλήλοις, i.e., being in the identical ratio to each other], they will all be one" [ἕν]). The opposite of integrative unity is "discord (στάσις)" whether among the parts of the soul or the parts of any natural whole. See for example, *Soph*. 228A4–B4. Also, "disharmony (διαφωνία)." See for example, *Lg*. 3.689A1–B4. The phrase "integrative unity" is meant to encapsulate the common meaning of a variety of terms used by Plato including (σύν)τάξις, κόσμος, ἁρμονία, and συμφωνία. Scholars who have written with exceptional insight about integrative unity are Hampton 1987; Miller 1990; Desjardins 2004, 18ff. See also the still-interesting Lodge 1928, 145–155, on integrative unity as a criterion of moral evaluation resting ultimately on the Idea of the Good. Lodge, however, 305–306, 476, identifies the Idea of the Good with "mind." This mind is presumably that of the Demiurge.

[43] Hall 1963, ch. X, focuses on what he calls the "differentiated unity of the soul," emphasizing the differentiation that pertains to the immortal or rational part of the soul. The differentiation refers to "the pleasures, desires, and other affections appropriate to the cognitive or rational faculty, and the division of that faculty into reason and opinion." I am more concerned in this book with the unity of the embodied soul, both as an endowment and as a potential achievement.

Suppose that Socrates' interlocutors agree that courage is a virtue and virtues are one type of good. Or suppose that these very same interlocutors insist that money or power or pleasure are goods, too.[44] In the first case, it is certainly reasonable to ask why becoming good by becoming courageous is good for me. In the second case, it is also reasonable for Socrates to ask whether these admitted goods are good for someone to have. In general, for anything that is a good, where "good" is an end or goal, it is always open to question whether it is good for one to have *that*.[45] But if all seek their real, not apparent, good, there can be no question of whether it is good to have that. So, many suppose that when Socrates gets his interlocutor to agree that virtue is good, then whether or not the interlocutor realizes it, he has lost. For he agrees that virtue is good and that he wants his good; therefore, he wants to be virtuous. But this conclusion is far too easily reached, and easily rebutted. For there are many goods, often competing goods, and virtue is just one of the competitors. If it turns out that virtue is destined to win every single competition, that will not be for any reason to which a prudentialist is privy. It will be because there is a superordinate Idea of the

---

[44] See the controversial passage *Ap.* 30B2–4: Οὐκ ἐκ χρημάτων ἀρετὴ γίγνεται, ἀλλ' ἐξ ἀρετῆς χρήματα καὶ τὰ ἄλλα ἀγαθὰ τοῖς ἀνθρώποις ἅπαντα καὶ ἰδίᾳ καὶ δημοσίᾳ ([Socrates proclaims:] it is not from material possessions that virtue comes to be, but from virtue all material possessions and other [goods] come to be good for human beings both in private and in public). One may, implausibly, take this passage to mean that if you are virtuous, then you will be rich. More likely, the passage means that if you are virtuous, then goods like money will be good *for* you. I take it that Plato here distinguishes between goods and what goods are good for or for whom they are goods, so to speak. On this interpretation, it makes sense to ask whether some good, that you may or may not possess, is good for you. Cf. *Protag.* 333D9–10, where it is asked if certain "goods (ἀγαθά)" are "beneficial (ὠφέλιμα)" for human beings. Also. *Gorg.* 452B1, C5, D3–4 on the use of τοῖς ἀνθρώποις ("for human beings") in this way. At C1–2, it is asked whether there is a greater good than wealth for human beings (picking up the τοῖς ἀνθρώποις of B1, and then made explicit at C5). In *Republic*, as we shall see, it is the Idea of the Good that makes virtue itself beneficial or useful; so, too, for other goods. The words "good for" are a simple gloss on "beneficial and useful." Also, see *Lg.* 1.631B–D, where the goods of health, beauty, strength, are deemed "human" goods over against the "divine" goods of virtue. But it is beside the point to make them conditional on other things or to grade them. For wisdom might at times direct the pursuit of the conditional over the unconditional or the "human" over the "divine." Even if something is the most important thing in life, that doesn't mean that other things are of zero importance or that they can never, under any circumstances, take precedence as the goal of an action. It is no small task for Plato to show that the good of life is absolutely to be subordinated to the good of justice. Socrates does not actually argue for this claim in *Crito*; he merely asserts it.

[45] A moral realist who is also a naturalist, such as Brink 1989, holds that "goodness" just refers to the human goods that are naturalistically grounded such as health, pleasure, and so on. It is not clear, however, how a survey of goods which excludes a Good over and above counts as *moral* realism. Health may well be a good, but why ought I to value it in another? Brink, 65–66, tries to bridge the gap between naturalism and morality by supposing that "values" are things discovered by us naturalistically. The "location" of these "naturalistic" values is obscure, to say the least. I take it that Brink does not suppose that they are found in the Platonic intelligible world at the apex of which is the Idea of the Good.

1.2 How Should We Classify Plato's Ethics?

Good and it is *that* that everyone desires to possess in some sense. And unlike any human good, including virtue, it is actually *incoherent* to ask whether it is good for me to pursue the Good.[46]

My hypothesis is that Plato identified the One, the first principle of all, with the Idea of the Good because the first principle, being a principle of integrative unity, was the Good that all sought. What Plato supposed he could show was that a virtuous person who does in fact become one out of many is in a position to understand that it is incoherent to ask why someone wants to become one or an integrated unity. This is because becoming one is achieving the Good, insofar as that is possible for anything that is not itself that Good. Thus, the One must be identical with the Good, the Good from which all things come and toward which all things aim.

The elevation of Good to superordinate status beyond that of generic predicate solidifies the universality of Good. Whether "good" as a predicate of "when" or "good" as a predicate of "how much" is univocally predicable or not, recognizing that something is thus good does not require one also to recognize the universality of "good." It may be claimed that this is true, but only for the apparent good; it is not true for the real good. That is, one cannot recognize that "x is good" is true without wanting to pursue it in comparison to an alternative that is not so recognized. But this claim relies upon a failure to distinguish what is in fact good from what appears to be good. Even one who pursues what is in fact good does so because it appears to him to be good. Whether the apparent good is really good is a metaphysical question, not a question that is answered introspectively. So, one who acknowledges that something appears to him to be a real good is still in a position to wonder if that supposedly real good should be pursued.[47] How could it be otherwise when the content of the putative real

---

[46] See Zhao 2020, who argues for what he calls "teleological moral realism," which has a strong affinity with the Platonic view, though Zhao says nothing about a superordinate Idea of the Good. Interestingly, Zhao, 660–661, does situate his view alongside Stoicism, Christianity, Confucian ethics, and Aristotle's ethics, without identifying it with these.

[47] Thus, in this way Platonic ethics is essentially externalist rather than internalist. That is, the mere recognition that something is good is not a sufficient "internal" motivation because this recognition could only be of what appears to one to be good. See Brink 1989, ch. 3. The prudentialist reading of Plato's ethics is, by contrast, internalist. All that is necessary for motivating someone to act is the knowledge that so acting is good for oneself. Externalism becomes internalized, as it were, when one identifies one's own good with the Good, that which all desire. See below Chapter 3, Section 3.1 regarding prudentialists' misleading use of the word "knowledge" in this regard. See Watson 2003, 177–181, on internalism versus externalism. The contrast is not, after all, so helpful in explicating Plato's doctrine, as I understand it, owing to the complexity of embodied agency. Our will (βούλησις) is permanently oriented to the Good, but multiple goods can be objects of desires which are in open conflict with our will.

good is, perforce, located at a particular time and place and set of circumstances? Only someone who refuses to make a separation between "good for me" and "good" is in a position to say that if x is good for me then x is good and *that* is what I want.[48] Similarly, if he recognizes that x is good, he immediately knows that x is good for him. But most people assume that "good" and "good for me" can sometimes at least diverge. This would be impossible to deny unless "good" refers to a manifestation of the superordinate Idea of the Good and "good for me" just means that. If there were no superordinate Good, identified with its manifestations as in "good for me," then there is no reason in principle to exclude the possibility that an acknowledged good is *not* good for me here and now.[49] Only if what is acknowledged to be good is acknowledged to be identical with what is good for me are we in a position to deny that what is good may not be good for me. But this means that the Good really must be beyond essence. This is the core insight of G. E. Moore in concluding that "good" refers to a "simple" and "indefinable" quality.[50]

Why, though, if the Good is beyond essence, is it not arbitrary to identify it with the evidently contentful "good for me" where the content resides in what "good" is predicated of? The answer is, again, found in the

---

[48] See Blanshard 1961, 143, who argues that Plato collapses "right" and "good for me," where "right" stands for Good, that is, what is distinct from self-interest. It is true that Plato "collapses" these, but not in such a way that the interest of anyone else could possibly be harmed by my pursuit of self-interest. Thus, Plato refuses to accept what is an underlying assumption of the supposed conflict of duty and self-interest. Stated otherwise, Plato's moral realism short-circuits the frequently deployed distinction between agent-neutral and agent-relative normative theories. Every instantiation of the "agent-neutral" Good is "agent-relative" to all agents. This short-circuiting affects the distinction between consequentialist versus nonconsequentialist normative theories. For Plato, if a good is pursued independently of consequences, it cannot thereby reconstitute a distinction between "good" simpliciter and "good for me." If, for example, a nonconsequentialist theory maintains that a certain practice is good or ought to be performed come what may, Plato will maintain that if the practice really is good, then it is good for everyone, that is, good in its consequences. See Dreier 1993 on the classification of normative theories in these two ways.

[49] Some things good in one circumstance may be bad in another and so, in themselves, indifferent. See *La.* 192B9–D9; *Charm.* 160E7–11; *Protag.* 359E5–7; *Me.* 87D–88C; *Euthyd.* 281B–D. The Stoics obliquely recognized this point in identifying the traditional goods such as health, beauty, power, money, and so on as indifferents. These are only made good when a universalizing principle of rationality is applied to them. That this principle cannot do the work of a superordinate Idea of the Good is an argument that I shall take up in due course.

[50] See Moore 1971 [1903], 9–10. See Murdoch 1970, 3–4, on a Platonizing defense of Moore against his critics. Butchvarov 1989, 66, argues that Moore's insight has to be supplemented "by holding that goodness is a generic universal." And, 63, "If we find in a person the property of being compassionate, we should not expect to find *in the same way also* the property of being good. But we can find the property of being good *in* the property of being compassionate, as we can find triangularity in an isosceles triangle and color in a shade of color." This is close to Plato's position if we add the qualification that since the Idea of the Good is "beyond οὐσία," it does not have, strictly speaking, an intelligible content.

identification of the Good with the One, where all the content in manifestations of the Good are found in integrative unities.⁵¹ But is it not the case that we can legitimately ask the identical question of a proposed achievement of integrative unity: Is it good for me? Of course, one can do so, but only by lapsing back into a distinction between "good" and "good for me." For example, suppose that "ideal human being" is the name for the integrative unity that the virtuous person achieves. The question "why is it good for me to strive to be an ideal human being?" only makes sense if the one who asks the question denies that she is a human being. If she acknowledges that she is a human being and that she desires her real good, then she cannot coherently deny that she desires to be an integrative unity. For her real good is just what being an ideal human being amounts to.

Naturally, one can unwind the argument, so to speak, down to the level of a particular act or practice and, assuming that one agrees that one wants to be an integrative unity, ask whether or not that act or practice contributes to its achievement. This is no doubt why Plato supposed that a certain philosophical expertise was required to answer such questions with authority. It is why he eventually identified avatars of the Good as beauty, truth, and symmetry. These are all, as we shall see in detail, criteria of integrative unity.

The Idea of the Good is productive and so, though it is – uniquely – beyond essence, whatever it produces possesses essence. The connection of all things produced to their producer is that they manifest their producer each according to their own essence. This follows straightforwardly from the uniqueness of the superordinate superessentialistic Good and from the fact that the effect must somehow be "contained" within the cause. If we know what a Form of Justice or a Form of Circularity is, we know that it is. Its existence is *a se*.⁵² But this does not preclude the fact that the existence of a Form of Justice or Circularity is really distinct from the nature that "Justice" and "Circularity" name.⁵³ The contribution of the Good/One

---

⁵¹ Kraut 2011, 93, in arguing against the very idea of absolute good, thinks that this idea entails that there is a good "the value of which does not reside in [its] being good for anyone." This is not the position I am attributing to Plato. For Plato, "the absolute good" is good for *everyone*, including those who do not avail themselves of it. See Hurka 1987, 71; 2020. It should be added, though, that for Plato, unlike Hurka, the identity of "good" and "good for me" does not support consequentialism.

⁵² This is true even if we can only come to know what Justice is by encountering instances of Justice and inferring their diminished reality in relation to their paradigm as, for instance, in the Recollection Argument in *Phaedo*.

⁵³ See *Parm.* 142B5–6.

can be precisely expressed as providing the unity of existence and essence in the Form.[54] From this fact, it will follow that achieving an integrative unity is the opposite of suffering the dissolution of existence and essence for anything that participates in a Form. If the virtuous person becomes one out of many, the vicious person is dissolved or deconstructed or "exploded" without limit.[55] The ideal state exists as an integrative unity and its opposite is literally torn apart by factions.

As Aristotle reports, Plato posited the Indefinite Dyad or the Great-and-Small along with the One as principles.[56] There are many unresolved, and perhaps irresolvable issues in the interpretation of the two principles. But several features of the report and of Plato's own accounts are salient and sufficiently well established. The first is that the Indefinite Dyad cannot be a principle co-ordinate with the One if only for the logical reasoning that the One's absolute simplicity guarantees its unique status. That is, if there could be two absolutely simple principles, there would need to be something in each to differentiate it from the other. But then this would entail internal complexity in each, the internal complexity consisting in the "thing" and the putative property that differentiates it from the other. From the absolute simplicity of the One, we can infer the relative complexity of the Indefinite Dyad even as an existing principle of limitlessness. The second is that the Indefinite Dyad is necessary for the hylomorphic composition of any integrative or potentially integrative unity. This is the import of the passage in *Philebus* to which we shall return, in which we learn that everyone that now exists is composed of limit and unlimited.[57] If a whole consists of an integration of parts, then either the parts are unities themselves or else they are limitless substrata. In the first case, they can themselves be analyzed into limit and unlimited; in the second, we have already arrived at limit and unlimited.

For our purposes, the most important feature of the Indefinite Dyad or the Unlimited is its normative role. Just as unqualified or perfect unity is an asymptote or terminus along the axis of grades of goodness, so "perfect"

---

[54] I use the expression "Good/One" with full recognition of its unredeemable ugliness. I apologize to readers who share my distaste. My only defense – and, obviously, I think it is a satisfactory defense – is that "Good" and "One" need to be always considered together. I would suggest that we think of the first principle of all as the absolutely simple One insofar as it is the source of everything and as Good insofar as it is the goal of everything. These are inseparable, as I show below, but conceptually distinguishable depending on context.

[55] See, in *Rep.* Bk. 9, the powerful description of the dissolution of the soul of the tyrannical man.

[56] See Aristotle, *Meta.* A 6, 987a29–988a1; M 6, 1080a12–30, 1080b4–33; 7.1081a12–17, 1081a21–25, 1081b17–22; 8.1083a20–b19; N 2, 1089a31–b15.

[57] See *Phil.* 23C–26D.

disunity or decomposition is the other terminus. The Indefinite Dyad is the principle of unlimitedness just as the One is the principle of limit or measure.[58] Unlimitedness gives us as perspicuous a way of making normative judgments as does limit. This is fairly obvious for all that pertains to the incarnate tripartite soul poised between integrative unity and dissolution.[59] It is not quite so obvious in relation to cognition, understood as a unificatory process. We shall, in due course, see how Plato combines the psychical and the epistemological. For example, we shall be able to see how exactly knowledge is virtue.

1.3 Moral Realism vs. Naturalism

A well-canvassed complaint against all forms of moral realism is that it depends upon there being moral truths, propositions that express truths that are not reducible naturalistically. But no putative moral truth is a part of any explanation within a naturalistic framework.[60] This argument has been challenged by some who try to show that moral facts do enter into the explanations for certain empirical facts.[61]

According to most versions of naturalism in ethics, moral properties are either identical with or constituted by natural properties. If this is so, however we construe the identity or reduction of the moral to the

---

[58] See *Phil.* 66A6.
[59] See Rist 2002, 67–72, for some perceptive remarks on dissolution of integration and evil and especially how a resolution of a conflict among goods can exemplify the "trajectory" of the soul along a dynamic continuum of agency.
[60] See for example, Harman 1977, §1. According to Railton 1995, 171, 185, there are "moral facts" but these are constituted by "natural facts" of which they are a subgroup. See also Sturgeon 1988, 2006; Clarke-Doane 2012; Hayward 2019. Hayward argues, interestingly, that a nonnatural moral realism is actually *immoral* since it conditionalizes moral claims on the existence of moral nonnatural facts. But, according to Hayward, our moral obligations should not be so construed that if we should come to believe that there are no nonnatural moral facts, then these obligations would cease and nihilism would ensue. For a criticism of the incompatibility of moral realism and naturalism, see Rea 2006. The gist of Rea's argument, 216, is that a naturalist, following scientific methodology, can only accept moral realism if she is a theist, which contradicts naturalism, or at least scientific methodology. Against Rea, I would deny that the only plausible alternative to naturalism is theism, understanding by that term the personalizing of the first principle of all. I would also be inclined to argue that Platonic metaphysics is not antithetical to scientific methodology, so long as that is not limited to empiricism.
[61] See for example Brink 1989, 156–167. Boyd 1988, 201, draws an analogy between moral realism and scientific realism, basing the naturalism of the former on the latter. The truth-makers within this naturalistic moral realism are, basically, human needs. Accordingly, the criterion for moral judgments is frankly consequentialist. The plausibility of a moral realism based on "human needs" diminishes when we confront real-life conflicts among these needs. Who is supposed to be the arbiter of the conflicts, especially when the procurement of one need precludes the procurement of another?

nonmoral, what such a view definitely excludes is the moral realism which has its truth-maker in a supernatural principle. But before we consider Plato's case for this extraordinary truth-maker, we should mention one strategy Plato has available in order to counter naturalistic reductions in any form. Plato claims that, for example, beauty is univocally predicable of bodies, souls, institutions, laws, and sciences.[62] The same is true for good. A good horseman is not the same as a good shoemaker even though good is univocally predicable of both. If univocity of moral predicates across vastly diverse instantiations makes any sense, then reduction to naturalist properties does not. Helen's beauty cannot be reduced to her bodily parts if, say, an institution can also be called beautiful. Of course, the naturalist will receive this objection with equanimity, maintaining that univocity in predication is no more plausible than is nonnaturalistic moral realism. The Platonic defense of predicational realism generally is the topic for another discussion.[63] And yet we might reasonably hypothesize that the evident mismatch between the range of moral predicates and their putative naturalistic bases is not obviously resolvable in favor of naturalism.[64]

The principal reason for contesting the possibility of a naturalistic moral realism is that the putative naturalistic accounts of moral properties and propositions always speak generally as opposed to universally. For example, one influential naturalistic account of moral properties and propositions is evolutionary. According to this account, moral claims are rooted in the evolutionary benefit of members of the species "internalizing" prescriptions and injunctions that are conducive to evolutionary success.[65] But evolutionary success can only be construed epidemiologically, so to speak. It deals with populations, not with individuals. And the individual exception is precisely the correct focus for the one who challenges the absoluteness or universality of moral claims. This is as true for a Socrates who refuses to flee from prison as it is for a Thrasymachus. Even if the "community" benefits from cooperation in its evolutionary march, this

---

[62] See *Symp.* 210A–212B.   [63] See my 2020, ch. 3, §3.
[64] Putnam 2015, 313, argues for a "liberal naturalism" that recognizes the "epistemic and ontological objectivity of normative judgments" at the same time as he rejects "a Platonic realm of normative facts independent of human practices and needs." Without engaging in a critical examination of views of this sort, I simply wish to note at this point that it is a caricature of Plato's moral realism to maintain that it posits normative facts "independent of human practices and needs." Indeed, for Plato, the overwhelming human need is for the Good to infuse human lives, including human practices. This is a normative fact about human desire, namely, the normativity of the ends or goals of desire.
[65] See for example, Ruse 1989, 261–262: "Morality is a biological adaptation no less than are hands and feet and teeth."

might certainly not be true for the individual who is not particularly interested in the success of the community, who indeed even sees its success as inimical to his own. I would suggest that being a naturalistic realist about moral properties probably entails divesting the term "moral" of its usual meaning.

Plato, of course, does not try to refute the naturalist while remaining within a naturalistic framework. His uncompromising antinaturalism universally rejects the adequacy of naturalistic explanations of the sort that, for example, Anaxagoras sought to provide. What is distinctive about Plato's metaphysical moral realism is that all explanations, including those for moral facts, terminate in the unhypothetical first principle of all. This is a feature of Plato's theory that is easy to miss, especially when it is represented in a truncated form according to which the Good is not the One and goodness is not instantiable as integrative unity. Ultimately, the explanation for why certain types of behavior are wrong or right and why certain natural phenomena occur as they do is the same. It is not that the Good preempts the explanatory role of Forms; rather, the explanatory role of Forms is cast in terms of instrumentality for the Good or One. Thus, for example, participation in Justice is one way to attain the benefit flowing from the Good since it is the Good that makes just things beneficial.

Although this sweeping claim may seem implausible in the extreme, consider again the way *Philebus* connects the Good with beauty, symmetry, and truth.[66] We shall return to this passage at some length in Chapter 6. Here, it should suffice to indicate that beauty, symmetry, and truth are each and all together ways of characterizing the Forms whose being is explained by the Good. So, it is not just the case that, say, Helen's beauty is explained by the Form of Beauty, which is in turn explained as a product of the Good, and the justness of a just act is explained by the Form of Justice, which is itself caused to be by the Good, but *all* Forms serve as explanations insofar as they are eternally being produced by the Good.[67] It is because Plato's moral realism is situated within a hierarchical metaphysical structure that naturalistic arguments against the relevance of moral realism as having any explanatory role can have no purchase against it.[68]

---

[66] *Phil.* 65A–B.
[67] The verbs at *Rep.* 6.509B5–9, παρεῖναι ("to be present to") and προσεῖναι ("to come to") with the genitive ὑπὸ τοῦ ἀγαθοῦ ("by the Good") and ὑπὸ ἐκείνου ("by that") indicate the causal or productive relation.
[68] See Leiter 2015; 2019, who rightly emphasizes the historical, Platonic connection between metaphysics and morality. Leiter, as a naturalist, sees the abandonment of metaphysics as entailing the abandonment of morality. I think Plato would wholeheartedly endorse this claim.

1.4 The Priority of Good to Right

Various forms of moral realism either prioritize right or duty over good or insist on right as a primitive notion irreducible to good.[69] Insofar as the concepts of right and duty can be mapped on to Plato's theory, it should be clear that Plato's good is conceptually prior to both. The term τὸ δίκαιον, which is usually translated as "just," is often appropriately translated as "right."[70] So, the topic of *Republic*, namely, whether it pays to do τὸ δίκαιον, has a broader meaning which is more perspicuously expressed as a question about whether it pays to do the right thing. Plato, of course, wants to argue that it always does pay to do the right thing, according to both popular and philosophical metrics. But there is no doubt as to *why* doing the right thing always pays. It is because the Idea of the Good makes doing the right thing beneficial and doing what is beneficial for us is what we all unequivocally and without exception desire. There is no scenario under which doing the right thing might not be desirable, because the Idea of the Good eternally provides the Form of Justice (the Form of "the right thing to do") with the property of being beneficial or useful.[71] If good is a property of right, then by contrast we may assume that doing the opposite of the right thing can never have as a consequence the good that we seek. If this is so, then the Good's overflowing of goodness to all the Forms would seem to preclude the possibility of a Form of Evil or Injustice. I think this is in fact what Plato believes, though we require more by way of argument than an arbitrary stipulation of the necessary connectedness of right and good.[72]

For Plato, it does not seem possible that doing the right thing can be anything other than optimific, a term I introduce to include the possibility that the best that is achievable among all the alternatives, even if the best has undesired side effects. Therefore, doing the right thing cannot have an independent pull on us regardless of the consequences. But this is as much

---

[69] See, for example, Prichard 1968 in "Does Moral Philosophy Rest on a Mistake," 4–5, who says that it is false that "our sense that we ought to pay our debts or to tell the truth arises from our recognition that in doing so we should be originating something good." Also Ross 1930, 132–133, "if we contemplate a right act alone, it is seen to have no intrinsic *value*." That is, "good" should not be attributed to it.

[70] Sometimes, as at *Rep.* 7.517C1, the adjective ὀρθός is used synonymously with δίκαιος. Cf. *Lg.* 2.659D4. Elsewhere, for example *Eu.* 12C3, we find δέος.

[71] It is a mistake to substitute "knowledge" or "wisdom" for the Idea of the Good in answer to the question, "what makes health, pleasure, friendships, etc., good?" Still, one needs to know how to provide the conditions for the manifestation of the Good.

[72] Apelt 1912 argues that the fundamental principle of Plato's ethics is the Form of Justice. Apelt takes this as intrinsically regulative, thereby ignoring the superordinate Idea of the Good. For Apelt, too, the right is prior to the good.

as to say that it can never *be* the right thing to do something that does not instantiate or manifest the Idea of the Good. One who exhorts others and himself to do the right thing come what may either implicitly supposes that the right thing is right because it is good, or else he is making a hollow gesture supported only by some parochial fiat. So, the question "why should I do the right thing?" is an entirely reasonable one supposing that one wants one's own good, that one's own good is identical with the Good *simpliciter*, and the Good is instantiated in doing the right thing *now*.

The priority of the good to the right in Plato's moral realism enables us to see the intellectualism which is inextricable from the whole project. For in order to know if this is the right thing to do, one must know whether it instantiates the Idea of the Good indirectly by participating in one or other of the Virtues. There is no question of directly instantiating the Good since the Good is "above οὐσία" and so not identifiable with any particular property. One cannot simply do the "good thing." But even if one does know what, say, Justice is and that the Good makes Justice beneficial, there is no guarantee that one will thereby be an infallible guide to determining whether something is just or the right thing to do. And yet the only alternative to infallibility is not ignorance. One who knows the Good may be better placed than one who does not in recognizing where the Good is and is not manifested, although such a claim will need to appeal to some heuristic to be made plausible. "Infallibility" attaches only to this knowledge, however, not to any belief – true or false – about the sensible world or the instantiations of the Good.

The prioritization of the right over the good, or at least their separation, is done on behalf of a desire to protect morality from contamination by egocentric interest. Immanuel Kant and Kant-inspired philosophers have skewered prudentialists and consequentialists alike for their misunderstanding of the irreducibility of the moral to anything else. Perhaps one reason that Plato's moral theory does not fit neatly into any of the traditional taxonomies is that the contrast between morality and self-interest or between deontology and prudentialism or consequentialism has no meaning within that moral theory.[73] Of course, the contrast has considerable meaning for Socrates' interlocutors, whose tepid interest in a universal Good is almost always undermined by their eagerness to have the answer to the burning question, "what's in it for me?" As most readers of Plato will recognize, it is typical of him to employ a kind of philosophical

---

[73] See Butchvarov 1989, 123–128, especially 128, "The question whether Plato, Aristotle, or Augustine were ethical egoists is simply not well defined."

judo on these interlocutors of Socrates: "Let us by all means try to discover what is unequivocally and unashamedly in one's personal interest. We won't at the end, however, cavil if it turns out that it is impossible for one's personal interest to be served if it is at the expense of anyone else. Will we?"[74]

1.5 The Distinction between Good and Value

It is not uncommon for some defenders of moral realism to identify the truth-makers for moral propositions as values, sometimes called "intrinsic."[75] The supposed objectivity of these values is hard to disentangle from the subjective recognition of them, which is in turn hard to disentangle from subjective and hence variable valuation. By contrast, if we distinguish the truth-makers for propositions in morality from values, we can agree that values depend on human beings without drawing the conclusion that these propositions would no longer be true (or false) if human beings did not exist. The latter view is Plato's. There is no obvious word in ancient Greek for an abstract noun "value" understood as referring to a human judgment of a certain kind. It is a confusion, I believe, to suppose that Plato's truth-makers are the objective correlates, so to speak, of our values. It is perfectly in line with Plato's philosophy to hold that values are subjective, in the contemporary meaning of that term. It is not one's valuing something that makes it good or bad. This is true generally for any belief. Once we distinguish values from goods, the subjectivity of value does not even preclude the relativity of goods. But as we have seen, if all goods were relative, then the Platonic version of moral realism would be defeated.

Plato treats values and valuing within the framework of apparent goods. If, say, you value money over justice, this is because it appears to you that your real good is found in acting according to this preferential ordering. But since Plato's moral realism focuses on the real good, not the apparent good, he is not tempted to plumb the depths of preferential orderings to discover the good that all seek. One's preferential ordering may or may not

---

[74] See *Rep.* 1.335E5–6, the conclusion of the refutation of Polemarchus' definition of justice as helping your friends and harming your enemies: οὐδαμοῦ γὰρ δίκαιον οὐδένα ἡμῖν ἐφάνη ὂν βλάπτειν (For it has become clear to us that it is never just to harm anyone). The ultimate justification for this claim is, at this point in the dialogue, still far in the distance.

[75] See for example, Railton 2003, 46. Railton, 5, holds that moral properties are "objective, though relational." So, presumably, "good for me" (i.e., "relationally") can be objective, though on this basis, morality may still be relative.

reflect a strategy for achieving some manifestation of the Good. But for the philosopher's or ruler's task of determining if and when the Good is manifested, the preferential ordering of individuals – their values – are mostly irrelevant. For at the level of the individual, orderings are subjective and ordinal. If this is true, consequentialism as a *political* doctrine is incoherent. Even if an individual can accurately represent to himself his relative values, there is in principle no way of commensurating these with anyone else's. In the seventh chapter, I shall explore Plato's attempts to derive political applications for his moral realism.

Values, as apparent goods, may or may not have truth-makers, depending on whether the apparent goods are or are not real goods. That is, what we value may or may not be valuable. The subjective ordering of values certainly gives the appearance (to oneself and to others) of a judgment aiming to match up what appears to be good with the real Good that we all seek. I value A over B now because I think that attaining A rather than B is the way to attain the real good that I seek. Such a valuation does not, of course, force us to maintain that B is not a good. Indeed, there are very few actions in life that do not involve privileging one good over another good. This obvious truth is but another way of making the point that the Good that we all seek cannot be itself an οὐσία even if that οὐσία is indisputably good, like, say, Kant's "good will." For the effort to cultivate a good will must inevitably be set within the framework of goods the subjective ordering of which is only possible if these goods are commensurable. Each person will decide whether cultivating a good will or, say, cultivating a fat bank account is to take priority. Whatever one decides will be perforce an apparent good and the question of the connection of that apparent good with the real Good has an answer independent of human values.

There is a certain resemblance between the contemporary notion of value and Plato's notion of good or goods, that which human beings typically pursue as ends. The list of these goods is not long, nor much in doubt. There is no canonical version, but the list mainly consists of: health, pleasure, wealth, beauty, excellence (or: virtue), friendship, self-esteem, and the esteem of others. One's "values" at a particular time and place consist of a preferential ordering of achieving or contributing to one or another of these. The inevitable conflicts that arise among our "values" and our responses to these conflicts indicate only how the manifestation of the Good – that we unequivocally desire – appears to us at this moment. To choose one good over another on one occasion does not suggest incoherence if this preferential ordering is reversed on another occasion. Since the appearance of a manifestation of the Good does not entail its reality, it is always legitimate, so to speak, to question whether one's ordering in a particular case achieves the desired result. None of Socrates' interlocutors *disvalue* excellence or virtue, though admittedly, they tend to have a less refined notion of the human virtues than does Socrates. But these interlocutors typically and understandably bridle at a mere assumption that always privileging the practice of virtue over other goods does in fact achieve the real good that we desire. Maybe today, but not tomorrow; maybe in this case, but not in that case. For Plato, the *only* way to escape the imputation of arbitrariness in Socrates' urging the privileging of his preferential ordering over that of anyone else – the good of virtue over any other good – is to posit a superordinate Idea of the Good.

CHAPTER 2

The Idea of the Good

2.1 The Idea of the Good as the First Principle of All

In *Republic* Book 6, Socrates says:

> You have at least often heard it said that the Idea of the Good is the subject of the most important study, since it is that by means of which just things and other useful things actually become useful or beneficial.[1]

There are many issues raised by this passage including how the Idea of the Good is to be studied and how it actually makes justice and other things useful or beneficial.[2] It does seem beyond doubt, however, that what is here being claimed is, minimally, that the Idea of the Good has a fundamental role to play in Plato's moral realism. I put this claim in this anodyne manner not because I do not think that a much stronger claim can be substantiated; I do so because even such a claim has been widely rejected, especially but not only in the English-speaking world for well over a century.[3] It is held that the Good is redundant because justice and other

---

[1] *Rep.* 6.505A2–4: ἐπεὶ ὅτι γε ἡ τοῦ ἀγαθοῦ ἰδέα μέγιστον μάθημα, πολλάκις ἀκήκοας, ᾗ δὴ καὶ δίκαια καὶ τἄλλα προσχρησάμενα χρήσιμα καὶ ὠφέλιμα γίγνεται. Cf. *Gorg.* 474D4–E7, where the connection is between ὠφέλιμα and τὸ καλόν or ἡδέα (pleasures) and τὸ καλόν. If something is thought to be καλόν and is not pleasurable, then it is so because it is beneficial. Also, *Protag.* 333D9 where the connection is between τὸ καλόν and ὠφέλιμα alone. The words πολλάκις ἀκήκοας ("you have often heard it said") suggest that the doctrine of the Idea of the Good antedates *Republic*. We should not forget that Socrates is here – on any interpretation – expressing Platonic doctrine. So, the words "often heard" can reasonably be taken to at least include intra-Academic discussions or Plato's oral teaching.

[2] See Adam 1921, v.2, 51, *ad loc.*, who rests his claim that the Idea of the Good is Plato's "Deity" on this passage. I shall return to this interpretation in several places later in this book though I think it is mistaken.

[3] See the works referred to in the previous chapter, n. 5. White 2013, 25, says that "the concept of goodness" is the central concept for Plato's ethics. White cites *Rep.* 7.534B8–D1 in this regard, where the question is explicitly about the Idea of the Good, *not* a concept of goodness. If the Good were a concept, it would not even be clear that Plato is a moral realist. Delcomminette 2006, 604ff, argues that the Idea of the Good has no formal role to play in dialectic and that it has no content. Accordingly, it has no substantive role to play in ethics.

virtues are good by definition. That is, the Good does not add anything to knowledge of the Forms of the Virtues. This possibility seems challenged by the fact that the study of the superordinate Good is "the most important study." Indeed, as we learn a bit later in the passage on the Divided Line, the study of the Good is the greatest study at least because without knowing it, we cannot even know the definitions of the Virtues, let alone know that it is good or beneficial for us to possess instances of them.[4]

Recognizing that the Idea of the Good makes justice useful or beneficial, one may object that then it cannot be the case that justice is intrinsically good; rather, goodness will be external to justice in some way.[5] Such an objection arises from a limited conception of how Plato conceives of the relation between the Good and the Forms. The Good is the explanation for the existence and essence of all the Forms.[6] Goodness is as intimately present to the Form of Justice as is its own οὐσία, if for no other reason than that whatever causal role the Good has in relation to Forms, it has eternally. The Good is also intimately, albeit indirectly, related to any instantiation of the Good via an instantiation of Justice and the other Forms. As a synonym for "instantiation" we might use "manifestation" or even "expression," bearing in mind that instantiation is not instrumentality but, for Plato, participation.[7] In the eternal or intelligible realm, all

---

[4] See *Rep.* 6.511B2–C2; cf. 7.533C3–6. In fact, the prior necessity of knowing the Idea of the Good is not limited to the Forms of the Virtues; this is the case for all the Forms. See Dorter 2006, 198. The Idea of the Good is by Plato explicitly embedded in a metaphysical framework larger than that required by moral realism.

[5] See Penner and Rowe 2005, 260–269, for some salutary remarks on the unsuitability of the modern notion of "intrinsic goodness" for interpreting Plato. Their key insight is that intrinsic goodness is usually identified with morality as distinct from happiness. Thus, something can be intrinsically good and therefore morally obligatory even if it does not bring happiness. I treat the supposed conflict of morality and happiness in Chapter 4, Section 4.4.

[6] *Rep.* 6.509B5–9: Καὶ τοῖς γιγνωσκομένοις τοίνυν μὴ μόνον τὸ γιγνώσκεσθαι φάναι ὑπὸ τοῦ ἀγαθοῦ παρεῖναι, ἀλλὰ καὶ τὸ εἶναί τε καὶ τὴν οὐσίαν ὑπ' ἐκείνου αὐτοῖς προσεῖναι, οὐκ οὐσίας ὄντος τοῦ ἀγαθοῦ, ἀλλ' ἔτι ἐπέκεινα τῆς οὐσίας πρεσβείᾳ καὶ δυνάμει ὑπερέχοντος (And say that for the things that are knowable, their being known is present to them owing to the Good, but even their existence and essence belong to them owing to it, the Good itself not being essence but beyond essence, exceeding it in seniority and power). See Gerson 2020, 120–127, for more details on this and related passages. Some scholars, for example, Gould 1955, 170, take the words ἐπέκεινα τῆς οὐσίας to mean "beyond reality," thereby justifying the claim that Plato's intentions here are impenetrable. Of course, such an interpretation depends on what is meant by "reality." The Good is certainly beyond *finite* reality, meaning any limitations imposed by essence or οὐσία. But that it is not beyond reality in the sense of being nothing at all is refuted by the fact that the Good is "the happiest of that which is (εὐδαιμονέστατον τοῦ ὄντος)" (526E4–5), that it is "more beautiful (κάλλιον)" than knowledge and truth (509A6), and that it is "the brightest of that which is (τοῦ ὄντος τὸ φανότατον)" (518C9). See Ferber and Damschen 2015 on why the Good, though it is "beyond οὐσία," is not "beyond ὄν (being)." The authors, however, 202–203, reject the reality of the Good, instead claiming it to be a "chimera" or *ens verbale*, that is, "something one can not imagine but can only formulate."

[7] See Timmermann 2019, 101.

relations are internal including the relation between that which participates and that which is participated in. So, Justice is intrinsically beneficial, not because of what the word "justice" means, but because of its eternal participation in the Good. And since this eternal participation is an internal relation, goodness is constitutive of the identity of Justice and the other Forms, too.

If the Idea of the Good is not relevant to the acquisition of virtue or anything else that is beneficial, or to the knowledge of it, then the following problem arises. It is a problem to which I have already alluded. Our paradigmatic malefactor, the tyrant, can without reservation concede that virtue is a good. He can also concede the supposedly "Socratic" point that what may seem to be a good is not really so if one does not know how to use it.[8] So much hardly steps outside the bounds of ordinary ancient Greek language and common sense. A virtue is good just because it is one of the things that people aim for, alongside health, wealth, beauty, pleasure, power, friendship, security, and so on.[9] They may well dispute what the virtue consists in or what its definition is, but the fact that someone pursues it means at a minimum that it is an apparent good, that is, a goal the achievement of which appears to the agent to be one that he or she truly desires. Even if the tyrant refuses to accept that some states or practices are virtues, for example, piety or justice, he can hardly wish to deny that there are *some* virtues including say, courage and endurance. And these will be at least prima facie goods. But at the same time, it is always open to the tyrant to say that, though some virtues are indeed goods, it is not good for him to have them or to practice them at this time and

---

[8] See *Rep.* 1.340D2–341A4, where Thrasymachus is eager to agree that only the correct use of power is advantageous. Admittedly, "correct use" is ambiguous, although we cannot assume without argument that the correct use of power will always be to the disadvantage of the tyrant *as he sees that*. As Chappell 1993, 13, shows, Thrasymachus does have his own list of virtues: strength (ἰσχύς), liberty (ἐλευθερία), and dominance (δεσποτεία) (344C5–9), plus shrewdness (εὐβουλεία) (348D2). Chappell argues that Thrasymachus does not include justice (or injustice) on this list. But insofar as he is prepared to consider justice or injustice at all, he does so according to the criterion of whether or not it is useful or beneficial to him. So, even if Thrasymachus conceded that justice in some sense is a virtue, it must be set alongside other goods and judged according to its usefulness in relation to the others. Plato's Idea of the Good is explicitly introduced as the explanation for what makes any virtue useful or beneficial. For Plato, the only alternative to this explanation is Thrasymachus' one, namely, that what makes some good useful or beneficial is one's personal "interests," whatever these may be. This is about as far from universality as one can get. See also Rist 1998.
[9] On good as goal or τέλος, see, for example, *Gorg.* 468A–B, 499E; *Phil.* 20D; *Euthyd.* 279A–C. Goals are a constituent of actions including those of the vicious and the acratic. This remains true even if it is also true that everyone desires the Good. Matching the achievement of the goal to the Good is, alas, not inevitable.

under these circumstances.[10] Another way of putting this point is that what may appear to be goods to some people are not good for him. Or at least, they are defeasible goods when measured against others.

Given the subjectivity and the ordinality of the valuations that people – ordinary people as well as tyrants – make, it is entirely possible to recognize virtue as one good among many. Sometimes, the self-interested calculations of people lead to the practical conclusion that in certain circumstances a good other than virtue needs to be prioritized. After all, it is not unreasonable to hold that A is the most important thing *ceteris paribus*, but that B has *some* importance too, and that from time to time, one should act to attain B rather than A. To be instructed by a "Socratic" critic that there are more important things in life than B is to invite the reply, "not here and now there aren't." Something like this must have been going through the mind of Crito in his eponymous dialogue when, at a critical moment, he hears Socrates' decision to privilege the good of virtue over the good of human life. Socrates' decision in this regard does not automatically invalidate or reduce to absurdity a contrary decision by someone else.

Just a few lines after the passage quoted at the beginning of this chapter, Socrates provides what I take to be the conclusive reason for the centrality of a superordinate Idea of the Good in Plato's ethics. This is the passage indicating the Good as that which all desire and the fact that everyone divines that it is something, although they do not know what it is.[11]

---

[10] Brown 2007, 56, makes the perceptive observation that the good that Glaucon wants Socrates to show that justice is, is different from the good that Socrates shows it to be. This good is still mapped onto self-interest. But Brown thinks that the task is completed by the end of Bk. 4 of *Republic*, thereby ignoring the role of the Idea of the Good in identifying the universal Good with one's own interest. If *Republic* is taken to be framed by Glaucon's challenge, this is not finally met until the end of Bk. 9 or, arguably, the end of Bk. 10, where the indispensability of philosophy to happiness is reaffirmed. See Annas 2015, especially 56–58, for a similar reply to Brown. In reality, there is no opposition between the egoistic and the altruistic; the opposition is in appearance only.

[11] *Rep.* 6.505D5–E5. There are many texts in the dialogues in which Socrates indicates that people seek what is good for themselves and avoid what is bad. See *Me.* 78A6; *Gorg.* 468B1–4; *Symp.* 205A6–7; *Protag.* 358C6–D2; *Euthyd.* 278E3–6; *Lys.* 222C3–5. All of these texts contain a possible ambiguity that is in fact easily removed. One may desire what appears to be good even if it is not, and one may desire the real good because it appears to be so. The ambiguity is between nonveridical and veridical appearances. The determination of whether the appearance of good is veridical or nonveridical is a matter for metaphysics, not human psychology. This ambiguity is distinct from the possible ambiguity that arises from failing to distinguish "good" as a generic Form and "good" as indicating a superordinate Idea of the Good (see the next section). That people "divine" the Good to be something strongly suggests that the good being talked about here is not a mundane good, like pleasure or physical health, whose existence and essence require no divination. Contra Rowe 2007, 145, who thinks the good here is just that which is useful and beneficial. Burnyeat 2006, 18, takes this passage, correctly, to refer to the superordinate Good, but then claims that this is in conflict with the doctrine rejected with the tripartition of the soul of Bk. 4. The rejected doctrine is that of the so-called

2.1 The First Principle of All

Suppose that it is *not* the Idea of the Good that makes justice really good for oneself as opposed to merely being apparently good. If that which does this is not above οὐσία, then it is or has an οὐσία of its own. For example, say that what makes justice good for oneself is that the Form of Justice partakes of another Form, the Form of ἀταραξία (absence of anxiety). It is then open to the tyrant to ask why absence of anxiety should be the stopping-point. That is, why should it be assumed that absence of anxiety is really good for oneself? Or *always* good for oneself? It seems that for the possession of an instance of any οὐσία, the question of the real good for oneself continues to remain open. Hence, in order to avoid begging the question, the "good at which all things aim" must be beyond οὐσία.[12]

Terry Penner has argued that the Idea of the Good is just the Form of Advantage.[13] This seems to be taken by him to be synonymous with

---

Socratic intellectualism. I treat of this further in Chapter 4, although it should be mentioned in passing that a radical doctrinal difference between Bk. 4 and Bk. 6 of *Republic* is not very likely.

[12] The quotation is, of course, from the first sentence of Aristotle's *Nicomachean Ethics* A 1, 1094a2–3: διὸ καλῶς ἀπεφήναντο τἀγαθόν, οὗ πάντ' ἐφίεσθαι δοκεῖ. It is natural to suppose that the word ἀπεφήναντο ("they pronounced") refers to Plato and others in the Academy. If so, Aristotle might be taken to be agreeing with Plato's argument that the Good must be unique and superordinate though he denies that the Good is beyond οὐσία; in fact, it is, for Aristotle, the primary referent of the meaning of οὐσία. See *Meta.* Λ 7, 1076a26–28 on the identity of the primary object of intellection and of desire. See Baker 2017, 1840–1841, on the irreducibility of "good" in this sentence to "good in a kind or good for something." Also, Baker 2021, 400.

[13] Penner 2007a, 93. Penner, 104, takes this claim as the central feature of his interpretation of Plato's ethical theory as "pure prudentialism," which he is careful to distinguish from "ethical egoism" since sometimes the prudential choice is other-regarding. So, too, Rowe 2007, who emphasizes the continuity between the meaning of what Rowe calls "agent-centered good" in the so-called early dialogues and in *Republic*. Sidgwick 1902 [1896], 22–31, is perhaps one of the early proponents of a prudentialist reading of Socratic ethics. Shorey 1895, 213ff, arguing against Sidgwick, resists the conflation of morality and prudence, but it is not clear to me why he does so. It should give pause to one holding the prudentialist interpretation of Plato's ethics that the most clearly anti-Platonic philosopher in antiquity, Epicurus, was himself explicitly a prudentialist. See, for example, *Principal Doctrines* V and the more expansive expression of prudentialist justice at XXXI–XL (D.L. 10.139–154). See Rist 2002, 45–50, on the anti-Platonism of Epicurean ethical theory. As Mitsis 1988, 77–78, points out, Epicurus' prudentialist conception of justice is in all likelihood consciously directed against a supersensible foundation for justice in Plato. One may state the difference between Epicurean prudentialism and the sort of prudentialism that fits within Plato's larger metaphysical picture by pointing out that the former is defeasible, and the latter is not. For Epicurus, as opposed to Plato, it is prudent to be virtuous – for the most part. When virtue does not result in pleasure, there is no prudence in virtuous behavior. Epicurus' position clearly reflects the position of Democritus. See Nill 1985, ch. 4. It is also reflected in David Hume's *An Enquiry Concerning the Principles of Morals*. Another clear example of pure prudentialism that is patently anti-Platonic is found in Joyce 2001, ch. 7, who argues for fictionalism, the view that all moral claims are false, though sometimes useful. This view overlaps with a variety of views under the heading "evolutionary ethics," where "usefulness" is parsed as "value to survival of the species." Joyce acknowledges that the fictionalist must eschew universality. He, 185, urges one to "keep using [moral] discourse but do not believe it." Joyce, 221–222, concedes that Gyges in *Republic*, in possession of the ring that makes him invisible, has no reason to embrace the pragmatic benefits of a moral stance. Does anyone really

a putative Form of Happiness. So, in answer to the question of why one should be just, Socrates (or Plato) would say, "because you want what is really good for yourself and what is really good for yourself is advantage, which is equivalent to happiness." Set aside for the moment the implausibility of this interpretation based solely on the fact that the Idea of the Good is what makes *all* Forms knowable and provides truth to them, not only the so-called ethical or normative Forms.[14] How a Form of Advantage makes, say, Circularity knowable is, to say the least, mysterious. Penner is correct, of course, in supposing that Plato believes that all human beings desire to be happy and that for them, the real good is happiness.[15] Socrates insists that happiness is found in virtuous living. The tyrant protests that this might be so for the many but not so for the few. For those who are up to the challenge, the life of the tyrant is to be preferred. It is in *that* life that happiness is to be found. Penner's Socrates is in no position to reply that it is impossible for a tyrant to be happy. This is so because either happiness is a purely formal term or else it has content, presumably, the content of Virtue. If it is a formal term, then a "prudential" Socrates has no grounds for excluding the exceptions to his rule that the tyrant claims. If the Form of Advantage has content, namely, Virtue, the tyrant, it seems, can still legitimately ask why being virtuous is more than merely apparently good.[16] Or he can ask why the demands of virtue are not defeasible.

The Idea of the Good has to be above οὐσία in order to attain to the universality of an ethical theory, at least for any theory that is even remotely plausibly Platonic.[17] Stated otherwise, the unhypothetical first principle of

---

suppose that such a view would appeal to the Socrates of the dialogues, who, we must not forget, adheres to his absolutist moral stance in the face of his own impending death?

[14] See *Rep.* 6.508E1–4 with 508A9–B7, 6.509B6–7; 7.517B7–C4. The text says that the Forms are "known (γιγνωσκομένοις)," not "knowable." The justification for the inference is (a) that the Good gives the "power (δύναμιν)" of knowing to knowers, which seems to imply that the Forms are *knowable*; (b) in the following analogy with the sun, the sun is said to make objects "seen (ὁρωμένοις)" not "seeable," too. But it stretches credulity to refrain from inferring that these objects are thereby made *seeable*. See Hitchcock 1982, 69, "the Good is only indirectly the cause of the power to know, by being the cause of the power of known objects to be known. The relationship between the Good and knowledge reduces to the already described relationship between the Good and truth."

[15] See, for example, *Symp.* 204E.

[16] Barney 2010a, 366, raises the question of whether or not τὸ καλόν and τὸ ἀγαθόν can have the identical "content," namely, a certain order or τάξις. But the Good cannot have a defined content if it is above οὐσία. Barney is right in finding an extensional equivalence between beauty and goodness as predicates. What unites the two "contents" is their relation to the first principle of all whose simplicity precludes predication. See Irani 2021, 358–359, n. 20, who rightly compares Epicurus with Callicles, the "enlightened hedonist."

[17] See Plotinus, *Enn.* V 5 [32], 4.13 Henry-Schwyzer, who says that the One-Good is μέτρον ... αὐτὸ καὶ οὐ μετρούμενον (measure ... not itself measured). This slogan neatly encompasses the main point: If the Good were not the principle of measure but that which is measured according to that

all has to be the Idea of the Good if Plato is to have an ethical theory of any kind. Eliminating the Idea of the Good or discounting its ontological significance is tantamount to saddling Plato with the inability to advance beyond rhetoric in Socrates' exhortations to his interlocutors to live a certain kind of life. It is a mistake to conflate the universality of the Idea of the Good with the universality of any Form. For it is the uniqueness of a superordinate Idea of the Good that alone provides the requisite universality for moral realism.[18] This universality must be "unhypothetical" because it is a stopping-point or first principle. Only that is something sufficient (τι ἱκανόν) as an explanation, in the present case for the truth of moral claims. The explanatory stopping-point is then identical with the goal or τέλος of all action.

2.2 The Idea of the Good and the Form of the Good

There are a number of passages in the dialogues in which Plato speaks about a Form of the Good which appears to be coordinate with other Forms as opposed to being "above" all Forms.[19] By "coordinate" I mean one οὐσία among many.[20] So, the obvious question arises as to why a coordinate Form of the Good is not sufficient to do the job that Plato needs the Idea of the Good to do. I have already suggested the answer to this question along the lines of the absolute priority of the first principle of

---

principle, then the question of whether *that* measured thing should be pursued or not overall would remain open. The Good must be unqualifiedly the principle of measure and not measured. Another way of understanding the point is to note that if the Good were measured, it would be a contentful predicate. We could judge (by some other measure) whether that which had "good" predicated of it was in fact good. That which would measure and not be itself measured would in fact be the Idea of the Good. See Rawson 1996, who rejects what he calls "the Neoplatonic interpretation of the Good because Plotinus thinks that the Good or One is beyond being altogether." This view is very difficult to square with many passages in *Enneads* including those in which Plotinus says that the Good or One, for example, "brought itself into existence (ὑποστήσας ἑαυτόν)," VI 8 [39] 10.34.

[18] Penner 2003, 192–194, complains that on the interpretation of the Idea of the Good that he rejects and that I and others accept, the Idea of the Good "is itself perfectly good, impersonally good, and non-relationally good." See contra Annas 1997, 146, who says, "Plato parts company with someone who believes that for something to be good is always for it to be good *for* X, or *from Y's point of view*, or *a good* Z." Penner's interpretation is misguided for a number of reasons, but primarily because of the fact that since the Good is beyond οὐσία, it does not have "predicates," including the predicate "good." It is a principle of goodness analogous to the way that "one" is a principle of number (ἀριθμός) and so therefore not itself a number. Even though something may be good because it participates in a Form and the Form participates in the Good, the Good does not contain the "content" of the Form as a distinct part.

[19] This section is based on Gerson 2015. See *Phd.* 65D4–7, 75C10–D2, 76D7–9; *Tht.* 186A8; *Parm.* 130B7–9; *Rep.* 6.507B4–6, 10.608E4–5. Cf. *Epin.* 978B3–4.

[20] On Forms as οὐσίαι see, for example, *Eu.* 11A7; *Phd.* 65D13, 77A2, 78D1; *Crat.* 386E1; *Parm.* 133C4; *Sts.* 283E8.

all. But a stronger reply can be formulated if we include the reason why a superordinate Idea of the Good does not preempt a coordinate Form of the Good such that the latter becomes otiose.

Proclus in his remarkable book of essays on *Republic* sees clearly the need to distinguish a coordinate Form of the Good from a superordinate Idea of the Good.[21] Proclus identifies the former as the genus of perfections (τελεώσεις) and the latter with the unhypothetical first principle of all.[22] The genus of perfections is distinct from the genus of substances (οὐσίαι). Among these are Human Being and Horse. Among the "species" of the genus of perfections are Beauty, Justice, Health, Strength, and so on.[23] What the latter all share is there are various ways in which a human being can be perfected or completed. That is, there are various ways in which we strive to bridge the gap between our human endowment and the achievements that comprise our fulfillment as human beings.[24] Proclus thinks it obvious that perfections as different as beauty and virtue have, nevertheless, a generic unity. This is analogous to the specific unity that, say, physical beauty and intellectual beauty have in *Symposium*. But there is an important reason why this coordinate Form of Good, the genus of perfections, cannot substitute for the superordinate Idea of the Good.

The coordinate generic Form of the Good is an οὐσία in which all its species participate. Things or states that are bad or neutral do not participate in it. Thus, the Form of the Good lacks the universality of the superordinate Idea of the Good. Its nature is absent from things that do not participate in it. This is owing entirely to its being a limited nature in

---

[21] See Proclus, *Commentary on Plato's Republic*, Essay 10, 1.269.4–287.17 Kroll. Cf. *In Parm.* III 811.6–7 Steel, where the distinction is between τὸ οὐσιωδὲς ἀγαθόν and τὸ ὑπερούσιον ἀγαθόν. Baker 2017, 1849, n. 23, points out that Aristotle's attack on a Form of the Good in *EN* A 6 is an attack on a univocal Form of the Good and not, at least intentionally, an attack on a superordinate Idea of the Good which, being beyond οὐσία, is "beyond" univocity. See also Menn 1992, 548–549; Shields 2015, 86–87; Herzberg 2017; Broadie 2021, 51–52.

[22] *Commentary* 1.278.22–279.2. See 1.270.29–271.25. The source of the distinction appears to be Plotinus. See VI 7 [38], 25.12–14 Henry-Schwyzer, where Plotinus references *Philebus* in distinguishing the good for human beings from the Good as first principle of all. Cf. Iamblichus, *De myst.* I 5, 15.5–11 Segonds.

[23] *Commentary* 1.269.19–270.20.

[24] See *Lys.* 221E3–6: Τοῦ οἰκείου δή, ὡς ἔοικεν, ὅ τε ἔρως καὶ ἡ φιλία καὶ ἡ ἐπιθυμία τυγχάνει οὖσα (So, it seems that what belongs to us is what love, friendship, and appetite happen to be of). "What belongs to us (τὸ οἰκεῖον)" expresses precisely the relationship between endowment and achievement. The achievement is ours, but it is not us now. Plato often uses οἰκεῖον synonymously with συγγενής ("akin to") as in *Rep.* 10.611D8–612A6, where if we could see the disembodied soul, we could see that its true nature is akin to the intelligible world. The fundamental human achievement and task is the recovery of our true nature or authentic self. The state of the soul when embodied is our endowment; the ideal state of the soul is found only when it is disembodied. A disembodied soul that retains remnants of its embodied state has not yet achieved the ideal. See *Phd.* 82Eff.

2.2 The Idea of the Good and the Form of the Good

which participation or lack of participation is possible.[25] By contrast, the superordinate Idea of the Good is not limited in any way. Everything with an οὐσία of any sort participates in it including things with radically disparate natures. It is true that Plato does not make explicit the distinction between the Form of the Good and the Idea of the Good, but since he does explicitly make the latter "beyond οὐσία," it is not, I think, unreasonable to suppose that he means to distinguish it from anything that has an οὐσία including the coordinate Form of the Good.

The coordinate Form of the Good is the eternal foundation for facts of a particular sort.[26] Whether someone is or is not virtuous or healthy is an objective fact, quite independent of his or her own perceptions or beliefs. This is true generally for all the coordinate Forms which provide the explanation for the real or objective samenesses and differences in the sensible world. But the validation of a claim to objective fact, for example, that Socrates is virtuous and Callicles is not, does not and cannot answer any questions about normativity. When Plato lays down the principle that everyone desires the real good, he is not making the banal claim that everyone seeks to perfect themselves according to their own ideas of what perfection consists of. The presence of a real good as opposed to a merely apparent good is determined according to a norm, not a fact. The norm is set by nature as an achievement as opposed to an endowment. It must be a real, not a merely notional norm. Without an ontological foundation for the norm, though objectivity may still be supported, universality is not. An anti-Platonic scientific approach to ethics can be content to endorse a pallid form of normativity based, for example, on evolutionary biology or sociobiology. Or no normativity at all. Without the superordinate Idea of the Good, this is the right approach to take. On this approach, there is no room for Socrates' absolutism. In this regard, Penner's prudentialism is actually closer to an anti-Platonic position than to Plato's own as expressed in the dialogues.

---

[25] Miller 1985, 182–183 with nn. 23–24; 2007, 328–339, takes the Good to be "perfection as such." According to my reading, this confuses the co-ordinate Form of the Good, the genus of perfection, with the superordinate Idea of the Good. As we shall see, though, in Section 2.6 below, there is a close connection between perfection and unity, particularly integrative unity according to kind, that Miller himself acknowledges.

[26] Dorter 2006, 188, distinguishes between the co-ordinate Form of the Good and the superordinate Idea of the Good as objects of διάνοια and νόησις, respectively. See *Rep.* 7.534C4–5 for an explicit distinction between the Idea of the Good itself (αὐτὸ τὸ ἀγαθόν) and any other good (ἄλλο ἀγαθόν). I take it that since there can only be one superordinate Good, an "other good" must refer to something with the property of being good, that is, manifesting the Good. A failure to distinguish these could, for example, lead someone to reason that because x is good, it is the Good. According to Plato, this is how the hedonist reasons.

A multiplicity of universal norms runs up against the problem canvassed above, namely, that they will each have to have content, thereby leaving necessarily open the motivational question.[27] Mere objectivity is strictly compatible with relativism whether at the individual or group level. Only universality can yield exceptionlessness, like the exceptionlessness of mathematics; but only the unique universality of the superordinate Idea of the Good can yield normative exceptionlessness. There is no way to achieve normative universality or absoluteness without a unique normative principle that transcends "content." In a hierarchical metaphysics, this principle is bound to be the first principle of being. No matter how bizarre or even repugnant one may find this view, it seems to be the view that Plato holds.[28]

There is a fairly obvious objection to this view, an objection found as frequently among those sympathetic to Plato's ethics as among those who are not.[29] The objection is that the universality here outlined is entirely inappropriate as a foundation for the rich, contextual human world.[30]

---

[27] Crombie 1962, v.1, 273–275, defends Plato against the charge that his "concept of good" commits the "naturalistic fallacy" by Plato's identification of this good with one form of content or another. Crombie, however, does not defend Plato on the quite obvious ground that his Good is "beyond οὐσία" and so without specific or defined content; rather, he defends him on the odd ground that Plato uses "good" to commend different sorts of behavior, thereby evading the imputation of the naturalistic fallacy. The criterion of commendation is consistency. Crombie concludes his discussion of Plato's ethics, 281–292, by focusing on *Republic*, a discussion in which he says nothing about the Idea of the Good.

[28] Wreen 2018, 338–339, suggests that absolutism should not be contrasted with relativism, but rather with what is prima facie good. But as I am using the terms, all absolute or universal moral claims are defeasible by showing one exception. That would not be, strictly speaking, relativism, but if something is good but not absolutely good, presumably it is good for one or more but fewer than for all. I take it that that amounts to relativism of some sort. Wreen 2018, 340, concedes that what is relatively good is metaphysically grounded, that is, in what is true "for" one or more, but not for all.

[29] Annas 1999, 102, claims that "it is unpromising to look in the *Republic* for a direct way in which [the theory of Forms] has impact on the content of the dialogue's moral theory." She does this because she maintains that, even if ethics requires a metaphysical basis, the Idea of the Good is not adequate for providing this. She adduces the Stoics as arriving at similar notions of virtue with a "quite different metaphysical account." Apart from the dubious claim that the Stoics, as materialists, have *any* metaphysical account to offer, it is the identification of the Good with the One that gives the former its ethical content. Annas claims, 111–116, that "to think that ethical conclusions can be obtained from metaphysical premises is thus to be in a muddle about what ethics and metaphysics are." This view would, in my opinion, have some force if we were not talking about a superordinate first principle of all, which is identical with the One. This is the principle in which metaphysics and axiology converge.

[30] See, for example, Rowe 2007, 131–132, who raises this problem as besetting only those who take the superordinate Idea of the Good as the necessary metaphysical foundation of ethics. Rowe 2007, 145, n. 59, rejects an "ultra-transcendent good," arguing that the Idea of the Good is in fact nothing but the personal or human good that is the focus of virtually all of the earlier dialogues. I agree with Rowe that "my good" and "the Good" are identical, analogous to the way that, for example, Beauty and the beauty in Helen, or Largeness and the largeness in a building, are identical. I deny that the Good is thereby to be discounted or stripped of its "ultra-transcendence." The differences between

2.2 *The Idea of the Good and the Form of the Good*

An exhortation to strive for and embrace the superordinate Idea of the Good should only be met with derision by anyone struggling to do good and avoid evil in real life. Plato's response to this objection is twofold. First, the Good is instantiated here below via the Forms. And the Forms are the paradigms of all possible intelligible content. That is, *any* ethical theory will ultimately need to appeal to the definitional content of Forms in order to make intelligible its normative claims. Second, the precise way in which, say, the Form of Justice is to be instantiated is not, alas, immediately entailed by a recognition of a superordinate Idea of the Good that makes just acts useful or beneficial.[31] One naturally struggles to find some heuristic to apply the results of having engaged in "the most important study." There seem to be at least three.

First, if Good is universal, then it is not possible that something, say, some action, should be good for A and at the same time not good for B. The obvious parallels are found in the truths of mathematics. Another way to put this is to say that if the Good is instantiated here and now, it is otiose to add "for me" to the proposition that represents the good state of affairs. Thus, if benevolent kingship is good for Athens, then it is true, but also needs no saying, that it is good for me, an Athenian citizen, that a benevolent king rules. More interesting and related to the role of the Good in illuminating the Socratic paradoxes, if it is good that I be punished for my wrongdoing, then it is good for me that I be punished for my wrongdoing. Conversely, if it is good for me that I obtain something or do something, then we can infer that it is good *simpliciter* that this occur.

How does this logical point about the universality of Good yield a heuristic? If I am right in believing that, say, just deeds are good owing to the Idea of the Good, then I can infer that they are good for me. Similarly, I can infer that it is bad for me to do an unjust deed.[32]

---

us are not trivial or merely a matter of semantics. I claim that only with the Idea of the Good in its full-strength ontological status can the universality of Plato's moral realism be preserved. Without that, we must fall back upon prudentialism, whose "universality" is a naive hope rather than the conclusion of a philosophical argument. It is as naive as the hope that a "decent" human being like Protagoras, having ascended to power, will do the "right" thing.

[31] One might object that the relation of instantiation of the Good or the Good via Forms turns normative predicates into instruments. See, for example, Timmermann 2019, 101. I doubt that Plato would take this as a serious criticism since the bringing about of any good *is* supposed to be an instrument for attaining the Good. That is why it is good in the first place.

[32] At *Ap.* 31C4–D6, Socrates explains how his daemon works: it "turns him away (ἀποτρέπει)" from doing things, but never "encourages (προτρέπει)" him to do anything. Someone who believes that goodness is one thing and that life is not a zero-sum game is going to have a demonic devotion to not interfering in the lives of others. I am assuming, of course, that Socrates' vigorous practice of

Then, my doing an unjust deed can never be in my interest. Plato surely believes this on any account of his ethics. But on the prudentialist account, it does not follow that doing just deeds is in everyone's interest even if Justice, like all the Virtues, is a species of perfection. Thus, I can never achieve my good by being unjust to anyone else. Clearly, knowledge of what justice is is crucial to the task of being just and of benefiting oneself. But this knowledge is only dispositive in determining action on behalf of my good if the Form of Justice participates in the superordinate Idea of the Good which is the object of my will. Suppose that knowledge of what Justice is includes, minimally, knowledge that intentionally harming an innocent person cannot constitute a just deed. If that is so, the heuristic indicates that one refrain from aggressing against anyone. Needless to say, agreeing to this would amount to a huge concession on the part of the tyrant. His devotion to the idea of life as a zero-sum game leads him to think that his own good can often only be advanced at the expense of others.

Let us dig a bit deeper for a more problematic case. Someone employing a utilitarian calculus might argue either that (a) if the greatest happiness of the greatest number is attained, then injustice done to the few is good or that (b) if the greatest happiness of the greatest number is achieved, then no injustice is thereby done whatever is in fact done to a few. It seems that on the basis of the universality of the Good, Plato would decisively reject both alternatives. The first is rejected in Socrates' absolutist prohibition of injustice in *Crito*.[33] The rejection of the second alternative follows from Socrates' refutation of Thrasymachus' definition of justice as the advantage (συμφέρον) of the stronger.[34] This claim is rejected for all cases of "the stronger" including the majority in a democracy. Attaining advantage for the majority presumably entails disadvantage for the minority, that is,

---

dialectic does not constitute interference. At *Rep.* 6.505E2, a passage quoted above, every soul "divines (ἀπομαντευομένη)" that the Good is "something (τι)," even though they cannot quite say what that is. There is, I suggest, a connection in the use of the religious language of daemons and divination. It may also be that the capacity for "divining" something is owing to our disembodied knowledge, which we struggle to recover through recollection. See *Rep.* 7.523A8, 531D5; *Phil.* 64A2–3; *Tim.* 41E2–3, where every soul is, prior to birth, shown the nature of the cosmos and its laws.

[33] See *Cr.* 48C6–49B6, esp. 49A4–5: Οὐδενὶ τρόπῳ φαμὲν ἑκόντας ἀδικητέον εἶναι, ἢ τινὶ μὲν ἀδικητέον τρόπῳ τινὶ δὲ οὔ (Do we say that one must not willingly do an unjust deed in any way or do we say that one must do an unjust deed in one way but not in another?). I am assuming that the rejected second alternative would permit a utilitarian calculation that required the harming of the few for the good of the many.

[34] *Rep.* 1.338C2ff. Note that Thrasymachus contrasts seeking "one's own benefit (τὸ αὑτῇ συμφέρον)" with "the good of another (τὸ ἀλλότριον ἀγαθόν, 343c2–3)." This is the false view that the introduction of the Idea of the Good corrects.

2.2 The Idea of the Good and the Form of the Good 41

the weaker; otherwise, it would be for the advantage of all. According to Thrasymachus, the advantage of the majority (if it is stronger) is just for all.[35] The rejection of this position by Socrates entails the rejection of (b). If this is so, here is a strong, albeit negative, heuristic based on the universality of the Good.

This heuristic is also sharply circumscribed since the possibility of doing something apparently good that has adverse consequences for someone sometime is considerable. And the "greater" the good that one aims to do, the greater the chance of bringing about these consequences. In the face of this, one might attempt various strategies. For example, one might introduce degrees of goodness. So, one doesn't calculate whether doing something to A has or has not a bad effect on B, but whether bringing about A-B is, on balance, a greater good than not doing so. In other words, one tries to contextualize the effects of acting and then shape the demands of virtuous behavior accordingly. Alternatively, one might introduce a doctrine of unintended consequences or of "double effect." According to such a doctrine, if doing something good to A has the unintended effect of producing something bad for B, then this does not "count" as a failure of virtue. Admittedly, both of these strategies are fraught with possibilities for abuse. It should also be noted, however, that truly unintended side effects of one's behavior – if they are *unforeseeable* – cannot, *ex hypothesi*, be part of a calculation regarding doing good and avoiding evil. But often, and especially at the political rather than personal level, unintended side effects are reasonably foreseeable. At this level, it is difficult to see how an absolutist prohibition of wrongdoing would not be violated. The cascading consequences of behavior and the circumscription of the first heuristic suggest a certain skepticism about instantiating the Good or at least of trying to do so via laws or rubrics. Understandably, Plato hoped that a philosopher with knowledge of the Good would be best placed to make circumstantial judgments about how the Good should be brought about case by case.

The second heuristic for the instantiation of the Good follows from the necessary absolute or unqualified simplicity of the unhypothetical first principle of all and from its being identified with the Idea of the Good. As Plato says in *Republic*, "the virtuous person becomes one out of many (ἕνα γενόμενον ἐκ πολλῶν)."[36] I shall have much more to say about the

---

[35] See *Rep.* 1.338E3–4.
[36] See *Rep.* 4.443E1; cf. 5.462B1–2; 8.554D9–10; *Phd.* 99B5–6; *Phdr.* 246A6–7.

Good as One later in this chapter, but for now it should suffice to indicate that unification according to kind or integrative unity is a standalone criterion of goodness for Plato even though its effective implementation depends on having at hand definitions of the natures whose unity is sought, including species of living things and forms of association like a state or a family.[37] The optimal state for any natural or even for any artificial construct is integrative unity.[38] In nature, integrative unity maps the steps from endowment to achievement, from the kind of thing one is by nature to the fulfillment of that nature.[39] The diversity of types of integrative unity once again indicates the necessity for the first principle of all to be beyond οὐσία. The Good or One is a principle of integrative unity, and in its absolute simplicity, it is beyond any need for an integration of parts. But for this to be more than merely notional, the Good or One must be, as Plato says explicitly, the source of the being of everything that has the complexity of an existent with an essence. In eternity, endowment and achievement of integrative unity coincide; in the temporal world, where being is "spread out" across time (and space), integration is not inevitable. But it is the only way that the Good is achievable.

The third heuristic is offered in *Philebus* where we learn that the Good cannot be grasped on its own.

> So, if we are not able to capture the good in one idea, let us get at it with three, with beauty, symmetry, and truth, and say that we would be most correct to treat these as in a way one and responsible for what is in the mixture [of the elements in the good life], and that it is owing to this being good that it becomes so.[40]

---

[37] See Krämer 1959, 135; 535–541, on the centrality in Plato's philosophy of integrative unity, called by Krämer "Einheit in der Vielheit"; Beierwaltes 2002, 127–130.

[38] See *Gorg*. 506E1–4: Τάξει ἄρα τεταγμένον καὶ κεκοσμημένον ἐστὶν ἡ ἀρετὴ ἑκάστου; – Φαίην ἂν ἔγωγε. – Κόσμος τις ἄρα ἐγγενόμενος ἐν ἑκάστῳ ὁ ἑκάστου οἰκεῖος ἀγαθὸν παρέχει ἕκαστον τῶν ὄντων; – Ἔμοιγε δοκεῖ. (Therefore, it is due to order that the virtue of each thing is something that is ordered or arranged, isn't it? – I would say so – Therefore, when a certain appropriate arrangement comes to be in each thing, that provides the good of each of the things that are? – It seems to me so.) Cf. 455B8, 503E4ff. See Krämer 1959, 130–138, citing a number of texts in the dialogue focusing on or alluding to integrative unity as an idea. Also, see Hoffmann 1996, 15–22, on the centrality of the concepts of τάξις and κόσμος in Plato's metaphysics, epistemology, and ethics.

[39] See Sedley 2009, 157–158: "If you make the best decision and unify your self with your intellect, you are making yourself identical with that in you which is immortal." Also, see Jorgenson 2016, following Sedley, with some incisive remarks about achieving immortality as achieving an integrative unity.

[40] See *Phil*. 65A1–5: Οὐκοῦν εἰ μὴ μιᾷ δυνάμεθα ἰδέᾳ τὸ ἀγαθὸν θηρεῦσαι, σὺν τρισὶ λαβόντες, κάλλει καὶ συμμετρίᾳ καὶ ἀληθείᾳ, λέγωμεν ὡς τοῦτο οἷον ἓν ὀρθότατ' ἂν αἰτιασαίμεθ' ἂν τῶν ἐν τῇ συμμείξει, καὶ διὰ τοῦτο ὡς ἀγαθὸν ὂν τοιαύτην αὐτὴν γεγονέναι. Treating the triad "as in a way one" does not imply homogenization or the effacement of the three criteria. Integrative unity *according to kind* preserves the natural complexity of the kind. Cf. *Tim*. 87C5–6.

2.2 The Idea of the Good and the Form of the Good

I shall have more to say about this triad of criteria in Chapter 6. Here I only want to emphasize that this triad is potentially the most powerful heuristic of all in determining whether or not the Good is being instantiated. It indicates implicitly integrative unity ("treat these as in a way one"), but it also indicates the *relational* properties of truth, beauty, and symmetry: Truth is the property of being in relation to our intellects, beauty is the property of being in relation to our desire or appetite, and symmetry is the property of being in relation to authentic imaging of it in the sensible world.[41] Thus, in reflecting on the truth, the beauty that attracts us, and the symmetry of the parts of real images of Forms, we have something of a guide to action.

The Idea of the Good provides truth to the intelligible world, thereby making its inhabitants knowable.[42] It is itself "more beautiful (κάλλιον)" than this world, drawing things to itself by drawing them to the intelligible world.[43] In short, the Good is the principle of beauty and truth. It is puzzling how symmetry (συμμετρία) fits into this picture until we see the Good as the One. For symmetry is virtually identical with integrative unity. All genuine symmetries are "true" images of the first principle, the paradigm of all being.[44] The Good or One is virtually all the intelligible world.

These three heuristics, even when used together, fall short of a comprehensive formula for determining how to live a good life or how to act so

---

[41] See *Soph.* 235D6–E2 where εἰκαστικὴ τέχνη, in producing "the symmetries belonging to the paradigm (τὰς τοῦ παραδείγματος συμμετρίας)," is distinguished from φανταστικὴ τέχνη (see 236C4), the latter "saying farewell to the truth" (236A4). Perhaps discoveries in higher mathematics provide the most vivid examples of the rough unity of beauty, symmetry, and truth. No doubt, biology is, too, a rich source of examples, especially of symmetry among subsystems operating together in the larger organic framework. For example, an ecological niche evinces the sort of balance that Plato evidently has in mind. Recent spectacular advances in the application of computational science to microbiology are particularly illuminating. It is now possible to predict the three-dimensional structure of a protein molecule on the basis of its DNA pattern or syntax alone. I think Plato would wholeheartedly endorse the claim that the three-dimensional "projection" of the DNA structure is a startling example of symmetry. A purely intelligible structure is manifested in the sensible world in bodies that are "symmetrical" with it.

[42] *Rep.* 6.508D10–E2.   [43] *Rep.* 6.508E4–5.

[44] See *Rep.* 7.540A9, where the Good is referred to as παράδειγμα ("paradigm"). Broadie 2021, 58, denies that the Good serves as a paradigm at all; instead, "since the form of the good is identical with the forms of the virtues or the complex of them, finding out what they are is identical with exploring the nature of the good." Broadie rejects the paradigmatic status of the Good in part because she rejects the identification of the Good with the One. See below Section 2.6. Hence, she can see no independent paradigmatic status for the Good. If, however, the Good is the One, "then integrative unity according to kind" is a perspicuous way of talking about that status.

that the Good is instantiated in it. Political τέχνη is indispensable in this regard. Nevertheless, these heuristics in fact exclude a great deal from consideration – such as utilitarianism and relativism – and are action-guiding in countless ways. Most important, these criteria make no sense without the superordinate Idea of the Good. They make no sense if achieving one's own good cannot be grounded in super-sensible metaphysics, in particular in a principle that is both without specific essentialistic content and at the same time, explanatory for all the intelligible content that there is.

I shall conclude this section with one additional consideration in favor of the necessity for distinguishing a coordinate Form of the Good and the superordinate Idea of the Good. The latter, as we have seen, makes Justice and other Forms "useful or beneficial." The superordinate Good is not required to make any "perfection" a good. Unless we distinguish the Idea of the Good "from everything else," we are powerless to answer the question of whether the possession of one or more of these perfections is actually useful or beneficial.[45] Wisdom or knowledge does not determine whether, for example, pleasure or health is a good, but only whether it will be circumstantially useful or beneficial to us to have that good. Conflating the coordinate Form of the Good and the superordinate Idea of the Good forces one to say that physical health is not something that human beings desire, *ceteris paribus*, since it is undoubtedly true that a fully healthy vicious person can do more harm to himself and to others than if he were prostrate with illness.[46] Conflating the coordinate Form of the Good with the superordinate Idea of the Good would also threaten the argument in Book 4 of *Republic* that justice is desirable in itself (i.e., good) just as is physical health. By contrast, distinguishing the Form and the Idea allows us to recognize and endorse the obvious fact that people want pleasure and health and so on without conceding that the unalloyed Good that they seek is identical with either of these. And indeed, achieving this Good might even require us to forgo one or more of these goods.

---

[45] See *Rep.* 7.534B8–C1: ὃς ἂν μὴ ἔχῃ διορίσασθαι τῷ λόγῳ ἀπὸ τῶν ἄλλων πάντων ἀφελὼν τὴν τοῦ ἀγαθοῦ ἰδέαν (unless someone can give an account of the Idea of the Good, distinguishing it from everything else). Presumably, the term λόγος is being used loosely here, since there can be no λόγος τῆς οὐσίας for the Good. See Broadie 2021, 73–75, for a similar view, though her reasoning is somewhat different.

[46] See, for example, *Rep.* 6.496B–C, where Theages evidently benefits from being sick because his sickness keeps him out of politics.

2.3 The Idea of the Good as Beginning and as End

The Idea of the Good is "in a certain sense the cause of all things (τρόπον τινὰ πάντων αἴτιος)."[47] Its causality is represented by the metaphor of "overflowing (ἐπίρυττον)," an activity that is unlimited in any way since the Good is beyond οὐσία.[48] It is also, as we saw in Section 2.1, that at which everything aims. The simple conjunction of these two claims yields a particularly powerful conclusion. Apparently, it was a conclusion that Speusippus, Plato's successor, could not accept. For according to Aristotle, he maintained that the good for human beings must be separate from the first principle of all, the One.[49] Presumably, Aristotle mentions this because he thought that Speusippus held this position in opposition to Plato. If this is so, this supports the claim that Plato identified the Good as source with the Good as goal.[50] Why is the cyclicity of the identification of the beginning and the end so importantly different from the centrifugality of the Speusippian position? With the view of Speusippus or anything like it, the source of all being is no guide to the attainment of the good for human beings or for anything else. On this view, the only possible guide to that which is really good is how that appears to each one. By contrast, for Plato the source of being is the *only* guide to the attainment of the Good, whether through one or more of the three heuristics discussed in the previous section or in some other way. No doubt, this is why the Good is the object of "the most important study." The situation of ethics within a metaphysical framework and therefore the rejection of its autonomy sets Plato's ethical theory apart from most others.

Later Platonists made much of the coincidence of the first principle of all and the real Good that we all seek. Plotinus famously insisted that in order

---

[47] *Rep.* 7.516C1–2. This is inferred from the analogy of the sun, which is the cause of all things in nature. See 6.509B1–3. Bury 1910, 274–279, takes the Good as "the ultimate end of the universe" as well as "the principle of order, intelligibility, and reality." Denyer 2007, 284–285, seems to identify the productive role of the Good with its role as explanation for the intelligibility of its products. The idea is that if one claims that it is good that something exists, then one has thereby explained why x exists. But the "why" is here radically ambiguous. For if it were to apply exclusively to goals, then the productivity of the Good would have to be explained similarly by a goal. But the Good's putative goal in producing x can hardly be achieved by the existence of x, if for no other reason than that the Good is insufficiently complex to have goals or at least to have goals external to itself. The Good is "happiest" because it is utterly self-sufficient. See Leslie 1979 and Leslie 2019 on the deduction of the world from the primacy of the Good. Also, Miller 1985, 190, on the productive consequence of the Good's self-sufficiency.
[48] *Rep.* 6.509B6–7. Verdenius 1954, 250, inexplicably, claims that the Good "erniedrigt sich nicht, wie der christliche Gott, sondern er lässt sich nur anschauen."
[49] See Aristotle, *Meta.* Λ 7, 1072b31–34.
[50] See Berti 1983, 318, n. 13; Ferrari 2001; 2003, 287–290.

to know who we are we have to know where we come from.⁵¹ And, naturally, we have to know who we are in order to know how to achieve our own good.⁵² Nevertheless, in order to escape the suspicion that Plato has simply stipulated that the beginning is the end by giving them the identical name, it is necessary to ask for some rationale within a Platonic framework for this far-reaching claim. Here are the assumptions I find operating beneath the seemingly cavalier conflation of the answers to two questions: What is the first principle of all and what is the good life for a human being?

First, as I have already suggested, Plato is very much in line with all ancient Greek thinkers in taking nature (φύσις) to have a dual aspect. That is, there is a distinction between nature as an endowment and nature as an achievement. Normativity is found in the interstice between the two and depends on a first principle of normativity that explicitly transcends appearances.⁵³ What is good for someone, or some thing, is to become what it is in the fullest possible way. With this assumption, Plato takes his own path in arguing that the paradigms of the natures of things are eternal Forms.⁵⁴ But since there must be a first principle of all, which is the cause or explanation for the combination of existence and essence that constitutes any Form, this principle is in a way the paradigm of the natures here below.⁵⁵ It is uniquely paradigmatic since it is "beyond οὐσία."⁵⁶ The first principle is the goal precisely because of its unique paradigmatic status.

---

⁵¹ See *Enn.* V 1 [10], 1.1ff.
⁵² See Kahn 1987, 103, "At the limit, knowing the good and loving it will be only notionally not psychologically distinct." Kahn says this in response to the claim that whereas beliefs aim to conform to the world, desires aim to make the world conform to us. If this were true, the claim that the Good is the beginning and the end would be undermined. For Plato, attaining true belief, and ultimately, attaining knowledge, automatically infuses desire. This is what the so-called Socratic intellectualism maintains. But without the Idea of the Good as goal *and* as source, the intellectualism is quixotic.
⁵³ See Jordan 2019 for an account of "natural normativity" rooted in the dual aspect of nature as endowment and as achievement. *Moral* normativity requires rationality or the ability to discern a gap between one's endowment and what excellent achievement is. Normativity for, say, plants is analogous, though nonmoral. See Korsgaard 2009, 27, on the necessary connection between normativity and integrated unification. "The principles of practical reason serve to *unify and constitute us as agents*, and that is why they are normative" (my emphasis). We should, of course, add a further distinction between actual and ideal achievement.
⁵⁴ See *Parm.* 132D2. ⁵⁵ See *Rep.* 6.509B5–9.
⁵⁶ See Santas 2002; Delcomminette 2006 on the Idea of Good as generic Form or Form of Forms. Both these scholars reject the plain meaning of the text that places the Good beyond οὐσία. Similarly, Sayre 1995, 178, who takes the Good to be "the interconnected field of eternal Forms"; Seifert 2002, 413–418. Gosling 1973, 118, says that "the vision of how everything fits in is the vision of the Form of the Good." And yet, a vision of the first principle of all is not identical with the object of the vision. It is not Plato's vision that caused the Forms to be.

2.3 *The Idea of the Good as Beginning and as End*

The principal alternative to Plato's assumption of the dual aspect of nature is this. Someone with a human endowment fulfills his or her nature every day no matter what he or she does. On this view, it is a mistake to separate endowment and achievement normatively. On this view, it would still be possible to retain a distinction between first and second actuality, but the latter would have no normative significance. Even if there were a Form of Humanity, there is nothing we could do, short of dying, that would cause us to divest ourselves of our natural bodily endowment. We are fulfilling our nature at every moment. So, whatever good we seek is bound to diverge from a unique and universal first principle of all since that good can only be a function of our idiosyncratic individual desires.[57] On what other basis could I seek my own good? On what other basis could I discover that what appears to me to be my good is in reality not so? For I can have in principle no other guide to my real good than what appears to me to be that.

The basis for Plato's rejection of this alternative is found in Socrates' "autobiography" in *Phaedo*.[58] Naturalistic explanations for things being the way they are and for it being good that things are the way they are as provided by Anaxagoras are inadequate. A turn from naturalistic explanations to metaphysics is required. These sorts of explanation have a natural stopping-point in Forms, but ultimately require a stopping-point in "something adequate (τι ἱκανόν)." For example, if it is asked why Socrates is sitting in prison when he could escape death, the naturalist will provide an explanation in terms of anatomy and physiology whereas Socrates argues that he is remaining in prison because he believes that it is good for him to do so (even though, of course, dying unnaturally is not a good). Leave aside for now the explanations for things and events that stand outside human ethical considerations and appear to have no connection to the Idea of the Good. If it is indeed good for Socrates to remain, without this good being explained ultimately by the Idea of the Good, it is very difficult to see why it is good for Socrates to give up his life as opposed

---

[57] Stocker 1979, 745, claims that "something can be good and one can believe it to be good without being in a mood or having an interest or energy structure which inclines one to seek or even desire it." Thus, one can desire the bad. This view, in part directed against Plato, does not seem to me to take into account two things: (1) that Plato uses "good" as part of the analysis of the nature of action such that it is not logically possible to act for the bad (even in cases of *akrasia*, as we shall see) and (2) that the good for which we must act is always apparent, even when it is really good. Apparent goods are always in need of contextualization, especially a temporal dimension, to be understood. Taylor 1924, 82, would seem to be more accurate in reference to Plato's doctrine when he says, "he who chooses evil in preference to good does so not *because of*, but *in spite of* its badness."

[58] *Phd.* 92A4–102A9. See Gerson 2020, ch.3.3.

to fleeing and perhaps fighting again another day. But perhaps he believes that it is good for him to remain just because that is the way he is. Perhaps he wants to stay because of some pathological psychological state. If that is the case, then the issue morphs into a question of relativism.

If relativism turns out to be unsustainable, then the desire for the real good for oneself can only be the achievement of one's nature, the paradigm of which is the Form of Humanity whose paradigm in turn is the Idea of the Good. So, fulfilling one's nature is to approach the ideal.[59] But the ideal is itself only an ideal expression of the first principle of all. It is only an instrument of the first principle, which exceeds all οὐσίαι in "power (δυνάμει)." It does so because it is uniquely self-explanatory and unlimited in its activity. As we can see in the Divided Line, it is not even possible to know the Forms without "ascending" to the unhypothetical first principle of all.[60] If the good we all seek for ourselves were other than an instance of the Idea of the Good, the first principle of all, then there could in principle be no explanation for why something is really, as opposed to apparently, good for us. For a process of reasoning that led me to conclude that something was really good for me would still leave me with the fact that it can only appear to me that it is really good for me. If it is indeed good for me, that is not *because* it appears to me to be so. The successful defense of the claim that all human beings seek the real good requires that the real good is identical to the ultimate and "adequate" explanation or αἰτία for the being of anything.

Every Form is, of course, unique. But the uniqueness of the Idea of the Good is not the uniqueness of a Form and that fact should restrain us from taking it to be unequivocally a paradigm, even the "ultimate" paradigm. It is only analogously so. The Good is not eminently all things; if it were, we might be enticed to say that it has the predicate "paradigmatically good." If that were so, it could only be because the Good participated in *another* paradigm. It is a paradigm only in the sense that it stands to everything else

---

[59] See *Lys.* 522IE3–6 (quoted above in n. 24) which makes the point clearly enough.
[60] That the "unhypothetical first principle of all" at 6.511B5–6 is the Idea of the Good and not, for example, the Law of Non-Contradiction as a few have proposed, is clear from a comparison with 7.532C6–7, where "the best among beings" does not, obviously, refer to a logical principle, and 533C9, where the ἀρχή of all is referring to the previous passage and 534B8 where the Good is explicitly invoked. Broadie 2021, 68–71, is I think, correct in maintaining that the Forms are not "deduced" from the superordinate absolutely simple first principle. Instead, the vision of the Good, understood to be the One, is of the "internal" connectedness of all intelligible reality, that is, as an intelligible unity. Nevertheless, she is incorrect in maintaining that the text does not indicate that an ascent to the Good is necessary for knowledge of the Forms. Subsequent to the ascent, there must be some sort of descent, even if this is not straightforwardly deductive. More on this below in Section 2.6.

2.3 The Idea of the Good as Beginning and as End

analogous to the way the real paradigms – the Forms – are paradigms of the intelligible samenesses and differences found in the world. It is virtually everything, analogous to the way that "white" light is virtually all the colors of the spectrum. The relevance of this unique, quasi-paradigmatic status for moral realism is as follows. The Good, although it makes things beneficial or useful, does not provide "content" to things such that when they are good, that is because they participate in that content. The Forms are "Good-like (ἀγαθοειδῆ)" not because they participate in the "content" that is the Good but because their being is the effect of the eternal causal activity of the Good.[61] There is, as we shall see later in this chapter, an indirect way in which things participate in the Good by achieving integrative unity according to kind.

The charge frequently made against the interpretation of Plato according to which the Idea of the Good is the focal point of his moral philosophy depends upon the unquestionable truth that the Good is devoid of content in the sense that it is beyond οὐσία and is, therefore, absolutely simple. But for the charge to work, two additional premises are needed, namely, that which is absolutely simple can have no effects and that it cannot be an object either of desire or of thought. The Platonic rebuttal of both of these premises must be the same: The Good or One is essentially productive. It cannot produce what it is incapable of producing. Since it is ultimately the cause of everything, it is capable of producing everything. From the vast and complex array of intelligible beings in the world, we can immediately infer that the Good/One has the power to produce these. That is why it exceeds all intelligible being in its power.[62] The supposed content of which the Good/One is bereft is actually the entire intelligible world, so long as this is understood to be an effect rather than an explanatory terminus. The Good that we all seek must be the Good from which we all come because any putative content sought for other than the Good can always be "deconstructed" as effect and not as cause. As such, the question still remains as to what makes this effect good. The answer to this question is always: the Good in which it partakes. And it is that that we are seeking. The Good is not "empty"; it is the cause of the being of all there is. Its productive causality consists in its "overflowing," which it does eternally. Everything desires the Good

---

[61] See *Rep.* 6.509A3, which actually refers to knowledge and truth as Good-like. Knowledge and truth come from the Good, 6.508D10–E2, and are extensionally equivalent with the Forms or intelligible being.
[62] See *Rep.* 6.509B8–9. *Soph.* 247E5 gives us power (δύναμις) as a criterion (ὅρος) of being. The Good infinitely exceeds the power of anything with οὐσία.

because the Good is the principle of one aspect in the duality of nature, the aspect of achievement. It could only be this if it is also the source, "containing" in itself virtually everything it produces. The Good produces all the things whose goods consist in the fulfillment of their natures, natures which are what the Good is virtually. To achieve one's end is to arrive at one's source.

2.4 The Idea of the Good and the Demiurge

In *Timaeus*, Plato introduces "the maker and father of this universe (τὸν μὲν οὖν ποιητὴν καὶ πατέρα τοῦδε τοῦ παντός)," the Demiurge.[63] This maker is "good (ἀγαθός)."[64] And because he is good, he is not "grudging (φθόνος)."[65] Therefore, he "willed (ἐβουλήθη)" that the cosmos he was about to create should be good, too, as near to being like himself as possible.[66] In fact, he desired that the cosmos should be as good as possible.[67] On the basis of this description alone, many Platonists throughout history have been irresistibly drawn to the conclusion that the Demiurge is to be identified with the Idea of the Good.[68] It is hardly

---

[63] *Tim.* 28C3–4. [64] *Tim.* 29E2, E1.
[65] *Tim.* 29E2. A lack of grudging follows necessarily from being good since the Good is a principle of ungrudgingness in its eternal overflowing. The more something is "Good-like" the more it is ungrudging or overflowing in goodness. The Good is not ungrudging itself because it has no properties including this one.
[66] *Tim.* 29E2–3. [67] *Tim.* 30A1–2.
[68] See especially Krämer 1967 [1964], who gives a detailed account of the "*Nus* Theologie" of many (but not all) Middle Platonists. Also, Boys-Stones 2018, 148–149, with translations of some of the most relevant texts, and Ferrari 2020. Alcinous, *Handbook of Platonism*, ch. 10, is an outstanding example of this view, calling the intellect that the Demiurge is "the primal god (ὁ πρῶτος θεός)" (164.22 Whittaker). He leaves no doubt about the identification of the Demiurge and the Good (164.36). See also 179.41–42. Alcinous is undoubtedly representative of one standard Middle Platonic interpretation. Verdenius 1954, 243, 247–250, identifies God with the Idea of the Good, but realizes that the Demiurge must be subordinate to the Good, principally because the Demiurge does not create the Forms. But contrary to Verdenius, the very reason for denying the supremacy of the Demiurge is the reason for denying the supremacy of all the Forms, namely, that they are derived from the Good. See Van Riel 2016, ch. 3, on the Aristotelian basis for this interpretation and on the various modern interpretations. See also Bordt 2006, 145–187, who argues for the identity of the Demiurge and the Good, stressing the nonidentity of the Demiurge and the Living Animal. Benitez 1995, 119–140, takes a slightly more nuanced approach to the identification of the Good and the Demiurge, though finally affirming their extensional equivalence. Benitez, however, bases this false interpretation on the sound insight that Plato wants to identify ultimate efficient and final causes. Rist 2012, 231, following Guthrie 1975, 512, claims, "But if the Demiurge is pure Mind – that is, a purely immortal and immaterial substance – he is by that closer to being identified with what is all along and undoubtedly purely immaterial – namely, the Good itself." This view is developed in the following pages, 232–241. See Solmsen 1942, 72, for a sounder evidence-based conclusion, "For the philosopher, the source, standard, and criterion of good is not God, but the Idea of the Good." Long 2021, 77–78, largely follows Adam and Bordt in making the Good Plato's "supreme god." Rice 2000, chs. 4 and 5, argues for an "abstract conception of God" that he identifies with goodness. But,

2.4 The Idea of the Good and the Demiurge

surprising that early Christian Platonists should be drawn to this conclusion, too. The principal reason for this is that if the Demiurge and the Good are conflated, then the Christian God can more plausibly be identified with both.[69] So, God is the first principle of all and God is provident and has or is an intellect. But in *Timaeus* itself, the text seems implicitly to deny this identification. In the course of a discussion of the principle of necessity and of the world prior to its being made a cosmos, Timaeus says,

> We are not now going to speak of the first principle or principles of all, or however we are to speak of these, if for no other reason than because of the difficulty of clarifying these matters given our present method of proceeding.[70]

Since the Demiurge has already been spoken of extensively, it seems straightforwardly to follow that the Demiurge is not the first principle of all.[71] The only thing that might lead us to hesitate in drawing this conclusion is that Timaeus refers to "first principle or principles." One might suppose that "principles" cannot refer to the first principle and hence not to the Good. But the ambiguity is easily resolved on the basis of Aristotle's testimony, according to which Plato posited two principles, the One and the Indefinite Dyad, identifying the former with the Good. For our purposes, we can leave aside for now in what sense the Indefinite Dyad is a principle. However exactly it is related to the Good, identified with the One, does not change the fact that the Demiurge is *not* the unhypothetical first principle of all, and therefore is not God, understood in the Christian

---

according to Rice, this abstract God is capable of interacting with persons and so is itself a person. This identification is not shared by Plato.

[69] This is the idea that seems to be behind the argument of Cook 1896, section 3. Cook completely ignores the Idea of the Good in his construction of the metaphysical basis of Plato's ethics. Nettleship 1961 [1897], 232–233, makes the observation that "'the form of the good' in the *Republic* occupies the place in regard both to morals and to science which the conception of God would occupy in a modern philosophy of morals and nature, if that philosophy considered the conception of God as essential to its system." See Adam 1921, v.2, ad 505A2, who endorses the widely held nineteenth-century view that the Good is to be identified "with [Plato's] philosophical conception of Deity."

[70] *Tim.* 48C2–6: τὴν μὲν περὶ ἁπάντων εἴτε ἀρχὴν εἴτε ἀρχὰς εἴτε ὅπῃ δοκεῖ τούτων πέρι τὸ νῦν οὐ ῥητέον, δι' ἄλλο μὲν οὐδέν, διὰ δὲ τὸ χαλεπὸν εἶναι κατὰ τὸν παρόντα τρόπον τῆς διεξόδου δηλῶσαι τὰ δοκοῦντα; cf. 53D4–7. See Szlezák 1997, 198.

[71] See De Vogel 1986, 210; Enders 1999, 158–160; Perl 2014, 61–65. Contra Seifert 2002; Lavecchia 2006, 116–117, 216–222. Benitez 1995, 129, takes the reference to "principle or principles" to be a reference to Forms. It would be surprising if Plato were here telling us that he is declining to speak about Forms. And to what would the singular "principle" refer? Presumably, the "present method of proceeding" is to be contrasted with the method of dialectic as explained in *Republic*.

sense, nor is he the source of normativity. For he is good, not the Good.[72] Furthermore, because he is an intellect, he has an οὐσία.[73] And thinking all the Forms contained within the Living Animal means, minimally, that his intellect is informed by these in all their complexity.[74] Hence, he cannot be beyond οὐσία or absolutely simple in the way that the Good must be.

Perhaps the most important consideration militating against the identification of the Demiurge and the Good is this. The Demiurge is required to work on the Receptacle and the precosmic chaos in order to bring about the best possible image of the intelligible world. He is undoubtedly *constrained* by the circumstances presented to him. He is confronted with "necessity (ἀνάγκη)."[75] He is constrained because he has or is an intellect which is his οὐσία. That is what he is. His οὐσία is, by definition, a principle of limitation: to have an οὐσία is to be *this* and *not that*. These constraints indicate, or more accurately, define the nature of the Demiurge. He can do only what he can do with the material at hand because he is the good intellect that he is. Since the Good is beyond οὐσία, there is no way to attribute a definitional limitation to it. To say that it was constrained by the precosmic chaos would be to imply that there is something about its nature or οὐσία that makes this precosmic chaos a constraint on it. So, in addition to the other reasons given above, it seems quite clear that the Demiurge cannot be identified with the Good, the first principle of all.

This leaves us with the question of how the Demiurge is related to the Good and specifically, what role the Demiurge plays in Plato's moral theory. The refusal to conflate the Demiurge and the Good yields some fairly obvious conclusions.[76] First, providence is not to be attributed to the Good. This is solely within the purview of the Demiurge and the gods he creates.[77] Second, the goodness of the Demiurge means that he is not a principle of normativity, but rather that he conforms to it.[78] So, an

---

[72] As emphasized repeatedly by Proclus, *In Tim.* I 304.5, 305.8, 359.20–360.4 Diehl. And he is "a happy god (εὐδαίμονα θεόν)," 34B8, not like the Good in *Republic* which is "happiest."

[73] See *Tim.* 39E7–8, 47E4.   [74] See *Tim.* 30C2–31A.

[75] See *Tim.* 47E5–48A5 where it is clear that the Demiurge must work to persuade (πείθειν) necessity, though he cannot completely overcome it. See Ilievski 2014, 215–222. As Ilievski notes, 220, "[the Demiurge] is omniscient and omnibenevolent, but not omnipotent as well."

[76] At *Phil.* 22D7–8, we learn that νοῦς is "more akin to (συγγενέστερον)" and "more like (ὁμοιότερόν)" that which makes good things good than is pleasure. The "proximity" of νοῦς to the Good reinforces their actual nonidentity.

[77] See *Tim.* 40E3–4 on the γένεσις of the traditional gods.

[78] Atticus, fr. 12 des Places (= Proclus, *In Tim.* I 305.6–16 Diehl), notes explicitly that the Demiurge is called "good" and not "the Good." Nevertheless, he proceeds to conflate them. Ferrari 2020, 244–245, points out in defense of Atticus' position that *Tim.* 37A1, in reference to the Demiurge (τῶν

2.4 *The Idea of the Good and the Demiurge*

investigation of normativity can appeal to the Demiurge as a supreme example of goodness, but he himself is only an example. His goodness is not self-explanatory; it is derived. Third, such "personal" attributes as the Demiurge has, including being ungrudging and desirous of the goodness of his creation and deliberating about how to achieve his goal, do not belong to the first principle of all. It is true that the Good is called in *Republic* "most happy (εὐδαιμονέστατον)."[79] But this term does not necessarily indicate anything personal. The most salient feature of happiness in Greek thought is self-sufficiency, and though this is typically attributable to persons or gods, it is not implausible that the self-sufficiency of the Good follows from its absolute simplicity, not from its having attained whatever it needs, since it is impossible that the Good needs anything.[80] It is precisely the absence of absolute simplicity that produces *insufficiency*, especially in such things, like human beings, in whom there is a gap between endowment and achievement and in whom ungrudgingness is an achievement not an endowment.

If the Demiurge is irreducible to the Idea of the Good, this fact raises the obvious question of what purpose the Demiurge serves. The principal one seems to be to account for the order or intelligibility of the cosmos.[81] This is what νοῦς and only νοῦς is able to do. The cosmos is intelligible to us because intelligibility was put into it by an intellect. Intelligibility is essentially communication among or between intellects. That is what "dialogue (διά-λόγος)" is. The Good alone cannot account for this because the Good does not have intelligibility strictly speaking, that is, it is not an οὐσία. The Demiurge is the locus of all intelligibility represented by the Living Animal which it eternally contemplates.[82]

νοητῶν ἀεί τε ὄντων ὑπὸ τοῦ ἀρίστου [by the best of beings among eternal intelligibles]), and *Rep.* 6.532C6–7, in reference to the Good (τοῦ ἀρίστου ἐν τοῖς οὖσι [the best among beings]), could be taken to refer to the same thing. So, too, Lavecchia 2010, 58–59. What Atticus evidently misses, however, is that the Demiurge is the best "among intelligibles," and the Good, which is beyond intelligibility because it is beyond οὐσία, is the best absolutely. See Perl 2014, 64.

[79] *Rep.* 7.526E4–5, referring to E2.

[80] See *Phil* 20D4–6: ΣΩ. ἱκανὸν τἀγαθόν; ΠΡΩ. Πῶς γὰρ οὔ; Καὶ πάντων γε εἰς τοῦτο διαφέρειν τῶν ὄντων (Soc.: Is the Good sufficient? Pro.: How could it not be? It certainly differs from all beings in this). At 67A5–8, it appears that "sufficient (ἱκανόν)" and "self-sufficient (αὐτάρκης)" are being used synonymously of the Good. These are what the Good possesses or, rather is, and neither intellect nor pleasure possesses. Jaeger 1943 [1936], v.2, 286–288, takes the happiness of the Good to indicate not its self-sufficiency but its virtue since Plato identifies the virtuous with the happy. This cannot be correct since the Good, beyond οὐσία, is beyond virtue.

[81] See Mohr 1989, 299–300, on the crucial and unique role of the Demiurge in the introduction of measures or standards into the phenomenal world. As Mohr shows, these measures and standards constitute the intelligibility of the sensible world.

[82] See Diès 1927, v.2, 550, who felicitously expresses the distinction between Demiurge and Forms as "le Sujet par excellence" and "l'Objet par excellence."

The point of all this for moral theory is that while knowledge (ἐπιστήμη) may in some sense be both necessary and sufficient for virtue, this is only the case if that knowledge somehow reaches beyond the intelligible Forms and beyond the Demiurge to the Good itself. The Good does not just make the Forms to be the intelligible entities that they are but it also makes them knowable and makes participating in them beneficial. The normativity of moral realism is mostly a bluff or a charade without the superordinate Good. This is the lesson of the Divided Line and the surrounding texts in Book 6 of *Republic*. Hence, desiring the real, as opposed to the apparent, good requires that there exists a real Good over and above all the Forms. The role of Forms is instrumental to the imposition of normativity in nature, as is the νοῦς that effects the imposition. It is never sufficient to know what the Form of Justice is. It is also necessary to know that being just is one way to instantiate the Good. If anyone desires anything, it is because it is a prima facie manifestation of the Good.

What is true for the Demiurge is, a fortiori, true for the gods he generates. These gods are two removes from the principle of normativity. Their being providential and benevolent, as explained in *Laws* Book 10, is not because they are normatively or ontologically fundamental but because, like all living things, they desire the Good and are themselves good insofar as they achieve what they desire.[83] Hence the old chestnut, deriving from *Euthyphro*, which inquires whether something is good because the gods desire it or the gods desire it because it is good, is answered decisively by the latter alternative.[84] The gods do not make virtue good by loving virtue or practicing it. These gods are powers in the cosmos, obviously more powerful than us since they are immortal. But they are not determinants of what is good and evil. And insofar as they can be imagined to be involved in punishing the wicked and rewarding the virtuous, they are servants of the well-run cosmos instituted by the Demiurge. In the matter of ethics, Plato draws his principles from metaphysics, not from theology.

2.5 Assimilation to God

In the so-called digression in *Theaetetus*, Socrates delivers an exhortation to the distinguished mathematician Theodorus regarding the aims of philosophy.

---

[83] See *Rep.* 2.379B–C, 380C; 10.617E.   [84] See *Eu.* 10A2–3.

Evils, Theodorus, cannot be left behind, for there is of necessity something always opposed to the Good, nor are evils located among the gods; rather, they loiter around the mortal nature and the world here by necessity. For this reason, we should try to flee from this world to the divine world as quickly as possible. And this flight is assimilation to god as much as is possible, assimilation meaning to become just and pious with wisdom. But, my good man, it is no easy thing to persuade people that pursuing virtue and shunning vice are not to be done for the reason that people give. The reason for pursuing the one and shunning the other is not that the one is useful and the other is not just for the purpose of appearing not to be evil and appearing to be good. That is just an old wives' tale, or so it seems to me. Let us state the truth in this way. God is in no way unjust; on the contrary, he is as just as possible, and no one is more assimilated to him than one who becomes as just as possible.[85]

For ancient students of Plato, the words "assimilation to god (ὁμοίωσις θεῷ)" express pithily the culmination of Plato's ethics.[86] The flight from evils is in the direction of the Good; it is the return to the source, as we have just seen. That flight consists in the practice of virtue with the addition of wisdom, precisely the wisdom that was absent in the man in *Republic* Book 10 who was virtuous merely by "custom (ἔθει)" "without philosophy (ἄνευ φιλοσοφίας)."[87] It is clear from this passage, however, that fleeing toward the Good does not mean something like a mystical union with it. The successful flight puts one in the company of the god or gods who themselves are subordinated to the Good. That this is the result follows from the nature of the assimilation, or more literally, the "making the same as." For one does not transcend οὐσία by the assimilation; on the contrary, one

---

[85] *Tht.* 176A5–C2: Ἀλλ' οὔτ' ἀπολέσθαι τὰ κακὰ δυνατόν, ὦ Θεόδωρε – ὑπεναντίον γάρ τι τῷ ἀγαθῷ ἀεὶ εἶναι ἀνάγκη – οὔτ' ἐν θεοῖς αὐτὰ ἱδρῦσθαι, τὴν δὲ θνητὴν φύσιν καὶ τόνδε τὸν τόπον περιπολεῖ ἐξ ἀνάγκης. διὸ καὶ πειρᾶσθαι χρὴ ἐνθένδε ἐκεῖσε φεύγειν ὅτι τάχιστα. φυγὴ δὲ ὁμοίωσις θεῷ κατὰ τὸ δυνατόν· ὁμοίωσις δὲ δίκαιον καὶ ὅσιον μετὰ φρονήσεως γενέσθαι. ἀλλὰ γάρ, ὦ ἄριστε, οὐ πάνυ τι ῥᾴδιον πεῖσαι ὡς ἄρα οὐχ ὧν ἕνεκα οἱ πολλοί φασι δεῖν πονηρίαν μὲν φεύγειν, ἀρετὴν δὲ διώκειν, τούτων χάριν τὸ μὲν ἐπιτηδευτέον, τὸ δ' οὔ, ἵνα δὴ μὴ κακὸς καὶ ἵνα ἀγαθὸς δοκῇ εἶναι· ταῦτα μὲν γάρ ἐστιν ὁ λεγόμενος γραῶν ὕθλος, ὡς ἐμοὶ φαίνεται· τὸ δὲ ἀληθὲς ὧδε λέγωμεν. θεὸς οὐδαμῇ οὐδαμῶς ἄδικος, ἀλλ' ὡς οἷόν τε δικαιότατος, καὶ οὐκ ἔστιν αὐτῷ ὁμοιότερον οὐδὲν ἢ ὃς ἂν ἡμῶν αὖ γένηται ὅτι δικαιότατος. Cf. *Rep.* 6.500B8–C8; *Phdr.* 252C3–253C6. Note that the central books of *Republic* are said by Socrates, 8.543C4–6, to be a digression as well.

[86] See especially Lavecchia 2006, 293–296. Also, Drefcinski 2014. In the Platonic tradition, much turns on whether the recognition of this fact is or is not coupled with the identification of the Demiurge and the Idea of the Good. See Männlein-Robert 2013, who argues that it is only in later Platonism beginning with Plotinus that the formula "assimilation to god" takes on prominence. I rather doubt this. It is prominent in both Plato and in Aristotle, for a start. And there are many Middle Platonic references to the idea. See Lavecchia 2006, 418, n.4 for some of these. Also, Karamanolis 2004.

[87] *Rep.* 10.619C8. Cf. *Phd.*82A10–B3. I am assuming that "to become just and pious" stands for all the virtues. See, for example, *Gorg.* 507A5–C7 where it is said that the "just and pious (and, therefore, courageous)" man is "perfectly good (τελέως)."

reverts to or appropriates one's own divine nature. That nature is the nature of an intellect, eternally contemplating intelligible being. Thus, we are made to be like the Demiurge by engaging in intellectual activity. And, as is also the desire of the Demiurge, we are made like the Living Animal by being cognitively identical with all the Forms it contains. That is, for example, the *only* way that an intellect can be made to be the same as a hippopotamus or a triangle.

In light of the *Republic* passage, we are obliged to say that wisdom or philosophy is an essential addition to virtue in order for assimilation to occur. Why? A by-now-venerable answer to this question is that the knowledge is an essential addition because this knowledge reveals how to be virtuous or how to put virtue into practice. It is the knowledge of a τέχνη. This interpretation is unsupportable for several reasons. First, as *Republic* Book 10 shows, the character without philosophy who chooses the life of a tyrant is already virtuous. That he is so by custom does not change the fact that he is not in need of knowledge of a τέχνη of how to do virtuous deeds. If it is objected that what he needs is not this sort of knowledge, but the knowledge of how to *be* virtuous, that is, how to have a virtuous disposition, it is far from clear what sort of τέχνη this is supposed to be.[88] The knowledge that, added to virtue, makes one like the gods, and that turns mere virtuous behavior into true virtue, is the knowledge that philosophers seek in *Republic* and in *Symposium*. It is knowledge of the Good, which is not esoteric knowledge of some secret "content," but knowledge that the Good is the One, virtually all intelligible being. Knowing that the Good or One is universal, we at least know that our happiness, our real good, cannot be achieved at the expense of anyone else. Practicing ordinary or "demotic" virtue is a simple and useful technique that contributes to achieving this goal. But it could never be sufficient without the knowledge – not belief – that one's own good is the good of an intellect, not that of an embodied human being. This knowledge is not otherwise available to human beings than as the culmination of philosophical education and it alone results in the self-transformation that consists in "becoming one out of many."[89] And

---

[88] See *Protag*. 339E5ff, where in the interpretation of Simonides' poem, Socrates says Simonides distinguished between "becoming (γένεσθαι)" and "being (ἔμμεναι)" "good (εσθλόν)" (340C4–5). As Frede 1992, xiii, points out, citing several passages in Thucydides, the word "becoming (γένεσθαι)" seems to be used here to refer to behavior, whereas the word "being (ἔμμεναι)" refers to the disposition to behavior.

[89] See Murdoch 1970, 84, "anything which alters consciousness in the direction of unselfishness, objectivity and realism is to be connected with virtue." Murdoch's view of the Good is sufficiently unlike that of Plato to have led her to assume an opposition between selfishness and unselfishness. If

2.6 The Idea of the Good and *Erōs*

it follows from the possession of this knowledge that one's true good cannot be achieved at the expense of anyone else.

2.6 The Idea of the Good and *Erōs*

Seen in the light of all the above, Diotima's speech in *Symposium* takes on a new clarity. Diotima instructs Socrates that love (ἔρως) is for beautiful things (τῶν καλῶν).[90] But this amounts to, says Diotima, a love for good things (τῶν ἀγαθῶν), that is, the possession of good things.[91] And the result of possessing good things is happiness (εὐδαιμονία), which all human beings wish for (βούλεσθαι).[92] So, love is nothing but the desire or appetite (ἐπιθυμία) for good things or for happiness.[93] The nexus of concepts here follows without deviation from what we have already seen in *Gorgias* and *Republic*. We all desire what is in fact good for ourselves and nothing else. A sharp distinction needs to be made between the things that seem or appear to be good for ourselves but are not and the things that really are. What *Symposium* adds is the extraordinary identification of the desire for good things with the love of beautiful things.[94] Ἔρως evidently includes both the desire for the apparently beautiful and the desire for the really beautiful. This last point is a crucial part of the puzzle since the cycle – remaining (μονή), procession (πρόοδος), and reversion (ἐπιστροφή) – needs to include everything there is.[95] No one does not desire to possess manifestations of the Good insofar as this is possible. But people, including lovers and tyrants and ordinary folk, do not frame their desires in this way. The answer to the objection that not all desire the Good by their own showing is that ἔρως is a common feature of all living things and ἔρως is nothing but a desire to possess the beautiful (whether merely apparent or real), which is in fact identical with a desire for good things. People desire the apparently beautiful because they suppose that it is really good.

---

my good and any manifestation of the Good are identical, this opposition disappears. I take it that unselfish behavior is what one would expect in someone who is virtuous "by custom" without philosophy. Plato thinks that for such a person, unselfishness is defeasible *in extremis*.

[90] *Symp.* 204D4; cf. 201E5. At 206E2, we have the singular τοῦ καλοῦ, instead of the plural τῶν καλῶν.

[91] *Symp.* 204D7. I take it that Plato assumes that beautiful things and good things are extensionally equivalent. That is, what makes something good, integrative unity or fullness of being, is what makes it beautiful or attractive and vice versa.

[92] *Symp.* 204E6–205A3; 205E7–206A4. Cf. *Euthyd.* 278E3–6, 282A1–7; *Me.* 88C3; *Phil.* 20C–21A.

[93] *Symp.* 205D1–3.   [94] See Krüger 1948, 158–164.

[95] The cyclical triad, remaining, procession, and reversion, often acknowledged as a central feature of Neoplatonic metaphysics, is rooted as firmly in the texts of the dialogues as any interpretation could be. The Good, while remaining eternally the Good, overflows ("processes"), and all things, both eternal and temporal, desiring the Good, revert to it.

The representation of ἔρως as midway between immortal and mortal – a daemon – is quite explicitly intended to establish its unifying role. "Being in the middle of the two [immortal and mortal], they [daemons] complete the whole and bind fast the all to itself."[96] Love is essentially a unificatory process like higher cognition.[97] In fact, as we learn at the completion of the higher mysteries, the highest expression of love *is* the highest form of cognition. And, of course, this is why the philosopher is the quintessential lover and why philosophy uniquely has the unificatory and transforming effect on the person.[98]

Another important feature of Diotima's discourse is her claim that the work (ἔργον) of love is birth in beauty, whether in body or soul.[99] It is misleading to translate ἔργον as "object" or "goal" as if ἔργον were synonymous with τέλος. For artifacts, the working or operation of that artifact may well be equivalent to its goal. The question "what does it do?" can be equivalent to the question "what is it for?" but this is not the case for things that exist by nature. The ἔργον of a human being is rational living; the τέλος of a human being is happiness. These are of course closely related, though nonetheless not identical since in the dual aspect of nature, rationality is an endowment whereas happiness is an achievement. What ἔρως does is give birth in beauty or, more expansively, in the presence of the beautiful. The τέλος of ἔρως is, as we have already seen, different; it is the possession of good things or happiness.[100] That ἔρως is naturally productive is a crucial feature of the entire system. For the Good is eternally productive and eternally happy, that is, self-sufficient. So, possession of the Good or any manifestation of it has the result of being productive.[101]

---

[96] *Symp.* 202E6–7: ἐν μέσῳ δὲ ὂν ἀμφοτέρων συμπληροῖ, ὥστε τὸ πᾶν αὐτὸ αὑτῷ συνδεδέσθαι. Cf. *Phd.* 99C5–6 on τὸ ἀγαθὸν καὶ δέον which binds (συνδεῖν) and connects (συνέχειν) everything. See Krüger 1948, 154.

[97] See *Phil.* 15D4: φαμέν που ταὐτὸν ἓν καὶ πολλὰ ὑπὸ λόγων γιγνόμενα περιτρέχειν πάντῃ καθ' ἕκαστον τῶν λεγομένων ἀεί, καὶ πάλαι καὶ νῦν (we say, I suppose, that it turns out always that in each of the statements we make one and many come to be identical by means of the statements, in the past and even now). In a simple predicative statement, e.g., *Soph.* 263A2, "Theaetetus is sitting," the "many" ("Theaetetus" and the predicate "is sitting") are also "one" ("Theaetetus is sitting").

[98] *Symp.* 204A1–B5.   [99] *Symp.* 206B1–8.

[100] See Penner 2011, 268, who conflates ἔργον and τέλος in the case of science or expertise, of which virtue is one. So, the ἔργον of the virtuous person is just the τέλος. The conflation seems inevitable if the superordinate Good is left out of the analysis or, like Penner, is understood as "the Form of Advantage."

[101] Mackie 1977, 23–24, takes it as a *reductio ad absurdum* of Plato's view that acquaintance with the Idea of the Good will provide sufficient motivation for virtue. This acquaintance with the Good is indeed the knowledge that is sufficient for virtue, though we must add the proviso that the knowledge is in fact of the identity of my own good and the Good itself. Knowledge of the Forms alone, were this possible, would not be, as Mackie insists, sufficiently motivating. See Cooper 1999, 145–148; Kahn 1987, 102; Singpurwalla 2006b, 279. This interpretation is disputed

2.6 *The Idea of the Good and Erōs*

It is an indication of the Good's universal causal scope that the vast variety of natural desires all result, with their satisfaction, in production.

But in addition to the differences between beautiful things, the difference between the apparently beautiful and the really beautiful matters to what is produced. That is why only the philosophical lover, when possessing the Good, produces true virtue.[102] Everyone else produces at best images of virtue or, at a further remove, images of themselves.[103] The possession of the Good that produces true virtue is, of course, the knowledge of τὸ καλόν.[104] This knowledge or vision is usually understood to be a reference to the Form of the Beautiful, although the question of why this Form alone should produce true virtue is rarely asked. Would not knowledge of a Form of Virtue or of the individual Forms of the Virtues be a more plausible object of knowledge productive of true virtue? We have, though, already had the claim that makes it implausible to say that the philosophers' achievement of the object of his love is a single Form. The love of beautiful things is nothing but the love of good things. And every Form is good insofar as it participates in the Good. It seems much more plausible to suppose that τὸ καλόν should be read attributively, that is, as a sort of synecdoche, "that which is beautiful," referring to all the Forms or to Being. Knowledge of Forms as requiting the love of beautiful things only makes sense, I believe, if the Good is virtually all of these.[105] If this were not the case, then the achievement of the philosopher would not clearly entail the possession of good things where "possession" indicates the real good that everyone wills (βούλεσθαι).

The production of true virtue which results only from the knowledge of Being further elucidates the articulation of the system. The Good is essentially diffusive. What it produces is unqualifiedly Good-like including both the Demiurge and Being. Here there is no virtue, but only the paradigm of virtue. True virtue is what goodness looks like in the sensible,

---

by Vasiliou 2015. He thinks, 45–47, that it is the desire for immortality that motivates the lover to give birth to true virtue. This view seems to me to misunderstand the text at 212A2–6, where it is the knowledge of Beauty that produces true virtue. The words γενήσεται τίκτειν ("he will give birth") are taken by Vasiliou to mean "will be able to give birth" and somehow to be irrelevant to the desire for immortality. But the claim is assertoric, not conditional. The true virtue is in the philosopher and the "cultivation (θρεψαμένῳ)" of it will produce virtuous deeds. No further motivation is needed since producing virtuous deeds is the achievement of one's own good.

[102] *Symp.* 211E4–212A7. See Destrée 2017, who rightly emphasizes the moral and political transformative effect of the knowledge of Forms.
[103] Price 1989, 51, takes these images of virtue as "ersatz" virtue, though he goes on to describe them as in fact the popular or political virtues of *Phaedo* and *Republic*, that is, virtuous practices without philosophical underpinning.
[104] *Symp.* 211D1–3.   [105] See Robin 1908, 223; Price 1989, 43; Gerson 2006, 62–64.

temporalized, and transitory world. "Illusory" or "popular or political" virtue are deviations from this.[106] The reason why wisdom is required to be added to the moral virtues in order to "assimilate to the divine" is clear. So, too, is the reason why "being virtuous without philosophy" in *Republic* Book 10 is as likely as not to produce dolorous results.

Beauty is a relational property of Being, specifically, the property of attracting us or stimulating our desire.[107] Considered as a unity along with symmetry and truth, it comprises the triad that best represents the Good.[108] The love of the beautiful encapsulates the reversion to the Good. Accordingly, the multiple beautiful things encapsulate the variety of manifestations of the Good.[109] The distinction between appearance and reality works in parallel for both: Apparent beauty stands to real beauty as apparent good stands to real good. Presumably, the prevalence of nonveridical appearances is entirely the result of embodiment. Whatever appears beautiful or good has to be scrutinized by intellect as to its *bona fides*. Integrated unity is an index of realness as opposed to mere appearance.[110]

Plato, I suppose, focused on the ubiquity of ἔρως to indicate the transcendent and ultimate power of the Idea of the Good. This ubiquity

---

[106] True virtue and popular or political virtue in relation to the paradigm of virtue in the intelligible world stand, respectively, as εἰκαστικὴ τέχνη and φανταστικὴ τέχνη in relation to their paradigm in *Soph.* 235D6–E2 with 236C3–4. True virtue is "symmetrical" with the intelligible world because it represents it as an integrated unity; popular or political virtue is not; it only appears to be. Being "symmetrical" with the intelligible world is the result of "assimilation to god."

[107] See Ferrari 1992, 260, "the beautiful is ... the quality by which the good shines and shows itself to us." In Aristotle, e.g., τὸ καλόν also has a derivative sense indicating our evaluation of an action or institution, and so on. So, at *EN* B 3, 1104b31, he says that there are three aims of choice: the noble (τὸ καλόν), the useful (τὸ συμφέρον), and the pleasurable (τὸ ἡδύ). The use of καλόν here should be situated within the dual aspect of the general meaning of φύσις as endowment and achievement. To call something καλόν is indicative of the achievement. So, for example, virtue is καλόν because it names that which fulfills our nature. See, for example, *La.* 192C–D; *Protag.* 349E; *Gorg.* 474D4. I call this sense derivative (at least for Plato) because the fulfillment of our nature is always correlated with the attainment of being, particularly, the integrative unity according to kind. See *Hip. Ma.* 295C2–3 where καλόν is defined as that which is beneficial (χρήσιμον). Here is perhaps a tertiary sense indicating that which contributes to the achievement.

[108] *Phil.* 65A1–5.

[109] McCabe 2005, 192–193, rather grudgingly admits that Plato posits a superordinate Idea of the Good but goes on to claim that its objectivity diminishes the importance of the agent. Also, see Kraut 2011, 80–81, along the same lines. See Murdoch 1970, 103, who seems to me to have a better grasp of what Plato is doing: "And when we try perfectly to love what is imperfect our love goes to its object *via* the Good to be thus purified and made unselfish and just." Also, see Kronqvist 2019, especially 991, for some penetrating remarks on how the apex of philosophical achievement does not involve the transcending of the personal, but rather its transformation in the light of the Good.

[110] Most evident in Aristophanes' myth in *Symp.* 189D2–193C5. The speeches of Phaedrus, Pausanius, and Eryximachus, and the dialectical interchange with Agathon all in their own ways cast light on the fundamental themes of true versus defective virtue and integrative unity. For example, the speech of Eryximachus at 186B–C invokes the universality of ἔρως, even including plants. The nature of ἔρως as desire for the Good is then explained by Diotima. See Kronqvist 2019, 979–986.

is the best way of acknowledging that the universal desire for the Good must originate in it. Plato saw that the immediate object of ἔρως, the beautiful, is a manifestation of the Good, whether real or apparent. If beauty is a relational property of Being, it follows that love of the beautiful is nothing but the desire for Being, which in turn is, in the consummation of love, just how the desire for the real Good is satisfied. If someone confines himself to the merely apparently beautiful (that is, the nonveridical appearance), none of these facts change. But in that case, it is not possible or perhaps just not likely for someone to grasp that "good is one," that one's good is not a goal in a zero-sum game. The charge that, in the higher mysteries of *Symposium*, the philosopher transcends that the personal is not a charge entirely without merit, though it is ultimately misplaced. For transcending the idiosyncratic personhood of the other is no more necessary than is transcending one's own idiosyncratic personhood, supposedly constituted by idiosyncratic and incommensurable goods. The one who wonders whether the good that is virtue is beneficial or more beneficial than any other good is assuming that the criterion for an answer to this question is personal advantage. One who is no longer tempted to think that personal advantage can be achieved despite the advantage of anyone else has transformed the personal and thereby achieved real happiness.

2.7 The Idea of the Good and to *philon*

Plato's dialogue *Lysis*, devoted to the theme of friendship (φιλία), can be read as a companion to *Symposium*.[111] It introduces φιλία into the structure of moral realism just as *Symposium* introduces ἔρως.[112] One well-trodden path used in explaining how this is done focuses on an important passage near the end of the dialogue, in which the idea of a πρῶτον φίλον ("primary friend") is introduced.[113] According to this approach, the

---

[111] By "companion" I mean that neither dialogue negates nor corrects anything in the other. See Thesleff 2009, 296–297, who concludes that "the various allusions in *Lysis* can be read as implying those of the *Symposium*."

[112] See *Lys.* 221B7, which seems to treat φιλία and ἔρως as overlapping, if not synonymous. This closeness in meaning is even more explicit at 5221E3–6, where ἔρως, φιλία, and ἐπιθυμία are said to be of what is οἰκεῖον to us, that is, what belongs to our natures. Undoubtedly ἔρως has a sexual connotation that φιλία does not necessarily have. And yet, embedding ἔρως in a metaphysical framework has a "desexualizing" effect that makes it even closer to φιλία. Other terms used as practically synonymous with φιλεῖν are ἀσπάζεσθαι (217B4), ἀγάπαν (222D2), and προτιμᾶν (219D7).

[113] The term φίλον is highly resistant to English translation. "Dear" is tepid; "friend" is too limited. I am going to leave it untranslated, noting only that it refers to any object of φιλία, one type of

πρῶτον φίλον is a reference to the Idea of the Good.¹¹⁴ This view is sometimes misrepresented as holding that Plato hereby introduces Forms into his discussion of φιλία, not a Form of Friendship, but a Form of the Good or perhaps a Form of Beauty.¹¹⁵ As argued above in Section 2.2, Plato distinguishes a superordinate Idea of the Good from a generic Form of the Good. And as I shall try to show now, and in the light of *Symposium*, we should insist on the likelihood that the πρῶτον φίλον refers to the former and not the latter. Here is the relevant passage:

> Medicine, we say, is φίλον for the sake of health – Yes – then, is health also φίλον? – Indeed, it is – Therefore, if it is φίλον, it is for the sake of something – Yes – For the sake of something φίλον if we are to follow our previous agreement – Indeed, it is – Then is not that for the sake of which it is φίλον also φίλον? – Yes – Then aren't we either going to have to give up going on like this or else get to some starting-point (ἀρχήν) which does not carry us on to another φίλον, for the sake of which all the others are said to be φίλον, but to a first φίλον for the sake of which all the others are said to be φίλον? – Necessarily – This is in fact what I am talking about, lest all the other things which we said to be φίλον for the sake of that deceive us, as some kinds of images of that first, which is truly φίλον.¹¹⁶

Clearly, the issue here is the identity of the πρῶτον φίλον.¹¹⁷ Perhaps the most obvious answer to this question is: the person who is dear or φίλον,

---

human desire which is not necessarily sexual or appetitive and whose various manifestations are an indication of the ubiquity of the Good in all types of being and our natural affinity for it.

¹¹⁴ See, for example, Krämer 1959, 499–501; Szlezák 1985, 117–126; Reale 1997, 277–283.

¹¹⁵ See Vlastos 1973, "The Individual as an Object of Love in Plato," appendix I, 35–37, in which Vlastos argues that there is no textual basis for assuming transcendent Forms to be present in *Lysis*.

¹¹⁶ *Lys.* 219C1–D5: ἰατρική, φαμέν, ἕνεκα τῆς ὑγιείας φίλον. {–} Ναί. {–} Οὐκοῦν καὶ ἡ ὑγίεια φίλον; {–} Πάνυ γε. {–} Εἰ ἄρα φίλον, ἕνεκά του. {–} Ναί. {–} Φίλου γέ τινος δή, εἴπερ ἀκολουθήσει τῇ πρόσθεν ὁμολογίᾳ. {–} Πάνυ γε. {–} Οὐκοῦν καὶ ἐκεῖνο φίλον αὖ ἔσται ἕνεκα φίλου; {–} Ναί. {–} Ἆρ' οὖν οὐκ ἀνάγκη ἀπειπεῖν ἡμᾶς οὕτως ἰόντας ἢ ἀφικέσθαι ἐπί τινα ἀρχήν, ἣ οὐκέτ' ἐπανοίσει ἐπ' ἄλλο φίλον, ἀλλ' ἥξει ἐπ' ἐκεῖνο ὅ ἐστιν πρῶτον φίλον, οὗ ἕνεκα καὶ τὰ ἄλλα φαμέν πάντα φίλα εἶναι; {–} Ἀνάγκη {–} Τοῦτο δή ἐστιν ὃ λέγω, μὴ ἡμᾶς τἆλλα πάντα ἃ εἴπομεν ἐκείνου ἕνεκα φίλα εἶναι, ὥσπερ εἴδωλα ἄττα ὄντα αὐτοῦ, ἐξαπατᾷ, ᾖ δ' ἐκεῖνο τὸ πρῶτον, ὃ ὡς ἀληθῶς ἐστι φίλον. See McTighe 1983, 76–79, for the slight textual difficulty in this passage and for the solution which I have followed. But the principal point is unchanged, namely, the identification of the πρῶτον φίλον with an ἀρχή of some sort. Cf. *Gorg.* 467C–468E for the basic logic of the argument: People only want specific means to ends because they want the ends themselves. If there were no ends, but only putative means, there could not then be means to ends. This is why Aristotle says that choice is *always* of means to ends; ends themselves are not chosen. They are given, principally by our natures. See *EN* Γ 5, 1112b11–12, b32–34, 7.1113b3–4. Price 1989, 8, takes the πρῶτον φίλον to be happiness, though he adds in a note, "Plato tends to count as truly 'good' not *eudaimonia* itself but what reliably yields or produces it." As *Symposium* says, happiness is the *possession* of the Good.

¹¹⁷ See Kahn 1996, 266, "No reader who comes to the *Lysis* without knowledge of the doctrine expounded in the *Symposium* could understand what is implied by 'the primary dear, for the sake of which everything else is dear.'" And, 267, "the *Lysis* points the way not only to the Beautiful itself in the *Symposium*, but also to the Form of the Good in the *Republic*."

2.7 The Idea of the Good and to philon 63

not for utilitarian reasons, but for "his own sake." The most well-known proponent of this view is Gregory Vlastos, who argued that "loving someone for his own sake" means to love them without regard for one's own sake."[118] As I have already argued in this chapter, the dichotomy between "for another's sake" or "for one's own sake" is undercut by the identification of the Good and one's own good, meaning *not* that the Good just is my own good or your own good distributively, but that their identity guarantees that it is not possible that my own good should be achieved at your expense. If that is so, then it is pointless to contrast altruism with egotism. Your good is never betrayed as I successfully seek my own, nor is my good betrayed when you are seeking yours. Needless to say, this claim applies *only* to the real good. Obviously, it frequently *appears* to one that one's own good is at odds with the good of another, even if this cannot possibly be so.[119]

It might be objected that the universality of the Good thus understood does not in fact efface the contrast between egotism and altruism. On the contrary, it is possible to be selfish and to be unselfish. These are real motives for action. Plato's moral realism does not deny this. Every ostensibly selfish or altruistic act appears to the agent to be a manifestation of the Good that she seeks. If that act turns out in fact to be good, then it is good for the agent and for everyone else that it is good for the agent. The implication of Plato's position is that describing an act merely as egotistic or altruistic does not give us enough information to be able to determine whether the appearance of good in this case (to the agent) is veridical or nonveridical. People certainly do act selflessly and selfishly. But in each case, the act takes its characterization from the rational desire or intention of the agent. Among other things, the metaphysical foundation of ethics undercuts the assumption that such desires or intentions are dispositive with regard to the question of the instantiation of the Good.

---

[118] See Vlastos 1973, "The Individual as an Object of Love in Plato," who claims that the πρῶτον φίλον *should be* a person who is loved for his or her own sake, though Socrates does not spell this out. In fact, 30, what Socrates pursues is "spiritualized egocentrism." We need to recall that Vlastos thinks that *Lysis* is among the so-called Socratic dialogues in which Socratic philosophy is expressed. When Plato begins to express his own philosophy in the so-called middle dialogues (along with the so-called transitional dialogues), he resolutely rejects any thoughts or altruism in loving or friendship, making it completely self-related. In the *Lysis* passage, Vlastos appeals to *Symposium* to understand the "images" of φιλία as analogous to "images of virtue" in *Symposium*. A true φίλον would be analogous to the true virtue of the successful philosopher. See Kosman 1976 for a perceptive response to Vlastos's criticism of Plato's "egocentric" conception of love.

[119] See *Lg.* 5.731D6–732B4 where Plato claims that "excessive self-love (τὴν σφόδρα ἑαυτοῦ φιλίαν)" is the greatest cause of human evils because this self-love "leads us to think that we should always honor our own self more than the truth (τὸ αὑτοῦ πρὸ τοῦ ἀληθοῦς ἀεὶ τιμᾶν δεῖ ἡγούμενος)."

A different proposal is advanced by Terry Penner and Christopher Rowe, who argue that the πρῶτον φίλον is knowledge, that is, knowledge of whatever it is that would produce my maximal happiness at this moment and under these circumstances.[120] Without wishing to discount the importance that Socrates places on knowledge, it seems far-fetched, to say the least, to focus on knowledge as the πρῶτον φίλον as opposed to what knowledge is supposed to be of. If that is so, "whatever maximized my happiness" would be the πρῶτον φίλον. But this result faces a problem alluded to earlier, namely, that it does not exclude the possibility that my happiness should be achieved at your expense. If, however, it is stipulated that it does exclude this possibility, then this would be because my happiness and your happiness are the same thing, not numerically, of course, but in principle. My argument has been that the only way this could be so – apart from sheer unaccountable luck – is if the Good is uniquely beyond οὐσία. *That* surely is the πρῶτον φίλον, knowledge of which is, as *Republic* makes explicit, and *Symposium* supports, what produces true virtue in everyone and anyone.[121]

In *Lysis*, ἐπιθυμία of what we lack is the cause of φιλία; in *Symposium*, ἐπιθυμία of what we lack is the cause of ἔρως.[122] And what we lack and so desire is, nevertheless, οἰκεῖον to us.[123] Further, our desire for the Good is desire for it as beautiful (καλόν).[124] Penner and Rowe are right to recognize that knowledge is the achievement of what is οἰκεῖον to us. And they are also right to emphasize the importance of being able to apply this knowledge to our own lives. But the Good is not the knowledge; rather, it is what the knowledge is of. And this Good is a metaphysical principle, not its contingent instantiation. Indeed, without the metaphysical principle, there could be no instantiation of it at all.

---

[120] See Penner and Rowe 2005, 273–278. For a similar interpretation see Vlastos 1991, 117, n.49; Irwin 1995, 54.

[121] See *Lys*. 220B7: ἀλλ' ἄρα τὸ ἀγαθόν ἐστιν φίλον; Ἔμοιγε δοκεῖ (Is then the Good φίλον? It seems to me to be so). Penner and Rowe 2005, 278–279, seem to acknowledge this claim when they concede that the πρῶτον φίλον could be reasonably identified with the *Form* of the Good, so long as that was understood to be the Form of One's Own Happiness. But if the Idea of the Good is meant, I do not see how it could be identical with my own happiness unless it was also identical with your own happiness, too. As Penner and Rowe insist, anyone's happiness is entirely circumstantial, and since circumstances differ, it is very difficult to see how my happiness and your happiness cannot ever conflict on their account of what the Idea of the Good is. The only motivation I can discern for this interpretation of the Idea of the Good is that it is required by the prudentialist principle.

[122] See *Lys*. 221D3; *Symp*. 207D1–3. See Robin 1908, 48–49, on the many striking parallels between *Lysis* and *Symposium*.

[123] See *Lys*. 222C3; *Symp*. 205E6–7.   [124] See *Lys* 216D2; *Symp*. 204E1–2.

2.7 *The Idea of the Good and* to philon

The last line of our passage makes the important point that the things that we think are φίλον because they are instrumental to the πρῶτον φίλον would only be deceptive images if there were no first. In other words, something derives its character of being φίλον from the first. Why, though, would we ever be in danger of being deceived by things that are φίλον but not the first? Within the metaphysical framework already adduced, there is a readily intelligible answer to this question. It is that if you do not grasp anything supposedly φίλον as related to the first, then you are likely to be deceived by it because the features of it that you identify as making it φίλον are in fact misidentified or misleading. If, to recur to *Symposium* once again, you identify beauty with certain physical features, the deception would be in thinking that something without those features could not be beautiful. This does not mean that the thing deemed beautiful is not so; it means only that unless you see it as an instance of the Form of Beauty, you will be misled – perhaps disastrously misled – in how you respond to that. So, unless you acknowledge the πρῶτον φίλον, and therefore, that every other thing said to be φίλον is δεύτερον (secondarily) φίλον and φίλον at all only because it participates in the first, you are likely to be deceived.[125]

In *Republic*, philosophers are distinguished from "lovers of sights and sounds" not by their knowledge – after all, they are seeking knowledge, not proud possessors of it – but by the fact that they understand that knowledge has as objects the intelligible world of which the sensible world is only an image.[126] Philosophers do not mistake the sensible world for the really real world. What this means in practice is that they will not misconstrue images of the real for the real itself; they will not take the "material" out of which the images are constructed as constitutive of the essential structure of the real. The false dialectic of the nonphilosopher is even more vividly at play when a secondary φίλον is mistaken for a primary one. The mistake consists in a doomed exploration of what exactly it is that makes the φίλον so. It is doomed because it presumes to find the answer in, as Vlastos puts it, "the individual as love object." The idiosyncratic attributes of the individual are not illusory or even insignificant. After all, even the apparently beautiful attracts us to the Good. But these idiosyncratic attributes

---

[125] Vlastos 1973, "The Individual as Object of Love in Plato," appendix 1, 37, denies that the images in this passage need to be interpreted within a metaphysical framework. Vlastos rejects the comparison with *Symposium* for obscure reasons. He says that the true virtue of the philosopher as a result of knowledge of the Forms is only "true" virtue as compared with virtues that are not genuine. This is hard to construe since it is certainly not the case that instances of the Form of Beauty are not true instances of it, though as we learn from *Republic*, they are sensible images.

[126] See *Rep.* 5.476A10–D5.

cannot amount to what the πρῶτον φίλον is. Loving persons as individuals or "for themselves" is no more excluded from the moral realism developed here than is altruism. Nevertheless, there is a fundamental divide between the love of persons as a function of the love of the πρῶτον φίλον and the love of persons as a *substitute* for that.

The dialogue *Lysis*, whatever its compositional place is in relation to *Symposium* and *Republic*, provides a revealing, albeit limited, account of the logic of transcendence. All desire aims at a goal or τέλος, that which satisfies the desire. The goal is either the πρῶτον φίλον or it is not, in which case it is a means to the πρῶτον φίλον. How are we to tell whether something is just φίλον because it is a means to the πρῶτον φίλον or whether it is itself the πρῶτον φίλον? The criterion provided in the above text is whether we can or cannot say of it "on account of something else (ἕνεκά του)." If we can, it is not the πρῶτον φίλον; if we cannot, it is. The Good is clearly φίλον in the latter sense. The manifestation of the Good in my case is my happiness, just as the manifestation of the Good in your case is your happiness. But if your happiness is subordinated to mine, then your happiness becomes only instrumentally φίλον to me; it is no longer a manifestation of the πρῶτον φίλον. In principle, this is perhaps the way the world works sometimes. It is surely not the way Plato thinks the world works. For the manifestation of the Good in A – let us call it x – is distinguishable from the material out of which x is constructed, just as Helen's beauty is distinguishable from her flesh and bones.[127] So, if the Good is manifested in how A acts in relation to B, though the λόγος of A's acting is different from the λόγος of B's being acted upon, if A's acting in relation to B is a manifestation of the Good for A, then there is no logical space for its being other than a manifestation of the Good for B. That impossibility would not be like a case of Helen's flesh and bones being ugly in different circumstances or in comparison to Aphrodite. What makes something a manifestation of the Good is always distinct from the agential circumstances and peculiarities of the agent, even though the Good cannot be manifested in us other than through our agential circumstances and peculiarities.

The result is that the πρῶτον φίλον must be over and above any manifestation of it. But unlike, say, the Form of Justice, it cannot have any essentialistic content. For on the assumption that it had such a content,

---

[127] In *Republic* 1.331C–D, the justice in an act of returning someone's property to someone is distinct from the physical act of returning the property. This is demonstrated by showing that the identical physical act of returning someone's property can be in other circumstances unjust.

one could always ask whether that content is good, that is, if the presence of that content is just φίλον "on account of something else" or the πρῶτον φίλον. If the prudentialist wants to maintain that a just act is the πρῶτον φίλον because it is constitutive of one's happiness, then that act could never be inimical to the happiness of someone else even if that person were indifferent to it. But for all we know, the same could be said for an unjust act when performed by the aspiring tyrant. The only way to short-circuit the realization of this possibility is if the πρῶτον φίλον is super-essentialistic. My happiness manifests the Good if and only if that manifestation cannot simultaneously negate the manifestation in another.

2.8 The Idea of the Good and the One

My principal concern in this section is answering the question, "what does the testimony according to which Plato identified the Idea of the Good with the One contribute to our understanding of Plato's moral theory?" Those who insist that the answer to this question is "nothing," seem to me to have an exceedingly weak case. Those who hold this view are inexorably led to say that the superordinate absolutely simple unhypothetical first principle of all has no relevance to Plato's moral theory because they cannot conceive of how the Good could provide knowability to the Forms, much less be the explanation for their existence and essence. They have no way of explaining how the Good makes Forms useful and beneficial.[128] By contrast, the recognition of the identification of the Good with the One by Plato does give us a powerful and comprehensive way of untying all these knots.[129] Finally, it should be emphasized that this

---

[128] Penner is an exception because he identifies the Idea of the Good with the Form of Advantage or Usefulness. The implausibility of this has been addressed above. See Krämer 1959, 487–551, for the seminal analysis of how the Good becomes identified with the One as the result of Plato's encounters with his Presocratic predecessors, especially Parmenides. I would add to this Plato's early encounter with Pythagoreans in Southern Italy.

[129] See Krämer 1959, 135, on the requirement that a principle of order, understood as integrative unity, be the One, and not simply the Good; Szlezák 2003, 109–131; Halfwassen 2015, 96–100. See also, for example, Murdoch 1970, 94–95, on the Good as a principle of unity and order in the moral life; Burnyeat 2000, 76–77, on the centrality of unity, as a principle of mathematics, for Plato's ethics and politics. Burnyeat assumes that this unity is identical with the Good. Burnyeat, however, does not clearly reject the unsupportable idea that the Good is the Form of Unity or Oneness. Broadie 2021, 176–195, raises some penetrating objections to the arguments of Burnyeat and others that the results of mathematical training is actually constitutive of dialectic. These objections are based on her diffidence in regard to the identification of the Good with the One. Lavecchia 2010 argues for a distinction between Good and One, wherein the latter (along with the Indefinite Dyad) are subordinated to the former. In effect, the One is identified with the One-Being of the second hypothesis of the second part of *Parmenides* (142Bff).

identification has considerable support from the dialogues, apart from the testimony of Aristotle and the indirect tradition.[130]

In chapter 6 of Book A of *Metaphysics*, Aristotle moves from a survey of Pre-Socratic philosophers to Plato, whose "treatment (πραγματεία)" of ultimate causes is a centerpiece of Aristotle's dialectical history.[131] Aristotle begins by distinguishing the ethical philosophy of the historical Socrates from the metaphysics of Plato, which begins with the positing of separate Forms as the objects of knowledge. He adds that in addition to Forms and sensibles, Plato posited Mathematical Objects, which are "intermediary" between the two.[132] He then reports:

> Since the Forms are the causes of other things, he thought that the elements of Forms are the elements of all things. As matter, the Great and the Small are the principles; as essence, it is the One. For from the Great and the Small and by participation in the One come the Forms and these are Numbers. In saying that the One is essence and not another thing that is said to be one, he spoke like the Pythagoreans, and also like them in saying that Numbers are causes of the essence of other things.[133]

The evidence that Plato did indeed identify Forms with Numbers in some sense is extensive.[134] Aristotle does not introduce this identification as a late "development" in Plato's thinking; indeed, Aristotle throughout the corpus and the scores of references to Plato's philosophy never even suggests that that philosophy is not a unified system. The reduction of

---

[130] At *Rep.* 6.506D7–E1, Socrates declines to discuss the essence of the Good (τί ποτ' ἐστὶ τἀγαθόν). The direct and indirect tradition is unanimous in reporting that the essence of the Good is found in the One itself (αὐτὸ τὸ ἕν).

[131] See esp. Miller 1995 on *Parmenides* as a major source of this testimony.

[132] *Meta.* A 6, 987a14–18. See also B 1, 995b15ff; Z 2, 1028b19–21; K 1, 1059b2; Λ 1, 1069a33ff; M 1, 1076a19ff; 9, 1086a11–13; N 3, 1090b35–36.

[133] *Meta.* A 6, 987b18–25: ἐπεὶ δ' αἴτια τὰ εἴδη τοῖς ἄλλοις, τἀκείνων στοιχεῖα πάντων ᾠήθη τῶν ὄντων εἶναι στοιχεῖα. ὡς μὲν οὖν ὕλην τὸ μέγα καὶ τὸ μικρὸν εἶναι ἀρχάς, ὡς δ' οὐσίαν τὸ ἕν· ἐξ ἐκείνων γὰρ κατὰ μέθεξιν τοῦ ἑνὸς τὰ εἴδη εἶναι τοὺς ἀριθμούς. τὸ μέντοι γε ἓν οὐσίαν εἶναι, καὶ μὴ ἕτερόν γέ τι ὂν λέγεσθαι ἕν, παραπλησίως τοῖς Πυθαγορείοις ἔλεγε, καὶ τὸ τοὺς ἀριθμοὺς αἰτίους εἶναι τοῖς ἄλλοις τῆς οὐσίας ὡσαύτως ἐκείνοις· Ross 1924 *ad loc.*, argues for omitting τὰ εἴδη. Jaeger 1957 and others, including Primavesi 2012, omit τοὺς ἀριθμούς. Berti 2017, retains both. Neither omission is found in the mss. Steel 2012, 186–188, argues that neither omission is desirable or necessary.

[134] Cf. A8, 990a29–32.; Z 7, 11.1036b13–25; Λ 8, 1073a18–19; M 6, 1080b11–14; M 7, 1081a5–7; M 8, 1083a18; M 8, 1084a7–8; M 9, 1086a11–13; N 2, 1090a4–6; N 3, 1090a16. M 4, 1078 b9–12 is especially important because it makes a clear distinction between an early (ἐξ ἀρχῆς) phase of the theory of Forms and then a subsequent reduction of Forms to Numbers. There is, however, no indication by Aristotle of when in Plato's career this reduction occurred. For this reason, it is left to students of Plato to discover indications of the reduction in the dialogues. See Gerson 2013, ch. 4, where this evidence is discussed at greater length. Also, see Richard 2005, 211–218; Krämer 2014 [1969], 206–207.

2.8 The Idea of the Good and the One

Forms to Numbers is not presented as a development but rather as an integral part of Plato's causal analysis.

The testimony continues:

> It is evident from what has been said that he [Plato] uses only two causes, the cause of the whatness and the cause according to matter (for the Forms are cause of the whatness of the other things, and the cause of the whatness of the Forms is the One). It is also evident what the underlying matter is, in virtue of which the Forms are predicated of the sensible things, and the One is predicated of the Forms; this is the Dyad, or the Great and the Small.[135]

So, Aristotle's testimony is that the ultimate principles of Plato's philosophy are the One and the Indefinite Dyad. It is not unreasonable to infer that this One must be another name for the first principle of all, the Idea of the Good. This inference is supported by the following passage:

> Among those who posit immovable substances, some say that the One itself is the Good itself; at least they thought the essence of the Good to be, most of all, the One.[136]

A number of features in the above report deserve attention. First is the claim that Plato viewed Forms as having elements.[137] Second is that these elements are the One and the Great and Small, also called "the Indefinite Dyad (ἀόριστος δυάς)" as the next passage indicates.[138] The third feature of the above account is Aristotle's expression of the two principles as matter

---

[135] *Meta.* A 6, 988a8–14: φανερὸν δ' ἐκ τῶν εἰρημένων ὅτι δυοῖν αἰτίαιν μόνον κέχρηται, τῇ τε τοῦ τί ἐστι καὶ τῇ κατὰ τὴν ὕλην (τὰ γὰρ εἴδη τοῦ τί ἐστιν αἴτια τοῖς ἄλλοις, τοῖς δ' εἴδεσι τὸ ἕν), καὶ τίς ἡ ὕλη ἡ ὑποκειμένη καθ' ἧς τὰ εἴδη μὲν ἐπὶ τῶν αἰσθητῶν τὸ δ' ἓν ἐν τοῖς εἴδεσι λέγεται, ὅτι αὕτη δυάς ἐστι, τὸ μέγα καὶ τὸ μικρόν.

[136] *Meta.* N 4, 1091b13–15: τῶν δὲ τὰς ἀκινήτους οὐσίας εἶναι λεγόντων οἱ μέν φασιν αὐτὸ τὸ ἓν τὸ ἀγαθὸν αὐτὸ εἶναι· οὐσίαν μέντοι τὸ ἓν αὐτοῦ ᾤοντο εἶναι μάλιστα. A bit further on, 22–25, Aristotle contrasts this position with that of Plato's successor as head of the Academy, Speusippus, who, owing to problems with the identification of Good and One, abandoned this, claiming that good arises from the One; it is not identical with it. The contrast seems to support the surmise that Plato (among others) is the one who is referred to in this passage as holding the identity of Good and One. Cf. also *EE* A 8, 1218a15–32, which refers to those who hold that τὸ ἕν is αὐτὸ τἀγαθόν. See Brunschwig 1971 for a comprehensive argument that this crucial *EE* passage is focused on the metaphysics of Plato, not that of Pythagoras or Xenocrates. Also, Krämer 2014, 262–264.

[137] The "elements" of Forms cannot be the superordinate One and the Indefinite Dyad but must be the One of *Parmenides* 2nd hypothesis (H2) and the Indefinite Dyad. The superordinate One is above elemental status. Aristotle, *Meta.* Δ 3, 1014a26–27, says that an element is that out of which a thing is composed. But this is distinct from an ἀρχή or principle. See 1, 1013a7–8. An element is an internal constituent; a principle is not that, but rather external to the elements and their composition.

[138] See *Meta.* N 7, 1081a22, and so on, where whoever is the subject of Aristotle's criticism, it is clear that "Dyad" is a shortened form of "Indefinite Dyad." At A 6, 987b25–6, Aristotle says that Plato differed from the Pythagoreans in making the Indefinite a duality. See *Phil.* 16C1–17A5, 23C–27C on the Unlimited and the Limit.

and essence or form. We must assume that Aristotle knew that the Idea of the Good is specifically said by Plato to be beyond essence. If the Good is the One, in what sense is it the essence in relation to matter? The explicit use of Aristotle's own terminology to explain Plato's position both raises a question about the accuracy of the testimony and about Plato's view regarding the relation of the two principles.

My suggestions for an answer to these questions are, briefly, this. Plato posits the Good and the Indefinite Dyad, later to be reflected in the distinction between Limit and Unlimited in *Philebus*, as the principles of a sort of Platonic hylomorphism.[139] Plato's version is to be distinguished from Aristotle's by the fact that while Aristotle affirms, Plato denies that the essence of a substance is identical with that substance. The One is not the essence of any kind of thing because the One is beyond essence. But it is the principle of essence for the nature of anything.[140] An analogous remark can be made for the Indefinite Dyad. The One or Good is certainly not the essence of oneness; rather, things are or belong to one kind rather than another because of the One. The principle of unity or oneness is not one. But without being one, nothing exists as the one thing it is. So, if we can make sense of how the One serves as a principle of Forms, and so indirectly of everything else, we have no reason to deny the accuracy of Aristotle's testimony.

The identification of the Good with the One is also supported by a fragment from a student of Aristotle, Aristoxenus, in his *Elementa Harmonica* in which he says that in a public lecture *On the Good*, Plato defied the expectations of his audience and instead of talking about traditional human goods such as wealth, health, and strength, he discoursed on mathematics, culminating in the claim that Good is one.[141] These words are most naturally taken to indicate the uniqueness of the

---

[139] The irreducible compositeness of everything but the One follows from the unique absolute simplicity of the latter. If the Good/One were a Form, it would be composite like all the Forms. See *Parm.* 142B5–6.

[140] See Krämer 1959, 135, 474ff, 535–551, who presents the most forceful step-by-step account of why the superordinate Idea of the Good must be identified with the absolutely simple One, linking virtue as order (τάξις) or integrative unity according to kind with unqualified unity as the ultimate principle of order.

[141] Aristoxenus, *Harm. Elem.* 2.30–31 (= *De bono*, p.111 Ross). Brisson 2018 tries to deflate the value of this testimony. The words ὅτι ἀγαθόν ἐστιν ἕν (that good is one) (without the definite articles) can certainly be understood in the anodyne sense according to which Plato is reported to have said that good is one as opposed to being many or diverse, as most people think. Plato does of course believe that. But these words conclude the account of what Plato talked about, namely, mathematics and astronomy, with the conclusion that "good is one." This brings to mind the education curriculum of Plato's rulers, culminating in their vision of the Good. But "good is one" would be a rather odd way to describe this conclusion. Given Aristotle's own testimony, it seems more reasonable that

2.8 The Idea of the Good and the One

Good, so to speak. "Good is one" means that Good is not one *and* many, as the Forms are said to be. None of the things that manifest the Good thereby "pluralize" it.

The glaring problem in understanding this testimony is not the identification of the Good with the One, but with the postulation of the Indefinite Dyad as a supposedly coordinate principle.[142] If the Good/One and the Indefinite Dyad are distinct principles on the identical ontological level, then each must possess sufficient complexity to be distinct from the other. But then the absolute simplicity of the first principle of all is destroyed along with the rationale for positing such a principle in the first place.[143] The interpretive and philosophical choices seem to be either somehow to subordinate the Indefinite Dyad to the Good/One or else to subordinate both the Indefinite Dyad and the Good/One as coordinate principles of the Form Numbers to another superordinate Good/One. In the latter case, we can maintain the interpretation of the first hypothesis (H1) of the second part of *Parmenides* as referring to a remote, uncognizable first principle and the second hypothesis (H2) as referring to the One-Being and its coordinate Indefinite Dyad.

The path to a solution to this problem should begin with a recognition that the Indefinite Dyad has its own sort of unity. It has a unity which nevertheless entails complexity of some sort since the One is uniquely simple. And it is the One's simplicity that entails its absolute priority. Accordingly, the Indefinite Dyad cannot be really coordinated with the

---

Aristoxenus is reporting that. It should be noted that Aristoxenus says specifically that he got his information from Aristotle. A passage in *Magna Moralia* should also be considered here, even if this work is not genuine. See A 1, 1182a27–30: τὴν γὰρ ἀρετὴν κατέμιξεν εἰς τὴν πραγματείαν τὴν ὑπὲρ τἀγαθοῦ, οὐ δὴ ὀρθῶς· οὐ γὰρ οἰκεῖον (for he incorrectly mixed in virtue with the treatment of the Good, for that is inappropriate). This πραγματεία would seem to be a reference to a technical lecture on the Good such as the one Aristoxenus mentions; otherwise, it would be bizarre for Aristotle – or the author of this work, if a student of Aristotle – to criticize Plato for connecting the study of good with virtue. This is confirmed by the next line: ὑπὲρ γὰρ τῶν ὄντων καὶ ἀληθείας λέγοντα οὐκ ἔδει ὑπὲρ ἀρετῆς φράζειν· οὐδὲν γὰρ τούτῳ κἀκείνῳ κοινόν (for when speaking about beings and truth, he should not have spoken about virtue, for the two have nothing in common). It should be added that Simplicius, *In Phys.* 151, 6–19; 453, 22–30; 545, 23–25 Diels, who endorses the identification of Good and the One, cites three distinct accounts of Plato's lecture or lectures by Aristotle, Speusippus, and Xenocrates. See Berti 2004, 38, for a similar argument.

[142] See Gaiser 1963, 12–13, on the centrality of this problem for understanding Plato's doctrine of principles and Halfwassen 2015, 109–131, 151–155, for its most plausible resolution. See also Lavecchia 2010, ch. 3, whose elegant solution identifies the One-Being of the second hypothesis of the *Parmenides* as the locus of the One and Indefinite Dyad, with the Good transcending that. He calls the Good a "*Metaprincipio*."

[143] See Plato, *Parm.* 140A1–3: ἀλλὰ μὴν εἴ τι πέπονθε χωρὶς τοῦ ἓν εἶναι τὸ ἕν, πλείω ἂν εἶναι πεπόνθοι ἢ ἕν, τοῦτο δὲ ἀδύνατον (if, however, the One has any property apart from being one, it would have the property of being more than one, but this is impossible). This consequence also follows if the One is one where "one" is a predicate.

primary One.[144] The Indefinite Dyad *is* a coordinate principle of One-Being, but the first principle of all is beyond Being. Undoubtedly, this alternative involves its own severe problems.[145]

Why, though, is the Indefinite Dyad a principle at all? The simple answer is that the Indefinite Dyad is the principle of πλῆθος or magnitude or size, which includes both continuous and discrete quantities.[146] With the principle of number alone, there could be no lines or planes or solid figures.[147] So, the apparent paradox facing Plato is this: If everything is generated from the One, then so is the Indefinite Dyad. But magnitude cannot be generated from the One. For example, a line is not generated from a point or an aggregation of points. The paradox is mitigated to a certain extent by the fact that One-Being is not number, but the principle of number, in which case number is generated from One-Being as much as is magnitude. This is why number and magnitude are both generated in H2 of *Parmenides*. They are coordinate principles of One-Being. It is simply not the case that the Indefinite Dyad is coordinate with the One, first principle of all. The general idea, I think, is that generation of Numbers up to the generation of three-dimensional volumes may be conceived of as a geometrical construction eternally carried out and eternally completed by a divine intellect, that is, the Demiurge. Plato does not

---

[144] See Aristotle, *Meta*. N 1, 1087b9–12, who says that the Great and Small is one, although the proponents of the principle do not say if it is one in number or in λόγος, too. Cf. Sextus Empiricus, *M* X, 261; Simplicius, *In Phys*. 454, 8–9. See Halfwassen 1997 on the combined monism and dualism of principles in *Parmenides*. This is, 16, "a monism in the reduction to an absolute with a dualism in the deduction of being." That is, a dualism subordinate to the primary monism. There is dualism *within* being and monism in the explanation for the generation of being. This dualism is the basis for Plato's hylomorphism, the combination of Limit and Unlimited.

[145] Already Aristotle, *Meta*. Λ 10, 1075b18–20, notes that those who posit Forms need a superordinate principle as cause of participation by sensibles in Forms. This causal role, however, does not seem to be easily assumed by an absolutely simple first principle.

[146] Thus, πλῆθος can refer to a plurality of units or "ones." See *Parm*. 132B2, 144A6, 151D3; *Phil*. 16D7. But it can also refer to a continuous quantity. See *Parm*. 158C4; *Phil*. 29C2. In the latter sense, πλῆθος is used synonymously with τὸ ἄπειρον. See 26C6. Also, it can be used synonymously with μέγεθος. See *Parm*. 149C5, 150B8. This is quantity or extension apart from number.

[147] Sextus Empiricus, *M*. X, 281–283, describes two ways in which the generation of bodies from numbers was thought to occur by different Pythagoreans (including Plato). The first mentioned describes the generation of bodies from numbers via the usual dimensional levels using the verb ῥυεῖν (to flow) which, it will be recalled, is the root verb used for the Good in its activity of "overflowing." It is hardly surprising that if like produces like, the mode of production will be like in all cases. How, say, a line "flows" from a point (or an indivisible line, as Aristotle explains, *Meta*. A 9, 992a20–22, M 8, 1084a37–b2) is a special case of how a many is derived from a one. That is, the reduction of bodies to numbers is the epistemological inverse of the generation of bodies from numbers. Everything that exists along this line of reduction/generation is ultimately accounted for by the unlimited fecundity of the first principle of all. The proof of the unlimited fecundity is just the existence of bodies. See Richard 2005, 190–205, for some helpful remarks about the complexities, and pros and cons, of the various accounts of generation from the first principle.

2.8 The Idea of the Good and the One

have to worry about how lines are composed out of points; rather, lines are constructed from a starting-point in thought, planes from a given line, and so on. The ontological hierarchy is manifested by constructive mathematical analysis. The generation of bodies in time is that of an image of this mathematical order. Without the Indefinite Dyad, not only could bodies not exist, but not even their paradigmatic geometrical volumes could exist. Neither could the Mathematical Objects. In fact, without the Indefinite Dyad, there could not even exist that which is minimally complex, that in which existence and essence are distinct. But complexity is, apparently, maximally instantiated. In that case, the One (from H1) and One-Being (from H2), which is composed of the Indefinite Dyad and the array of essences with which an eternal intellect is cognitively identical, must exist.

Aristotle's testimony regarding the reduction of Forms to the principles of the One and the Indefinite Dyad is, along with the texts in *Republic* on the Good as unhypothetical first principle of all, the most important piece of evidence for the claim that Plato's philosophy is systematic.[148] This evidence also informs us that the system is a *Derivationsystem*, hierarchical in terms of logical or substantial proximity to the first principle.[149] Simply stated, the greater unity there is, the closer something is to the first principle. And the identification of Good and One means that unity is also an index of goodness, or at least of proximity to the achievement of goodness.

It is often supposed that Plato did at some point in his career identify the Good with the One, but that this is a later development.[150] I think it is just

---

[148] See Merlan 1953, 166–177, for a concise survey of the evidence for Plato's system of derivation of all being from first principles (Merlan uses Zeller's term *Ableitungssystem*) and his qualified support for a positive answer to the question. Hermann 2007, 225, recognizes that the Idea of the Good has a unique and primary explanatory role to play, but he then goes on to claim that it would be wrong to "systematize" this Idea and the Forms into a unified hierarchy. See also Sedley 2007, 269–271, who accepts that "Plato's account of the Good would have been a highly mathematical one." But he is, I think, mistaken in going on to identify the Good as "ideal proportionality." As we will see below in the discussion of *Philebus* in Chapter 6, ideal proportionality is indeed one way that the Good is manifested. But ideal proportionality cannot be what the Good is for the simple reason that ideal proportionality is or has an οὐσία and the Good is beyond οὐσία.

[149] See *Rep.* 6.511B8 on "the things that depend (τὰ ἐχόμενα)" on the first principle; Aristotle, *Meta.* M 8, 1084a32–34, on the "things that follow (τὰ ἑπόμενα)" the first principle. Here together are dependence and hierarchy. If the Forms depend on the Good for their being and knowability, the Good cannot represent a property of these Forms, for example, their goodness. This is how Rowe 2007, 149–150, seems to understand the causality of the Good so that it turns out that a property causes that of which it is a property. Theophrastus, *Meta.* 6b11–16, speaks of a γένεσις of Forms and Numbers from the principles, but no further information is supplied. See Krämer 2014.

[150] See Ross 1951, 54–55, who thinks that their identification follows the writing of *Republic*. So, too, apparently, De Strycker 1970, 464–466.

as likely that Plato was from his early acquaintance with Pythagoreans in southern Italy inclined to identify the One as the first principle of all and that as he began to think about the ontological foundation of his moral realism, he saw the need to identify the One with a superordinate Good.[151] Nothing in my overall argument requires that this is the sequence of doctrinal developments. Nevertheless, I suspect that it was well before writing *Republic* that Plato moved toward the confluence of the Good and the One.

---

[151] Diogenes Laertius III 6, tells us that Plato was twenty-eight when he visited Philolaus and other Pythagoreans. If this is the case, his Pythagorean interests seem to antedate the writing of any dialogues. See also II 106, on Euclides of Megara, a student of Parmenides. Diogenes says that Plato and others visited him after the death of Socrates. Notably, Euclides held that "the Good is one."

CHAPTER 3

Virtue, Knowledge, and the Good

3.1 How to Read the Socratic Paradoxes

Plato tells us in a number of dialogues probably written over decades that "no one does wrong willingly."[1] This claim can be taken in a way such that it is plainly tautologous. The word ἁμαρτάνειν ("does wrong") indicates more accurately that someone is aiming at a target of some sort and yet fails to hit it.[2] Obviously, if you aim at a target and fail to hit it, you did not do so willingly since "aiming at" implies "willingly." So, we should probably assume that Plato intends to make a claim with more content than this interpretation would allow. If we set the claim within the context of an elementary account of human action, we can easily see what this content is. An action begins with a desire, a desire to achieve a goal consisting, roughly, in being in a state different from the state that one is currently in.[3] If there were no desire to be otherwise situated, there would be no action. The good that Plato says that people desire is, generally, just such a state or result that all desire is for. Whatever the desire is a desire for, it is a desire to achieve a state that one prefers to the state that one is currently in. So, even if one's desire can be characterized as altruistic, it is still a desire for one's own good, that is, a desire for the achievement of a state that one prefers to the state that one is currently in. An action arising from a desire

---

[1] Οὐδεὶς ἑκὼν ἁμαρτάνει. *Me.* 77C1–2; *Ap.* 37A5; *Gorg.* 488A3; *Protag.* 345D8, 352C2–7, 358B6–C1; *Rep.* 9.589C6; *Tim.* 86D7–E1; *Lg.* 5.731C–D. The range of dialogues within which this claim appears makes it implausible that the emphatic acceptance of the possibility of ἀκρασία in *Republic* should be accurately interpreted in a way such that Plato came to think that sometimes "no one does wrong willingly" is false. Because our βούλησις is permanently oriented to the Good, wrongdoing must be otherwise explained. See Šegvić 2000 on the ambiguities of the claim that no one does wrong willingly.
[2] See, for example, *Protag.* 345D9–E6 where in the interpretation of Simonides' poem, the claim is so understood.
[3] One can, of course, desire to remain in one's present state, choosing not to do something that alters that state or refraining from acting. But the state we desire to remain in is still temporally distinct from one's present state.

for the good of others that does not have as a goal a state superior to the state that one is presently in would in fact be no action at all. If, though, we understand the "wrong" in "no one does wrong willingly" as indicating a state contrary to the state that is the intentional object of desire, then another tautology threatens. That is, of course no one willingly "goes for" a result other than the result they desire; what they "go for" is determined by the desire, the starting-point of the action. And it is here that Plato's claim appears other than tautologous, indeed even paradoxical. For "wrong" is not intended by Plato to indicate a state contrary to the one desired, but a state that is wrong independently of what one desires.

With this interpretation, we perhaps veer from platitude to manifest falsity. For it seems that people habitually do things that are in fact wrong, not merely wrong independently of what they desire, but in spite of their being wrong. That is, they willingly desire what is wrong.[4] And if this is the case, then it is not even plausible to suppose that they never do wrong willingly. In order to show that Plato does avoid this apparent absurdity, one must show that there is a logical connection between the good that every desire is aimed at and the good that is independent of what one in fact desires. There are two radically different ways of making this connection. According to the first, it is something like a law of nature or even a happy coincidence that the good that one desires is never out of line with the good in fact, that is, the good independent of what one desires.[5] So, it is never in my interest to do wrong, where "interest" specifies the goods when and insofar as I desire them. According to the second, there is a metaphysical connection between "good" as an object of my desire and "good"

---

[4] At *Cr.* 49A4–5, we read: Οὐδενὶ τρόπῳ φαμὲν ἑκόντας ἀδικητέον εἶναι, ἢ τινὶ μὲν ἀδικητέον τρόπῳ τινὶ δὲ οὔ: (Do we say that one must not willingly do an unjust deed in any way or do we say that one must do an unjust deed in one way but not in another?). The injunction not to do wrong willingly suggest the possibility of doing so, at least if "ought" ("ought not") implies "can." Does this possibility contradict the claim that no one does wrong willingly? I believe it does, *unless* we take the injunction as directed to someone who, wanting the good, thinks that he or she can achieve this by doing something admittedly wrong or evil. For instance, consider someone who says that in order to achieve global justice, some individual acts of injustice will have to be committed. This is the view of Nagel 2005, 146: "for this reason, I believe the most likely path toward some version of global justice is through the creation of patently unjust and illegitimate global structures of power that are tolerable to the interests of the most powerful current nation." And, 147, "the path from anarchy to justice must go through injustice." Socrates firmly rejects this sort of utilitarian calculation. I take Socrates' injunction in the *Crito* passage to be absolutist and so anti-utilitarian. Hanann 2020, 16–17, thinks the *Crito* passage shows that Socrates is not yet committed to the claim that no one does wrong willingly.

[5] Perhaps it is not unfair to compare this appeal to a law of nature to Hecuba's hopeful reflections on divine justice in Euripides' *Trojans*, where she invokes Zeus, who is either to be identified with "the necessity of nature (ἀνάγκη φύσεος)" or with the "intellect of mortals (νοῦς βροτῶν)." Hecuba hopes that Zeus will punish Helen. See Euripides, *Trojans* 886. A pious and vain hope, as it turns out.

independent of my desire. That metaphysical connection may be expressed provisionally as extensional equivalence. If this is so, then the good I desire cannot in principle diverge from the good *simpliciter*. So, it is not possible that the good I desire for myself, since it is identical with the good *simpliciter*, could ever not be consonant with the good for someone else, which is, of course, also extensionally equivalent to the good *simpliciter*.

The first approach has obvious attractions. The principal one is that it makes no recourse to what may appear to be a highly implausible claim. For though it may be in some sense a law of nature that doing wrong does not ever benefit me, laws of nature, as opposed to mathematical laws, do, in many cases, admit of exceptions.[6] Accordingly, opting for the first approach, one can say that it is (almost) never the case that the good I desire is achieved by doing something wrong. On this approach, the alternative implausibly assimilates a law of nature to a mathematical law, which of course does not admit of exceptions. So, for example, the claim made by Socrates against Polus in *Gorgias* that tyrants do what seems best to them but not what they will, should be read as: Tyrants will their own good (like everybody else), but it is a law of nature that their own good probably cannot be achieved by the practice of tyranny – assuming, of course that tyranny is wrong.[7]

Nevertheless, this interpretation of the argument made against Polus faces an obvious objection. Admittedly, the tyrant is presented by Polus as an extreme case, a case of someone who apparently gets just what he wills because of his tyrannical power. The interpretation that maintains that the tyrant does not in fact will what he thinks he wills ("what seems to him to be best") can only rely on the putative law of nature that is supposed to be a general truth about human life. To say that a tyrant does not do what he wills to do just because what seems best to him is wrong must simply ignore the tyrant's implicit protest that he *is* the exception to the rule. The supposed law of nature may well cover the weaklings who are tyrannized, but it is precisely those with exceptional ability and strength of character

---

[6] At *Gorg.* 483E3, Callicles introduces the radical idea of a νόμος τῆς φύσεως (a law of nature), which he contrasts with human positive law. He thinks that it is a "law of nature" that the strong rule the weak. Those who contend that it is a law of nature that the strong never benefit from that rule are, presumably, using the word "nature" in a different, prescriptive sense. The nonmetaphysical basis for this sense is obscure.

[7] See *Gorg.* 466A4–467C4. Cf. *Rep.* 9.577D13–E1. See Penner 1991 for the most sophisticated attempt I know of to read this argument according to the first approach. Also, see McTighe 1984; Šegvić 2000, 6–11; 40–45, which includes her criticism of Penner, along lines similar to my own, though Šegvić argues that what I identify as the Good is "the right thing to do," thereby obscuring the metaphysical foundation for "right thing."

who are exempt from this law. So, to express confidence that the tyrant never does what he wills insofar as he acts like a tyrant, even though he does what appears to him to be what he wills, is to simply sidestep the problem with a prudentialist interpretation of Plato's ethics. But the prudentialist, who eschews metaphysics, has nothing else to appeal to.

Consider another case. Socrates maintains that it is better to suffer than to do wrong.[8] If your *only* choice in a particular situation is to be the hammer or the nail, you should unhesitatingly opt for the latter. I suppose that one might legitimately respond to the claim that if this truth rests upon a law of nature, then this is an amazing law! It is a law that does not merely generalize regarding the properties of agents, including their desires, but also explicitly lays down a norm. It is *better* to suffer than to do evil. Better for whom? Presumably, better for most, acknowledging possible exceptions. But the exceptions are not just exceptions, leaving the law intact, as it were. For if there are any exceptions at all, then anyone can claim to be one of those, for a whole host of reasons. The paradox that it is better to suffer than to do evil is certainly not presented by Socrates as a rule of thumb that, admittedly, alas, sometimes does not hold.[9] Rather, it is presented as an absolute truth, just like the mathematical truths that the prudentialist says are illicitly offered as an analogy to the moral truths of Socrates in the dialogues. Although the absolutist claim entails the truth of the prudentialist claim, the reverse is not the case.

The attempt to justify the Socratic paradoxes as resting on a law of nature draws its plausibility from the objectivity of a law, irrespective of the deviant desires of people. But objectivity is not enough to make this interpretation plausible. For it may well be objectively true for A that suffering injustice rather than doing it is best, while the opposite is objectively true for B. It is indeed implausible to suppose that moral laws are just like mathematical laws, but it is not implausible or at least not impossible that moral laws can have the exceptionless universality of

---

[8] See *Cr.* 49B–C. Cf. *Gorg.* 473A2–475E6; *Rep.* 4.444E6–445A4; 9.591A10–B7. At *Gorg.* 476A2–D4, Socrates argues that the one who is justly punished is benefited. This argument provides strong support for the universality of the Good. The just punishment of B by A is necessarily a benefit to B if the instantiation of Justice is universally good. Only if the miscreant is incurable is punishment not a benefit to him, in which case it would presumably not be just for someone to inflict it on him. See 512A–B, 527C1–2 with C5–6. Brickhouse and Smith 2002 make the sensible point that if there are incurable souls, then pure intellectualism seems misguided. See O'Brien 1967, ch. 1; Santas 1979, ch. 6; Brickhouse and Smith 2006 for helpful introductions to the so-called paradoxes.

[9] It may well be that Xenophon understood Socrates in this way. I doubt very much that Plato did.

mathematical laws.[10] To maintain this, however, is to maintain that moral laws are not generalizations regarding the outcomes of human behavior. Someone might argue, for example, that certain sorts of behavior are preferable on utilitarian grounds, the justifications for which are rooted in human nature, however that is conceived. More important than the problems with this view is that it has nothing to do with what Plato actually says.

The Platonic theory according to which there is no conceptual space between "good" and "good for oneself" does not imply that there is no psychological space between these two. It is certainly possible that one should desire something, believing it to be good for oneself, when in fact it is not, which entails and is entailed by its not being good *simpliciter*. The psychological gap is what produces the astonishment in Socrates' interlocutors when he presents to them arguments for the paradoxes. It is the elimination of the ontological gap that shifts the focus to the psychological gap. It is this that justifies claims that in some sense, knowledge is sufficient for virtue.[11] For, presumably, when one knows that one's own good is never achieved at the expense of anyone else, one has no motive to act otherwise than virtuously. One has no motive other than to seek out what is good and to avoid evil in every circumstance since the good is identical with that which is good for oneself. We should note, however, that this knowledge cannot amount to the knowledge that, say, justice is a good, since even acknowledging this, one may well go on to insist that it is still not good *for me* to be just. Here is a plausible story about how this claim can be made. Yes, justice is a good and, *ceteris paribus*, I would desire to do the just thing. But health is a good, too. And so are pleasure, wealth, beauty, and power.[12] And sometimes there are conflicts of good. These conflicts mean that it is not always possible to realize one without forgoing or even acting contrary to the other. Plato no doubt believes that such goods can be hierarchized in some way.[13] But that is neither here nor there unless he can show that his

---

[10] In fragment 286f of Euripides' *Bellerophon*, we hear the atheist complain that the wicked obviously prosper and the virtuous suffer. This is the *reason* for denying the existence of the gods. See Cornford 1923, 153, for a translation. So, too, Shakespeare: "Some rise by sin, some by virtue fall," *Measure for Measure*, Act 2, Scene 1. The prudentialist's view is like the atheist's view in eschewing supernatural justification, but unlike the view of commonsense that the prosperity of the wicked and misery of the just are all too real. The appeal to a law of nature either conceals a metaphysical foundation or is, it seems to me, remarkably naive.

[11] See Irwin 1977, 78; Vlastos 1991, 214–231; Penner 1992, 129; 1997; Benson 2000, 156–157.

[12] See *Rep.* 2.367C8–9 where Adeimantus is speaking and is expressing a commonplace in reference to seeing, hearing, thinking, being healthy, and whatever else is good "by nature (φύσει)" and not merely "by repute (δόξῃ)."

[13] See *Phdr.* 237D6–9, where Plato distinguishes between a desire for pleasure and an "acquired belief (ἐπίκτητος δόξα)" pursuing what is "best (τοῦ ἀρίστου)." Cf. *Phd.* 66B3ff; *Tim.* 88A8–B2.

ranking of these goods is universalizable. And the requisite universality is not attained by a generic good which includes goods like wealth, health, beauty, and power since all these can be "internally" hierarchized, so to speak. That is, one can recognize all of these as goods while at the same time insisting that from time to time the acquisition of one may be prioritized over the acquisition of another. Even if it is the case, as Socrates argues in Book 4 of *Republic*, that psychical health is as intrinsically desirable as is physical health, such a claim does not even begin to address the problem that arises when it is not possible to have both of these at once.[14]

For this reason, we should pronounce inadequate the prudentialist or nonmetaphysical reading of Plato's ethics which assumes that the knowledge that is sufficient for virtue is the knowledge of the definition of virtue or even the knowledge that virtue is a good, a knowledge that must in turn rest upon the knowledge of what virtue is. Even if one knows what the Form of Justice is and can therefore give a λόγος of it, and even if this λόγος includes the property of being a species of the generic Form of Good, this is not sufficient to make someone always desire to do the virtuous thing as opposed to pursuing some other good in despite of its being inimical to virtuous behavior here and now. This does not make the knowledge of the Form of Justice otiose. Far from it. For assuming that one knows that "good" and "good for me" are extensionally equivalent, that still leaves wide open the question of what I ought to do here and now. How is my good (*aka* the Good) to be instantiated? The emptiness of the reply, "by doing what is just" is patent. What, then, is the content of the requisite knowledge?[15]

It should be added that prudentialism draws its plausibility from the fact that it is, from a narrow perspective, true. Being virtuous is in fact in one's interest or to one's advantage. But the prudentialist, in stopping here and in refusing to seek out the metaphysical foundation for the truth of this claim, leaves him- or herself open to the obvious objections and

---

[14] See *Rep.* 4.444D12–E1. Cf. *Gorg.* 477B34.
[15] Grube 1935, 255, writes, "The object of the supreme knowledge is clearly the Ideas. And a knowledge of the Ideas means not only an understanding of Truth, of the structure of the world, but also of the moral and aesthetic realities in it, of its purpose and the reason why in all things. It then includes what we should call a sense of true values; the knowledge of good and evil, of beauty and goodness as well as of truth." It is not clear to me that the phrase "moral realities" points to anything beyond the definitions of the Virtues; it certainly does not include a recognition of a superordinate Idea of the Good. Grube, 258, struggles to answer the question "why someone with this knowledge cannot but do good" and gives an answer that gestures in the direction of the unity of goodness.

counterexamples that I have canvassed above. Prudentialism must suffice for a materialist like Democritus or Epicurus. But like it or not, that is not Plato's view.

3.2 Knowledge of the Idea of the Good

In *Republic*, Plato says as plainly as possible that the superordinate Idea of the Good makes the Forms knowable.[16] That is, the knowledge that is supposedly necessary and perhaps also sufficient for virtue is not possible without "ascending" to the Idea of the Good.[17] The claim being made here is stronger than the claim that we cannot know whether Justice, say, is good without knowing how Justice participates in the Good. In fact, we cannot know Justice at all unless we see it as following from the Idea of the Good.[18] So, someone who needs to be persuaded that doing justice is in her own interest must be shown that the real good that she seeks is identical with the Good. This is shown if it is the case that the Idea of the Good provides being or essence to Justice.[19] The argument seems to be this:

Everyone desires their own good;
One's own good is identical with an instantiation of the Idea of the Good;
Therefore, everyone desires the instantiation of the Idea of the Good.

Of course, "desires" must be understood in a transparent context, meaning that one must know what the instance of the Good is. But how is that which everyone desires "attained?" If the Idea of the Good provides being to the Forms, then the Forms are at least "Good-like (ἀγαθοειδές)" according to the principle that the effect must be like its cause.[20] Therefore, one attains the Good that everyone seeks by attaining the Forms. This attainment is, of course, knowledge. According to this line

---

[16] *Rep.* 6.508E1–4 with 508A9–B7, 6.509B6–7, 511B8–C2; 7.517C2–3.
[17] *Rep.* 6.511B6–7. The ascent is clearly epistemological and consists in a mental seeing of the first principle in its relation to the Forms. Cf. *Symp.* 212A1–3. See Szlezák 2003, 80–81.
[18] At *Rep.* 6.511B6–7, it is said explicitly that the Forms are derived from the first principle (τῶν ἐκείνης ἐχομένων). How exactly Justice is deducible from the Good is a key question, the answer to which will determine in what sense Plato's ethics rests upon his metaphysics.
[19] See *Rep.* 6.509B5–9. If Plato were committed to a Form of Injustice, he would be faced with the problem that the Idea of the Good would also provide being or essence to it, thereby presumably making it beneficial, too. But if injustice is the absence of justice where justice could be present, no such Form is needed.
[20] See *Rep.* 6.509A3, where it is said that knowledge and truth are "Good-like." But truth, which is provided by the Good to the Forms, is ontological truth, not semantic truth. It is a property of being in relation to an intellect, the property of being transparent to an intellect. "Transparency" here is the *ne plus ultra* of "clarity (σαφηνεία)," the criterion according to which the objects of the Divided Line are graded. See 6.509E6–510A3. See Ferrari 2003, 303–308.

of reasoning, the knowledge that produces virtue or virtuous behavior is the knowledge of Forms, but this knowledge is only possible when the Forms are seen to be derived from the Good.

One possibility sometimes advanced is that the knowledge that is necessary and perhaps sufficient for virtue is a kind of "know-how," that is, practical knowledge. This is suggested by Socrates talking about knowledge as a craft (τέχνη).[21] It is also suggested by his talk about virtue as the knowledge of goods and evils.[22] It is reasonable to suppose that one who has ἐπιστήμη as described in *Republic* would thereby have the craft which consisted in applying that knowledge in particular circumstances.[23] It seems a mistake, though, just to conflate the knowledge and the craft. What differentiates a craft from a knack (τριβή) is that a craft rests upon universal principles, whereas a knack does not.[24] Since a craft deals with particulars, if a craft were not attached to knowledge of these principles, then a craft would not be distinguished from a knack. The craft is not the knowledge, but the application of the knowledge. Focusing on the application of the knowledge and not the knowledge itself only occludes the metaphysical foundation of the entire edifice.

But even if we decline to identify ἐπιστήμη with a craft, we are still left with the problem that the relevance of ἐπιστήμη to ethics is obscure. The problem can be articulated in the form of a dilemma. Either the Good makes an essential contribution to our knowledge of, say, Justice, or it does not. If it does not, then why be persuaded that knowing how to be just as opposed to being unjust is my real good? If it does, and if knowing Justice means somehow knowing that it is derived from the Good, how does this direct action? How, in other words, can we make judgments regarding the justness of an action or, generally, the instantiation of "goods" and the avoidance of "evils?" Doing the just thing would be as empty as an exhortation to do good.

The relationship between the Good and the Forms which makes the ἐπιστήμη of the latter depend somehow on cognition of the former must be something subtle enough to allow one to pass between the horns of this dilemma. I suggest the following interpretation, additional support for which will be adduced in subsequent chapters. Aristotle accurately

---

[21] See, for example, *Ap.* 22B9–D4; *Gorg.* 465A, 501A; *La.* 184E11–185E6, 194C7–D9, and so on. See Irwin 1977, 71ff.
[22] See, for example, *La.* 199C4–D1; *Protag.* 319; *Gorg.* 507B1–3. Among those who hold that virtue is to be understood thus are Irwin 1977, 89; Brickhouse and Smith 1994, 71, 108; Annas 1999, 97.
[23] See *Sts.* 267A8–C3 on ἐπιτακτικὴ ἐπιστήμη (directing knowledge).
[24] See, for example, *Phdr.* 260E5–6.

3.2 *Knowledge of the Idea of the Good*

represented Plato as identifying the Idea of the Good with the One.[25] He criticizes Plato for conflating two senses of "one." According to the first, "one" indicates a measure of a quantity; according to the second "one" indicates simplicity or absence of complexity.[26] For example, "one" used for counting a number of items – one book, one cat, and so on – does not indicate the complexity or lack of complexity of one of these items. By contrast, to say that something is one in the sense of simple is to indicate its lack of complexity relative to another item or, at the extreme, to indicate its unqualified lack of complexity. Plato actually accepts the conflation of these two senses for the first principle of all. It is a feature, not a bug, in his system. The first principle is absolutely simple because it is beyond οὐσία. But anything that is Good-like (or One-like) is so not by being absolutely simple, for absolute simplicity is uniquely instantiable. It is Good-like by being one as a measure, a measure of a kind. The kind is, of course, denominated according to a Form. The realm of ethics is in the "gap" between endowment as a participant in a Form and achievement as an ideal integrative unity according to kind.[27] The virtuous person who, as Plato says, "becomes one out of many," is just one example of something that is one (as a measure or unit of perfected humanity) achieving an ideal state by assimilating to simplicity or absence or complexity relative to the kind of thing it is.[28] Not surprisingly, integration of parts within a whole admits of degrees. As we shall see, Plato treats virtues as scalable. The stages of integration are quite well articulated in the dialogues.

Assuming this interpretation for the moment, we can perhaps see how ἐπιστήμη is supposed to be sufficient, and even necessary, for virtue. "Ascending" to the Good is equivalent to seeing the integrative unity of the Forms. It is seeing that they constitute a web of internally related

---

[25] See my 2020, ch. 5, §6.
[26] See Aristotle, *Meta.* Λ 7, 1072a32–34. This objection is not explicitly directed to Plato, but I take it to include him given what Aristotle says later at M 8, 1084b13–1085a2, which is a part of an extended criticism of Plato's theory of principles.
[27] Sedley 2009, 156–158, represents one application of the distinction I am making as one between "conferred immortality" and "earned immortality." He adds, 158, "If you make the best decision [about what life to lead] and unify yourself with your intellect, you are making yourself identical with that in you which is immortal."
[28] See *Rep.* 4.443E1. The phrase "one out of many (εἷς ἐκ πολλῶν)" is a sort of slogan representing an idea deeply embedded in Plato's normative framework. Cf. 4.423D3–6, applying both to the individual and to the city and 5.462A2–B3, where something is made as good as possible by being made one. Also, 9.588B–590A on the ideal unity of the soul. For a human being to become one out of many does not, of course, mean to become absolutely one or simple since this would be the destruction of the kind whose integrative unity is being sought.

essences. They are what perfect Being (τὸ παντελῶς ὄν) is.²⁹ Since everyone desires the true or real good, when one sees this integrative unity, one sees that, say, being just is an instance of Justice, which is that of which the Good is the principle. To practice justice is to achieve a sort of integrative unity, the motivation for which is the desire for our own good that is hardwired in us.³⁰ It is knowledge alone, thus understood, whose attainment does not beg the question of its relevance to the good I seek. Knowledge is necessary for virtue because without it, virtue is mere correct behavior and does not touch on the integrative unity of the person. It is sufficient because once possessed, one knows wherein one's own good lies, never in opposition to the good of anyone else.³¹

If one could know Justice independently of knowing that it is derived from the first principle of all and therefore internally related to all the other Forms, presumably one would be able to recognize instances of Justice in the sensible world. But one would not thereby necessarily be motivated to pursue justice or to pursue it over against all other goods. The identical point can be made even if it is recognized that Justice is a species of a generic Form of the Good. But one has all the motivation one needs once one recognizes that Justice is "Good-like" because it is produced by the Idea of the Good. It is Good-like because it is a type of integrative unity or a measure of it. More precisely, justice is a human virtue that integrates the soul of the human being and therefore brings it closer to its source. It is the identical integrative unity variously instantiated in the state in individuals, in institutions, and practices, and so on.³² But when we descend to the level of public policy or to the level of individual action,

---

[29] This is the upshot of the dialectic regarding Parmenides' One in *Soph.* 244B–245E. The unity of τὸ παντελῶς ὄν, the multiplicity of Forms along with the Intellect thinking them, requires a principle that is "over-and-above." This is the Idea of the Good/One. The Good/One is beyond the Being that implies essence or οὐσία. Plotinus, *Enn.* VI 7 [38], 2 Henry-Schwyzer, provides the most incisive characterization of the interrelatedness among intelligibles. See also V 8 [31], 4.4–11.

[30] This is the import of the argument at *Me.* 77B2–78B2.

[31] Penner 2007a, argues that the knowledge that is sufficient for happiness is the knowledge of virtue, a type of knowledge which he treats as propositional. But being able to give a λόγος of the Form of Virtue does not close off the question of whether being virtuous is good for oneself. Penner somehow thinks that it does. If Penner says that the knowledge is not just of the Form of Virtue but of the fact that being virtuous is to one's advantage, that is a pious assertion and not an argument.

[32] See *Rep.* 4.435B1–2. Disunity is variously characterized, for example, "sickness (νόσος, νόσημα)" at *Rep.* 3.391C4, 4.439D2, 5.470C5–10; "internal discord (στάσις)" at *Rep.* 8.544C7. Any (organic) complex is endowed with an integrative unity at its inception (γένεσις) and the unity is undone at its destruction (φθορά). The integrative unity that is an endowment is one "side" of the dual aspect of nature; the other is achievement or perfection. One cannot become a perfected human being unless one is a human being to begin with. But endowment could not coincide with achievement amidst the images of the really real. The sensible world, and everything in it, is essentially dispersed or, relatively speaking, disunified.

success hardly seems likely to flow merely from knowing that an integrative unity is sought. As we shall see in a later chapter, the idea of the φρόνιμος (practically wise person) as the person who can discern the universal in the particular instantiation of it has its germ here.

We are familiar with the simple and powerful argument advanced by Socrates in *Euthyphro*, and elsewhere: I cannot know if x is f unless I know what F-ness is. Conversely, if I do know what F-ness is, I can recognize its instances here below. At the very least, in trying to discern whether x is f, I have a better chance of coming up with the right answer if I know F-ness than I do if I do not. The relevant knowledge is frequently glossed as the ability to give a λόγος of F-ness. There are a number of reasons why this is likely not to be true. First, if knowing F-ness were equivalent to being able to give a λόγος of F-ness, then presumably, that λόγος can be given to someone who receives it and then can give it to someone else. But then the knowledge of F-ness would be a commonplace, like the knowledge that fire burns or that night follows day.[33] It would certainly not be rare or only the result of rigorous philosophical exercise. A second and related point is that only one who knows F-ness knows if a particular λόγος is in fact a λόγος of F-ness. If you know F-ness, but I do not, then why should I suppose that your λόγος was in fact correct? But for the same reason, I cannot know if my λόγος is correct unless I know F-ness. From this it follows that the knowledge of F-ness is not reducible to the ability to give a λόγος of F-ness; rather, that ability is an expression of one's knowledge, an expression that is, alas, not productively accessible by anyone else who does not have that knowledge.

The above argument is offered in support of the claim that the knowledge of F-ness is the mental seeing of a one that is itself part of a whole. That whole, Being itself, is unified by the Good/One. Being is an integrative unity. That is why it is Good-like. The articulation of the "parts" of Being is just what the method of collection and division aims at. It aims at seeing the multitude of integrative unities manifested here below in a diminished way.

Plato insists in *Republic* that knowledge is only of the intelligible world.[34] He also insists that belief or δόξα is the relevant mode of cognition

---

[33] As Simmias plaintively says when Socrates dies, at *Phd.* 76B9–12, he fears that no one will be alive who can give an account (διδόναι λόγον) of a Form. Clearly giving an account cannot just be saying the words that would be contained in a true account. If this were so, Socrates could give it to Simmias, who could give it to anyone else. Presumably, this point was not entirely grasped by whoever composed the Pseudo-Platonic *Definitions*.

[34] Those who distinguish the "Socratic" ethics of the "early" dialogues from Platonic ethics naturally take the (Socratic) knowledge that is necessary and sufficient or virtue to be "nonmetaphysical." For example, Vlastos 1991, 113–114, claims that Socrates seeks and attains "elenctic knowledge," which is equivalent to something like justified true belief. But there seems to be a strong tendency among

for the sensible world of diminished, though not negligible intelligibility. This, I take it, is the main lesson of the argument with the lovers of sights and sounds.[35] Those expositors of Plato's ethics who renounce or ignore the relevance of metaphysics to ethics typically discount this claim when they are reflecting on the necessity and sufficiency of knowledge for virtue.[36]

Naturally, if one knows F-ness, then one is in a better position to arrive at a true belief about whether x is f than one who is ignorant of F-ness. But there are no grounds in the dialogue for turning the belief into the knowledge itself. This mistake is the burden of those alone who are allergic to metaphysics. It is true, as we learn from *Meno*, that for practical purposes, a true belief is as good as knowledge.[37] The problem, of course, is in applying a criterion for determining a true belief from a false one. Knowledge alone can fill this role. But this knowledge is not necessary to motivate action; believing that something is good for oneself will do that. In fact, a *false* belief will do it as well as a true belief. But a belief that doing something is in one's own interest is an unreliable guide to true virtue absent the knowledge of the Good and the attendant knowledge that one's own good and the Good are identical. Believing that it is in one's own interest to, say, obey the law, motivates behavior until the time comes when it doesn't. The philosopher's knowledge is the only guarantor of virtuous behavior, that is, of the true belief of what virtuous behavior is in any case. Insisting on the necessity or sufficiency of knowledge for virtue

---

those who make no such distinction to minimize or eliminate the metaphysical basis for Plato's ethics. See, for example, Hardy 2014, who takes the knowledge that is necessary and sufficient for virtue to be a comprehensive knowledge of one's own psychological constitution.

[35] *Rep.* 5.476A9–480A13. See Gerson 2003, ch. 4.

[36] Irwin 1977, 217–226, acknowledges that knowledge is of intelligibles, but he denies that this knowledge requires "ascending" to the superordinate Good. Instead, he argues, 225, that the Good is just the "system" of Forms. So, on this view, knowing what Justice (or at least knowing Justice among the other Virtues) is should be sufficient for desiring to be just. See *Gorg.* 460B10–13: ὁ δίκαια μεμαθηκὼς δίκαιος (the person who has learned about justice is just). But as we have seen, this is not so. The knowledge of Justice cannot be motivating independent of the knowledge that being unjust can never be in one's own interest because one's own interest is only achieved by instantiating the Good via Justice. Irwin's view is repeated in 1995, 272. Following Irwin is Annas 1999, 108. Kahn 1996 seems to suppose that the knowledge that is virtue is not knowledge of intelligible reality. He seems to treat it as a form of τέχνη. So, too, Gosling 1973, ch. 4. I presume Kahn and Gosling mean by "knowledge" a true belief about the instantiation of the Virtues. According to Plato, however, what makes the belief true is that it is a belief about an instantiation of a Form. And what makes the instantiation of that Form good for me is that the Form is derived from the Good and so "Good-like."

[37] See *Me.* 97B1–7. In this passage, the knowledge that the one with true belief is missing appears to be of the same thing as that of the true belief. But the identical point applies for knowledge of a Form and true belief about an instance of it.

3.3 Virtue, Knowledge, and Other Goods

makes little sense outside of the metaphysical framework in which the Idea of the Good is the first principle of all.

3.3 Virtue, Knowledge, and Other Goods

In *Euthydemus*, there is a well-known passage which highlights some of the issues being treated here. It does so in a way that will, I think, illuminate some of the differences among treatments of Platonic ethics. Here is Socrates drawing a conclusion in regard to the discussion of knowledge and other things:

> So, in summary, Cleinias, I said, it turns out that for all the things which we at first said to be good,[38] the correct account is not that they are by nature good in themselves, but it is this: if ignorance is in charge of them, they are greater evils than their opposites, to the extent that they are more prone to being controlled by an evil ruler, whereas if prudence or wisdom are in control, they are greater goods. In themselves, neither one of them is worth anything. – It appears, he said, to be as you say. – What, then, follows from what has been said? Is it anything other than this: that none of those other things are good or evil in themselves, whereas there are two things, wisdom which is good, and ignorance which is evil. He agreed.[39]

The point of the passage is evidently to differentiate goods that are not good "in themselves" from the one good that is, namely, wisdom. Furthermore, it is the presence of the latter alone that makes the others good; and its absence, assumed to amount to ignorance, makes them evil.[40]

The passage has tempted some scholars to make Socrates here a Stoic *avant la lettre*.[41] For the Stoics, virtue is the only good; all other putative

---

[38] These are health, beauty, noble birth, political power, and honor. See *Euthyd.* 279A8–B3. The passage goes on, B4–C4, to list individual virtues as additional goods. Of course, as Socrates goes on to argue, a good like, say, health needs to be used wisely in order for it to be good for us or for our happiness. Cf. *Gorg.* 507C2–3.

[39] *Euthyd.* 282D2–E5: ʼἐν κεφαλαίῳ δʼ, ἔφην, ὦ Κλεινία, κινδυνεύει σύμπαντα ἃ τὸ πρῶτον ἔφαμεν ἀγαθὰ εἶναι, οὐ περὶ τούτου ὁ λόγος αὐτοῖς εἶναι, ὅπως αὐτά γε καθʼ αὑτὰ πέφυκεν ἀγαθὰ [εἶναι], ἀλλʼ ὡς ἔοικεν ὧδʼ ἔχει· ἐὰν μὲν αὐτῶν ἡγῆται ἀμαθία, μείζω κακὰ εἶναι τῶν ἐναντίων, ὅσῳ δυνατώτερα ὑπηρετεῖν τῷ ἡγουμένῳ κακῷ ὄντι, ἐὰν δὲ φρόνησίς τε καὶ σοφία, μείζω ἀγαθά, αὐτὰ δὲ καθʼ αὑτὰ οὐδέτερα αὐτῶν οὐδενὸς ἄξια εἶναι. {—} Φαίνεται, ἔφη, ὡς ἔοικεν, οὕτως, ὡς σὺ λέγεις. {—} Τί οὖν ἡμῖν συμβαίνει ἐκ τῶν εἰρημένων; ἄλλο τι ἢ τῶν μὲν ἄλλων οὐδὲν ὂν οὔτε ἀγαθὸν οὔτε κακόν, τούτοιν δὲ δυοῖν ὄντοιν ἡ μὲν σοφία ἀγαθόν, ἡ δὲ ἀμαθία κακόν; {—} Ὡμολόγει.

[40] Cf. *Ap.* 30A10–B4; *Charm.* 173A7–D5. More precisely, as per *Rep.* 7.517C3–4, no one can act wisely without knowing the Good. So, the Good's causal role is prior to knowledge of it in explaining how something is good.

[41] See Annas 1993, 58. In this regard she is objecting to Vlastos 1991, 229, n. 96. Also, Senn 2005, 3, "The virtue Socrates makes so much of, is the sole intrinsic good, the sole constituent of happiness."

goods are in fact neutral.⁴² The extreme nature of this position is, the Stoics believed, mitigated by a distinction among "neutral" or "indifferent" goods between those that are "preferred (προηγμένα)" and those that "dispreferred (ἀποπροηγμένα)."⁴³ So, whereas health is in itself neutral, it is a preferred neutral whereas sickness, also neutral, is dispreferred. The idea of being "preferred" and "dispreferred" is, roughly, that of being the object of a natural inclination or disinclination taken in abstraction from any context. So, whereas we naturally tend to want to be healthy, if being healthy conflicts or impedes the only good thing, namely, virtue, then, though health is preferred, it is not good for us. It is actually evil.⁴⁴

This Stoic defense of the sufficiency of virtue for happiness does not appear in Socrates' argument. Even if it is true that Socrates can plausibly be thought to be arguing that a wise person who is sick is better off than an ignorant person who is healthy, it is far from plausible that he is arguing that a wise person who is healthy is no better off than a wise person who is sick. In other words, being healthy is "in itself" a good of some sort. But this seems to go directly against the text itself, which claims that the putative goods are in themselves neutral.⁴⁵ How is this problem to be addressed?

I would suggest that the solution is to recognize the way that "good" conceals an ambiguity that is eliminated in *Gorgias* by distinguishing "what seems best" to someone and "what he or she wills." As we have seen, the tyrant does what seems best to himself and not what he wills, which is his own good. But in order to distinguish what is good as the object of his will from what is good as the object of his desire, we had to show that what the tyrant wills is the Good which is universally instantiated when it is instantiated at all.⁴⁶ Consequently, if what seems best to the tyrant is different from what he wills (which is in fact the Good), then we know that he does not will what seems best to him. By contrast – just to be perfectly clear – if what seemed best to him was in fact a manifestation of the Good, then that would be identical with what he willed.

What we find in the *Euthydemus* passage is "good" used to indicate both an object of desire ("what seems best") and an object of will ("the Good in

---

⁴² See, for example, Diogenes Laertius, VII 101–103. See Annas 1993, 63.
⁴³ See, for example, Stobaeus, *Ecl.* 2.84.18–85.11.
⁴⁴ See, for example, Sextus Empiricus, *M.* XI, 64–67.
⁴⁵ See Korsgaard 1983, 179, who is defending a Kantian position which is very much in line with the Stoic one, "Power, riches, and health are good or not depending upon what use is made of them."
⁴⁶ See *Gorg.* 467E4–6, where health and wealth and "other such things" are said, along with wisdom, to be good in themselves. Things truly "neutral," that is, neither good nor bad in themselves, are said to be, for example, "sitting," "walking," "running," and "making sea trips."

itself"). It will always seem to one that health is desirable. The virtuous person does not stop desiring health. The use of "good" for "what seems best" is indeed very close to the Stoics' "preferred indifferents." It is not unlikely that Zeno's "preferred indifferents" are equivalent to "what seems best" in *Gorgias* and elsewhere and that he derived this idea from his Academic teachers. But in any case, the way that the knowledge that is virtue transforms a "neutral" into a real good without claiming that the neutral is neither desirable nor undesirable is if what is really good is determinable otherwise than by consulting what seems to us to be desirable. And this, I would claim, should lead us to abandon prudentialism. If what the tyrant wills is incommensurable with what seems best to him, there is no scenario in which he could find that, say, his health is to be preferred to what he wills, namely, the Good. The key is incommensurability.[47] But that is only achievable if there is no personal or subjective scale of values that would on occasion privilege health over virtue and thereby achieve what one wills. If, for example, health is not "intrinsically" good, we would have to count as a failure the argument in *Republic* that justice is "intrinsically" good, just as is health.[48] Health is intrinsically good to the subject who seeks it. Its goodness is negotiable for the subject who wills nothing but the Good or instances of it. Embodiment makes us destined to be both subjects; but it is only the latter that wills the Good.[49]

Here is another way of approaching the distinction I am urging is to be found in this passage. All the things ordinarily counted as goods, like health, beauty, pleasure, and so on, are human goods, things that human beings naturally desire. Whether or not any one of these goods is an instance of the Good we will now is a separate question. If it turns out not to be so, that is, if it turns out that physical health is being used unwisely, then though that is not what we will, this does not change the fact that physical health is a human good and so intrinsically desirable. One

---

[47] Annas 1993, 66, indicates the incommensurability by making a distinction between moral and nonmoral values.
[48] *Rep.* 4.443B–444E. On the analogy between body and soul, cf. *Cr.* 47D–E; *Charm.* 156E–157E; *Gorg.* 477B–480E, 504B–505B; *Phdr.* 270B–C. If physical health were not "intrinsically" good, then the claim that Glaucon and Adeimantus' challenge is met by showing that psychical health is analogous to physical health would be pointless. See 2.357C2–3 and 367C6–D3, where seeing, hearing, and thinking are added to being healthy as intrinsic goods.
[49] Aristotle, *EE* Θ 3, 1248b40–1249a5, marks the relevant distinction as between things that are good naturally (φύσει), though not καλόν, like health and pleasure, and things that are good *and* καλόν, like virtue. For a virtuous person, things naturally good will also be noble because they are put to noble use.

might accept this and still maintain that the superordinate Idea of the Good is otiose. For the distinction between a human good and an instance of the putative Good is just a distinction between something "neutral" and its transformation into a real human good. My objection to this deflationary position is its implausibility as an interpretation of Plato's moral realism. For physical health is better than sickness even for one who is wise or virtuous. And if that is so, then it is better for one who is not virtuous, too, independently of how it is used. And, of course, it can be misused. But in order to be able to determine its misuse, we need a criterion of goodness separate from the criterion of the human goods, which is just that human beings naturally desire these. If it is to be a universal criterion, then it looks like it will have to be the superordinate Good beyond essence as opposed to a co-ordinate Form of the Good, for reasons given in the previous chapter. A reversion to the Stoic interpretation of Socrates' words rather obviously follows from the imposition of a non-Platonic naturalism on the text. This is a form of moral realism that eschews metaphysics. Some might well say that that is exactly what Socratic, as opposed to Platonic, ethics requires. I have tried to show earlier in this chapter why there is little or no evidence for such a division.

The goods that human beings habitually desire may or may not be instances of the Good, which is what human beings always and everywhere will. If they turn out to be instances, then their appearance is veridical; if not, then nonveridical. But even a nonveridical appearance of an instance of the Good may be a good. That is, it may be an instance of a human perfection. These perfections are the kinds of things that human beings normally desire and pursue. The misuse of one or another of these does not change this fact. The characterization of them as "goods" is therefore independent of their possible misuse. Ultimately, what makes "nonmoral goods" and "moral goods," as Annas puts it, incommensurable is that the subject desirous of the first is a human being, whereas the subject of the second is, as Plato puts it, the "human being inside the human being."[50]

The transformative virtue in our passage is clearly related to wisdom (σοφία) or knowledge of some sort.[51] The reason why our passage maintains

---

[50] *Rep.* 9.589A7–B1: τοῦ ἀνθρώπου ὁ ἐντὸς ἄνθρωπος. Cf. *Alc.* I 130C1–3, where the human being is identified with the soul, not the composite of soul and body. From this it follows that what is good for the human being may not be good for the composite and vice versa. It is upon this distinction that the doctrine of grades of virtue depends.

[51] See *Me.* 87C5–89A6, where the conclusion is that virtue is either partly knowledge or the whole of it. Also, *Protag.* 361B5–7 on knowledge as the whole of virtue.

3.3 Virtue, Knowledge and Other Goods

that virtue is transformative of neutrals is that it involves the skill (τέχνη) of using them correctly. By contrast, ignorance would cause us to, say, misuse our health or wealth. But this can hardly be the whole story. As has been noted, if wisdom or knowledge were just the source or cause of good, then it would be instrumental to the very goods that are supposed to be inferior to it. Wisdom must also be good in itself independent of its instrumental value.[52] This wisdom seems to amount to or entail the knowledge of the identity of one's own good and an instantiation of the Good itself.[53] As we learn in *Republic*, only one who sees the Forms in the light of the Good has this knowledge. That is why philosophy itself is transformative.[54]

Most scholars would agree that the Stoic view is an exaggeration of Plato's own position. Plato does not hold that virtue is the only good, as do the early Stoics. I would suggest that the Stoics came to their radical position precisely because they rejected the superordinate Idea of the Good. Their rejection of it is the counterpart of the prudentialist's rejection of it.[55] Set aside the Idea of the Good. In that case, what are the grounds for denying that, say, health and wealth are goods along with virtue? Even if they are inferior goods according to some hierarchical criterion, it is not difficult to imagine a scenario in which our own good is served by privileging health over virtuous behavior. In this case, it is surely not adequate to appeal to the Stoic mantra "live in agreement with nature," an exhortation which could no doubt inspire some version of Socrates to escape from prison. Only if health is not at all a good and if virtue is the only good does it follow that in pursuing our own good we should look to nothing but virtuous behavior. For Plato, physical health (and much else) is good for a human being. But human beings are not what we truly are. The power of wisdom or knowledge is not the power to transform a "neutral" into a good. It is the power to transform sel-identification by discovering what one's true good is and that this is identical with an instantiation of the Good.

---

[52] See McCabe 2005, 209.
[53] Stalley 2000, 276, finds this identity as early as *Charmides*, "We all want the good and think we know what sorts of thing are good, but our judgment is generally distorted by our appetites and desires. To know the good is to know what we ourselves really want." Knowing what *we* want is inseparable from self-knowledge, that is, knowing who we really are, not soul-body composites, but rational souls.
[54] See McCabe 2005, 211: "Plato's metaphysics of morals ... rests on the account of the person who is wise and that person is who the philosopher is becoming." As McCabe, 212, goes on to stress, the mutual dependence of ethics and metaphysics is no more evident than it is here.
[55] See Boys-Stones 2018, 463, who points out that Middle Platonists like Numenius argued that Stoics were incapable of grounding their pursuit of the apparent good in what "objectively and absolutely *is* good."

The explicitly metaphysical basis for Platonic ethics is rejected by the explicitly naturalistic positions of Epicureanism and Stoicism. Epicureanism and Stoicism, each in their own way, pose a challenge to the Platonic view that moral realism requires a first principle of all that is "beyond οὐσία." Against the Stoics, Plato will in *Philebus* claim that pleasure is a good, albeit not the supreme good for a human being. Against the hedonism that Epicurus defends, Plato will also argue in *Philebus* that to say that pleasure is a good that is not contentious; but to say, as Epicurus does, that it is *the* good that is in incoherent position if there are other goods. In *Protagoras*, he will argue that to identify pleasure and the good is to make it impossible to explain how we can pursue pleasure despite our awareness that it is not the good. Plato does not, I think, allow that there can be any compromise between a metaphysically based moral realism and a host of incoherent alternatives.

3.4 Virtue and Philosophy

In *Republic*, Glaucon and Adeimantus challenge Socrates to prove that justice is not only "desirable in itself (αὐτό τε αὐτοῦ χάριν)" but also desirable "for its consequences (τῶν ἀπ'αὐτοῦ γιγνομένων)."[56] It is natural to read the challenge as urging Socrates to show, first of all, that justice is intrinsically valuable. But the proof could only show that someone who understood that Justice is Good-like would value a just deed over an unjust one whenever the occasion for doing the one or the other presented itself. That is, the valuing is always within the framework of a subjective ordering of preferences. The ordering is necessarily always of actions that appear to one to be good. We need not waste our time trying to discover the chimerical intrinsic property of value in a just deed. There is no one property in seeing, hearing, thinking, and being in a state of health that is isolated by calling all these intrinsically valuable.[57] Rather, what is desired in all these cases is the state that results from having or exercising them. By contrast, the supposed consequences of being a just person are the

---

[56] *Rep.* 2.367A6ff. See Anderson 2020, who argues that the positive consequences of justice concern the rewards and prizes coming from others. Anderson's argument depends on identifying the effects of justice in Bk. 9 as benefits of justice "in itself" and the beneficial consequences only in Bk. 10. I think that Bk. 9 gives us beneficial consequences in this life and Bk. 10 beneficial consequences in the next life.

[57] *Rep.* 2.367C8–9. This list of states good "in themselves (αὐτῶν)" "by nature (φύσει)" has no discernible unity other than that people want them independent of their consequences. Issues arise, however, when there is a *conflict* among these and one may have to be sacrificed for another. Not surprisingly, the priorities of people differ. The subjective variation becomes critical when, for instance, health and pleasure or wealth and virtue conflict.

"externals" that result from a supposedly desirable state such as wealth, reputation, power, pleasure, and so on.

Socrates' analogy of justice and physical health is supposed to illustrate an irrefutable claim, namely, that no one, *ceteris paribus*, would choose vice over virtue just as no one, *ceteris paribus*, would choose sickness over health. The rather obvious problem with the analogy taken as a substitute for the conclusion of an argument is that it is never the case, in the real world, that all other things are equal. Of course, no one would prefer achieving a desired end along with sickness over achieving that identical end with health. But many people would prefer the risk of sickness in order to achieve the end rather than abandon it. And some people would welcome sickness if it were a necessary condition for achieving some cherished goal. As much can be said for the state of the soul that is supposed to constitute psychical health, that is, justice. The analogy between physical health and psychical health makes this evident. If one has to choose between health and doing an unjust deed (granted that justice, like health, is intrinsically desirable or valuable), it is far from obvious that there is only one rational or defensible choice. When a preferential ordering of goods is made, it is the embodied human subject who is making them. The goal of philosophy is the achievement of transformative wisdom. This transformation results in our identification with a subject incommensurable with the subject pursuing and ordering human goods.[58]

Prudentialism takes the analogy between health and justice as morally dispositive. Because justice is psychical health, no one in their right mind would willingly do the things that would impair that health. This seems to be empirically false, but also contrary to the line of argument in *Republic*. For the conclusion that justice is analogous to physical health is reached at the end of Book 4, not even halfway through the dialogue. In addition, that conclusion takes no account of philosophy. This is important because at the end of *Republic* in the Myth of Er, we are told the story of the virtuous man who, given a choice of lives, opts for the life of a tyrant. This is because he was virtuous "by habit, without philosophy (ἔθει ἄνευ φιλοσοφίας)."[59] It seems plausible that the introduction of philosophy at the beginning of Book 5 suggests that the virtue defined in Book 4 is "without philosophy." In that case, prudentialism depends upon an incomplete or deficient representation of Plato's own account of how virtue is conducive to

---

[58] By "incommensurable" I mean that there is no all-things-considered judgment that enables us to compare these supposed goods and to decide which one is best.
[59] *Rep.* 10.619C8. Cf. 7.518D9–519A5; *Phd.* 82A10–B3. See Gerson 2019 for further argument regarding this passage.

happiness. Insofar as philosophy is necessary in order to transform mere popular or political virtue into philosophical virtue, and insofar as philosophy seeks out knowledge, we would expect that that knowledge is what the unnamed virtuous person in Book 10 is lacking. And as we learn in the Divided Line passage, the knowledge of Forms sought by philosophers is not possible without ascending to the Idea of the Good. Indeed, the Idea of the Good is introduced immediately before the Divided Line. So, it is hardly surprising that the account of Plato's ethics could never be adequate without integrating the Idea of the Good into that account. Thus is Plato's ethics inseparable from his metaphysics.[60]

In addition, as we learn in Book 6, it is owing to the Idea of the Good that just things (τὰ δίκαια) become useful and beneficial.[61] So, it is the Idea of the Good that is the bridge between the provisional answer to the question about the benefits of justice at the end of Book 4 and the complete answer at the end of Books 9 and 10. Without adducing the Idea of the Good, there is no satisfactory answer to Glaucon and Adeimantus.[62] For to say that being psychically healthy is analogous to being physically healthy and that, all things being equal, no one would prefer either psychical or physical sickness to health, does not even touch the central problem. The variable subjective ordering of goods or "values" never amounts to the absolutist conclusion that Plato manifestly wants to reach. Only if the real good that I seek can never require the privileging of my health (or any other good) over my personal rectitude will Plato's goal be achieved. And *that* is

---

[60] Putnam 2005, Lecture 1, characterizes Platonism, especially its ethics, as based on "inflationary metaphysics" or "inflationary ontology." I suppose that Plato would reply to Putnam that he, Plato, is providing exactly as much ontology as is needed to make true universal moral judgments. And no more.

[61] *Rep.* 6.505A2–4. This passage seems to reference 4.444E6–445A4, where Socrates says that what remains is to show that justice "benefits (λυσιτελεῖ)" us. The answer to the question of *why* justice is beneficial requires us to "ascend" to the Idea of the Good. Note that the question is not: Is justice a good? One can grant that justice, like all the virtues, is a good without conceding that it is always useful or beneficial to practice it when other goods are at stake.

[62] Some scholars assume that it takes the definition of the Form of Justice in Bk. 4 to be more or less the end of the matter, at least with regard to the first part of the challenge of Glaucon and Adeimantus. Psychical health is intrinsically valuable and whatever we can say about justice and its consequences after that does not change this. See, for example, Vlastos 1971b, 68, n. 7, who says the argument that justice pays in Bk. 4 is a "self-contained one"; Kosman 2007, 121, "the end of Bk. 4 is meant to register the success of that project [proving that justice is valuable in its own right]"; Santas 2010, ch. 5. But even if this is true, the intrinsic value of justice must be set alongside the intrinsic value of other goods sought for their own sake, like physical health. My contention is that when we do this, if we ignore the Idea of the Good, we can at best arrive at a prudentialist position which must countenance the possibility that justice is not always the winner in a decision process leading up to the prioritization of different intrinsically valuable goods. For all we can tell, sometimes a preference for justice over physical health is imprudent.

only possible if my good is identical with an instantiation of the superordinate Idea of the Good which is at once without limited or defined content and universally present in all its effects. The identity of one's own good and an instantiation of the Good holds for everyone, but it takes a philosopher to know this.[63]

In order to show that philosophy is relevant to virtue, it is not enough to maintain that knowledge is necessary for virtue and that knowledge is of Forms. As we have already seen, knowing what Justice is is not sufficiently motivational for the would-be tyrant.[64] Even knowing that Justice is a kind of good, that is, that it is a species of the Form of Good is not sufficient. For insofar as Justice is a species of Good, Good must have some content. But there is, I think, no plausible response to the complaint that there can be no explanation for why one must desire that content. It is always possible to question whether that content is the real good that one seeks.[65] For example, assume that being just is being good because justice is one type of perfection. One might well ask why it is supposed that being perfect in this way is the real good that one seeks. The real goods that one seeks are manifestations of the Idea of the Good that is "beyond οὐσία." How is one to leverage the desire for one's own good, whatever that turns out to be, into a desire for that which is beyond essence?

Here is a sketch of how the argument goes. When people become aware of their own desires, they implicitly identify not only an object of desires but also a subject of desires. This is not a trivial point, since when a *conflict* of desires arises, this is perforce a conflict of subjects of desire. The idea of a conflict between reason and "appetite" so much discussed in the literature is not, I think, even intelligible unless the terms "reason" and "appetite" are shorthand for the subject who is reasoning and the subject who is having the appetite.[66] These subjects are manifestations of an identical soul, so they are the same, but they are numerically different. They are individuated by their particular states. Conflicts within the soul reveal the indeterminacy of subjectivity, at least the subjectivity of embodied individuals.

---

[63] See *Rep.* 3.412D4–7 where the rulers, *as rulers*, are emphatically characterized as those who regard their own good and the good of the *polis* as identical.
[64] See, for example, Foot 2001, 9, who argues that acting morally is part of practical rationality. Foot can only mean by "rationality" reasoning according to moral norms, which makes her claim a tautology. See also Korsgaard 1996, 93; Lott 2014.
[65] See Stemmer 1988, 545–549.
[66] See *Phd.* 94C9–D6 for a vivid description of a soul "having a conversation (διαλεγομένη)" with appetites, rages, and fears "as if with a separate thing (ὡς ἄλλη οὖσα ἄλλῳ πράγματι)." A conversation assumes rationality on both "sides." Only a rational agent with an appetite is persuadable by a "separate" rational agent. See Beere 2011, 263–264.

So, while all agree that they pursue their own good as they see it, they can without difficulty be made to admit that the "their" in "their own good" is problematic. But until this is determined, the pursuit of one's own good – whether or not this is identical with the Good *tout court* – cannot be reliably achieved. When Plato says that the virtuous person becomes "one out of many," it is not only the virtuous person for whom this is true. The vicious person or tyrannical man, his polar opposite, also tends to become one out of many, a single subject of his basest appetites.[67] Adding philosophy to virtue is, accordingly, a process of self-discovery, that is, discovery of one's true or ideal self. But what this self desires is knowledge, as Plato repeatedly insists. The self-transformation brought about by achieving philosophical knowledge amounts to the desire for one's own good being identical with the desire for the Good. The reason – or, one reason – why the Good must be beyond οὐσία is that only if it is so does the question "is it good for me to achieve x?" where x names some οὐσία, loses meaning. In this case, "x" is knowledge of intelligible reality. But knowledge of intelligible reality requires the ascent to the Good. Having one's own true good means "having" the Good as object of knowledge.[68]

The effectiveness of philosophy in the transformation of popular or political virtue into true virtue must consist in the power of knowledge.[69] But this is not what most scholars take this power to be. It is usually supposed that the knowledge is the knowledge of the definition of a Form, specifically, the Form of a Virtue. So, if one knows what Justice is, then this is sufficient for being just. Of course, if this claim is to be even remotely plausible, one must add: Knowing what Justice is includes somehow

---

[67] See *Rep.* 9.575E2–576A6, where the tyrannical soul is ruled by the "monarch" eros, the mirror image of the aristocratic man who is ruled by reason. Eros here is evidently a mythical representation of the subject of erotic desire. If eros is powerful enough to impel the philosopher up to the Good, it is powerful enough, when misdirected, to lead one down to destruction. It is not without significance, I think, that the antecedent of the tyrannical man, the democratic man, is completely dispersed in his subjectivity. The "downward" trajectory in the typology of states and individuals ends in a complete inversion of the integrative ordering of the aristocratic state and soul. The tyrant's soul is the last remnant of unity prior to dissolution into complete disorder or limitlessness.

[68] At *Rep.* 6.504D2–505A4, Socrates says that the study of the Good is the "greatest study (μέγιστον μάθημα)" for humankind. It is "something greater than (τι μεῖζον)" the study of Forms. It is implausible to suppose that, as some have argued, the study of the Good is greater than the study of Forms because the Good is just the sum of Forms. For the study of the Good is greater, that is, more important, than the study of all the virtues. Should we suppose that what is meant here is that the study of the Good adds, say, the study of mathematical Forms to the "greatest Kinds" of *Sophist* and that *that* constitutes the greatest study for humankind? Even if the study of *all* the Forms is greater than the study of some of them, are we to suppose that the text can bear the interpretation according to which that is all the Good indicates? If nothing else, "sums" do not cause their "parts" to exist.

[69] See Sedley 2013, 82–83.

knowing that being just is in one's own interest. I take it, though, that this is exactly what people like Callicles and Thrasymachus deny.⁷⁰ There is no suggestion in the dialogues that the definition of Justice will include the property of its being in one's interest to be just. Indeed, the text says just the opposite, namely, that it is the Idea of the Good that makes being just in one's interest. And as we have seen, even if we suppose a genus "Good" (that is, perfection) such that Justice is one species of perfection, we still do not have the requisite motivational premise. For one can intelligibly and even plausibly ask why achieving perfection is in one's own interest. Perhaps, after all, the perfect is the enemy of the good, that is, one's own good.

Realizing that the superordinate Idea of the Good is the key to the argument about virtue and knowledge still leaves us with the glaring problem of how that which is above οὐσία is not actually empty of content. In that case, the study of it adds nothing to the study of Forms. In an important though neglected paper, David Hitchcock argues that, independently of the testimony of Aristotle and the indirect tradition, it is possible to see in *Republic* the assimilation of the Idea of Good to the One, the principle of unity and simplicity.⁷¹ There is in fact good textual support for the claim that Plato takes virtue, both in the individual and in the state, as the achievement of integrated unity according to kind.⁷² By "integrated unity" I mean the parts of a whole working together optimally. By "according to kind" I mean that optimal operation is indexed to essence. So the virtuous person who becomes one out of many is or has the optimally integrated human soul. In Book 4 of *Republic*, this appears to require the rule of reason, "controlling" the integrative unity. But as we have seen, the virtue in Book 4 is not the virtue of a philosopher, who is not revealed as the possessor of true virtue until Book 8. So, the integrated unity of the virtuous nonphilosopher is suboptimal. And it is easy to see why this is so. For the nonphilosopher has not undergone the self-transformation that

---

⁷⁰ See *Gorg.* 491E8; *Rep.* 1.344A3–6, B1–C2, 347E2–4, 352D2–4. See Vasiliou 2015, 61–62, who makes the identical point, not from the perspective of the tyrant, but from that of ordinary people. But Vasiliou does not regard the Idea of the Good as the starting-point for the solution to this problem.
⁷¹ See Hitchcock 1982.
⁷² For the individual, the most important text is *Rep.* 4.443E1, where the virtuous person "becomes one out of many." Adam 1921, v.1, *ad loc.*, notes that the phrase "one out of many (εἷς ἐκ πολλῶν)" is a sort of "Platonic motto." Cf. 4.423D3–6, applying both to the individual and to the state and 5.462A2–B3, where something is made as good as possible by being made one. For the state, there are a number of texts: 4.423B9–10, D4–6; 8.551D5–7. See Shields 2007, 74, on the gradations of virtue and vice in *Republic* as degrees of unity. See Chan 2021, 1372–1376, on "kind-based" integrated unities as manifestations of a "platonic," "kind-independent" criterion of goodness.

consists in seeing the Forms in the light of the Good. Seeing or knowing that, say, Justice is a species of Good would not be enough, as becomes evident in Book 10 for the unnamed virtuous would-be tyrant. The rule of reason is adequately manifested in someone who simply obeys the laws, when these are *good* laws. But the sort of justice thereby achieved is merely prudential justice, part of popular or political virtue, the probably defeasible view that being just is, as a matter of fact, more likely to be in one's own interest than being unjust.[73]

It may well be supposed that integrative unity according to kind is an exceedingly thin normative criterion. What could the goal of achieving integrative unity tell us about the correct response to the many ethical conundrums that human beings face? I think there are three levels of response to this question. According to the first, if the Idea of the Good is the first principle of all, and if my good is identical with a manifestation of that, then it is not possible for my good to be achieved by doing or being something that impedes the achievement of manifestations of the Good by anyone else. This is why, though Socrates endorses self-defense, he insists that one must not return an injustice for an injustice. His absolutist prohibition of doing injustice follows from the facts that (1) injustice does not manifest the Good; (2) all seek the real Good; and (3) manifestations of the real Good and my own good are identical. So, naked aggression against anyone is pretty clearly prohibited.

The second level of response will seek to discover whether there are more subtle forms of aggression and what these are. At this level, I find Plato's response mostly conventional and unsatisfactory. For example, he is apparently uninterested in the question of whether paternalistic legislation could possibly be unjust. I will return in Chapter 7 to issues surrounding the connection between Plato's ethics and his political philosophy.

The third level of response faces the question of the positive responses to the achievement of integrative unity as the Good. Merely refraining from naked aggression does not tell us how a person becomes one out of many. I take it that the answer to this question is found in those passages in which Plato discusses the affective and cognitive training on behalf of the

---

[73] See *Rep.* 4.430E7–431A6, where ἐγκράτεια ("continence" or "restraint") is characterized as "self-mastery (κρείττω αὐτοῦ)," which does not seem substantially different from the definition of the virtues of wisdom (441E3), self-control (442D2), and justice (443D4) later in Bk. 4 as the rule of reason in the soul. As we shall see in the next section, the virtue of the philosopher is not equivalent to continence; she has no bad appetites in need of restraint. For the nonphilosophically virtuous, continence is one in reality with the virtues, although it differs in λόγος from them. That is, the continent person will *behave* exactly as will the truly virtuous one in the identical situation.

3.4 Virtue and Philosophy

cultivation of practical and theoretical reasoning. From the *in utero* physical training of the unborn, to the musical and physical education of children, to the development of practical skills and theoretical reasoning, to the philosophical education of the rulers of the ideal state, every practice and strategy is geared to integrative unity. Without the last step, such integrative unity as is achievable is unstable. What for Aristotle is the distinction between self-control and virtue is for Plato the distinction between popular or political virtue and philosophical virtue. It is only the one practicing the latter who can distance himself sufficiently from the subjects of appetitive and emotional desire. Embodied persons can never do this completely; this is the burden of embodiment after all. But it is possible – or so Plato thought – to achieve a sufficient distance from these ephemeral subjects to be able to look at them without prejudice in their favor.[74]

If this analysis of the levels of casuistry still leaves much that is indeterminate, that does not seem to me to be uniquely Plato's problem. For example, we should not suppose that the systematic construct of ethics will yield a definite answer to the questions that Plato apparently asked himself about the appropriate response to the political problems that his friend Dion faced in Syracuse or the problems of how he should have treated Dionysius II. That Plato took one course rather than another tells us nothing about its ethical superiority over any other. Thus, there is a certain level of skepticism beneath the absolutism expressed by Socrates in many places. This skepticism is occluded by Plato's enthusiastic partaking in imaginary lawmaking. All of these laws – sometimes implicitly, but more often explicitly – are presented as following from moral principles. To what extent this is justified will be considered in due course.

That integrative unity is normative for Plato follows from the identification of the Good with the One. The normativity is expressed systematically within Platonism by the articulation of the cycle remaining (μονή) – procession (πρόοδος) – reversion (ἐπιστροφή).[75] Since this "cycle" is typically taken to be a hallmark of Neoplatonism, it is important to insist that, although the terminology is late Platonic, the elements of the cycle are as

---

[74] Socrates' calmness in the face of death, a death he could have avoided, was exemplary in antiquity and indeed afterward as well. This is the aspect of Plato's ethics wholeheartedly embraced by Stoicism. The many characterizations in the tradition of Socrates as heroically virtuous implicitly recognize and valorize the distinction between philosophical virtue, on the one hand, and popular or political virtue, on the other.

[75] See Proclus, *Elements of Theology*, Props. 25–39 Dodds. See Chlup 2012, 64–69. Also, see Gersh 1973, 49–53 for concise expressions of the doctrine.

firmly rooted in the texts of Plato as could be. The Good "remains" because it is eternal.[76] It "proceeds" by "overflowing (ἐπίρυττον)." The reversion is to the Good that all desire. Reversion is according to kind because the Good produces everything via the instrumentality of the Living Being which is articulated into Kinds. Everything, in striving to fulfill its nature, thereby strives to attain the Good in the only way it possibly can. The fulfilling of one's nature is just the achievement of integrative unity for that kind. For human beings, it is fairly clear that the watershed in the passage to integrated unity is the metaphorical separation from the body and the subjectivity that embodiments forces upon us.

3.5 Gradations of Virtue

Because integrative unity is normative, it is possible to grade virtue according to proximity to the One. That virtue *is* gradable for Plato hardly seems in doubt. The distinction between "popular or political" virtue and philosophical virtue implies gradation, not a contrast, between real and unreal.[77] So, too, virtue with philosophy added is graded more highly than virtue "without philosophy."[78] In addition, the virtues of courage and self-control are inferior to the virtue of wisdom because they are associated with the body.[79] How this happens we have seen above. Here I want to

---

[76] See *Tim.* 42E5–6 for the "remaining" of the Demiurge who also produces because he is good.

[77] See *Phd.* 87A11–B3. I take it that the "illusory" virtue in *Phd.* 69B6–7 is not like fake diamonds in relation to real diamonds, but like the images of Forms in relation to the Forms themselves. The "true" virtue that a philosopher produces after a vision of the Beautiful in *Symposium* 212A5–6 is not contrasted with "fake" virtue but with the inferior form of virtue found in those who have not benefited from philosophy. See Petrucci 2017 for an illuminating analysis of the distinction between philosophical virtue, on the one hand, and popular and political virtue, on the other, in *Menexenus*. Petrucci shows that it is only the former that comes with knowledge, whereas the latter is purely habitual. See Boys-Stones 2018, 463–465, on Middle Platonic recognition of gradations of virtue. See Reed 2020 on what he calls "deficient virtue" in *Phaedo*. As Reed aptly points out, there is a striking similarity between deficient virtue and the prudentialism of Epicurus. This is exactly the result we should expect from stripping metaphysics from "Socratic" ethics.

[78] See *Rep.* 10.619B7–D1; cf. 4.443C9–D1, *Phd.* 82A10–B3. Virtuous behavior alone is clearly not perfect virtue, though it is virtue nonetheless. At *Phd.* 68C5–69A3, the difference between true virtue (69B3) and the "shadow (σκιαγραφία)" of true virtue (69B6–7) is described in terms of motivation for behavior or practices. The motivation for the latter turns out to be a desire for bodily preservation at all costs. See Centrone 2021, 275–279.

[79] See *Rep.* 7.518D9–10. At *Lg.* 1.631C5–D1, there is a gradation or hierarchy of virtue that excludes philosophy and so seems to be equivalent to popular or political virtue. Cf. 4.710A5; 12.968A2. The hierarchy is practical wisdom (φρόνησις), self-control (σωφροσύνη), justice (δικαιοσύνη), and courage (ἀνδρεία). These are called "divine goods," in contrast to the "human goods" of strength, beauty, wealth, and health. It seems that here φρόνησις is now used by Plato as Aristotle will use it, for the intellectual virtue having to do with action instead of its earlier use by Plato for theoretical wisdom or σοφία. Cf., for example, *Symp.* 202A9. The desired virtues of the citizens of Magnesia

focus on how a nonmetaphysical interpretation of Plato's ethics tries to handle gradation of virtue.[80]

The grades of virtue are not degrees of virtue, like the comparatives taller and shorter, higher and lower, and so on.[81] Hence, the problem of defining the virtues arises. This is, in general, the problem of trying to define the paradigm starting from the image. This is not exactly the problem of defining the perfect by the deviant, as in the straight line by the curved line. A curved line is not an imperfect straight line. The politically virtuous individual, say, does not become philosophically virtuous by becoming maximally politically virtuous. And yet the political virtuous individual is not vicious. So, the virtues as defined in Book 4 of *Republic* are aspects of integrative unity. It is integrative unity that is gradable. But if virtue just is integrative unity, how can there be a higher grade of this?

The way Plato answers this question is to assume that virtue is transcategorical, so to speak. Just as a slave and a woman have their own virtues, so an embodied soul and a disembodied soul have their own virtues. What links the latter two is the fact that I, endowed with an embodied soul, am ideally a disembodied soul. Those rejecting a metaphysical interpretation of Plato's ethics want to lay great emphasis on the claim that knowledge is necessary and/or sufficient for virtue.[82] This is supposed to be knowledge of the virtues or, more exactly, knowledge of what the λόγος of a virtue is. But this so-called propositional knowledge could not possibly be necessary or sufficient for achieving philosophical virtue. At most, it could be so only

---

may be divine but they are not philosophical or informed by philosophy. As Gauthier-Jolif 1970, v.2, 466, note in an illuminating discussion of the history of the term φρόνησις, the practical meaning of the term antedates Plato, but Plato connects that with the theoretical meaning, culminating in the knowledge of the Good, the practical relevance of which is patent. Aristotle reverts to the primarily practical meaning.

[80] Vlastos 1971b, in an influential paper, treats virtue in *Republic* without gradation and hence without need for metaphysical supplement.

[81] See Irwin 1995, 234–236; Kamtekar 1998, who takes grades of virtue as *degrees* of virtue, that is, more or less complete virtue. Virtue does not admit of degrees, but rather of gradations, ultimately depending on grades of integrated unity. This is mainly because virtue is a limit; only things without limit, like pleasure, admit of degrees. Helen's beauty, for example, is no less an instance of beauty than is the beauty of a law or institution or science. But it is further removed from the One than these, owing principally to its being instantiated in a body with μέγεθος, that is, extension. The unity of something with extension is always going to be inferior to the unity of that which has no extension, such as intellect, but also to that which, though having no extension, is "dispersed" extensively, like the soul. I think we should gloss "Helen is more beautiful than Xanthippe" as an account of appearance, not of an intrinsic degree of beauty in one that is greater than that in another.

[82] See Aristotle, *NE* Z 13, 1144b28–30, who says that Socrates thought that the virtues were kinds of knowledge or, more perspicuously, areas of inquiry within which knowledge was possible. But Aristotle is here probably referring to the historical Socrates, whose reasons for holding whatever belief it was that he held are not available to us.

for the attainment of the popular or political sort. For example, suppose that someone truly believes that the definitions of the virtues in Book 4 of *Republic* are correct. Note that true belief alone is relevant here; knowledge, assuming it is more than true belief, is not necessary. But the true belief that, say, self-control, is acquiescence in the rule of reason in the soul could at most make someone a docile and obedient citizen.[83] How, though, even if this is true, would one then be in a position to give an account of the higher grade of virtue that the philosopher seeks to attain?

It is not just that the prudentialist view deprives itself of the resources to answer this question, but it is committed to taking what Plato himself regards as merely an image as the real thing. Thus, it places itself within the purview of the lovers of sights and sounds in *Republic*, those who are explicitly contrasted with philosophers. It is not likely that Plato's ethical teaching can be correctly identified with an approach which is opposed to that of philosophy and aligned with that of the purveyors of antiphilosophy.

Perhaps one will reply to this criticism by insisting that gradations of virtue can be accounted for by degrees of belief or commitment. So, the virtuous person who chooses the life of the tyrant only had a mild belief that virtue was good for him. What philosophy would have given to him is an unshakeable belief that this is so. One here might appeal to *Meno* and Socrates' distinction between true belief and knowledge, where the latter ties down the former with a bond that is unbreakable.[84] The distinction is between believing p and knowing why p is true, that is, having the explanation (αἰτία) for the truth of p. As I have argued, the explanation for the fact that my good is only achievable by doing what is good *simpliciter* is that there is a superordinate Idea of the Good that is the principle of all. And, in addition, that this Good is the absolutely simple One. But this of course means that the reply to the above criticism must concede the metaphysical foundation for Plato's ethics and therefore abandon prudentialism. Apart from this interpretation of the *Meno* passage, I do not see how moving from believing that virtue is good for me to knowing that virtue is good for me can be otherwise explained. For if knowing this means knowing that Virtue is a species of the Form of Good, the question of whether doing what is good is in fact good for me is not even addressed. There is no knowledge of virtue, upgraded from belief, that could explain why virtue is in my interest apart from knowledge of the

---

[83] See Monteils-Laeng 2014, 137–144.   [84] See *Me.* 97E–98B.

3.5 Gradations of Virtue

Forms, which as we have learned, is not possible without ascending to the Good.

In *Protagoras*, the question is raised regarding the unity of the virtues. Although an answer is not clearly arrived at in the dialogue, the question lingers. And many scholars have wondered whether in *Republic* Plato provides an affirmative answer.[85] I believe that Plato's actual view is obscured by a failure to distinguish grades of virtue. For in the highest grade of virtue, the virtues are mutually implicating and so unified; for the lower grade they are not.[86] That which makes any single virtue good for me is that which makes them all good for me. The unity of the virtues in the philosopher is owing to the fact that the philosopher alone knows that his own true good and the Good are identical and that therefore his own good is never achievable at the expense of anyone else. But the vices are exactly various ways of misperceiving one's own good in relation to others. Even if there were some person who happened to practice all the popular or political virtues, this would not establish their unity. For virtuous behavior in one area of human life does not entail virtuous behavior in another.[87]

It is not very difficult to imagine a person who excels in courage and fails in self-control. Attempts to deny this by sophistically claiming, for example, that the recipient of a Congressional Medal of Honor is not *really* courageous if he is also lacking in self-control seem absurd. The shred of plausibility in such a claim depends on switching between the two main grades of virtue, the nonphilosophical and the philosophical. So, the nonphilosophically courageous person may well be held to be philosophically not courageous just because he is philosophically not self-controlled. The mutual implication of the virtues at the philosophical level is owing to the integrative unity of the soul or self that is achieved.[88] For such a self, the

---

[85] See, for example, Vlastos 1973 [1972]; Penner 1973b; Devereux 1992; Cooper 1999, ch. 3.
[86] See Prauscello 2014, 57–73; Centrone 2021, ch. 10, on the grades of virtue in *Laws* and mutual implication of the philosophical virtues.
[87] See *Rep.* 5.477C6–D2, where the virtues are powers (δυνάμεις) each defined by its specific object. Like the five sense powers, these are not mutually implicating. At *Sts.* 305A12–B11, 306B9–10, it is apparently the "natural virtues (φυσικαὶ ἀρεταί)" of courage (ἀνδρεία) and self-control (σωφροσύνη) that are actually antithetical to each other. In *Republic*, the philosopher must possess virtues by nature. See 6.485A–487A, 503B–D, 560Cff. Cf. *Lg.* 1.631C, 696B, 4.709E, 12.963E. Cf. Aristotle, *EN* Z 13, 1144b1ff.
[88] See O'Brien 2003 on the complexities in determining what exactly the thesis of "the unity of the virtues" is supposed to mean in *Protagoras*. O'Brien, 129, concludes that at the end of the dialogue, while it is clear that Socrates holds that the virtues are mutually implicating, it is not clear how this is so. In particular, it is not clear how knowledge or wisdom is supposed to be related to the other virtues. The question of what the knowledge is is put off to another time (357B5–6). Answering this question would, I take it, create a path to the distinction between popular or political virtue, on the one hand, and philosophical virtue, on the other.

practice of each and every virtue is an expression of the Good, the only good that this self desires. For the self who is virtuous but without philosophy, there is no inevitability of virtuous practice in one area carrying over to another. This is because of the lessened degree of integrative unity of this self. The problem of a philosopher ruling in a *polis* is compounded by his or her ruling over people who, at best, practice a patchwork of nonphilosophical virtues along with various dispositions to vice.[89]

Additional support for gradations of virtue in Plato's ethics can be found in the conflation of virtue and continence (ἐγκράτεια) in *Republic* Book 4.[90] The virtue of self-control (σωφροσύνη) is identified with continence (ἐγκράτεια), the rule of the "better" part of the soul over the "worse." Someone who practices the popular or political virtues exercises self-control, but has no part in philosophy. Such a person might do what is good despite his or her desire to do otherwise. By contrast, according to Aristotle, continence is distinct from virtue. Doing the right thing is not sufficient for virtue; it must be one as the virtuous person would do it. That is, virtue does not belong to one who is continent and does the right thing even if it is not for an ignoble reason.[91] It might be suggested that there is merely a dispute between Plato and Aristotle on the semantic range of the words "virtue (ἀρετή)" and "self-control (σωφροσύνη)" and "continence (ἐγκράτεια)." But this semantic difference alone does not tell the whole story. For Aristotle, whether a deed is virtuous or not does not depend on whether or not the deed was done by a virtuous person or merely a continent person. For example, an anonymous act of charity is no less so for being anonymous. In response to the question of what makes the deed virtuous, I think Aristotle has no answer other than it is a deed that the virtuous person would have done. But it cannot be that *only* a virtuous person would have done that deed. So, Aristotle has no real answer to the question. By contrast, Plato's answer is straightforwardly that what makes the deed virtuous is that it instantiates the Good, which is one despite being variously instantiable. It instantiates the Good because it contributes to the integrative unity of the human person and nothing more. But such

---

[89] Thus, the puzzle originally posed by David Sachs 1963, "how can we be sure that the philosophically just person will be conventionally just?" is solved by the subsumption of the latter by the former.

[90] See *Rep.* 4.430A3–B2. Cf. *Phdr.* 256A5–B3, where the lovers practice self-control apparently because of their philosophical training. This use of ἐγκράτεια is either to be accounted for as an earlier semantic looseness on Plato's part or by the fact that the lovers are destined to be reincarnated again. They have not escaped embodiment altogether. Philosophy has not yet completely dominated their souls.

[91] See Aristotle, *EN* H 7, 1145b8–11, 1152a33.

contributions are gradable because integrative unity is gradable. The difference between one who is virtuous without philosophy and one who is virtuous with philosophy indicates such gradation. A nonphilosopher who performs a virtuous deed does so "customarily," unsupported by the knowledge that his own good is identical with a manifestation of the Good.

Popular or political virtue is the virtue of a human being; philosophical virtue is the virtue of the "human being inside the human being." What connects the two – apart from the dual aspect of φύσις discussed in Chapter 2, Section 2.6 – is the capacity for the embodied self to identify with the disembodied ideal. The identification of one's own good with the Good provides the metaphysical foundation for the possibility of the identification of the embodied self with the disembodied self. "Philosophy" is the name for the method of pursuing and achieving the identification. The knowledge that the philosopher seeks is just the knowledge of the unity of all intelligible reality, a unity provided by the Good. So, anyone seeking her own good comes to know what that really is when she knows that the Good is virtually all that is knowable. Knowing the λόγος of a Form of a Virtue turns out to be sufficient for being philosophically virtuous, if we realize that that knowledge is not propositional, but the mental seeing of the unity of all intelligible reality provided by the Good. Popular or political virtue is an image of true virtue because it excludes this knowledge; it is found in actions unmotivated by the appropriate knowledge.

3.6 The Metaphysics of Virtue

As Socrates says to Callicles in *Gorgias*, our discussion is about "how we should live (ὄντινα χρὴ τρόπον ζῆν)."[92] The choices are stark: the life praised by Callicles or the life praised by Socrates. These are the life in pursuit of pleasure and the life in pursuit of the Good.[93] As Socrates goes on to explain, the latter is characterized by structure (τάξις) and order (κόσμος), the former by their opposites.[94] Then, we get the identification of virtue (ἀρετή) with such structure or order:

> Is it, then, by the presence of pleasure that we experience pleasure and by the presence of good that we are good? – Yes, indeed – But, indeed, we and everything else are good by the presence of some virtue. – It seems to me to be necessarily so, Callicles. – But, then, the virtue of each thing, whether it be a tool or a body or a soul or, indeed, any living thing, is not best produced

---

[92] *Gorg.* 500C3–4. [93] *Gorg.* 500D6–10. [94] *Gorg.* 503D5ff.

by random, but by structure and rightness and craft, whichever belongs to each. Isn't this so? – I say it is. So, is the virtue of each thing structured and ordered by a structure? – I would say so. – Therefore, when some order arrives to each thing, its peculiar good is present in it. – So it seems to me. – And is a soul that has its own order better than one without? – Necessarily.[95]

This passage not only identifies something good with an integrative unity but also identifies that with its virtue. The nexus good–virtue–integrative unity could not be clearer. Regardless of the question of parts or forms of soul, it is also clear that the structure and order is provided by intellect, whether that of the individual soul for itself or that of another as a supplement or substitute. Something's or someone's virtue is achieved by the imposition of structure appropriate to a particular kind. We see here once again normativity in the interstice between nature as endowment and nature as achievement. The thing's good is present insofar as the correct ordering of parts is achieved. This correct ordering is indexed to kind, that is, to a Form. So, something is endowed with manifestations of the Good according to the kind of thing it is. In other words, it gets as much of the Good as something of that kind is able to get. Prima facie, manifesting the ordering dictated by the paradigm would seem to leave tremendous scope for personal idiosyncrasies. Nevertheless, the ideal integrative unity, which consists in identification with one's intellect and the attainment of cognitive identity with universal intelligible reality, necessarily transcends the idiosyncratic at least insofar as the idiosyncratic pertains to embodiment. The grades of virtue and of vice judged by their proximity to the One is where all that which is idiosyncratic is to be found.

Socrates at once extends his conclusions about integrative unity to the cosmic level.

> wise people say that community and love and order and moderation and justice hold together heaven and earth, gods and human beings, and this is the reason why they [the wise people] call the entirety a cosmos, my friend, not a "non-cosmos" nor a "disorder." You don't seem to me to pay attention to these matters, even though you are wise; rather, it has escaped your notice

---

[95] *Gorg.* 506C9–E5: Ἡδὺ δέ ἐστιν τοῦτο οὗ παραγενομένου ἡδόμεθα, ἀγαθὸν δὲ οὗ παρόντος ἀγαθοί ἐσμεν; {—} Πάνυ γε. {—} Ἀλλὰ μὴν ἀγαθοί γέ ἐσμεν καὶ ἡμεῖς καὶ τἆλλα πάντα ὅσ᾽ ἀγαθά ἐστιν, ἀρετῆς τινος παραγενομένης; {—} Ἔμοιγε δοκεῖ ἀναγκαῖον εἶναι, ὦ Καλλίκλεις. {—} Ἀλλὰ μὲν δὴ ἥ γε ἀρετὴ ἑκάστου, καὶ σκεύους καὶ σώματος καὶ ψυχῆς αὖ καὶ ζῴου παντός, οὐ τῷ εἰκῇ κάλλιστα παραγίγνεται, ἀλλὰ τάξει καὶ ὀρθότητι καὶ τέχνῃ, ἥτις ἑκάστῳ ἀποδέδοται αὐτῶν· ἆρα ἔστιν ταῦτα; {—} Ἐγὼ μὲν γάρ φημι. {—} Τάξει ἄρα τεταγμένον καὶ κεκοσμημένον ἐστὶν ἡ ἀρετὴ ἑκάστου; {—} Φαίην ἂν ἔγωγε. {—} Κόσμος τις ἄρα ἐγγενόμενος ἐν ἑκάστῳ ὁ ἑκάστου οἰκεῖος ἀγαθὸν παρέχει ἕκαστον τῶν ὄντων; {—} Ἔμοιγε δοκεῖ. {—} Καὶ ψυχὴ ἄρα κόσμον ἔχουσα τὸν ἑαυτῆς ἀμείνων τῆς ἀκοσμήτου; {—} Ἀνάγκη.

3.6 The Metaphysics of Virtue

that geometrical [i.e., proportionate] equality has great power among gods and humans, whereas you think one ought to practice greed. That is because you neglect geometry.[96]

Those who are reluctant to embroil Socrates and his ethics in Platonic metaphysics tend to ignore this passage or else to assign the entire dialogue to a mythical "transition period" in Plato's philosophical development. Thus, the accounts of virtue in the discussions with Polus and Callicles are Socratic, but this one passage is somehow not. There is, however, no need for these arbitrary expedients. The integrative unity according to kind that applies at the personal level is here assumed to be analogous to integrative unity at the cosmic level. And that "geometrical equality" is how integrative unity is achieved both for gods and for humans.[97] One may try to explain Socrates' confidence that the world is a cosmos and not a "non-cosmos" without recourse to Pythagorean metaphysics, but in my view the prospect of this being right is small. The accusation that Callicles neglects geometry is readily explained in the context of this metaphysics, but not so otherwise. Socrates gladly shares Callicles' insistence that their debate on the question of how one should live be conducted at the level of nature (φύσις) and not at the level of law (νόμος).[98] What Callicles actually means by "nature" is the greed (πλεονεξία) that he thinks motivates everyone. What Socrates means by "nature" is what is universally the case including in the cosmos itself. If the Pythagorean metaphysics this implies is not taken seriously, then Socrates has no answer to Callicles at the level of nature. He has only one opinion thrown up against another. For at the level of Callicles' nature, it is hardly disputable that there are exceptional

---

[96] *Gorg.* 507E6–508A8: φασὶ δ' οἱ σοφοί, ὦ Καλλίκλεις, καὶ οὐρανὸν καὶ γῆν καὶ θεοὺς καὶ ἀνθρώπους τὴν κοινωνίαν συνέχειν καὶ φιλίαν καὶ κοσμιότητα καὶ σωφροσύνην καὶ δικαιότητα, καὶ τὸ ὅλον τοῦτο διὰ ταῦτα κόσμον καλοῦσιν, ὦ ἑταῖρε, οὐκ ἀκοσμίαν οὐδὲ ἀκολασίαν. σὺ δέ μοι δοκεῖς οὐ προσέχειν τὸν νοῦν τούτοις, καὶ ταῦτα σοφὸς ὤν, ἀλλὰ λέληθέν σε ὅτι ἡ ἰσότης ἡ γεωμετρικὴ καὶ ἐν θεοῖς καὶ ἐν ἀνθρώποις μέγα δύναται, σὺ δὲ πλεονεξίαν οἴει δεῖν ἀσκεῖν· γεωμετρίας γὰρ ἀμελεῖς. Cf. *Me.* 81C9–D11. Also, Aristotle, *Phys.* Θ 1, 252a11–16; *DC* Γ 2, 301a5–12. See Mirus 2012, 504–506, on Aristotle's association of nature, order, and the good.

[97] See Dodds 1959, 338–339; Burkert 1972, 77–79, on the Pythagorean origins of the idea of a cosmos and its mathematical structure. Also, see Huffman 2005, 73, on the relationship between this passage and Plato's association with the Pythagorean Archytas of Tarentum. As Huffman points out, 209, the term "geometrical equality" is probably not being used by Plato here as a technical term; rather, it means "the sort of equality that is studied by geometers" but also the sort of equality that appears in politics in the proportional distribution of goods and power. See *Lg.* 6.757B–C. The most relevant point is the intrusion of mathematics into a discussion of virtue via the generalization regarding integrated unity. See also Schofield 2011, 44–47, on early Pythagorean influence on Plato along with an apt allusion to this early influence in *Gorgias*.

[98] *Gorg.* 482Cff.

individuals for whom popular or political – much less philosophical – virtue do not coincide with self-interest.

Callicles' position might be viewed as a form of moral realism given his claim that we should look to nature to determine how we ought to act. But his putative moral realism differs sharply from that of Socrates in one crucial matter. Although he recognizes that nature has a dual aspect in the way described in the last paragraph, he thinks that nature as achievement is indexed to nature as endowment rather than to a universal principle, the Good. So, his view belongs to a family of views, including those of Stoics and Epicureans, that introduce so-called Cradle Arguments, aiming to determine the ideal achievement for a human being based on how a baby acts, that is, matching that achievement as closely as possible to one's endowment at ground zero. As I conceded at the outset, talking about Plato's moral realism is anachronistic if the word "moral" is not used with extreme care. It seems to me, though, that due caution is abandoned if we classify Callicles' view and Socrates' view as different forms of moral realism.

There are a number of possible objections to this approach to virtue in *Gorgias*. First, one might well object that optimal order is not species-relative; it must be sought not at the level of species but rather at that of individuals. Perhaps my optimal level of dynamic structure is not yours. Second, it is not clear that even if the optimal order is species-relative, it will unqualifiedly require the dominance of reason. Perhaps the proper order requires a *balance* between reason and appetite, where this balance does not *always* require the domination of the former. Finally, how does reason supposedly produce this structure? It is easy to see that, say, a builder imposes a geometrical structure on building materials. But this is only possible if the building materials can assume that structure. And in fact they can insofar as they are extended bodies with their own quantitative properties. But it is not so clear how this analogy is supposed to work for souls. For the imposition of order by reason on appetite and emotions, broadly speaking, cannot operate in the same way.

The answer to the first two questions is the same. Reason operates universally. Its conclusions can be applied to individuals and to individual circumstances, but what constitutes optimal reasoning cannot itself be indexed to individuals. Practical reasoning is an intellectual virtue, the same for everyone. The choice or decision to subordinate reason to appetite or emotion is, of course, a use of reason. It is a choice regarding how to instantiate the Good, something that everyone wills. Instantiating the Good is equivalent to a contribution to the achievement of integrative

3.6 The Metaphysics of Virtue

unity according to kind. Just as the Good makes Forms useful or beneficial, so the Good, conceived in its absolute simplicity as the One, makes Forms each to be μονοειδές or uniform in nature. And it is by participating in a Form of, say, Justice that integrative unity is imposed on the soul. The presence of justice in the soul is equivalent to the rule of reason. But this still leaves the question of how reason does this.

The answer to this question requires a further excursion into metaphysics. Returning for a moment to the proponents of "Socratic ethics," the claim that knowledge is necessary and sufficient for virtue, even if true, does not tell us what virtue is. For Plato, no set of conditions amount to a cause or explanation. In fact, all the virtues are habits (ἕξεις) or dispositions (διαθήσεις). In general, they are states (πάθη) in the soul. The states of one who is practically or politically virtuous as in *Republic* or *Phaedo* are found in the appetitive and spirited parts of the soul. The state of wisdom and other intellectual virtues are found in the so-called rational faculty. So much seems clear. But apparently first in *Philebus*, we get a categorical description of these states.

> Let us divide all the things that now exist in the universe into two, or rather, if you like, into three. – In what way? – By picking up part of what was said previously? – What was that? – We said that god showed that among things there is the unlimited and the limit. – Yes, we did. – Let us take these as two kinds, and the third one a mixture of these two.[99]

Appetites and emotions arise from states of the soul.[100] An appetite for drink arises in the soul from the state of dehydration in the body; an appetite for pleasure in the soul arises from the state of deprivation or emptiness of the body. Every bodily state is a combination of unlimited and limit, where limit indicates a particular mixture of the elements going to make up that state. An optimal state of the ensouled body results from the imposition of the right or appropriate limit, which is a μέτρον. So, measure is a subset of limit. And as the above passage goes on to explain, the imposition of measure is always the result of the operation of intellect, whether human or divine.[101] The reason why measure is only within the purview of intellect is that measure is a norm controlled by the Good or One. Whatever imposes measure, as opposed to mere limit, must look to

---

[99] *Phil.* 23C4–D1: Πάντα τὰ νῦν ὄντα ἐν τῷ παντὶ διχῇ διαλάβωμεν, μᾶλλον δ', εἰ βούλει, τριχῇ. {ΠΡΩ.} Καθ' ὅτι, φράζοις ἄν; {ΣΩ.} Λάβωμεν ἄττα τῶν νυνδὴ λόγων. {ΠΡΩ.} Ποῖα; {ΣΩ.} Τὸν θεὸν ἐλέγομέν που τὸ μὲν ἄπειρον δεῖξαι τῶν ὄντων, τὸ δὲ πέρας; {ΠΡΩ.} Πάνυ μὲν οὖν. {ΣΩ.} Τούτω δὴ τῶν εἰδῶν τὰ δύο τιθώμεθα, τὸ δὲ τρίτον ἐξ ἀμφοῖν τούτοιν ἕν τι συμμισγόμενον. Cf. 16C7–D8.
[100] See *Phil.* 35C6–D3.   [101] See *Phil.* 26E1–31A10.

the Good or One as guide. The Demiurge will, of course, also look to himself, where he will find the array of intelligible Forms which provide the variety of possible measures. As Aristotle says, the science of X and the science of good X are the identical science. And as Plato already knew, science belongs uniquely to intellects.

As we have already learned, the Good or One is the principle of measure. What that means exactly is that virtue is achieved by the optimal imposition of limit on the unlimited, where "optimal" indicates an expression of what the Good or One is virtually. So, a courageous person is one who is disposed in a way that is neither excessive nor deficient with respect to the state of fearfulness or upset in the body. And "fearfulness" indicates a particular type of pain at the prospect of something harmful. So, being courageous is one way of instantiating the Good, since by participating in the Form of Courage one participates in Being, which is what the Good is virtually. That is why at the end of *Philebus* we learn that beauty (τὸ καλόν), symmetry (συμμετρία), and truth (ἀλήθεια), when taken as one, determine the presence of good in any mixture.[102] Together they operate like a litmus test.

The above analysis seems to pertain mostly to popular or political virtue. And indeed the discussions of virtue central to *Statesman* and *Laws* focus on this since it is the role of law and the lawgiver to control the appetites of the many. True virtue is reserved for the philosopher, who attends to the immortal part of the soul.[103] What is most important for this study is that Plato's moral realism never occurs outside a metaphysical context. In particular, the determination of virtue requires recourse to the intelligible world and ultimately to the Good or One. And, in addition, we have the second principle, the Indefinite Dyad manifested in the various cases of unlimitedness that make embodiment so perilous.

The relationship between limit (τὸ πέρας) and measure (τὸ μέτρον) gives concrete expression to the distinction between nature as endowment and nature as achievement. Everything with a nature is composed of limit and unlimited. Measure is the ideal limit. It is that which is imposed on the precosmic elements by the Demiurge. And in the construction of living things according to the Living Animal, the gods make kinds as good as possible within the constraints imposed by the Receptacle and its inchoate elemental contents. Humans, owing to embodiment, are responsible for

---

[102] *Phil.* 65A1–5. Cf. *Tim.* 87C5–6.
[103] See *Tim.* 90A–D. The view is endorsed by Aristotle in *EN* K 7, 1177b30–1078a3. The lawgiver focuses on popular or political virtue, even though the best sort of life, the divine life, is the life of contemplation, the life of the exercise of nonpractical intellectual virtue.

deviations from a measured life. What makes a measure good is the Good itself or the One; it is by integrative unity according to kind that measure is achieved.[104] In this perspective, it is obvious why the Good/One must be "beyond οὐσία." If it were not, it would not be the principle of measure, but a specific measure that consisted of whatever οὐσία was assigned to it. And then imposing that measure on the wrong kind would be disastrous. But it could not fail to be imposed on some wrong kinds since the unity of this putative measure would not match the diversity of kinds.

3.7 Plato and Kant on Motivation

Various forms of prudentialism or psychological egoism – whether these views are attributed to Plato or not – begin with a claim that human action can only be accounted for on essentially egoistic terms. Some scholars who wish to separate Plato from this view – whether by way of defending Plato or attacking him – think that if psychological egoism is false, there have to be nonegoistic motives. On my view, Plato eludes the dilemma of egoistic or nonegoistic motives. Everyone wills the Good which is, of course, one's own good. But this good can never be achieved at the expense of another's good. So, we might as well say that everyone who acts for their own *real* and not apparent good is acting, albeit unintentionally, for the good of others, too, even if it does not seem to him and to others that he is doing so. The plausibility of the view that one must *either* act from egoistic *or* nonegoistic motives is derived from an assumption regarding the unity of action. All action, it is thought, follows from an all-things-considered (ATC) judgment about how to achieve what appears to one to be good for oneself. Either one acts for one's own good or for the good of another. But the latter is at least implausible, and perhaps impossible.[105] Once we establish, though, that (a) what we will is our real good and (b) that there is no entailment from what appears to us to be our real good and what is in fact so (even when what appears to be our real good is in fact our real good), the commensurability that ATC judgments assume breaks down. It can appear to me that satisfying an appetite is my real good at the same time as it

---

[104] At *Lg.* 4.716C4–5, god is said to be the μέτρον of all things. I interpret this to mean that the Demiurge, which is identical with the Living Animal, is the locus of all paradigms. Here is the perfection according to kind which things here below strive to emulate. At *Phil.* 66A6–7, first place among the ranking of goods is τὸ μέτρον, τὸ μέτριον, τὸ καίριον, and so on. The Good as One is the principle of these. That is, it is not a good but the Good itself.

[105] It should be noted that a claim about the impossibility of altruistic behavior takes us beyond an empirically based description of human psychology into the metaphysical realm of modalities.

appears to me that satisfying it is not. How is this possible? It is possible because one wills something that is not determined by appetite, namely, one's real good. And yet one must look to what appears to be good to oneself in order to act to achieve the real good. One rule of thumb that is used is to consult one's desire or appetite. Some people are content to use this rule of thumb and hope for the best. Others are inclined to submit the putative sign of one's own good to critical reflection either accepting or rejecting its claim. Still others, whom Plato calls "philosophers," are disinclined to put much stock in appetite's "appearance" of the real good at all and to rely instead on thinking alone. There is no contradiction in its appearing to me that satisfying the appetite is my true good at the same time as it appears to me, on reflection, that satisfying the appetite is not my true good. This is because one appearance is nonreflective and one is reflective.[106] The subjects of each appearance are different, though the same, just as the beauty in Helen is different from the beauty in Aphrodite, yet the same.[107]

If it is indeed the case that everyone desires their own good, and it is also true that all action originates in desire of some sort, then it is not possible to act other than on behalf of the achievement of that good. This is so even if the good that is sought is in fact only an apparent good and not the real good. By contrast, Immanuel Kant argued that moral content is attributable to an action *only* if it is done from duty and not from self-interest.[108] According to the account of Plato's view of the motivation for moral behavior I have given, it is in fact not possible to act from duty, that is,

---

[106] See Price 1995, 44–45, who makes a similar suggestion, couched in terms of a "half-belief" and a "full belief."

[107] See *Rep.* 10.602C–605C on the conflicts in illusory appearances. The line at 602E4–6 is difficult. It reads: Τούτῳ δὲ πολλάκις μετρήσαντι καὶ σημαίνοντι μείζω ἄττα εἶναι ἢ ἐλάττω ἕτερα ἑτέρων ἢ ἴσα τἀναντία φαίνεται ἅμα περὶ ταὐτά (Often, however, when this [the calculative part of the soul] has measured and is indicating that one group is greater or lesser or equal to another, opposites to those identical things simultaneously appear to it). The τούτῳ appears to refer to τὸ λογιστικόν in the line above, which would make the division required in the next line in order to avoid attributing contraries to the same thing as per 436B8–C1, a division of the calculative part. So, Burnyeat 1999, 223, n.12. Adam 1921, v.2, 407–408, *ad loc.*, takes the line to be in fact a counterfactual. Thus, it *appears* that the calculative faculty has contrary beliefs at the same time. But, in fact, this is not possible. Therefore, the subject of the false or illusory belief is not at the same time the subject of the true belief. I can be the subject of an appetite and at the same time the subject of a thought that the appetite should not be satisfied because my embodied self is divided episodically, so to speak.

[108] See *Groundwork of the Metaphysics of Morals*, §2. See Bobonich 2002, 81–88, from whom I have drawn a number of points regarding the comparison of Plato and Kant. Cf. Bradley 1876, 63, "It is immoral to ask 'why should I be moral.'" In a note to this famous essay, 73, Bradley ends with a deeply Platonic point, namely, that the reason why the question "why should I be moral?" is immoral is that, ultimately, morality does coincide with self-interest. So, the real question is "what is the self whose interest I am always seeking?"

the real good insofar as it affects others, in spite of acting in one's own interest, even if one thinks that this is what one is doing. Has Plato refuted Kant *avant la lettre*?

Kant famously distinguished desire as a motive or incentive for action from the maxim according to which or under which the desire falls. If one acts solely from the desire – even if the desire is altruistic, say – then one is not acting according to the maxim. And it is only in the latter case that one acts morally. We have already seen that there is, here, a striking parallel with Plato's own analysis of action according to which a desire has to be combined with a universal judgment in order to yield an action. Kant thinks that acting according to a universalizing maxim guarantees the morality of the action, whereas acting according to desire excludes it. But Plato holds that all action originates in desire including what Kant would call a moral action that is done for no other reason than that it is one's duty.

The difference between Plato and Kant in this regard is clear enough. Kant thinks that all goods are ends for specific desires. The content of these ends excludes their universalizability. This universalizability is attainable only on the basis of a maxim according to which one wills that the principle upon which one acts is one upon which all should act. But no desire for a specific good, which is always by definition associated with a specific desire, could attain to this universalizability. Kant's critique of motivational desire assumes that goods are contentful in a way that excludes universalizability in acting to achieve them. Only a good will, bereft of specific content, qualifies. When, however, we consider the Idea of the Good, adding that the desire for the real and not apparent good is the desire for *this*, we can see at once that the Good has the requisite universality. To act for the real Good is not to act to satisfy a self-regarding desire no matter how elevated. Does this mean that Plato contradicts himself when he maintains that all action originates in the desire of the agent? I think not. Plato would no doubt point out to Kant that one who desires to do his duty and only his duty is still acting on the basis of desire. Plato might also point out to Kant that a desire to do one's duty is, however universalizability is parsed, still a desire for a specific good, and in this case, as in the case of all other specific goods, it is intelligible to inquire into whether doing one's duty is good, even good for oneself. Kant, however, to put it mildly, eschews metaphysics in his critique of practical reasoning. He thinks that in practical reasoning, morality requires that one just see the identity of the good and doing one's duty. Presumably, therefore, the question of whether doing one's duty is good is illicit. Plato would insist that the intelligibility of the question and the positive answer to it do not cause the doing of one's duty to devolve into venality. Doing one's duty because it manifests the Good and because one desires the Good does not disqualify the act from being moral. It does not do so precisely because the Good is always desired by everyone. And this is as much a claim about metaphysics as is the claim about the existence of the superordinate Good itself.

In *Crito*, Plato has Socrates express the argument of the laws of Athens to the effect that Socrates, as a citizen, is bound to do his duty to "persuade or obey" the law.[109] Since he has failed to persuade the law that he is innocent, he is bound to obey the verdict of the jury, which embodies the law. He must obey because it is just to do so. And doing justice is good not only because justice manifests the Good but also because the Good makes just deeds to be what they are and to be beneficial to the agent.

The discordance between desire and adherence to a moral maxim for Kant is recognized by Plato as a discordance between apparent and real desire, the former having no necessary ontological connection with the Good. But because apparent desire does have a contingent connection with the Good, when the apparent desire is the desire of the virtuous person and so coincident with a desire for the Good, it is possible to continue to maintain that the action of doing one's duty, as Socrates describes it in *Crito* and elsewhere, does derive from a desire. This desire, however, is only a desire for the Good if one recognizes that one's own good and the Good itself are identical. Kant was right to the extent that he presumed that all nonmoral desires originated otherwise than in a will to do one's duty. He was wrong to suppose that a desire for the Good is nonmoral because it is a desire; on the contrary, will (βούλησις) is a desire of the true, rational self. I take it that Kant separated desire and will because he believed that there is no superordinate Good, at least not as a constituent of our rational means–ends calculation. For Plato, desire and will can come apart owing to embodiment and the partitioning of the soul. If the tyrant does what he desires (or "what seems best to him") and not what he wills, then that is because he is or has a divided self. If the tyrant is reformed and he desires only what he wills, he does not then become immoral; he becomes an integrated self.

For Plato, the good is plainly prior to the right or to duty and for that reason doing one's duty can never be isolated from one's desire for one's own real good.[110] Plato outflanks Kant, so to speak, by insisting on the

---

[109] See *Cr.* 50C–51C.
[110] See *Rep.* 7.517C1, where the Good is explicitly said to be the cause (αἰτία) of everything right (ὀρθῶν). Hence, the priority. See Chappell 2014, 296.

externalist metaphysical claim of the unity and supremacy of goodness, which is added to the assumption that all action is aimed at the real, not apparent good. Insofar as the very conception of "morality" is thought to depend on the separation of the right from one's interest, as we saw in Prichard and many others, Plato's approach undermines the relevance and even the intelligibility of this conception. That is, no doubt, why discussions of Plato's "moral theory" from this perspective always seem to be off-kilter. It is also why, I suppose, when Plato has Socrates talk about his duty (τὸ δέον), he is blithely unaware of the possibility that this might be counter to his own interest. What might impel one to think that duty and self-interest never fall apart is that Plato has Socrates understand his own interest as a philosophically enlightened "human being inside the human being" who habitually "reverts" to the Good, the ultimate cause of his being.

CHAPTER 4

Socratic versus Platonic Ethics?

4.1 Socratic Ethics in Context

As is widely known, many distinguished Plato scholars have argued strenuously that in a rather loosely defined group of dialogues there is a distinct position, dubbed by them "Socratic ethics." This position is distinct from the one found in the rest of the dialogues and labeled "Platonic ethics." According to Gregory Vlastos and many others, the hallmark of the former is that it is an ethics without metaphysics. Socratic ethics in fact requires no metaphysics to be cogent and defensible. Furthermore, the author of these dialogues, Plato, probably concurred in the belief that this ethics needs no metaphysics for its defense.[1] Accordingly, when Plato does introduce metaphysical considerations, what he is doing is essentially extraneous to Socratic ethics. Alternatively, he introduces a new ethical position whose connection with the position of Socrates is open for debate. As should already be evident, I am in agreement with the view that Plato situates his ethical views within a metaphysical framework and that that metaphysical framework pervades every dialogue. However, scholars like Vlastos, Penner, Rowe, Irwin, Brickhouse and Smith, Benson, and many others do not think that the metaphysical framework provided by Plato for Socratic ethics is either necessary or desirable.[2] They think that Socratic

---

[1] See, for example, Santas 1979; Vlastos 1991; Nehemas 1999; Brickhouse and Smith 2000; Benson 2000; Penner 2005, 2011; Rowe 2007; Devereux 2008. Sidgwick 1902 [1886], 36, takes a rather unusual view: "The ethics of Plato cannot properly be treated as a finished result, but rather as a continual movement from the position of Socrates towards the more complete and articulate system of Aristotle; except that there are ascetic and mystical suggestions in some parts of Plato's teaching which find no counterpart in Aristotle, and which, in fact, disappear from Greek philosophy soon after Plato's death until they are revived and fantastically developed in Neo-Pythagoreanism and Neo-Platonism." Kahn 1992 [1981], 47, expresses the contrary view, which he further develops in Kahn 1996: "The dialogues belong to Plato and to the fourth century. So do the doctrines and arguments contained in them. Even where the inspiration of Socrates is clear, the dialogues are all Platonic."

[2] Most recently, see Callard 2017 who assumes that the principle that everyone desires the good, a principle enunciated in *Republic* among other places, is foundational for *Socratic* intellectualism.

4.1 Socratic Ethics in Context

ethics can stand on its own two feet. Indeed, the higher the firewall that can be constructed between Socratic ethics and Platonic metaphysics, the stronger does the former become.

In this chapter, I shall not defend the view that Socratic ethics was presented by Plato in the above package of dialogues, even though he, Plato, had at the time of writing these dialogues a metaphysics addition or two up his sleeve. I agree with Vlastos that Plato probably believed the philosophical claims advanced by Socrates and a few other leading interlocutors in the dialogues. Rather, my contention will be that the so-called early Socratic dialogues depend on Platonic metaphysics. I must here emphasize that my argument does not depend on a strict unitarianism according to which Plato never changed his mind or "developed" his views either in ethical or in metaphysical matters. I think it is fairly evident that Plato did change his mind on some subjects. He did develop increasingly nuanced views about human action, philosophical methodology, the articulation of the intelligible world, and the appropriate vocabulary within which to describe these. At least. But I maintain that he did so within a framework of a metaphysical ethics that did not substantially change. In fact, there is no evidence that Plato's principles changed at all; rather, our best, albeit inconclusive evidence, is that he held these views *before* he wrote any dialogues at all.[3]

My argument in this chapter is twofold. First, after exposing the position that describes a nonmetaphysical Socrates, I will show that the basis for this position is circular. That is, the selection of dialogues that are supposed to be "Socratic" and not "Platonic" depends on an unfounded prejudice regarding what is Socratic and what is Platonic. Second, I will show that there is no dialogue within the corpus wherein the claims of the proponents of Socratic ethics can be sustained. Even the relatively simple and probably early dialogues like *Apology* and *Crito* do not present us with defensible grounds for the positions that they clearly express. In every case, metaphysics – Platonic metaphysics – is needed to come to the rescue. So, we are left to conclude that Plato himself did not know how to give a competent defense of these claims, or that he did, but for reasons having to do with the construction of the dialogues and their purpose, he chose not to do so. Toward the end of this chapter, I shall make some remarks on behalf of the latter alternative. But my argument would still stand if,

---

Smith 2014 argues that the Socrates of the early dialogues *does* have a metaphysics, but it is not a metaphysics that includes separate Forms. A fortiori, it does not rest upon the superordinate Idea of the Good.

[3] See Gerson 2013, 56, n. 49.

against all plausibility, Plato, early in his writing career, had not seen how to defend those claims to which he was intuitively drawn.

4.2 The Nonmetaphysical Socrates

In an earlier book, I examined some prominent versions of the view that Socratic ethics is a philosophical position distinct from Platonic ethics. According to those who hold this view, what distinguishes Socratic ethics from Platonic ethics is that it relies on no metaphysical premises. It is, through and through, an ethical position resting solely on an analysis of the psychology of human action.[4] The three versions I considered were those of Gregory Vlastos, Terry Penner, and Christopher Rowe. Here, I shall only briefly summarize their positions and my reasons for rejecting these. I hope that this will clarify the grounds for maintaining that metaphysics is in all likelihood the foundation for everything that Plato writes about ethics.[5]

To begin, all those who want to distinguish Socratic ethics from Platonic ethics have in mind a collection of dialogues where Socratic ethics is exhibited. These supposedly include: *Hippias Minor, Charmides, Laches, Protagoras, Euthyphro, Apology, Crito, Ion, Gorgias, Meno, Lysis, Euthydemus, Menexenus,* and *Hippias Major*. Sometimes, *Republic,* Book 1 is included, too. A few remarks should be made regarding this list. First, the list excludes *Alcibiades* I which, though stylistically in line with the other dialogues, is excluded from the grouping because the doctrine found there does not cohere with the doctrine supposedly contained in the other dialogues.[6] Second, *Phaedo*, though obviously dramatically continuous with *Apology* and *Crito*, is excluded from this grouping because there is in it rampant metaphysics. Its inclusion would destroy the construct of the nonmetaphysical Socrates. Thus, it is excluded for that reason alone. Third, while *Gorgias* and *Meno* are placed in the grouping, they are widely acknowledged to contain doctrinal "elements" that are not Socratic. For this reason, and only for this reason, they are usually labeled as "transition" dialogues, meaning that Plato has, inexplicably, added extraneous metaphysical features to an otherwise purely Socratic ethical

---

[4] See Gerson 2013, 53–72.
[5] Gould 1955, ch. 1, dismisses out of hand any metaphysical foundation for "Socratic ethics." He says, 21, that "the essence of Socratic ἐπιστήμη ... is the conviction of knowing how to act." On this basis, Gould focuses on human action as a basis for understanding the Socratic paradoxes. He adds, 30, that for Plato as well as for Socrates, ἐπιστήμη is "a manner of behaving."
[6] See Ledger 1989, 79–80, on the early style of this dialogue. Note that Ledger groups *Alcibiades* I with *Hippias Major*, which *is* included in the above grouping. Those who, like N. Smith 2004, argue against the authenticity of this dialogue, do so mainly on the circular grounds that it does not fit into the "Socratic dialogue" pod.

4.2 The Nonmetaphysical Socrates

treatise. Fourth, the list of Socratic dialogues *always* excludes *Theaetetus* and *Philebus* owing to their manifest metaphysical content, even though Socrates, the principal interlocutor, says many "Socratic" things and follows a well-established "Socratic" methodology. I take these remarks to indicate the question-begging nature of the position that is here being examined. Unless and until there is a non-question-begging doctrinal criterion applied to the dialogues such that we can isolate a grouping based on doctrinal similarity, everything said about non-Platonic Socratic ethics should be held suspect.[7]

Gregory Vlastos argued that among the many differences between S_E (Socrates of the early dialogues) and S_M (Socrates of the middle dialogues), the Socratic reliance on "elenctic knowledge" is foundational.[8] Elenctic knowledge is the putatively justified true belief that one aims to arrive at as a result of practicing *elenchus* on Socrates' interlocutors. The epistemological justification, as Vlastos stresses, is purely inductive; there can be no certainty in this knowledge.[9] Nevertheless, this elenctic knowledge is the "final arbiter of moral truth."[10] Presumably, these truths are truths about human nature and human life. They can be epitomized in the so-called Socratic paradoxes.[11] Vlastos agrees that elenctic knowledge is not the ἐπιστήμη that Plato takes to be the goal of philosophy. This ἐπιστήμη is not only of Forms, but of Forms only intelligible in the light of the superordinate Idea of the Good.

Apart from the question-begging grouping of dialogues above, there are two main reasons why I would reject this attempt to found Socratic ethics (understood by Vlastos as the ethics held by Plato at the time of writing the Socratic dialogues). The first is that elenctic knowledge is only justified to the extent that the opinions of Socrates' interlocutors are sufficiently sophisticated to lead us to believe that their negation attains some profound truth. Second, and more important, elenctic knowledge is just a belief, albeit with some justificatory basis, but without any justification grounded in reality. For example, take as a fundamental "Socratic" ethical principle that it is better to suffer than to do evil. That Socrates can refute

---

[7] See Kahn 2002 on what we can and cannot reasonably learn from stylometric analysis of the dialogues. The most pertinent result of Kahn's analysis is that we cannot derive conclusions about doctrinal development from a putative chronology of the writing of the dialogues.
[8] See Vlastos 1991, 111, n. 23; 115, n. 39.   [9] See Vlastos 1991, 114.   [10] Vlastos 1991, 117.
[11] See Vlastos 1991, 117, where Vlastos sets forth his "grand methodological hypothesis," which is that Plato only allows Socrates to say what he, Plato, believes is true at the time of writing a work. So, Vlastos must discount Aristotle's evidence to the effect that Plato believed in a two-world metaphysics "beginning in his youth (ἐκ νέου)." See *Meta.* A 6, 987a29–b9. Smith 2014, 424 and 430, thinks that Aristotle's testimony pertains to the early dialogues and not to the historical Socrates. But there is no evidence for this view; indeed, in all probability, Plato's metaphysically committed "youth" (before the age of thirty) preceded the writing of *any* dialogues.

one who holds the opposite view – that it is better to do than to suffer evil – can hardly be said to be a relevant justification for this claim. One wants to know *why* this paradoxical claim is true, not merely why one who refutes someone who holds that it is false is somehow therefore justified in believing that it is true. The stipulated "nonmetaphysical" Socrates does not have the resources for countering someone who says that even if it is true for the most part that it is better to suffer than to do evil, there are important exceptions. Everyone thinks that he or she is an exception. But for all we know, heroes of tyranny really are exceptions, practically speaking.

Terry Penner wants to distinguish Socratic ethics from Platonic ethics on the basis of what he calls "Socratic intellectualism," which characterizes the former and is rejected in the latter. Penner characterizes Socratic intellectualism as a belief-desire theory "designed to explain voluntary action."[12] According to this theory, desire is for whatever constitutes one's own real good and also for whatever action is really the best means for attaining that end now. Thus, the only way that someone voluntarily deviates from the appropriate action is owing to a change of belief regarding which action will attain the desired end. It follows that the only reason for failing to act in a way that attains one's own good is that one holds a false belief, that is, a false belief about the means to one's own real good. The ethical consequences of this theory are: Virtue is knowledge, specifically the knowledge of good and bad, vice is ignorance, and no one errs willingly. Finally, knowledge is more stable than belief because belief can be overcome by pleasure, whereas knowledge cannot.[13] Penner takes this theory to be pure prudentialism. That is, there is no distinction between the good that maximizes happiness and a moral good, a good that could conceivably conflict with the maximizing of happiness.[14] Since there is no such distinction, Socrates is an ethical egoist.[15] For him, it is inconceivable

---

[12] See Penner 2002, 195–196; Penner and Rowe 2005, 216–230. See Stemmer 1988. In his 2007a, 117–119, however, Penner says that the ethics of Socrates is indistinguishable from the ethics of Plato. See by contrast Sedley 2013, 76ff, who argues that the so-called Socratic intellectualism is very much a part of the moral psychology of *Republic*, despite the tripartitioning of the soul. As we have seen, for its proponents, Plato's ethics is set apart from Socratic intellectualism by its introduction of "irrational" springs of human action. Sometimes, the term "psychological eudaimonism" is used by scholars instead of "Socratic intellectualism."

[13] Penner 2002, 197.

[14] Penner 2002, 198. Penner, 189, adheres to the traditional view that the beliefs expressed by Socrates in the putatively early dialogues are in fact more or less identical with those of the historical Socrates. However, Penner, 203–204, is frankly puzzled by the apparent mixture of contradictory Socratic and Platonic elements in *Gorgias*.

[15] See Mackenzie 1981, 218, who does not differentiate between Socratic and Platonic philosophy: "the core of Plato's moral theory is egoistic." Mackenzie, 238, locates the egoism in the account of justice

4.2 The Nonmetaphysical Socrates

that my good should ever conflict with the "moral" good as, for example, a Kantian would argue. As we saw in the previous chapter, Penner is right about the absence of such conflict, but only on the assumption of a first principle of all that is the Idea of the Good. For Penner, a science of good and bad is the supreme human science, but it is not the science of dialectic as described in *Republic* Book 6. It is the practical science of how to live, and it is for this reason that the unexamined life is not worth living.[16]

Penner, like Vlastos, assumes a question-begging grouping of the dialogues supposedly manifesting Socratic intellectualism, though Penner is admirably forthright in expressing his inability to make *Gorgias* fit into his theory. My principal objection to Socratic intellectualism as articulated by Penner is that it is just as true for the Platonic dialogues as it is for the Socratic dialogues. In other words, because Plato's ethics is intellectualist in some sense, there are no grounds for sharply separating it from Socrates' ethics. And since Plato's ethics explicitly rests upon a metaphysical foundation, so, too, should we suppose that Socrates' ethics – as presented by Plato in the dialogues – rests upon the identical foundation.

Penner believes that one of the most firmly grounded elements of his theory is that Plato abandons intellectualism in favor of what he calls "irrationalism."[17] This irrationalism rests upon Plato's argument that *akrasia* or incontinence is possible. Because it is possible, people can act

---

as psychical health or harmony in Bk. 4 of *Republic*. But this account will be explicitly folded by Plato into the broader metaphysically based account of justice in the rest of *Republic*. Mackenzie's view tends to conflate popular or political virtue with philosophical virtue. Cooper 1999, 140–141, seems to deny that what nonphilosophers possess can be called virtue at all. He identifies virtue with philosophical virtue. See n. 8, "for Plato only accomplished philosophers can be just."

[16] See *Ap.* 38A5–6; *Symp.* 211D1–3.

[17] Penner 2002, 194. Penner, however, 202–203, agrees that the statement at *Rep.* 505E–506A, that all desire the real good, is a statement of intellectualism. It is just that this statement conflicts with the recognition of the existence of the phenomenon of incontinence in Bk. 4. Penner 2007a seems to significantly qualify his sharp distinction between Socratic and Platonic ethical theory. Although he retains the distinction between intellectualism and irrationalism, he argues that Plato, especially in *Republic*, posits the Idea of the Good as the Form of "Advantage" or that which is purely prudential for the individual. He takes this to be Socrates' theory as much as it is Plato's. Penner denies that the paramount importance of individual human advantage, which aims at happiness, amounts to selfishness as opposed to ethical egoism, since an individual's happiness is necessarily connected to the happiness of others. But the latter point is purely speculative or aspirational. Penner is also correct in emphasizing the extensional equivalence of one's own good with the good itself. But for him that means only that the good itself is just (distributively) the good of all individuals. We may well wonder what makes it true that the good itself is identical with the good of all individuals without exception. Indeed, if we set metaphysics aside, it seems commonsensical to suppose that it is at least possible that one's good should be attained at the expense of another's. Mackenzie 1981, 162–163, thinks that the acceptance of the possibility of *akrasia* leads to a qualified or "diminished" form of intellectualism, where knowledge of the good is still essential for virtue. See similarly Kahn 1996, 226–227; Rowe 2007, 133–134.

otherwise than for what they believe is their own interest. So, whereas intellectualism finds the key to happiness in having true beliefs about what produces happiness, irrationalism requires in addition the training of appetites in order to prevent their thwarting the realization of one's true beliefs. As I shall argue in the next section, it is far from clear that we find a rejection of the phenomenon of *akrasia* in *Protagoras*, a dialogue Penner regards as Socratic. Even if this is not so, what I do want to argue in addition is that Penner is wrong in thinking that Socratic intellectualism is negated by what he calls Platonic irrationalism. If this is true, then there is no need to separate metaphysics from intellectualism. Indeed, there is every reason to insist on their inseparability.

It is troubling, to say the least, that Penner's strong contrast between intellectualism and irrationalism relies on an interpretation of *Republic* according to which an affirmation of irrationalism and an affirmation of intellectualism are found within a few pages of each other. The main problem with Penner's position is, I think, that he uses the word "irrationality" in a way that does not in fact correspond to Plato's usage.

Let us look briefly at the famous text, which is uncritically taken, I think, to indicate Plato's commitment to irrationalism.

> So, a particular type of thirst is for a particular type of drink. Thirst itself, however, is not for much drink or little, nor for good or bad drink, nor, in a word, for a particular type of drink; rather, it is, by nature, only for drink.[18]

The text goes on to distinguish the appetite for drink from the calculation that the drink is good *or bad*.[19] And indeed the calculative element in the soul is explicitly distinguished from the appetitive element, which is also called ἀλόγιστον.[20] Clearly, the issue here turns on the meaning of ἀλόγιστον. The word is not especially rare in Plato in either its adjectival or adverbial forms. It usually means something like "unreasonable," that

---

[18] *Rep.* 4.439A4–7: Οὐκοῦν ποιοῦ μέν τινος πώματος ποιόν τι καὶ δίψος, δίψος δ᾽ οὖν αὐτὸ οὔτε πολλοῦ οὔτε ὀλίγου, οὔτε ἀγαθοῦ οὔτε κακοῦ, οὐδ᾽ ἑνὶ λόγῳ ποιοῦ τινος, ἀλλ᾽ αὐτοῦ πώματος μόνον αὐτὸ δίψος πέφυκεν;. Cf. 4.437D8–E6. Sometimes, *Tim.* 77B1–6 is taken to indicate Plato's decisive rejection of rationality to the appetitive part of the soul. But this passage pertains to the souls of plants, not rational animals.

[19] The words "bad drink" are typically ignored in the analysis of this argument. I take it that they are added to "good drink" because Plato wants to indicate the evaluative sense of these predicates, that which is absent from the appetites. But this does not change the fact that all desire or appetite is for a good understood as that which will satisfy the appetite. See Weiss 2007, 89–90.

[20] *Rep.* 4.439D7. Many English translators (e.g., Shorey, Cornford, Bloom, Sterling and Scott, Grube, Reeve) succumb to the temptation to translate ἀλόγιστον as "irrational." Rowe has "unreasoning," which is a bit better. An exception is Allen who, more accurately in my view, translates it as "unreflective." Rational animals may certainly act unreflectively without thereby abandoning their rational nature.

is, counter to commonly accepted norms of rationality.[21] But far from suggesting an *absence* of rationality, this unreasonableness, or acting counter to the way one ought to act, presumes it.[22] n *Republic* Book 10, the term is used for the element of the soul in conflict with the element that calculates; the former "leads us to recollections of our sufferings and to lamentations, is incapable of having enough of them, is lazy, and is a friend of cowardice."[23] An appetite for drink or an appetite for wallowing in one's past sufferings is, I submit, not at all irrational except in what we might term the evaluative or normative sense.[24] That is, it requires someone with a rational soul to conceptualize the object of one's appetite and, surely, to conceptualize one's past experience as suffering, especially unjustified sufferings. The object is conceptualized within the framework of ends-seeking behavior. Another name for such ends is "goods."[25] Thus, what Plato is claiming is that it is *unreasonable* to pursue such goods, not

---

[21] See, for example, *Ap.* 37C7; *Phd.* 62E2; *Gorg.* 522E2; *Phil.* 63E8; *Lg.* 9.875B7–8, etc.

[22] So, too, τὸ θυμοειδές at 4.442C10–D1, which *agrees* with τὸ λογιστικόν on the latter's right to rule. In no sense can the nonrational or irrational agree (or disagree) with the rational. Scholars usually take the "agreement" to be metaphorical, but there are no textual grounds for this. For what, after all, would it be a metaphor?

[23] *Rep.* 10.604D9.

[24] See Aristotle, *DA* Γ 10, 433a28–29. See *Charm.* 167E1–5; *La.* 191C8–E1 where ἐπιθυμίαι are taken to be for pleasure without any suggestion that these are irrational desires. And yet they differ from βούλησις. The proponent of Socratic intellectualism is burdened with showing that texts like these in the so-called early dialogues do not allow the possibility of noncognitive behavior, but somehow the texts in *Republic* do. In the *Laches* passage, exactly the sort of conflict envisioned in *Republic* is assumed to be possible. For example, a courageous person is one who fights against the desire to run away. Presumably, such a person might succumb to the desire. Or, if we resist the idea that a courageous person would ever succumb, surely there are persons who aspire to be courageous, thinking that is how they should behave, and yet do succumb to the desire to flee. Such a person, like Leontius in *Republic*, can easily be imagined to feel disgust in himself as he runs from the battlefield. In other words, *akrasia* and continence are seen as possibilities in *Laches*, even though tripartitioning of the soul is not explicitly introduced.

[25] As Penner 2002, 203, notes, it is sometimes claimed, for example by Irwin 1995, 223–243, that Plato's explanation for the phenomenon of incontinence involves the introduction of "good-independent desires." That is, while the calculative faculty tries to determine what is good for the person, the appetitive faculty acts on desires that are independent of that determination. Annas 1981, 139, calls these desires "blind cravings"; Cooper 1999 [1984], 122, calls them "reason-independent." See also Devereux 1992, 778–783; 1995, 396–401. I think this is a mistake, easily made by overlooking a distinction between the appetite as a state (πάθος) and the awareness of the appetites, which is cognitive and which is, since it is the awareness of a rational animal, always oriented to what is good or, at least, to what appears to be good. So Kahn 1987, 85, although Kahn supposes that the faculties of appetite and spirit have their own "minimal" rationality; Frede 1996, 6–7; Moss 2008, 61–62; Moore 2015, 198–203; Ferber 2020 [2013], 19–21. See *Phil.* 35B3–4; cf. 41C4–7. An appetite qua state is indeed only for its object without consideration of whether the object is good or not. See *Rep.* 4.437D9–438A2. But the desire to satisfy the appetite is a desire for a good, namely, the satisfaction of the appetite whose object has to be conceptualized *before* it can be sought. This is just the point that Thomas Aquinas makes in *Summa theologiae* I–II q.1, a.6, *respondeo: quidquid homo appetit, appetit sub ratione boni.*

irrational.²⁶ Stated otherwise, it is unreasonable to pursue goods the acquisition of which betray our will to the manifestation of the Good. But it is only rational animals who can act unreasonably.

The distinction between nonnormative and normative rationality is parallel to the distinction between apparent and real goods, and thus apparent and real desires. A desire or appetite, for Plato, is a state of the embodied soul. "The desire for x" is elliptical for "S has or self-reflexively recognizes in herself a desire for x." A desire is the focus of a structure which must include an intentional object and a subject. There are no desires for food or drink or sex or money without subjects of those desires. These are the desires of embodied rational souls.²⁷ The intentional objects are conceived of by rational souls. Without such a conception, one could not undertake steps to satisfy the particular desire that one has. The desire for money is presented in *Republic* as a leading form of appetitive desire.²⁸ A moment's reflection should convince one that a desire – even an overwhelming desire – for money is not nonrational or irrational, except normatively. So, the subject of appetites is rational. And the intentional object of desire is an apparent good that one takes to be the real good.²⁹

---

²⁶ See Cooper 1984 [1999], who rightly stresses that the language of "parts" of the soul rather than "forms (εἴδη)" is highly misleading. If one "part" of the soul is the seat of rationality, then it is easy to suppose that the other parts are bereft of rationality. In fact, the three "forms" of soul are sources of motivation within a divided embodied self. All human motivation is the motivation of a rational animal, even those motives that are inextricably bound up with embodiment. See Watson 2004 [1975], 16–18, who endorses the Platonic notion of reason as an independent source of motivation, although Watson adheres to the idea of "good-independent" desires.

²⁷ See *Rep.* 4.436A8–B4, where the question is raised: whether "we" (plural subject) learn, feel angry, crave sex, and so on, with each part of the soul or with the whole soul. The question is left unanswered, but in either case, there must be a subject for the desire. See *Rep.* 10.611B1: the soul in its "truest nature (τῇ ἀληθεστάτῃ φύσει)" is revealed when disembodied. When embodied, the rational soul is "dispersed" or divided according to the three faculties of calculation, spirit, and appetite. This dispersal does not negate the rationality of the soul, as it were; it only dilutes or compromises it. See Monteils-Laeng 2014, 75–103, for some penetrating remarks along these lines, although she incautiously calls appetitive desires "irrationnelles."

²⁸ See *Rep.* 9.580E2–581A1 where the appetitive faculty is actually named "money-loving (φιλοχρήματον)." Money is an object of appetite (ἐπιθυμία) because it can be used to satisfy other appetites like food, drink, and sex. It is only in a normative sense (i.e., in relation to the real good) that an appetite for money can be thought or as "good-independent." After all, an exhortation by one person to another to the effect that he ought not to do something must be an exhortation to a rational animal. Such an exhortation is radically different from what would be an absurd exhortation to someone's autonomous nervous system or digestive system or to a nonrational animal.

²⁹ See *Rep.* 6.505E1–2: "Ὃ δὴ διώκει μὲν ἅπασα ψυχὴ καὶ τούτου ἕνεκα πάντα πράττει (That which every soul pursues [namely, the Good] and on account of this it does everything it does). Cf. *Gorg.* 468B1–4. Pursuing the Good as a practical goal means, of course, pursuing manifestations or instances of it, including all those things which appear to be good to the subject of appetites. Irwin 1977, 336, n. 45, takes this passage to conflict with the affirmation of "good-independent desires" from Bk. 4. There is no conflict according to the interpretation I am offering. Kamtekar

4.2 The Nonmetaphysical Socrates

That is, it is that which is *thought* to satisfy the desire or appears to the subject to do so. And yet, the argument for the tripartitioning of the soul reveals to us that one is capable of making second-order judgments about such desires. These judgments may also include explicit or implicit judgments about their subjects and objects. But these judgments are always normative judgments.[30] It is according to these judgments that one thinks that some desires ought or ought not to be satisfied.

Suppose someone acquires a novel appetite owing to a new and intense sensory experience, say, an appetite for a certain type of food.[31] This new appetite is now embedded into a complex framework of appetites and their relative prioritization. It requires memory and a conceptual context in order to recognize and strategize on behalf of the satisfaction of this appetite. The appetite, like all others, is also now susceptible to the normative judgment of reason. But this normativity does not suck up all the air of rationality from the subject of the appetite. Nor does the normative reflection of the rational subject suck up all the subjectivity of the agent of the appetite. Reflection on whether or not the appetite should be satisfied is not reflection on whether any appetite should be satisfied or the appetite of anyone else, but rather on the satisfaction of the appetite of

---

2006, 154, n. 52, thinks that "non-rational motivations" include "conceptions of the good." I doubt that "non-rational" and "conceptions" are terms intended by Plato to be coherently linked. Lorenz 2006, 41–52, discusses the pros and cons of making the appetitive part of the soul rational or nonrational. Lorenz, 47–48, though rejecting what he takes to be extreme positions, concludes that while the appetitive part of the soul "lacks the cognitive resources required to form desires for money" it can still "develop tendencies to form intense desires for things like money." This conclusion seems to me to be unpersuasive and leaves unexplained what money could possibly mean to a subject bereft of "cognitive resources." Exactly what "*non*-cognitive resources" are we to suppose are drawn upon by one who lusts after wealth?

[30] See Frankfurt 1971, 13, n. 6, who makes the influential distinction between first- and second-order volitions, noting that the latter are not necessarily moral. Frankfurt says a person may be capricious and irresponsible in forming these volitions. They are only evaluative in the sense that they express preferences. Plato's calculative faculty (= the source of Frankfurt's second-order volitions) are evaluative or normative for one decisive reason: Everyone desires the Good. The reflective judgment on appetites is, for Plato, always based on this desire. Hence, the normativity. It is possible, nevertheless, that the evaluation should be faulty and that in fact calculative reasoning has not led to a correct conclusion about how the Good is to be instantiated in one's own case. This does not compromise its normativity, but only the accuracy of the calculation.

[31] See *Symp.* 207E1–5 on the transitory nature of appetites and emotion and, implicitly, of the subject of these: καὶ μὴ ὅτι κατὰ τὸ σῶμα, ἀλλὰ καὶ κατὰ τὴν ψυχὴν οἱ τρόποι, τὰ ἤθη, δόξαι, ἐπιθυμίαι, ἡδοναί, λῦπαι, φόβοι, τούτων ἕκαστα οὐδέποτε τὰ αὐτὰ πάρεστιν ἑκάστῳ, ἀλλὰ τὰ μὲν γίγνεται, τὰ δὲ ἀπόλλυται (and these characteristics, habits, beliefs, appetites, pleasures, pains, fears are not only in the body, but also in the soul; each of these is never identical in each person, but some arise, and others are destroyed). As the passage goes on to explain, this is even true for tokens of knowledge. So, the embodied self is essentially transitory and caught up in time. Nevertheless, at *Phd.* 75E6–11, it is emphasized that knowledge (ἐπιστήμη), once acquired, remains with one throughout life, even if one forgets it. The recovery of knowledge is perforce the recovery of the self who knows.

the same person who is doing the reflecting. "I really shouldn't be obsessed with my desire for sushi" is not an exhortation to anything or to anyone that can intelligibly be termed "irrational." It is an admonition by a subject to the identical subject – a rational, albeit divided, subject. In reply to the objection that the distinction between two subjects precludes their identity, we can note the following. "Identity" in the formal sense in which it *would be* incoherent to speak of two identical subjects applies only to the Good. Everything else has a qualified or compromised identity since everything else is composite. The embodied soul is not only composite; it is also divided. It is divided among subjects of appetitive, affective, and cognitive states. The burden of embodiment is that of having a divided self. The ephemeral or episodic "selves" that respond to embodied desires are in a way avatars of the true rational self, oriented permanently to the Good, and for that reason the source of normativity in practical reasoning.[32]

Since the subject of an appetite is, by definition, as ephemeral as is the appetite, there certainly is a question about its identity and reidentification. Plato does not directly address this question but I am inclined to the view that such subjects are to be identified as a "product," so to speak, of embodiment and the objects of appetite. Thus, the one who desires food is a "food-desiring embodied subject." Like the lovers of sights and sounds in *Republic* Book 4 and the sights and sounds themselves, appetitive subjects are superficial temporary subjects inextricably mired in confusion. Whereas the objects of appetitive desire "are and are not at the same time" because they are constructed out of or infected by unintelligible material, so the subjects of appetitive desire conceive of goods that cannot be unqualifiedly good according to the canon of rationality that they themselves employ. That is, they desire objects as good for these subjects by means of the use of nonnormative rationality. But these are also susceptible to being overturned by normative rationality. The appetitive subject desires something and therefore takes it, precipitously, as good. But just as someone can ask whether something claimed to be a good is actually good for oneself, so the nonnormative good can be overturned by a determination – by the calculating subject – that that putative good is not in fact good for oneself; it is only apparently good for oneself insofar as one identified oneself with the subject of the appetite.[33]

---

[32] See Price 1989, 21–25, who focuses on Diotima's speech at *Symp.* 207D–208B to show the episodic nature of embodied subjectivity. Also, Ademollo 2018, 40–49, following Price and elaborating the analysis of 207E1–208A7, where embodied psychical identity is explicitly at issue.

[33] To say that an appetite is for an apparent good is to deny that the appetite is "neutral" or "good-independent." See Irwin 1995, 206–207; Kahn 1996, 244–245 for this position. My position depends on rejecting the interpretation of ἀλόγιστον as indicating a complete absence of reason.

4.2 The Nonmetaphysical Socrates

It seems that second-order desires are essentially normative and first-order desires are essentially nonnormative and that this is the primary way in which they are distinguished. However, there is a passage in Book 9 of *Republic* which threatens to wreck this clear distinction. In that passage, Socrates distinguishes three kinds of appetites (ἐπιθυμίαι), one for each part of the soul.[34] If the appetites of the calculative faculty belong to a subject who is employing nonnormative rationality and if the calculative faculty is also the locus of normative rationality, then this faculty would seem to be divisible in itself. But we need not accept this drastic conclusion. The distinction between nonnormative and normative rationality cuts across the distinction between the three parts or forms of soul. Both the calculative and appetitive parts or "forms" of the soul can be the source or starting-point for an action, each based on a different type of desire. Each of these requires rationality. But it is in the calculative part of the soul alone that the operation of normative rationality is to be found. It is, I take it, unproblematic that one can make a second-order judgment about a first-order desire to, say, engage in philosophical work, even a second-order judgment that it is not appropriate to do so here and now. This first-order desire is always embodied. The second-order normative judgment operates independently of the exigencies of embodiment even though it is the judgment of an embodied human being. It would seem necessary for Plato to maintain that the real or ideal self, the self that survives the destruction of the body, is the locus of normative thinking since in its ideal state it is contemplating the Forms and the source of their being, the Idea of the Good. Practical normative judgments for the embodied person are just an image of the theoretical normativity of disembodied contemplation.

Let us consider the case of Leontius. He believes that he ought not to gaze on the naked corpses and he desires not do so, but he also desires to do it. When he "gives in" to this desire, he is disgusted with himself. According to Penner and other proponents of Socratic intellectualism, there is no real conflict within Leontius. His all-things-considered (ATC) judgment is that he ought to gaze; if that judgment had been that he ought not to gaze, then he wouldn't have done it. This is because his ATC judgment is a judgment about his own good, which he wrongly (according to Penner) thinks is found in his gazing. Penner thinks that the phenomenon of *akrasia* is not real because it spoils the intellectualist argument. If, however, the phenomenon is real – whatever the consequences for *Socratic*

---

[34] See *Rep.* 9.580D6–7.

intellectualism – then it is Leontius' second-order judgment that gazing on the corpses ought not to be done even at the very moment that he has an appetite to do so. According to the above distinction, he employed non-normative reasoning in conceptualizing the object of his desire and he employed normative reasoning in making the judgment that he ought not to satisfy this desire.[35] This normative reasoning would take a form something like this: Whatever is ignoble is bad (not good) for me; gazing on the corpses is ignoble; therefore, it is bad for me.

Psychologically speaking, this is a plausible account of Leontius even if he is mistaken in believing that corpse-gazing is bad for him. That is, *akrasia* itself, though normally referred to in cases where some acts are contrary to correct normative reasoning, could just as well occur in cases in which someone acts against normative reasoning that is mistaken or perverse. Acting contrary to what you think is good does not entail that what you think is good is in fact so. So, without even knowing what norms the incontinent person is acting against, we can fault him for, well, incontinence, or even *mauvaise foi*. But the moral judgment made explicitly in regard to an incontinent individual and implicitly against him in praise of the virtuous individual is a judgment based on the fact that what the incontinent person thinks is normatively bad for him really is so. We certainly should not suppose that the only thing wrong with the neurotic is that he is not true to his warped principles. So, the normative reasoning of concern to Plato's ethics is that which arrives at judgments about that which is unqualifiedly good and bad.

How is the unqualifiedly good or bad related to the desire for what is good for oneself here and now, the only desire that Penner thinks is the basis for normativity? The superordinate Idea of the Good in *Republic* is the basis for saying that these are identical. It is not possible to achieve one's good without instantiating the Idea of the Good, which is identical for everyone. So, it cannot be the case that whatever I do that is truly good for me is not good for you. But I want to argue here that this patently metaphysical foundation for ethics in *Republic* is not a "middle period" innovation and that therefore the attempt to construct a nonmetaphysical Socratic ethics fails.

---

[35] See Ferber 2020 [2013], 96–98, who recognizes the cognitive aspect of Leontius' acting on his appetite, but for this reason denies that Leontius is acratic. That is, he denies synchronic *akrasia*, maintaining that Leontius is only diachronically acratic. The former requires that one act to achieve some end at the same time one believes that achieving that end is not good for oneself. So-called diachronic *akrasia* or weakness at the time of acting such that one's belief that one should not act is "inoperative," is not, in my view, even properly called *akrasia*.

Consider the tyrant of *Gorgias* who, Socrates shows, does what seems best to him but not what he wills.[36] For he – like everyone else – wills what is good for himself, but what seems best to him is actually not good for himself. Penner provides a powerful argument in support of the claim that tyrants do not do what they will.[37] By why is Socrates so sure that the life of the tyrant is *not* what the tyrant wills? On prudentialist grounds, one could of course argue that most people would be ill-advised to pursue a life of tyranny. Let us suppose this is owing to their pusillanimity. But we can easily construct a hypothetical tyrant who suffers from no such impediments to a thrilling, albeit dangerous life of infamy. He can even fully acknowledge the risks of his chosen way of life, while insisting that the rewards of tyranny are worth the risks. Why is Socrates so sure that the tyrant could not be doing what he wills when he chooses to be a tyrant? It seems to me that the most plausible explanation for his confidence is that Plato believes that what is good for the tyrant and what is good *simpliciter* are identical and that it is not possible for the tyrant (or for anyone else) to flourish at the expense of others.[38] Admittedly, prudentialism by its very nature is open to a probabilistic argument in defense of Socrates. After all, that is more or less what prudentialism is. A repudiation of tyranny of any sort is the best policy to follow for everyone, for the most part. Of course, there *may* be exceptions, but these are not predictable. Better safe than sorry. My principal reason for finding this interpretation exceedingly implausible is that the example of the tyrant is obviously intended as the extreme test case. That is, if even tyrants with unlimited power over other people do not do what they will but only what seems to them to be best, then surely this is so for everyone else. But the tyrant is exactly the sort of case that is disputable. And if the tyrant could be held out as an exception, I suppose that Plato thought that anyone else would not be hard put to discover their own exceptional qualities, those that make it at least possible that when they do what seems best to them, they in fact do what they will.

Consider Socrates' absolutist prohibition of wrongdoing in *Crito*.[39] Surely, this is more than rhetoric since Socrates is willing to give up his life rather than do wrong. It may well be the case that Socrates is the sort of person who could never live with himself if he escaped from prison. It is grossly anachronistic, though, to suppose that Plato has Socrates insist on

---

[36] See *Gorg.* 466B1–468E5. Cf. *Rep.* 9.577E1–2.   [37] See Penner 1991.
[38] See *Gorg.* 468B2, where Socrates moves from βέλτιον εἶναι (to be better) to 468B6, ἄμεινον εἶναι ἡμῖν (to be better for us), treating these as identical.
[39] See *Cr.* 49B8: Οὐδαμῶς ἄρα δεῖ ἀδικεῖν. (Therefore, one ought never to do injustice.); cf. 40A6–7, 48C6–D5; *Ap.* 28D6–10, 29B6–7; *Gorg.* 469B12, 508E. See Gerson 1997.

the absolute prohibition of wrongdoing as an expression of his own peculiar personality. Perhaps Socrates is morbidly scrupulous. If prudentialism eschews absolutes, it is at least possible on prudentialist grounds that escaping from prison would be in one's own best interests. That mere possibility seems to make a mockery of Socrates' absolutism. I claim that without metaphysics, there is no way to eliminate the sting of such mockery. On general hermeneutical grounds, I think Plato must have thought this, too. This is so even if *Crito* is, as proponents of Socratic ethics hold, an early dialogue and even if Plato was disinclined to articulate in detail the metaphysical framework which supports the prohibition.

Vlastos thought that the absolutism could be defended by the "sovereignty of virtue."[40] By this Vlastos meant that virtue is the supreme good "in our domain of value [and] its claim upon us is always final."[41] One is tempted to reply here that the sovereign claim of virtue is final for those for whom it is final. The use of "final" here is rhetorical, not substantive. It is not like the use of "final" in "he took his final breath at midnight" or "this is the final installment of payment." It is always possible for someone to question whether "our" domain of value ought to be embraced by oneself or whether it is good for oneself that one practices virtue, which is, we may grant, the supreme good in some sense. The problem with Vlastos' antimetaphysical account of Socrates' exhortation to virtue and his absolutist prohibition of wrongdoing is the same problem as with Penner's. The sovereignty of virtue can only be read prudentially, so to speak, without the sort of metaphysical foundation provided by the superordinate Idea of the Good. A genus of Good, that is, a Form with a generic nature cannot serve, for the essentially Moorean reason that one can always ask whether the substantive content of that generic Form is good for oneself. Moore thinks "good" refers to a nonnatural property, but Moore, too, eschews metaphysics. Only if "good" refers to the unhypothetical source of all properties will it serve the purpose behind all of Socrates' arguments and exhortations.

Absolutism sits uncomfortably with prudentialism, although the renunciation of the former makes entirely plausible the embrace of the latter. Thus Democritus and Epicurus. We, of course, know little or nothing of the reasons the historical Socrates had for holding whatever views he did hold. Plato's Socrates, however, was an absolutist. Plato gives us – explicitly in *Republic* and implicitly elsewhere – the metaphysical grounds for this absolutism. The "construction" of a prudentialist Socrates is pure speculation in regard to the historical figure and an easily refuted fiction in regard

[40] 1991, 210–212.   [41] Vlastos 1991, 211.

to the literary character, so long as we do not arbitrarily segregate a selection of dialogues which, with careful parsing, can be made to appear to be the expression of a prudentialist.

4.3 *Protagoras*, Intellectualism, and Normativity

One way to try to separate Socratic ethics from Platonic ethics, and hence, "Socratic intellectualism" from "Platonic irrationalism," is to identify the explanation for *akrasia* and the tripartite soul with the latter and the denial of the possibility of *akrasia* with the former.[42] Perhaps if *akrasia* is impossible, intellectualism, understood as the necessity and sufficiency of knowledge for virtue, would preclude the need to appeal to metaphysics, broadly speaking. I shall not here aim for anything like a comprehensive treatment of the difficult and complicated argument in *Protagoras* purporting to show the impossibility of *akrasia*.[43] Here I shall argue that the lengthy argument at *Protagoras* 352D–358D is intended to show the impossibility of *akrasia*, but only on the assumption of a specific version of hedonism.[44] Thus, the argument is: If hedonism is true, then *akrasia* is impossible; but if *akrasia* is possible, then hedonism is false.[45] In other words, the argument is

---

[42] See Aristotle on the historical Socrates as denying *akrasia*. For explicit references to Socrates as having denied the possibility of *akrasia*, see *EN* H 2–3; *MM* A 9, 1187a5–12, B 6, 1200b25–30; *EE* H 13, 1246b33–35. For explicit references to Socrates as having identified virtue with knowledge, see *EN* Γ 8, 1116b5, Z 13, 1144b18–20; *MM* A 1, 1182a15–17, 1183b9, 20, 1190b28, 34, 1198a10–13; *EE* A 5, 1216b3–10, Γ 1, 1229a15, 1230a8. See Frede 1992, xxx, who argues for the supposed fundamental difference between "Socratic intellectualism" and "Platonic irrationalism," which is introduced in *Republic*; Reeve 1988, 134–135; Rowe 2007, 133–134; Pasnau 2021, who shows that this dialogue does not yield an argument against *akrasia*. Pasnau thus distinguishes sharply the historical Socrates from Plato's Socrates in this dialogue.

[43] See Evans 2010, with numerous references to the literature, for an excellent survey of the strengths and weaknesses of the argument. I do not agree with Evans on several crucial points, which I shall indicate as we go along. See Callard 2014 for a similar argument against the view that Socrates is rejecting the possibility of *akrasia tout court*. According to Callard, 40, Socrates is not denying the possibility of *akrasia tout court*, but rather arguing against the account of *akrasia* that self-proclaimed hedonists give regarding their own actions. Also Callard 2016, 57–61.

[44] See Russell 2005, 239–248, for a survey of the literature regarding the putative hedonism of Socrates in *Protagoras*. I am arguing that it is the assumption of hedonism that makes an explanation for *akrasia* impossible. One major division among scholars is whether or not Socrates shares this assumption. See Guthrie 1975, 232, whose view that Socrates is arguing from the assumptions of his opponents is the one I share. Šegvić 2000, 23ff, argues that Socrates does indeed accept the impossibility of *akrasia*; Wolfsdorf 2006; Morris 2006.

[45] I shall assume throughout that the discussion pertains to synchronic *akrasia*, not diachronic *akrasia*. The latter is not Plato's worry, either in *Protagoras* or in *Republic*. See Santas 1966, 5, who shows that Socrates' argument is directed against the explanation of *akrasia* given by the many, not against the possibility of *akrasia*. See also Zeyl 1989. Haraldsen 2017, 113–114, agrees with the *reductio ad absurdum* nature of the argument, but he thinks that it is directed primarily against Protagoras himself and not just all hedonists in general or "the many."

not intended to show that *akrasia* is impossible. If that is so, then the explanation for the possibility of *akrasia* in *Republic* does not constitute a rejection of the position of the literary Socrates, even if it does so for the historical Socrates.[46] Consequently, we should reject attempts to separate Socratic intellectualism from Platonic irrationalism by attaching the denial of *akrasia* to the former and its acceptance to the latter. And as we shall see, the reason why a consistent hedonism leads to a denial of the possibility of *akrasia* is rooted in the metaphysics of the Good.

The argument that concludes with a denial of the possibility of *akrasia* claims that no one, whether knowingly or with mere belief, can act against what they regard as their own good.[47] The argument assumes what the "many" believe, namely, that the good is pleasure and the bad pain, and that acting against what they regard as their own good is nothing but acting to acquire less pleasure or more pain than they would have had otherwise.[48] More precisely, the hedonist is represented as maintaining that the good is nothing but pleasure, and the opposite of good, evil, is nothing but pain.[49] So, what the hedonist is forbidden from

---

[46] See Kahn 1996, 243–247. Kahn, 246, says that Plato (a) remains loyal to the paradox that no one does wrong willingly in *Republic* and that he does so (b) "after his explicit recognition of non-rational, value-neutral desires." Kahn is right about the former but not, as I argued in the last section, about the latter.

[47] See *Protag.* 358B6–C1, C6–D2. The argument is explicitly cast as a hypothetical: εἰ ἄρα τὸ ἡδὺ ἀγαθόν ἐστιν ... (if, therefore, that which is pleasant is good ...). The words at 355A1–2 εἴ πῇ ἔχετε ἄλλο τι φάναι εἶναι τὸ ἀγαθὸν ἢ τὴν ἡδονήν (if you are able to say that the good is in some way other than pleasure) confirm that we should not read this as a claim that pleasure is *a* good among others; rather, the claim is that pleasure and good are identical. Cf. *Rep.* 6.505B5–6, C6, referring to those who define the good as pleasure (οἱ τὴν ἡδονὴν ἀγαθὸν ὁριζόμενοι). Blackson 2015, 35, thinks that the denial of *akrasia* that the hedonist is led to maintain is based upon the primacy of beliefs for action. But he denies that Socrates assumes that there is a "standing desire for the real good." This interpretation seems to me to rest upon a false dichotomy between belief and desire. The desires initiating action are rational desires, that is, desires of rational animals. These rational desires are always for what appears to be one's own real good. That is, they are infused with beliefs. See Kahn 1987, especially 81–91.

[48] 354B5–7; cf. 355A1–6. Presumably, people do this because of "the power of appearances (ἡ τοῦ φαινομένου δύναμις)," 356A5–7. It must here be stressed that miscalculation based on appearances is not what *akrasia* is taken to be. This is important because correct calculation does not necessarily eliminate *akrasia*. Is the view of the many psychological hedonism or ethical hedonism? Both alternatives have been maintained. For psychological hedonism see Ferber 2020 [2013], 14–17; for ethical hedonism Taylor 1976, 182–186. But this modern distinction seems somewhat anachronistic to me and not helpful in understanding Socrates' intricate argument. Modern discussions of this distinction introduce a moral or ethical "ought," according to which the ethical hedonist holds that one ought to pursue pleasure and avoid pain. This "ought" is not in the text and generally presupposes a distinction between duty and self-interest, which we have already seen is un-Platonic.

[49] 354E8–355A2. Taylor 1976, 180–181, thinks that there is a fallacy in the substitution of "pleasant" for "good." But it is precisely the identification of the two that the many assume and that Socrates aims to show is incompatible with *akrasia*.

4.3 Protagoras, *Intellectualism, and Normativity*

doing is agreeing that "good" can name a normative criterion for action apart from "pleasant."⁵⁰

On this basis, the idea of being overcome by pleasure and for that reason failing to do what is best when one recognizes what that is absurd.⁵¹ The hedonist's position is incoherent insofar as he acknowledges that "doing what is best" could be something other than doing what is most pleasurable overall. If he refuses to acknowledge this, then the problem with his position is that "being overcome by pleasure" itself makes no sense. One could be "overcome" by pleasure, but only if "doing what is best" is thereby accomplished.

Socrates is here neither affirming nor denying the possibility of *akrasia simpliciter*. He is showing its impossibility under the assumption that pleasure is the good. I suspect that this is the reason why many scholars, including myself, have assumed that hedonism is not particularly germane to the argument. In fact it is not, but it is perhaps the most plausible ethical view that strictly identifies the Good with a single good, in this case, pleasure. Socrates himself does not avow hedonism here either.⁵² He aims only to show that if hedonism is true, then the most important thing in life would be the craft of measurement (ἡ μετρικὴ τέχνη), the craft which can compare prospects for pleasure and grade them according to size or intensity. Whether or not pleasures can actually be so graded is another question. But if hedonism were true, knowledge of the craft of measurement would be paramount in the best possible life. Ignorance of this craft would be disastrous.⁵³ Given that everyone wills only their own good, having the knowledge of how to measure pleasures would indeed be

---

⁵⁰ See Callard 2014, 48; Kamtekar 2017a, ch. 2; Vasiliou 2021, 236.
⁵¹ 352E5–353A2. The position of the many has three parts: (a) being overcome by pleasure; (b) failing to do what is best; (c) recognizing what is best. This is a canonical way of describing *akrasia*, even though that term is not used here or anywhere in the dialogue. Presumably, we are meant to assume that in (b), what is best, is different from (a) what is pleasurable. One might be overcome by pleasure, thinking that that is best. But this would be vice of some sort, not *akrasia*. In addition, "failing to do what is best," is, presumably, an admission that what would be best could be something other than what is pleasurable overall. See Pasnau 2021, 9–11.
⁵² See Gosling and Taylor 1982, 58–68, who hold that Socrates is in fact represented as a hedonist in *Protagoras*. In reply to the obvious objection that this is certainly not the case in *Gorgias*, Gosling and Taylor suppose that *Gorgias* is a later dialogue in which a radically new antihedonistic view is attributed to Socrates. As I have already argued, there is *no* evidence that in any dialogue Plato is presenting views other than his own. Irwin 2007, 35–36, thinks that *Protagoras*, in its supposed espousal of hedonism, was a (Socratic) precursor to Mill's own utilitarianism.
⁵³ As Socrates says at 357B5–6, we will conduct the inquiry into the nature of the craft of measurement at a later time. In fact, the falsity of hedonism does not undercut at all the urgency of acquiring this craft. See Freeland 2017, 126–134; Haraldsen 2017, 110; Pasnau 2021, 14–15.

sufficient for doing what is most pleasurable (or least painful) and so for doing what is good for oneself.

If, however, pleasure is not the good, and if therefore a criterion of good can be applied independently of whether or not something is pleasurable, then the possibility of *akrasia* remains open, where someone acts contrary to what they know or believe is good.[54] It is by no means obvious how this can be done. *Republic* shows the extreme difficulty of the problem. The foundation of so-called Socratic intellectualism is based on the assumption that everyone desires their own good.[55] The attribution of the term "intellectualism" means that the problem of how to attain one's own good is an intellectual problem, that is, a problem about figuring out exactly what this good is. For once one figures this out, then, given the fact that one's own good is what everyone always aims for, one cannot but "go for" that good. The claim that "no one does wrong willingly" neatly encapsulates this position, but contrary to what some intellectualists seem to intimate, this is a claim upon which Plato insists throughout his career. There is no evidence that he gave it up when he thought he discovered how to account for the phenomenon of *akrasia*.

As we have seen, the Idea of Good is itself a principle of measure (μέτρον).[56] But it cannot be this if my own good, which I necessarily seek, can diverge from the Good, universally conceived. But perhaps one wants to insist rather that the Good just is reducible to one's own good. And that would really eliminate metaphysics from ethical calculation and even from moral psychology. But then there is no criterion of good apart from pleasure, broadly conceived, of course. Socrates pushes his interlocutors, for example, Callicles, to admit that good is a criterion independent of

---

[54] Socrates characterizes the hedonistic "many" as taking a preponderance of pleasure over pain as a criterion of good. See 353D5–354E5. In the phrase πρὸς τέλος, 354D8, good is the goal and the πρός indicates a criterion being applied to whatever is proposed as conducive to that goal. So, the hedonists have no resources with which to judge whether or not doing something leads to the goal they seek other than a preponderance of pleasure over pain. This goal cannot be just achieving some good, since everyone recognizes that pleasure is good. It must be the real Good or its manifestations that all desire.

[55] See *Protag.* 358B7–C1, 358C6–D2; *Me.* 77A–78C; *Gorg.* 466A–468E; *Symp.* 205E7–206A4; *Rep.* 6.505E1–2; *Phil.* 20D7–10. See Barney 2010b.

[56] Cf. Aristotle's dialogue, *Sts.* fr. 2 Ross: πάντων γὰρ ἀκριβέστατον μέτρον τἀγαθόν ἐστιν (the most accurate measure of all is the Good). This fragment seems to confirm the reference at *Sts.* 284D1–2 as being to the Good as ultimate measure. Syrianus, *In Meta.* 168.33–35, says that Aristotle says this "explicitly (διαρρήδην)" in this work. I take it that Syrianus – who is defending Plato against Aristotle's criticisms – uses this word to emphasize what the reader might take to be the surprising agreement with Plato and an even more surprising use of the word "most accurate" for the Good. Protagoras and Plato can agree on the importance of the craft of measurement, while differing radically on its principle: the Good or a human being.

pleasure.⁵⁷ But as we shall see in the next section, it cannot be a criterion if it is identified with a substantive good. Even knowledge or wisdom will not serve in this capacity.

The conclusion of the argument that claims that no one knowingly or with belief acts other than according to what he knows or believes is better for him adds the words, "neither is being bested by oneself anything other than ignorance nor controlling oneself anything other than wisdom."⁵⁸ The words "being bested by oneself" and "controlling oneself" are meant to be a gloss on "overcome by pleasure" and its opposite, "resisting being overcome by pleasure."⁵⁹ It is clear that "overcome by pleasure" is shorthand for a result of "desiring pleasure," despite any other considerations; one is not, after all, being overcome by an external force.⁶⁰ The subject of the desire for pleasure pursues that pleasure. Evans thinks that the appearance of something as pleasurable can occur without belief.⁶¹ His example is of the Müller-Lyer lines, which appear to be unequal but are in fact equal. But such examples are not germane to the question. It is true that it can appear to someone that the lines are unequal at the same time as they believe that they are in fact equal. But it does not seem possible that the appearance can generate an action based on a belief that they are unequal at the same time as there is a belief that they are equal. In the relevant cases, we are talking about people engaged in actions to satisfy desires, and Evans has done nothing to show that it is possible to act without belief. What is not possible is that one should simultaneously believe and not believe that

---

⁵⁷ See *Gorg.* 495E2–499B3.
⁵⁸ *Protag.* 358C1–3: οὐδὲ τὸ ἥττω εἶναι αὐτοῦ ἄλλο τι τοῦτ' ἐστὶν ἢ ἀμαθία, οὐδὲ κρείττω ἑαυτοῦ ἄλλο τι ἢ σοφία.
⁵⁹ See 354E6–7.
⁶⁰ See 355B1, where the words ἀγόμενος ("being driven") and ἐκπληττόμενος ("being battered") implicitly refer to a psychical subject who is driven and battered, presumably by their own state of desire and the subject of that desire.
⁶¹ See Evans 2010, 16–21. Singpurwalla 2006a, 248–249, thinks that the possibility of acting against our beliefs about goodness requires that there be "some kind of irrational element at play in the case of mental conflict and weakness of the will." Singpurwalla, 249–254, goes on to argue that Socrates in *Protagoras* recognizes irrational desires and for that reason the supposed divide between Socratic intellectualism and Platonic irrationalism is bogus. But what Singpurwalla characterizes as "irrational desires" are "evaluative beliefs that are based on appearances and so may conflict with our other, well-reasoned beliefs about goodness." It seems odd, though, to call an evaluative belief or the desire that flows from it "irrational," except in the normative sense explained above. Singpurwalla is right, though, that the dedicated hedonist acts on a belief that the pursuit of pleasure is good for herself. Her mistake is in assuming that pleasure is *the* good and not *a* good, subject to evaluation according to the criterion of what is really good for oneself. Singpurwalla says, 253, "Motivational conflict is a conflict between our well-reasoned conception of the good, and a belief based on the way things appear to us." I would add that even in the case of our well-reasoned conception of the good, there is an appearance of the good.

satisfying the desire is good for oneself according to whatever criterion of good one deploys. What is entirely possible, however, is that one should have a desire for a pleasure and at the same time think that satisfying that pleasure is not good for oneself. The subject of the desire for the pleasure is and is not identical with the subject who thinks that satisfying the desire is not good.

Examples like the Müller-Lyer lines or, to adapt Aristotle's example, that of the sun that appears to be one foot across while we believe that it is much larger, do not show that we can believe p and not believe p simultaneously. Nor are these examples helpful in explicating the cognitive state of the acratic or encratic. Both examples of the optical illusions depend upon our ability to do something that we do not normally do, that is, distinguish between a nonveridical appearance and a belief contrary to that appearance.[62] Such a distinction itself depends on our being able to distinguish belief from knowledge, as for example when we deny that someone has knowledge even if they have a true belief because the belief was happenstance or arbitrary. Then, from the distinction between belief and knowledge we can easily infer that a belief can be held in abeyance as perhaps being false and so not knowledge, because the belief in itself does not announce itself as veridical or nonveridical.[63] But in the case of the optical illusion, when we know that it is an illusion or, in fact, merely believe that it is on the basis of good evidence, we can simultaneously say that it appears to be, that is, we believe it to be one way (nonveridically) while we know or believe it to be another (veridically).

The case of the acratic or encratic is different. The belief that the satisfaction of the appetites is good for oneself (*not* good-independent) can be held at the same time as a different subject holds that its satisfaction is not good for oneself.[64] Although it is not possible to simultaneously believe p and not-p, it does seem possible to believe not-p at the same time as acting as if p were true. This is because the belief that p is true is contextualized by an appetite. The subject "generated" by that appetitive state is sufficiently alienated from the subject "generated" by the belief that not-p is true such that the one can act independently of the other. And yet these are not two different selves or persons; rather it is one person divided

---

[62] The ambiguity is elegantly exposed in Greek: δοκεῖ μοι ("it appears to me") seems to entail that I have a δόξα (belief) that p; at the same time, I can have a belief that not-p because I believe that the appearance is nonveridical.
[63] See Callard 2014, 77, n. 38. The belief that does not announce itself as veridical or nonveridical is called by Callard a "simulacrum." Callard makes a similar point in 2017, 642, in reference to apparent goods that may or may not be really good.
[64] See *Rep.* 10.602D6–E2, where reasoning rules appearance.

into multiple subjects, each arriving at contradictory beliefs pertaining to the real good of that person. The phenomenology here is not so difficult to grasp. After all, we are all probably quite familiar with it. The more difficult question pertains to which subject is more likely to attain a veridical belief about the real good for the person.

While Socrates' argument in *Protagoras* should not be taken as conclusive as to the impossibility of *akrasia*, that does not mean that he should not be taken to uphold the power of knowledge.[65] But this is only so if "knowledge" is understood not as a form of belief.[66] For if knowledge is a form of belief, then it must be owing to some condition other than the belief itself from which knowledge draws its power. That cannot plausibly be taken to be either a truth condition or a justification condition. For beliefs can be true and justification need have no more psychological force than belief. Someone can believe something false with at least as much strength as someone who knows it to be so. Were this not the case, there probably would be no religious wars where we can say with confidence that at least one side has false beliefs. If, however, knowledge draws its power in the way suggested above, then the story is different. For the relevant knowledge is the identity of my good and an instantiation of the Good universally conceived. One who knows this could not possibly act in a contrary way, since such a person, like everyone else, desires his own good. The ubiquity of *akrasia* in human life suggests that this knowledge is indeed rare. Even the encratic is acting only on the basis of a belief, that is, an appearance, of what is good for himself. The knowledge that Socrates extols is stronger than any such appearance.

A person with this knowledge could not find in the subject of his own appetites a motive for action if the belief upon which that action was based contradicted the knowledge of the subject that one's own good and the universal good were identical and in the present case, that one's good was achieved by not acting. One who knew this could not be acratic or encratic; he would be virtuous. The possibility of *akrasia* and *enkrateia* both depend upon occurrent nonveridical beliefs that contradict a belief about one's own good. The possibility disappears in both cases when there is not belief, but knowledge about one's own good, namely, the knowledge that the Good is one thing and that it is identical to my good.[67]

---

[65] *Protag.* 352A8–C7. See Clark 2012.
[66] Penner 1997, 120, denies the special strength of knowledge just because he takes knowledge to be a type of belief.
[67] I should note that "the knowledge *that* the Good and my good are identical" is not, strictly speaking, what the knowledge is. It is not propositional; rather, it is a direct "mental seeing" of the array of Forms at the apex of which is the Good. Nevertheless, we embodied humans represent this

What exactly is the power of this knowledge? I suggest that it is the power to transform one's self-identification such that, having this knowledge, one only perhaps notionally identifies with the subject of appetites. One becomes alienated from the embodied subject. To have this knowledge is to identify with an intellectual subject who sees her own good practically exclusively as identical with the universal Good. There is, so to speak, no oxygen left for the subject of appetites to flourish. She can no longer see herself as seeking an idiosyncratic good except insofar as it manifests the Good and is therefore not in conflict with it.

4.4 Virtue and Happiness

When Socratic ethics is presented as different from, or even opposed to, Platonic ethics, the basis for this is sometimes that (a) the virtuous person alone is happy and that (b) virtue is knowledge or, more precisely, that one who has the craft of being virtuous will then be happy.[68] I have questioned (b) on the grounds that the putative relevant knowledge cannot plausibly yield the desired result. As for (a), there is a distinct problem with the claim that virtue is happiness, that is, that virtue is necessary and sufficient for happiness. The problem is with the very different ways that necessity and sufficiency are here treated. It is easy to make out a case for the necessity of virtue for happiness, so long as one holds it to be an a priori truth that the nonvirtuous person cannot be happy. And by "a priori truth" I do not mean a tautology. This would be analogous to the a priori claim that all actions aim at a goal because of the nature of an action. The necessity of virtue for happiness is the "Socratic" view that the Stoics embraced. Thus, someone who claimed to be virtuous but unhappy would be mistaking whatever it is he feels for the happiness that must result from his being a virtuous person. Or else, he would be mistaken in his claim to be virtuous. But the sufficiency of virtue for happiness is different. For people manifestly pursue goods, including so-called nonmoral goods, because they regard these as contributing to their happiness and they avoid certain "bads" or evils just because they think that these impede their happiness.

---

knowledge in λόγοι, including in λόγοι we direct to ourselves in thought, and therefore, propositionally. See Chappell 2008, 429–433, on the mental seeing in moral realism. Chappell emphasizes "pattern recognition," which I would connect to integrated unity.

[68] Irwin 1992 [1986] argues that Plato's ethics differs from that of Socrates because, whereas Socrates insists on the sufficiency of virtue for happiness, Plato denies this. Cf. 2007, 89–91, 98–100. A more plausible account of this distinction, I think, is that Plato always thought that virtue was sufficient for happiness, but when he came to acknowledge that there were grades of virtue, he denied that this was true for any but the highest grade.

One could say, as do the Stoics, that people who claim that these goods really make a difference to their happiness are just as deluded as would be the admittedly rare individual who was in fact virtuous but claimed to be unhappy. Alternatively, one could say, with Vlastos and others, that, though virtue is sufficient for happiness, the possession of nonmoral goods like health and wealth and social position can add to one's happiness, albeit minimally.[69]

Here, though, is the problem with the latter approach. If the evaluation of the contribution of nonmoral goods to one's happiness is determined by an individual and not objectively, as is the question of the a priori necessity of virtue for happiness, then why should we deny that the nonmoral consequences of doing a virtuous deed, for example, suffering death or torture, may be found by the same individual to be detrimental to his happiness? Stated otherwise, if the sufficiency of virtue for happiness is open to subjective valuation relative to other potential contributors, then what are the grounds for denying that Callicles or Thrasymachus could be legitimately said to be unhappy if he had to suffer the debilitating constraints imposed by practicing virtue? Or, even if Socrates would rather die than escape from prison because escaping from prison would be unjust, someone else might well claim that it is better to escape from prison and remain alive even if this entails doing an injustice than it is to die doing no such thing. So long as one is willing to allow that any goods other than virtue itself can contribute to happiness, then *this* understanding of what happiness is conflicts with the understanding of happiness according to which it is not possible to be virtuous and not happy.

Vlastos cites a number of "Socratic" texts in which he claims the usual interpretation is wrong.[70] According to this interpretation, Socrates is asserting the sufficiency of virtue for happiness, not just its necessity.[71] On this interpretation, the necessity and sufficiency is the analysis of the coreferentiality of "happiness" and "virtue." So, the presence of virtue and virtue alone guarantees happiness. Vlastos, however, wants to interpret these texts such that while virtue is necessary and sufficient for happiness, the terms "virtue" and "happiness" are not coreferential. If that is the

---

[69] See Vlastos 1991, ch. 8. The "minimally" is Vlastos' invention.
[70] See *Ap.* 29E5–30A2, 30A8–B4, 30C5–D5, 41C8–D2; *Cr.* 48B4–10; *Gorg.* 470E4–11, 507B8–C7; *Rep.* 1.335C1–7.
[71] Vlastos 1991, 214–218, rejects what he calls the "identity thesis" for virtue and happiness. He does this because he wants to maintain the necessity and sufficiency of happiness for virtue in a qualified manner. If "virtue" and "happiness" were coreferential, then the identity thesis would indeed follow. But since Vlastos wants to argue that nonmoral goods (that is, goods other than virtue) can contribute to happiness, albeit minimally, he has to deny identity.

case, then we can say that virtue is necessary and sufficient for happiness but, provided that virtue is present, certain nonmoral goods can enhance happiness, albeit minimally. Perhaps another way of stating this interpretation is to say that "virtue" is coreferential with "basic happiness" or that virtue is necessary and sufficient for basic happiness, but that "enhanced" happiness can include nonmoral goods.[72]

The claim is in effect that happiness admits of degrees. The problem with this claim is twofold. First, it is not clear what the threshold is that virtue reaches but that no other nonmoral good can reach alone. Second, it is not clear why the threshold cannot be reached other than by virtue. Perhaps it is the case that one or another nonmoral good adds little to happiness but that an abundance of nonmoral goods can achieve happiness independent of virtue. The obvious response to this is that if virtue is necessary and sufficient for happiness, then and only then when virtue is present do the nonmoral goods add anything. But this means that virtue and the nonmoral goods are commensurable in the sense that virtue alone is worth less than virtue plus even one nonmoral good. This commensurability, however, is not acceptable if virtue is a priori necessary and sufficient for happiness. If it is so a priori, this can only be because there is some connection between virtue and happiness independent of what anyone thinks. But the only reason for the "addibility" of a nonmoral good is precisely the effect it has on what someone thinks. For if, say, wealth added to happiness regardless of what anyone thought, then it would itself be part of what is necessary and sufficient for happiness a priori. It is not open to Vlastos or to anyone else holding this position to say that a nonmoral good adds to happiness but that it does so only if virtue is present. This is because virtue is sufficient for happiness as well as necessary.

Vlastos cites a well-known but contentious text whose natural interpretation supports his view. In *Apology* Socrates says:

> I go around doing nothing else but trying to persuade you, both young and old, to make your first and strongest concern not your bodies or your possessions but that your souls should be in the best possible condition. I do this by saying that virtue does not come from wealth, but through virtue, wealth and everything else, private and public, becomes good for people.[73]

---

[72] Aristotle may have such a distinction in mind when he suggests in *EN* that μακαρία (blessedness) is more than happiness (εὐδαιμονία).

[73] *Ap.* 30A5–B4: οὐδὲν γὰρ ἄλλο πράττων ἐγὼ περιέρχομαι ἢ πείθων ὑμῶν καὶ νεωτέρους καὶ πρεσβυτέρους μήτε σωμάτων ἐπιμελεῖσθαι μήτε χρημάτων πρότερον μηδὲ οὕτω σφόδρα ὡς τῆς ψυχῆς ὅπως ὡς ἀρίστη ἔσται, λέγων ὅτι Οὐκ ἐκ χρημάτων ἀρετὴ γίγνεται, ἀλλ' ἐξ ἀρετῆς χρήματα

4.4 *Virtue and Happiness*

Here it would seem fairly clear that nonmoral goods are made to be good by the presence of virtue. This is a point that even Thrasymachus can concede.[74] But it does not touch the question of happiness, in the sense of "happiness" according to which nonmoral goods add to happiness; rather, it is happiness in the sense according to which it is an a priori truth that virtue is necessary and sufficient for happiness. If wealth with virtue can enhance one's happiness, it is not clear why wealth without virtue cannot do so. It may be that virtue makes the possession of wealth a greater good than the good it would be without virtue. Thrasymachus can agree to this and still maintain that wealth or power alone makes a greater contribution to happiness than virtue alone. It seems indeed obvious that many persons in political power would be glad to exercise that power virtuously but would be nonetheless happy enough if the exercise of that power precluded virtuous behavior from time to time. Virtue would be the feather in a cap entirely desirable on its own.

On the view of Socraticists, the virtue that is necessary and sufficient for happiness cannot be the virtue that Plato in Book 9 of *Republic* assigns to the philosopher alone. This is because virtue thus construed requires the knowledge of the Idea of the Good, an explicit metaphysical requirement. So, either the virtue that Socrates is supposed to be talking about is the "popular or political virtue" of *Phaedo* that is "illusory virtue," or else it is an undefined use of "virtue" that is ambiguous between this inferior form and the philosophical form.[75] I assume that Socraticists would strongly resist the idea that the virtue in Socratic ethics is properly characterized as illusory. If it is philosophical virtue but not the philosophical virtue that requires knowledge of transcendent reality and the metaphysical foundation for this, then we must cast about for a sufficiently deflated meaning for "knowledge." Vlastos' "elenctic knowledge" is one such meaning. Another is the "craft knowledge" of how to instantiate the virtues. But neither elenctic knowledge nor craft knowledge is, as we have seen, necessary and sufficient for virtue. One may have this "knowledge" and still think that virtuous behavior is not only or exclusively in one's interest. If this knowledge is not necessary and sufficient for virtue, Socratic intellectualism cannot get off the ground. If they are, then since virtue is necessary and sufficient for happiness, knowledge is necessary and sufficient for happiness. If this knowledge is elenctic knowledge or craft knowledge, it

---

καὶ τὰ ἄλλα ἀγαθὰ τοῖς ἀνθρώποις ἅπαντα καὶ ἰδίᾳ καὶ δημοσίᾳ. See Vlastos 1991, 219–220, with note 73. See above p. 14, n. 44 for my understanding of this passage.

[74] See *Rep.* 1.340Cff. So, too, Callicles. See *Gorg.* 500A4–6.

[75] See *Phd.* 82A11–B1 on popular or political virtue and 82A10–B3 on illusory virtue.

does not seem necessary for one to be a philosopher to obtain it. At least one does not have to be a philosopher to live according to the dictates of one who has it. And that is, of course, the status of all the virtuous people in Book 4 of *Republic* who possess an inferior grade of virtue.

The inferior grade of virtue is virtue by custom or habit; it is behavioral. Such virtuous people do virtuous things because they have been accustomed or habituated or perhaps instructed to do so. From a Socratic perspective, they are lucky to have been raised this way. All they need to live their lives successfully are the true beliefs about what constitutes virtuous behavior, true beliefs that have been inculcated in them by family and the state. And as Socrates says in *Meno*, for practical purposes true belief is enough. But true belief is unstable unless or until it is tied down with the bonds of reasoning. This occurs by a process of recollection.[76] So, either we should say that the knowledge that Socrates thinks is necessary and sufficient for virtue is really just true belief, as is the case if the knowledge is elenctic or craft knowledge, or else the knowledge that is necessary and sufficient for virtue is something more. If it is, we begin to tread on metaphysical territory.

In line with the nonmetaphysical Socrates, let it be true belief. What is it that makes the true belief that virtue is necessary and sufficient for happiness true? Presumably, it is something nonmetaphysical. Let us suppose, then, that it is a law of human nature that the virtuous flourish and the vicious are miserable. We can give the genesis of this law whatever psychological or biological backing we like. One thing we can say for sure about such a putative law is that, unlike mathematical and logical laws, it will admit of exceptions. Perhaps Thrasymachus is such an exception, and neither do vicious practices immiserate him nor do virtuous practices elevate him.[77] This possibility seems to undercut the absolutist prohibition of wrongdoing that Socrates insists on. So, it is reasonable that true belief should go along with popular or political virtue, but it is unreasonable to think that it goes along with Socrates' absolutist argument. If, then, we turn to knowledge that is not true belief, we will be naturally inclined to identify this with the knowledge of the Forms, the expression of which constitute the definitions sought by Socrates in the early dialogues. But knowing what Justice is, say, and so being in a good position to have a true belief about what practices, laws, institutions, and so on are just is clearly

---

[76] *Me.* 97E–98B.
[77] Sextus Empiricus mentions the famous case of the slave of Alexander the Great who shivered in the sun and sweated in the shade. Socrates' moral absolutism cannot countenance cases in ethics analogous to this one.

not sufficient for motivating one to pursue these unless one thinks that one's own good is thereby achieved. But knowing that Justice is a species of a genus of Good will not be adequate, for the by-now-familiar Moorean reason that it is always possible to ask whether this or that good is really good for me. What is needed is the superordinate first principle of all. What is needed is to see that Justice is knowable only if one knows how it is related to this Good. On that basis alone, one would be in a position to maintain that such knowledge produces virtue, and that virtue is unequivocally in one's own interest. This is the philosophical knowledge that Plato makes explicit in *Republic*. This knowledge alone is necessary and sufficient for happiness. But it is happiness for a person or self who construes that happiness entirely in intellectual terms. Just as philosophical virtue is a higher grade of virtue than popular or political virtue, so is philosophical happiness a higher grade of happiness than the happiness available to nonphilosophers.[78]

Given all the above, it is a legitimate question as to why Plato withholds this metaphysical foundation in any dialogues, especially those in which Socratic ethics is supposedly at play. I find the hypothesis that best fits the evidence is the one advanced by Charles Kahn.[79] Kahn explains Plato's motive for "holding back" in his earlier dialogues as (1) the desirability, if not need, for an aporetic introduction to his systematic philosophy and (2) Plato's awareness of the unusual nature of that philosophy and hence of "the psychological distance" that separates his world view from that of his audience. Neither of these reasons would be nearly so persuasive if it were not for the fact that Plato does eventually "show his cards" with the postulation of the superordinate Idea of Good, the metaphysical foundation for his ethics. Still, as we have seen, he does not completely do this, assuming that Aristotle is right about Plato's teachings that were unwritten.

The proponents of a self-contained "Socratic" ethics, while acknowledging the metaphysical context of the so-called middle dialogues, want to insist that this is all unnecessary for genuine Socratic ethics. All that Socrates needs is a simple belief-desire model of human psychology. Within this austere nonmetaphysical framework, an analysis of the nature of desire and belief is sufficient to justify the paradoxes, even if it does not justify what they would take to be a spurious absolutism. So, on this analysis, desires are for one's own good and the relevant beliefs concern

---

[78] It is, I think, worth noting that when Aristotle, in his *Nicomachean Ethics*, privileges the happiness of the contemplative life over that of the political life, he is following Plato closely. See *EN* K 7–8.

[79] See Kahn 1996, 65–70.

the actions that do and do not achieve this good, all things considered. This, however, is not quite enough, even according to the most rigorous version of the austere framework developed by Terry Penner. For there has to be in addition a distinction between apparent and real good, and the desire must be for the latter and not merely the former. Thus, although it might appear to a tyrant that dominating others is the good that he wills to achieve, in fact it is not. The tyrant's confusion of the two is owing to his false belief. Were he to arrive at a true belief regarding his own good, he would immediately lose his desire to practice tyranny. I think that this is in fact Plato's view. But it is an expansive metaphysical doctrine that makes it so.[80] It is the doctrine that, when applied to the present case, claims that it is not possible that the tyrant's own good can be achieved by tyranny. I think this is as true in *Gorgias* as it is in *Republic*. Prudentialism has no resources to show that the tyrant is not an exception to the rule that crime does not pay. And as much can be said for the other Socratic paradoxes. Even if we can imagine Plato agreeing that it is a law of nature that benevolence redounds favorably to the beneficent, I do not see how he could, without metaphysical tools at his disposal, deny that this putative law of nature admits of exceptions. But the salient point of this entire debate is that everyone, faced with the challenge to exculpate themselves, claims an exceptional status. The prudentialist says, "you may not think so now, but in the long run you'll be glad that you acted justly and not unjustly." The tyrant replies, "your advice makes sense for the little people, but not for me." I focus on the tyrant here because everyone, when contemplating doing evil in order to achieve their own good, thinks of themselves in a tyrannical mode. That is, they think that petty tyranny is justified even if massive tyranny is not, and even if they do not possess the psychological resources of the great tyrants. The circumstances in which they find themselves indicate a surer path to their own good than bowing to the supposed ethical laws of nature.

The absolutism of Socrates' injunctions to virtuous behavior seems to require more than this. If it is indeed a law of nature that my good is never achieved at the expense of others, this could not be what we might loosely call a "social" law; rather, it must be a law rooted absolutely in the nature of reality. I wish to stress that what I am claiming is not a speculative flight of

---

[80] Aristotle certainly provides the most powerful implicit objection to the claim that an expansive metaphysical doctrine is necessary to exclude the possibility of a truly enlightened tyrant. See *EN* I 4 1166b2–29 for the wonderful description of the bad person who cannot live with himself, although it is worth pointing out that Aristotle diagnoses his problem as having "a soul at war with (στασιάζει) itself (b19)"; in other words, a lack of integrated unity.

4.4 Virtue and Happiness

fancy. The universality of the Good is explicit in *Republic*. What I have tried to show, however, is that excluding this universality as applicable to an arbitrarily selected group of dialogues for the sole reason that metaphysics is abhorrent to the purity of Socratic ethics is indefensible. It may have been the case that the historical Socrates did indeed refuse to flee from prison when his life was in the balance. And Plato may have thought that this Socrates had his own reasons for doing so. But our best available evidence for Plato's own view is that a defensible justification for this behavior is rooted in metaphysics.

The virtue that guarantees happiness is clearly that of the philosopher whose entire *métier* is metaphysics. The addition of philosophical knowledge to ordinary virtue transforms the latter because it transforms the self. The nature of this transformation is transparent provided that we recognize the centrality of the Idea of the Good. It consists in one identifying "good for me" with "Good" *simpliciter*. Doing this consists in refusing to identify oneself, except adventitiously, as the subject of bodily appetites and emotions. The idiosyncratic nature of these precludes the antiseptic assimilation of "good for me" to "Good." All of Socrates' benighted interlocutors who are aghast and amazed at his paradoxical-sounding arguments are manifestly among those who locate themselves principally as subjects of bodily desires. Of course, if my good is the good of such subjects, then it would be unthinkable to identify "good for me" with "Good."

It is not the practice of philosophy – "doing philosophy," as we say – that is transformative, but the successful outcome of this practice. For in success, one sees that the Good makes the Virtues Good-like. And in this comprehensive knowledge of intelligible reality or "perfect being (τὸ παντελῶς ὄν)," one sees one's true self. One's own good is *that* Good. Without the superordinate Good, none of this is possible. It is because of the successful attainment of knowledge of the Good that the philosopher in *Symposium* spontaneously produces true virtue.[81]

---

[81] See *Symp.* 212A5–6. Smith 2018 proposes a trilemma for understanding Plato's treatment of Socrates: (1) Socrates in an exemplar of virtue; (2) virtue is a kind of knowledge, and (3) Socrates lacks the knowledge in which virtue consists. Smith proposes to resolve this potential inconsistency by distinguishing grades of knowledge. Socrates does not have the knowledge of a god but he is far ahead of other human beings. Hence, 93, his virtue is not undermined by his ignorance. The knowledge he possesses, despite his ignorance, is in fact a skill (τέχνη) of living virtuously. It is a skill of soul-care. I am sympathetic with this approach. Nevertheless, if there is a skill of living well, it must rest upon ἐπιστήμη of the Good. I think Smith's view in fact comes very close to my view if we add that Socrates believes that life is not a zero-sum game, but the Good is one thing. His ignorance then would consist in his not knowing how to instantiate the Good of which he has no ἐπιστήμη. Perhaps a Socrates who is skeptical about this is not much different from a Socrates who is ignorant about this. But then what becomes of his vaunted skill?

Because the Good is the One, instantiating the Good is equivalent to producing integrative unity according to kind. Since all virtue, including the inferior kind, is a kind of integrative unity of the parts of the soul, the practitioner of political craft does not need to suppose that philosophical transformation of the self is the only desideratum. A well-ordered state is not an exiguous achievement. But even if metaphysics is remote from the minds of the state's denizens, it is metaphysics nonetheless that provides the rationale for the political ordering. Obviously, the best a political ruler could reasonably aspire to is popular or political virtue in the masses.

CHAPTER 5

Moral Responsibility

5.1 The Puzzle of Moral Responsibility

As we have already seen, the use of the term "morality" in reference to Plato's thought is problematic, especially if morality is understood as somehow opposed to self-interest.[1] Still, there is one use of "moral" that seems to work sufficiently well in characterizing Plato's view on human action generally. This is the use of the word "moral" in "moral responsibility." Although this phrase translates nothing in the Greek, it may well serve as a gloss for the use of the words "blameworthy" and "praiseworthy" when referring to actions.[2] The phrase "moral responsibility" has a fairly commonsensical meaning that conceals much. People are held to be morally responsible, especially for their actions, when it is thought that they "could have done otherwise" or when "they should have known better."[3] This sense of moral responsibility has its origin in Aristotle and is theorized

---

[1] See, for example, Mackenzie 1981, 218, "the core of Plato's moral theory is egoistic; he argues that virtue is in our interests." Mackenzie, 219, goes on to argue that on this basis Plato has no adequate reason to promote benevolence. With the positing of the superordinate Idea of the Good, the *opposition* of self-interest and benevolence disappears. True self-interest and true benevolence coincide; it is only in appearance that they conflict. Both excessive self-interest and excessive benevolence undermine the coincidence.

[2] The noun for "blame" is ψόγος and the verb ψέγω, both connoting something more than strict liability or unintentional responsibility. The opposite of "blame" is "praise (ἐπαίνω)." These words often appear together. In none of the 100 or so uses of these words in the dialogues is a clear "moral" meaning indicated. Things and people are praised or blamed for all sorts of reasons, especially as a device for altering behavior. Not surprisingly, such uses are typically found in educational contexts, but also in persuasive contexts such as the preambles to the laws in *Laws*. For example at *Lg.* 7.798D3–5 a law is aimed at changing "customs (ἤθη)" among people through "praise or blame."

[3] That someone "could have done otherwise" and that he "should have known better" are, of course, logically independent claims. But they are often introduced alongside each other in the assignment of blame and praise and punishment and reward. See especially van Inwagen 1986 on the logical connection between moral responsibility and alternative possibilities. Van Inwagen effectively rebuts attempts to separate these. His strategy is to focus on carefully specifying the particular action for which one can be held responsible, even if circumstances are such that attempting to perform the action would have been ineffective or unnecessary. The phrase "should have known better" will be seen to be more or less equivalent to the assignment of culpable ignorance.

extensively by the great Peripatetic commentator Alexander of Aphrodisias in his treatise *De fato*.[4] His Aristotelian defense is explicitly directed against Stoics, whose doctrine of what we have come to call "soft determinism" or "compatibilism" is supposed by Alexander to undercut moral responsibility. Leaving the Peripatetic–Stoic debate aside for the moment, I have used the word "moral" here promiscuously, since it nowhere appears in anyone's arguments about praise and blame or "what is up to us." What does "moral" add to responsibility? The obvious response, coming certainly from Plato himself, reflects a legal distinction between strict liability and *mens rea* or intent.[5] Most legal systems, including Plato's, distinguish between damage done by one person to another or to his property that is unintentional from damage that is intentional. It is the latter that is usually dubbed "criminal" and is thought to be the locus of moral responsibility, at least within a legal framework.

The idea of moral responsibility is closely connected to the idea of moral agency. The latter term refers, roughly, to the recognition of one's own moral responsibility. To the extent that one does not feel oneself to be in control of one's actions and intentions, that is, to be shorn of moral agency, to just that extent we are apt to deny that one is morally responsible, including for oneself. Within the Platonic context that I have been developing, moral agency requires the awareness that the real good is the object of one's will. Plato's observation *en passant* that everyone "divines" that the Good is something is both the precondition for this awareness and the guarantee that divesting oneself of moral responsibility can only be done by someone *else*, never by oneself. Thus, someone who says, "I am not morally responsible for my actions," if he understands the words he utters, is morally responsible. Moral responsibility would not even be possible without moral agency; moral agency would not be possible if all accurate accounts of agency were third person. That is, the putative primacy of third-person accounts of action excludes the first-person self-reflexivity necessary for one to be aware of being in some way in control of one's actions. Again, within the Platonic context, exercising control means that

---

[4] See Aristotle, *EN* Γ 4, 1136b6–7: ἐφ' ἡμῖν δὴ καὶ ἡ ἀρετή, ὁμοίως δὲ καὶ ἡ κακία (virtue is up to us and so is vice). Alexander of Aphrodisias, *De fato* 164.19, 169.13–15, 181.12–14, 199.8–9, 211.31–33; *Mantissa* 172.30–31 Bruns, thematizes the term τὸ ἐφ' ἡμῖν ("what is up to us") to indicate moral responsibility. If an action is up to us, that means that we could have done otherwise. His focus on the term is a response to the Stoics' severe limitation on what is "up to us." Among contemporary philosophers, the association of moral responsibility and "could have done otherwise" is still strong, though not unchallenged. See, for example, Frankfurt 1969; Goetz 2005; Widerker 2005.

[5] I leave aside the fine-grained distinctions that have developed within law regarding types of criminal intent, including negligence and recklessness.

one can apply some rational standard in the course of judging how to satisfy one's desires, where such satisfaction is supposed to be the attainment of one's real good.

The term "moral agency" also indicates that normativity is inextricably bound up with action. This follows straightforwardly from the fact that every action is undertaken in order to achieve an apparent good which is held by the agent to be an instantiation of the real good that she seeks. A tendency to separate normativity from agency seems to arise from the assumption that normativity is separable, and even, at times, inimical to the pursuit of one's personal interests. But what I "ought" to do on every occasion is to seek my own real good, which could only *appear* to diverge from an instantiation of the Good. Moral responsibility depends not so much on how things appear to me, but on my reliance on universal reason in determining this.

There are a couple of problems with this account. First, lining up moral responsibility with the law is not always going to work since people are typically held to be morally responsible for things on which the law does not speak. Indeed, someone may be held to be morally responsible for *obeying* a bad law, as Socrates implies in *Apology*. So, if moral responsibility is not entailed by intentionally disobeying a law, even if we "could have done otherwise," what does "moral" really add to "responsible?" In this chapter, I want to show that Plato's metaphysical commitments lead him to accept a distinction between intentional and unintentional behavior at the same time as he eschews a facile conflation of moral responsibility with "could have done otherwise."

If Plato is correct to insist that no one does wrong willingly (οὐδεὶς ἑκὼν ἁμαρτάνει), how can anyone be held morally responsible when they do wrong?[6] Yet, Plato does seem to assume that something like moral responsibility exists, if only for the obvious reason that he assigns rewards and punishments to the virtuous and the wicked in the afterlife.[7] Even if it is

---

[6] See *Ap.* 37A5; *Gorg.* 488A3; *Protag.* 358C7; *Rep.* 9.589C6; *Tim.* 86D7–8; *Lg.* 4.731B, 9.860D1–3. Penner 2011, 278–282, distinguishes "Socratic" ethics from Platonic ethics by the fact that the former contains no concept of moral responsibility, although the later "might" (see 279, n. 28; 289, n. 57). On Penner's view, it makes no sense for us to suppose that Socrates felt himself to be morally responsible for obeying a just law or for refusing to obey an unjust one.

[7] I am here going to assume that the mythical context of these rewards and punishments does not undercut the substantive point. After all, the myths are supposed to be plausible representations of what happens after we die. But if punishments are unjustified, so are rewards, and there would be no point in creating myths to perpetuate the misrepresentation, perhaps apart from some politically motivated "noble falsehood." It seems inconsistent with Plato's positive view of the gods that, as the agents of punishment and reward, they would be held to participate in delivering anything other than condign punishment. See Chapter 7.

the case that rewards and punishments can serve as deterrents for those still living, this can hardly negate the direct retributive function.[8] But if no one does wrong willingly, what purpose exactly does retribution serve? As we have seen, there is abundant textual evidence to support the standard view that unwilling wrongdoing occurs owing to ignorance, even though it is far from clear exactly what the ignorance is ignorance of. But whatever this ignorance is of, it is at least initially difficult to see why we are morally responsible for it. I will use the term "culpable ignorance" for the ignorance that would justifiably elicit blame or punishment. Whence the culpability?[9]

In the exposition of his penal code in *Laws* Book 9, the Athenian Stranger makes an apparently straightforward distinction between voluntary (ἑκούσιον) and involuntary (ἀκούσιον) harms (βλάβαι).[10] He adds the important qualification that not all these acts are injustices. Harms done involuntarily are in effect matters of strict liability.[11] A harm is unjust only when there is intent. Such harm is the locus of criminal law and punishment. But we may well ask how Plato can say at once that no one does wrong willingly or voluntarily *and* that there is a class of wrongdoing or harm that is voluntary.[12] An unjust act is voluntary insofar as it springs from the intent formulated in an unjust soul, but it is involuntary because unjust acts are never in anyone's own interest; they are done out of

---

[8] See Van Riel 2016, 113–114, who cites *Lg.* 10.903D3–E1 which sets forth clearly the reality of rewards and punishments for moral agents. The normative terms used are τὸ πρέπον (that which is fitting) and τὸ προσῆκον (that which is appropriate) to indicate the correspondence of rewards and punishments to that for which the agent is responsible. See also 904B8–D3. Roberts 1987, 34, tries, unsuccessfully in my view, to give a sense to "fitting" which does not entail culpability in the one receiving a "fitting" punishment. It seems to me implausible that Plato is using the words τὸ πρέπον and τὸ προσῆκον to indicate the nonmoral "correct" compensation for tortious behavior. For *that*, Plato typically uses variations of τὸ ὀρθόν ("that which is correct"). See, for example, *Lg.* 8.862A7, B7–8, C1.
[9] See Aristotle, *EN* Γ 2, 1110b24–30 on acting "in ignorance" where we can say that the person "should have known better." So, Aristotle seems to acknowledge a sort of culpable ignorance. But he provides no argument for the culpability, only a rhetorical appeal to common sense. One who denies the very existence of moral responsibility should have no difficulty in brushing aside this rhetoric as question-begging.
[10] *Lg.* 9.861E1–4. See Roberts 1987; Saunders 1991, ch. 5.
[11] *Lg.* 9.862B5–C4. In distinguishing between injustice (ἀδικία) and harm (βλάβη), and making the former depend on the character of the agent, Plato is significantly restricting the arena within which injustices may be declared. Thus, there are no unjust states of affairs or situations without unjust behavior by people with unjust dispositions. A situation, like a plague, might be deleterious, but it is not unjust unless there are unjust moral agents acting. Further, there could be no per se unjust institutions.
[12] Inferred from *Lg.* 9.862A2–B1 where the unjust nature of the action depends on its being voluntary. Indeed, the words at A7–B1 suggest that it is even possible for one to confer unjustly a benefit on someone else.

ignorance. A person with a disordered soul can intend to (that is, willingly) do harm even if it is the case that she does not intend to (that is, willingly) harm herself. This is possible just when one is ignorant that one's own good cannot be achieved at the expense of anyone else. This might be the plight of most of humanity, but the voluntary inflicting of harm on others is the result of an unjust soul. This seems clear enough. Nevertheless, this does not explain the culpability, if indeed there be such. For the circumstances producing the unjust soul might have been out of one's control.

The only thing that makes it possible that one can intend to do harm but do so involuntarily is ignorance.[13] What allows us to distinguish between involuntary acts of wrongdoing and voluntary acts of wrongdoing even though the latter are also in a sense involuntary is that the ignorance in this case is culpable. Somehow, culpable ignorance has to be associated with an unjust soul.[14]

It is important to see that we cannot easily avoid the question of culpable ignorance by adducing cases of incontinence or ἀκρασία. It is true that when someone acts counter to what they know or believe is the right thing to do, they are not acting in ignorance. Leontius certainly believes that gazing on the naked corpses is wrong even as he is doing it. So, he is not ignorant and yet he is blameworthy. Or so it would seem. But two things might lead us to resist this conclusion. First, it is not clear that insofar as he is blameworthy, he is acting against his own will. If Leontius believes that

---

[13] *Lg.* 9.863C1–D4. See Wilburn 2013, 116, who thinks that the way to understand criminal liability is to say that criminals voluntarily commit crimes but in doing so, do involuntarily what is bad for themselves. But this is only to say that what is done voluntarily is done out of ignorance. That there is ignorance involved here is hardly controversial. Nor is it problematic to insist that the criminal activity is counter to one's own βούλησις since this is permanently oriented to instantiations of the Good. What is at issue is whether one can be blamed for this ignorance. Nothing in Wilburn's analysis suggests that the ignorance is or could be culpable.

[14] The Athenian Stranger goes on to clarify his classification by adding anger and pleasure as sources of wrongdoing. See 9.863A7–B9. But these are not evidently sources of culpable wrongdoing, as *Tim.* 86B1–87B9 will explain in detail. Clearly, anger is the source of wrongdoing in the spirited part of the soul and pleasure is the source of wrongdoing in the appetitive part of the soul. See O'Brien 1967, 190–194; Mackenzie 1981, 245–249; Wilburn 2013, 113–119. Presumably, we must distinguish culpable ignorance from the ignorance ruefully acknowledged by Socrates. On Socrates' profession of ignorance see *Ap.* 20C1–3, 21D2–7, 23B2–4; *Charm.* 165B4–C2, 166C7–D6; *Eu.* 5A7–C5, 15C12, 15E5–16A4; *La.* 186B8–C5, 186D8–E3, 200E2–5; *Ly.* 212A4–7, 223B4–8; *Hip. Ma.* 286C8–E2, 304D4–E5; *Gorg.* 509A4–6; *Rep.* 1.337E4–5. This list, which I take from Smith 2018, n. 16, actually includes different sorts of ignorance not all easily fitted within a rubric of "not knowing how to give a definition of F," the traditional paradigmatic example of Socratic ignorance. But even when Socrates does clearly say that he does not know how to give a λόγος of F, it does not follow from this that he does not know F, say, nonpropositionally. In any case, it is not suggested anywhere in the dialogues that Socrates' self-professed ignorance is blameworthy or deserving of punishment of any sort. I should add that his ignorance, though it might preclude philosophical virtue, does not preclude popular or political virtue.

gazing is wrong and so in some sense does not want to gaze, he also wants to gaze. Apart from the problem that *this* occasions, insofar as he does not want to gaze, he is not doing wrong willingly and there is no straight path to his moral responsibility; insofar as he does want to gaze, he does wrong willingly, which would seem to violate the principle that no one does wrong willingly. Second, the principle that no one does wrong willingly must surely apply to the vicious at least as appropriately as it does to the acratic. But if the vicious person does wrong unwillingly, and if this is owing to his ignorance, again, whence the culpability?

It is difficult to imagine that the culpability is to be found in some substantial fact or rule, ignorance of which is blameworthy.[15] For the mechanisms – whatever they may be – that result in someone being ignorant of the truth of a proposition p do not seem to be able to be used to discriminate those propositions for which the resultant ignorance is nonculpable from those for which it is culpable. Social or economic or psychological circumstances could seem to prevent anyone from knowing or believing an infinite number of propositions – including normative ones – whether belief in these leads to morally blameworthy actions or morally innocent ones or even moral praiseworthy ones.

In order to answer our main question, it will be necessary to keep in mind exactly what wrongdoing is according to Plato. As I have argued, a wrong is perpetrated when someone does something in order to achieve his own good, when this putative good is achieved only at the expense of someone else. In such a case, one violates the principle of the universality of Good. It is not possible to attain one's own good at the expense of anyone else. Since everyone desires their own good, no one does this wrong willingly. The culpable ignorance is going to have to have something to do with the psychological state of one who acts in this way.[16] This, as we have just seen, is the state of an unjust soul. In an important clarification of the relevant ignorance, the Stranger says,

---

[15] Schöpsdau 1984, 113–114, thinks that the ignorance is not culpable because it amounts to a misunderstanding of the law. But this is implausible as an explanation for all cases. For example, there is no reason to assume that the tyrant is ignorant of the law.

[16] Arguably, the "ridiculousness" of being overcome by pleasure in *Protag.* 355A5ff is owing to someone simultaneously believing something to be bad for him and yet doing it willingly because he is overcome by pleasure. The culpable ignorance here would be in acting as if one were ignorant of that which one claims to believe, namely, that something is bad for oneself. See Clark 2012, 246, who argues that the ridiculousness consists in "attributing knowledge to an agent while also claiming that he has no such knowledge." It is in self-attribution that the culpable ignorance is found. Hugh Benson, in private correspondence, points out an alternative way of making the identical point: "if it is not possible to achieve one's good at the expense of others, then it is impossible to do so. So, if doing wrong is in fact aiming to achieve the impossible, one can only do so out of ignorance."

5.1 *The Puzzle of Moral Responsibility*   153

The different third category [of ignorance apart from anger and pleasure] is of hopes and beliefs – it is a mere shot at truth about the best.[17]

This very difficult bit of text at least seems to want to say that there is potentially culpable ignorance in hopes and beliefs about the best, where the "best" must indicate the concrete instantiation of the Good here and now.[18] These arise in the unjust soul, one in which reason does not rule. How are these hopes and beliefs blameworthy?

Here is my suggestion for how this works. When one acts to achieve any good, one does so on the basis of a reasoning process even if reason is not ruling in that person. That is, the initiating of the action is the conclusion of a practical syllogism, roughly, of the following sort: Actions of such-and-such sort achieve one's own good; this is such an action; therefore, let me act. The salient feature of this deliberation process is the recognition of the authority that one accepts for the content of the major premise, even if that premise is false. One acts *because* one believes true some universal proposition regarding action and the good achieved by that action. It is never the minor premise that provides the ἀρχή of the action. Even when Plato says in *Republic* that thirst is just for drink, not good or bad drink, when one acts to get a drink, this is because one thinks that this act is an instance of a rule or practice that the agent accepts. If that were not the case, then "going for" the drink would be a reflex, not an action. Of course, people do all sorts of things as a result of a reflex. But none of these are cases in which one can be said to morally err (ἁμαρτάνειν), for the simple reason that in order to err, one has to try to hit a target and fail. "Trying" is not the precise way to characterize what someone does when she takes her hand off a hot surface. "Trying" involves matching up a goal with steps to it under a general description that indicates that such steps are most likely to reach the goal.

The inseparability of the subject of the calculative faculty from practical reasoning along with the subject of embodied desire depends upon the

---

[17] *Lg.* 9.864B6–7: ἐλπίδων, δὲ καὶ δόξης, <του> ἀληθοῦς περὶ τὸ ἄριστον ἔφεσις τρίτον ἕτερον. Cf. 1.644C8–9; *Phil.* 12D3. See Saunders 1968, 433, on the text and the translation (slightly modified). Saunders 1991, 148, lists a number of other passages in *Laws* in which ignorance is the source of wrongdoing: the ignorance of atheists (10.886B, 903D1, 905B7, C2); the ignorance of those who think that the gods sanction theft (12.941B); the ignorance of those who believe that virtue and happiness are not mutually implicating (2.660Dff); the ignorance of those who believe that wealth is the good (9.870A–B); the ignorance of those who believe that wisdom points to selfishness (5.732A); hypothetical gods who are ignorant of their providential responsibilities (10.902A). It is not immediately clear why any one of these examples indicates *culpable* ignorance.

[18] See *Sts.* 294B1–2, where the principal defect in law as compared to the wise rule of the statesman is that it cannot possibly prescribe what is best or most just for everyone simultaneously (ἅμα). Some people are bound to be harmed as others are helped.

self-reflexivity of discursive thinking. That is, the dichotomy of unified subject or *homunculi* is false. Harry Frankfurt's first-order desire and second-order judgment is one way of representing the fact that one thinks about one's own desires and their satisfaction. The embodied divided self is morally responsible when it deliberates because there is no way to divest oneself of the authority of reason.[19] Even one who says, "let reason serve my appetites" is doing that from the perspective of a rational agent. Moreover, his attempt to recruit reason into the service of appetite is an implicit recognition of the authority or priority of reason; in the present case, the reasoning that leads to the conclusion that reason should be put in the service of appetite. So, attempts to divest oneself of culpability in acting require one to acknowledge the authority of that which guarantees culpability.

The culpable ignorance in the wrongdoer does not consist in him believing in the authority of the major premise and simultaneously disbelieving in it. That would be impossible. The culpable ignorance consists in *believing* in the authority of reason and *acting* as if reason is not authoritative.[20] You cannot really act at all if you do not believe in the practical authority of the major premise in the syllogism. We have already seen that Plato distinguishes between normative and nonnormative reasoning. The latter is employed whenever anyone thinks discursively, including when they engage in practical reasoning. But the recognition of the authority of reason in action is the recognition of the authority of normative reasoning.[21] Normative reasoning is how we prepare to act to achieve manifestations of the Good we seek. One believes that reason should rule if one believes in its authority. In action, it is *always* the authority of normative reasoning that is assumed. That is, one never acts

---

[19] See Cooper 1999, 125–126, "Thus the claim that the desire for the good is inherent in reason itself amounts to the claim that *anyone who possesses the power of reason wants to think out on his own, on purely rational grounds, what goals to pursue in life, and to achieve those goals. He wants, in other words, reason to rule in his life* [my emphasis]." As I understand Cooper, to disclaim moral responsibility requires one to accept the grounds for moral responsibility. This is in contrast to someone who might disclaim moral responsibility for another on the grounds that that person is incapable of showing a commitment to the authority of reason. Also, see Kauppinen 2019, 3, "rationality's demands seem to be somehow *authoritative* for anyone capable of meeting them, regardless of their desires or commitments."

[20] Someone who believed p and acted as if p were not true would be a clear example of a person exhibiting absence of integrated unity.

[21] See Wilburn 2013, 115, nn. 9–10. Wilburn cites *Lg.* 9.863E3, obviously referring to 1.644D7–645B1, the famous passage comparing human beings to divine puppets. The "golden cord" whose "pull" we ought to follow (δεῖν συνεπόμενον) is that of normative reasoning or βούλησις (863E3), which is oriented to the Good. The locus of culpable ignorance is in the practical thinking, the conclusion of which is not to follow the pull of the golden cord.

on the basis of a theoretical syllogism where the Good has no place. One always acts because one believes that the major premise is normative. It has the form: Such-and-such an action is good for me. But when one does wrong, one acts as if this authority does not obtain. That is why wrongdoing always has appetite or disordered emotion as its ἀρχή. One is culpably ignorant because one appeals to the truth of a proposition – the major premise in the practical syllogism – as the basis for acting, but then one acts as if reason were not authoritative. One acts to satisfy the appetite in spite of acquiescence to the authority of reason. If, by contrast, one were to act with the acknowledgment of the authority of reason, one would be unlikely to pursue the satisfaction of any appetite if in doing so one had to intentionally harm anyone else.

Related to the last point is something that has been discussed throughout the book. That is the problem for the embodied human being of determining his real or ideal self. The problem arises because of the ephemeral selves that come into being, along with appetites whose subjects they are, and go out of being as soon as the appetites are satisfied. In acknowledging the authority of normative reasoning in determining one's real, not apparent good, one at least takes a step in the direction of acknowledging one's real self. If this were not the case, it would indeed be irrational to appeal to reason to determine one's true good. It is as if one were to appeal to a book on fire to warm oneself. Of course, the result of thinking is only an apparent good, too, with the hope that it is a veridical appearance. But when what appears to the subject of appetite conflicts with what appears to the reasoning subject, just the recognition of the conflict amounts to an incipient self-knowledge and the attendant moral responsibility.

The tyrant who does what seems best to him but not what he wills acts according to a practical syllogism when engaging in tyrannical acts. But he appeals to a norm of behavior as authoritative. His culpability lies in being willfully ignorant. Or what amounts to the same thing; believing p and acting as if p were not true. He does this when an appetite is the ἀρχή of his action, not normative reason. The tyrant is not irrational in the sense that he does not employ reason. He is irrational only in the sense that he acts counter to the normativity of reason that he himself accepts, as do we all. Endowed with rational agency, wrongdoing amounts to acknowledging and at the same time disregarding that endowment. Who else could be to blame for that?

The obvious objection to this interpretation is that the major premise of the wrongdoer's practical syllogism is not an impersonal proposition about the Good but a personalized proposition about one's own good. The tyrant only has to recognize the authority of personal norms of reasoning. The tyrant can, it seems, heartily endorse Hume's claim that reason is the servant of the passions, not the master. And then, when he acts, there is no irrationality. And if we continue to hold that he does wrong unwillingly, there seems to be no culpability either. Why, then, is the tyrant blameworthy for his tyrannical acts?

We have already seen the force of the Moorean objection: For any claim that the good is x, it is always intelligible to ask whether x is good. The intelligibility of the question means that "good" cannot be identified with a particular good or with a kind of good.[22] One who appeals to a major premise in a practical syllogism makes a claim about the good. But the determination of whether or not the satisfaction of a desire is good for the one who has the desire is separate from the determination that the desire is present. The tyrant reasons, "dominating others is good for me; making arbitrary laws is dominating; therefore, let me make these laws." But whether or not it is good for him is not determined by the mere fact that he has the desire to dominate since it could conceivably turn out that dominating is not good for him. The acknowledgment of the authority of normative reason in the practical syllogism of the tyrant is not, therefore, gainsaid by the major premise containing the words "for me." That acknowledgment is of the authority of normative reason in expressing what is good, including what is good for oneself. The tyrant believes in an objective truth as determinable by the expert (ὁ τεχνικός). He acts as if there were no such experts, but that something like Protagorean relativism is true. That is, he acts as if desiring a good were the same thing as determining that it is good. This is simply a crazy view. If it were not, then no one would ever regret anything they had done. No one would ever have cause to say, "I thought it would be good for me, but it turned out not to be so." Deliberating about an action on the basis of "hopes and beliefs" is clearly indicative of the absence of knowledge. Hopes and beliefs do not determine the truth. Insofar as they contribute to action, they are idiosyncratic indicators of what seems to be good for oneself. In other words, someone who, for example, hopes that exercising an appetite for dominating others will not leave him worse off than before cannot divest himself of

---

[22] See *Gorg.* 499B4–500A6. The example here given by Socrates and accepted by Callicles is of pleasures – which are among goods – that are judged to be bad. One who judges a pleasure to be bad does so by appealing to the authority of reason, adherence to which is acknowledged by the agent to be necessary to achieve the real good that he desires.

5.1 *The Puzzle of Moral Responsibility*

moral responsibility for his behavior by claiming ignorance. For the ignorance is culpable.[23]

In *Laws*, there is a remarkable and well-known speech by the Athenian Stranger which includes a declaration on the source of culpable wrongdoing.

> The most serious vice innate in most persons' souls is one for which everybody forgives himself and so never tries to find a way of escaping. This vice is what they say is in fact a person naturally being his own friend and it is proper that it should be so. In truth, this excessive love of self is the explanation for each and every act of [moral?] error (ἁμαρτία) we commit. This love blinds the lover to the faults of the beloved and makes him judge badly regarding just and good and beautiful things, thinking that he should honor his self rather than the truth.
>
> Any would-be great person must cherish neither himself nor his own possessions, but just things, not only when they are his own, but especially when they happen to be done by someone else. It is because of this very [moral?] error that there arises in all things the appearance of wisdom when there is in fact ignorance. This is why we think we know everything when in fact we know nothing, so that owing to our not turning over to others what we do not know how to do ourselves, we are forced to err when we try to do these things ourselves. For this reason, then, every person must flee from excessive love of self, and instead always follow what is better than himself; and he must not be ashamed at the thought of abandoning his best friend. (Trans. Saunders with alterations)[24]

---

[23] Huemer 2013, provides an interesting anti-Humean argument somewhat akin to what I am proposing here. He argues that "facts of the form 'It is rational to Φ' and 'S has reason to Φ' *do* provide reasons for action, and they do so categorically, for all rational agents." It is rational for one to believe that there is a non-zero probability of the typical claims of moral realism. Recognizing this, one has a reason to act morally." Similarly, I am arguing that an appeal to the authority of reason in action – an appeal that every moral agent makes – is sufficient to make one morally responsible for actions. Plato would no doubt add that the fact that we all "divine" the Good to be something confirms this, since our actions are all aimed at achieving instantiations of this. Moral responsibility owing to culpable ignorance is part of our endowment as rational beings. Another part is our awareness that the Good is "something" and that that is what we desire.

[24] *Lg.* 5.731D6–732B4: Πάντων δὲ μέγιστον κακῶν ἀνθρώποις τοῖς πολλοῖς ἔμφυτον ἐν ταῖς ψυχαῖς ἐστιν, οὗ πᾶς αὐτῷ συγγνώμην ἔχων ἀποφυγὴν οὐδεμίαν μηχανᾶται· τοῦτο δ' ἔστιν ὃ λέγουσιν ὡς φίλος αὑτῷ πᾶς ἄνθρωπος φύσει τέ ἐστιν καὶ ὀρθῶς ἔχει τὸ δεῖν εἶναι τοιοῦτον. τὸ δὲ ἀληθείᾳ γε πάντων ἁμαρτημάτων διὰ τὴν σφόδρα ἑαυτοῦ φιλίαν αἴτιον ἑκάστῳ γίγνεται ἑκάστοτε. τυφλοῦται γὰρ περὶ τὸ φιλούμενον ὁ φιλῶν, ὥστε τὰ δίκαια καὶ τὰ ἀγαθὰ καὶ τὰ καλὰ κακῶς κρίνει, τὸ αὑτοῦ πρὸ τοῦ ἀληθοῦς ἀεὶ τιμᾶν δεῖν ἡγούμενος· οὔτε γὰρ ἑαυτὸν οὔτε τὰ ἑαυτοῦ χρὴ τόν γε μέγαν ἄνδρα ἐσόμενον στέργειν, ἀλλὰ τὰ δίκαια, ἐάντε παρ' αὑτῷ ἐάντε παρ' ἄλλῳ μᾶλλον πραττόμενα τυγχάνῃ. ἐκ ταὐτοῦ δὲ ἁμαρτήματος τούτου καὶ τὸ τὴν ἀμαθίαν τὴν παρ' αὑτῷ δοκεῖν σοφίαν εἶναι γέγονε πᾶσιν· ὅθεν οὐκ εἰδότες ὡς ἔπος εἰπεῖν οὐδέν, οἰόμεθα τὰ πάντα εἰδέναι, οὐκ ἐπιτρέποντες δὲ ἄλλοις ἃ μὴ ἐπιστάμεθα πράττειν, ἀναγκαζόμεθα ἁμαρτάνειν αὐτοὶ πράττοντες. διὸ πάντα ἄνθρωπον χρὴ φεύγειν τὸ σφόδρα φιλεῖν αὑτόν, τὸν δ' ἑαυτοῦ βελτίω διώκειν ἀεί, μηδεμίαν αἰσχύνην ἐπὶ τῷ τοιούτῳ πρόσθεν ποιούμενον.

There are a number of features in this passage that deserve close attention. First, is the claim that "excessive self-love is the source of [moral] error." This self-love is the source of the error, not the error itself. It focuses not on a part of the soul or the body or external circumstances, but the subject of action, the moral agent. Consider for a moment what Plato means by "self-love," leaving aside what makes it excessive. As we have seen, for Plato the self is the subject of desire. The subject of embodied desire is identified by the appetitive state that is discovered in one's soul. Self-love is as variable as the selves that turn up along with every appetite and usually disappear as soon as the appetite is satisfied. Love just is a form of desire, as *Symposium* tells us. All love is a form of desire to have desire's object. The lover of the beautiful boy in *Symposium* is a self-lover. What he desires is the satisfaction of his own appetite. What makes the self-love excessive is that it makes one judge badly matters of justice, goodness, and beauty. One judges these matters badly because one identifies with the subject of appetites and not with the subject of reasoning. Or worse, one employs reason to satisfy appetites indiscriminately. Just as the subject of appetites is identified by the appetite and its intentional object, so the subject of reasoning is identified by its desire to know. What it aims to know is what is universally and necessarily true. That is why honoring one's self more than the truth amounts to dishonoring one's real self. For nonphilosophers, honoring the truth means honoring the deliverances of philosophers or those who know. For philosophers, it means identifying the satisfaction of one's true desire with the knowledge of the truth.

Along these lines, at the end of the passage, the exhortation to flee from self-love and to follow what is superior to oneself (τὸν ἑαυτοῦ βελτίω) recalls *Republic* and the seemingly paradoxical idea of "self-mastery."[25] Socrates says that within the human soul there is a "better (βέλτιον)" part and a "worse (χεῖρον)" part. Self-mastery is the rule of the former over the latter. No doubt, this relationship between the better and the worse has its political analogue.[26] But in *Republic* and in the *Laws* passage, the better is the rational part of the soul. Its dominance is the antithesis of excessive self-love. A person who is not excessively self-loving does what he wills and not merely what seems best to him. He follows the real good and not the apparent good, where "apparent" refers to the beliefs that arise

---

[25] See *Rep.* 4.430E4–431A1.
[26] See *Rep.* 4.441A8–B2, where we learn that in childhood development, some develop rational capacity late and some not at all. The late development is apparently equivalent to its relatively weak dominance when it does develop. Hence the need for external control as a substitute for absent or defective self-control.

from affective states and states that occur in sense perception. The contrast is between the idiosyncratic and the universal. Excessive self-love is basically identical with the pathological identification of oneself with the subject of appetites. By contrast, the "right amount" of self-love results in one attending to one's appetites just so much and only insofar as reason determines is good.

But if no one commits an error willingly, why does Plato seem to countenance moral responsibility? We typically say that someone is morally responsible when they should have known better and could have done otherwise, though in a case like Aristotle's drunkard who acts "in ignorance," we could probably aim to divest him of moral responsibility for his propensity to get drunk. But the person who acts out of excessive self-love acts in despite of his manifest awareness of the authority of reason which provides the major premise in the practical syllogisms upon which he acts. He ignores his true self – while recognizing its authority in determining what is good for him – in favor of his ephemeral self whose appetites he habitually longs to satisfy. He believes in the rule of reason and nevertheless acts as if the rule of reason was not authoritative. That is, he acts to satisfy his appetites at the same time as he acknowledges the authority of universalizing reason. There is no possibility of exculpation even if there may be mitigation of responsibility. The one who says, "I really shouldn't be doing this" at the moment he is doing this is hardly in a position to abnegate moral responsibility as opposed to mere liability. He is also in no position to claim ignorance of who his true self really is.

This analysis seems to work better for the acratic than for the vicious person because the acratic acts against his own reason's commitment to the truth of a proposition about that which is good. By contrast, the vicious person's normative reasoning is more or less entirely relativized to what he determines is his own good alone. For this reason, the typology of the deterioration of aristocracy into tyranny and of the aristocratic person into the tyrannical person in *Republic* Books 8 and 9 is especially illuminating. The typology is, of course, not historical or suggestive of a necessary order of devolution. Aristocratic rulers could, presumably, raise democratic sons, not just timocratic ones. But the first crucial step in decline is represented by Plato as a struggle between τὸ λογιστικόν on the one side and τὸ ἐπιθυμητικόν and τὸ θυμοειδές on the other.[27] The moment of decay is when the son of the aristocratic person "hands over rule in himself (τὴν ἐν

---

[27] *Rep.* 8.550B1–7. Cf. *Phdr.* 237D6–9, where τὸ λογιστικόν is "desirous of the best (ἐφιμένη ἀρίστου)"; *Lg.* 9.864B7, cited above in n. 17: περὶ τὸ ἄριστον ἔφεσις.

ἑαυτῷ ἀρχὴν παρέδωκε)" to the middle element (that is, τὸ θυμοειδές). Who exactly is it doing the handing over? I take it that this must be the endowed self, the rational subject, compromised by embodiment, to be sure, but morally responsible for the decision.[28] Once the principle of the rule of reason has been breached, the path of deterioration is not certain, although it is perhaps predictable in particular cases. The ἀρχή of action is the embodied rational self. Moral responsibility cannot be removed from this self unless the power of assent (συγκατάθεσις, in the Stoic terminology) is removed. This is so because belief in a normative universal proposition entails assent to it.[29]

Moral responsibility just means that, because no one does wrong willingly, when wrong is done, it always involves ignorance that what one does is wrong. But this ignorance is culpable because acting to achieve a good for oneself requires a belief in the authority of normative reason at the same time as one is acting in despite of that authority. In effect, what belief in the authority of reason amounts to is a recognition of our real self, whose good reason is tasked with discovering. Obviously, this can be done more or less intentionally or with premeditation. It can be done for all sorts of physical reasons, as we shall see, some of which may be more mitigating than others. It is a mistake, I think, to try to make a strict correlation of rewards and punishments to degrees of moral responsibility as it is *not* a mistake to make compensations commensurate with harm done in tortious behavior. It is enough for Plato that all rational animals are morally responsible for their actions even if they do not do wrong willingly. The political or eschatological bases for scales of punishments and rewards do not necessarily pertain to the principles of ethics.[30] Politics only need require strict liability, not moral responsibility, and religion can offload the delicate question of postincarnate rewards and punishments to the gods and their supposedly unique access to the souls of human beings.

---

[28] See *Rep.* 4.443C9–444A2, where the endowed rational just self – who is also a moderate self-lover – governs himself, and then turns to external action (τὴν ἔξω πρᾶξιν). He is clearly the ἀρχή of action.
[29] The technical Stoic term συγκατάθεσις is used for assent to the contents of a sense perception. Plato says, *Soph.* 263E12–264A2, that in the course of thinking (διάνοια), belief (δόξα) includes, as Cornford 1934, 318–319, n. 3, puts it, "mental acts of assent (φάσις) and dissent (ἀπόφασις)" to "questions which the mind puts to itself." So, I interpret Plato to imply that in the reasoning process leading up to acting, one asks oneself for the relevant universal premise and then, having found it, assents to this. See Kauppinen 2019, 5, "what is distinctive of us as specifically *rational* animals is that we're capable of *responding* to reasons *as* reasons ... not only *reacting* to reasons." Why respond to these reasons if we do not think that they are instrumental in achieving our real good?
[30] I will return to this topic in Chapter 7.

5.1 *The Puzzle of Moral Responsibility*

Because we all desire the Good and because no one does wrong willingly, the presumed two-sided symmetry in "could have done otherwise" might not seem to work. Aristotle complains that it is absurd to hold someone morally responsible *only* for doing what is noble and not for doing what is disgraceful owing to a pursuit of pleasure. I take it that this is implicitly a criticism of Plato's position.[31] On the above analysis, however, the problematic phrase "moral responsibility" can be invoked bilaterally, just as in the Peripatetic position. It is, indeed, not "up to us" that our βούλησις is oriented to the Good. Nor is it up to us that we experience the dispersal of the real self into the ephemeral subjects of embodied desire. But as rational animals, we are able both to make and understand λόγοι, and to adduce them in action. The cognition of form universally, which is what thinking is, is essentially normative. The reason for this, once again, goes back to the Good which provides existence and essence to all the Forms. So, normativity is not just inseparable from our acting, but also from our commitment to its deliverances. If someone cannot give a reason for what they did, they are either dissembling or have not acted at all, as opposed to having moved reflexively. Even if it is a bad reason, indeed, even if it is the wrong reason, the presence of the reason – the normative reason – governs the action. Moral responsibility is either assent to the deliverance of normative reason, as we see occurring in Socrates in *Crito* when he adduces the reasons for not fleeing his prison, or it is dissent from the deliverance of normative reason, at the *same time* as we acknowledge its authority.

Oedipus is a stellar example of someone who acknowledges the authority of normative reason when he assents to a proposition of the form "oracles tell the truth." In his case, that oracle said that he would kill his father and marry his mother. But he tries to flee his fate, which makes no sense. If he had accepted his fate and had not tried to flee, he would have discovered that it is false that oracles tell the truth. Or else, if he had rejected the truth of the proposition about oracles, he would not have left home and he would not have been laid low. Oedipus acts as if the

---

[31] See *EN* Γ1, 1110b9ff; cf. 7, 1114a11ff. See Wolf 1986, 232, for a contemporary response to Aristotle along Platonic lines: "Determination, then, is compatible with an agent's responsibility for a good action, but incompatible with an agent's responsibility for a bad action." Wolf then adds the relevant corrective to the principle of alternative possibilities: "He could have done otherwise if there had been good and sufficient reason." Wolf explains further, 234, "The goal, to put it bluntly, is the True and the Good. The freedom we want is the freedom to find it. But such freedom requires not only that we, as agents, have the right sorts of abilities – the abilities, that is, to direct and govern our actions by our most fundamental selves. It requires as well that the world cooperate in such a way that our most fundamental selves have the opportunity to develop into the selves they ought to be."

proposition about oracles was not true, though he assents to its truth. According to Plato's lights, he did not do wrong willingly, although he is morally responsible for his peculiar brand of irrational behavior.

Oedipus is not vicious. Nor is he obviously acratic. Perhaps we should say that he is just illogical, and that this is his fatal error. But a vicious person, endowed, too, with a rational soul, adheres to a norm. It is, though, a norm that is warped. He "judges badly regarding just and good and beautiful things, thinking that he should honor his self rather than the truth."[32] Plato's exhortation to honor the truth more than one's self does not constitute a blanket condemnation of those who do the opposite. There is evidently room for mitigation and degrees of culpability. But outside of a legal context, are these degrees more than notional? For Plato, it seems enough to insist that rational animals have a rational desire for the Good alone, and that if they do not do what they will – what they *really* will – then they are at least prima facie blameworthy or morally responsible.[33]

If no one does wrong willing, that is because the wrong they do they do not will; they will only what is good for themselves. They could not will what is good for themselves if they did not have the rational ability to distinguish the goods that an embodied soul pursues from the real good, even when these coincide. In pursuing the goods of an embodied soul, they do not divest themselves of the rational ability that enables them to distinguish what seems good from what is actually so. And in appealing to reason to determine the real good, they at the very least have an inkling of whose real good is being sought. This ability is what makes them moral agents. Moral responsibility is the necessary burden of moral agency. Moral agency is a property of all those who participate fully in the Form of Humanity. Moral agency is what generates the normativity in the interstice between endowment and achievement.

---

[32] This phrase recalls *Rep.* 6.505D5–9, where the distinction is made between the Good, on the one hand, and just and beautiful things, on the other. In the case of the former, no one would accept the merely apparent good; in the case of the latter two, most would accept the apparent. Here just, beautiful, and good things are classified together in relation to how they are evaluated by the one who is an "excessive self-lover" and the one who is not. The excessive self-lover, while recognizing that she wants only the real, not apparent good, typically acts as an agent of appetite in pursuit of a merely apparent good that *could not be* the real good because it is part of the spoils in a zero-sum game. If I say, "I only want what is truly good for me" and then I act to attain something that I more or less acknowledge could not be truly good for me, then who else is there to blame? Within the realm of "more or less" are to be found, presumably, degrees of culpability, degrees perhaps too fine for human beings to reliably discriminate.

[33] See Kane 2019, 129–131, on degrees of moral responsibility, with an account of mitigation not unlike that of Plato.

5.2 How Does Embodiment Affect Moral Responsibility?

Plato must have always been aware that some people are not responsible for their behavior owing to madness. But Plato was also keenly aware that madness (μανία) is a plastic term that can be used contentiously or dubiously as exculpating in many situations. We are apt to say that "madness" is used metaphorically for the lover in *Phaedrus* or *Charmides*.[34] On a moment's reflection, however, it is not so clear that there is dividing line between one kind of madness and another in the matter of moral responsibility.

The exculpating words "I couldn't help myself" or, somewhat less suspiciously, "she couldn't help herself," are fraught with ambiguity. First, the counterfactual is obscure and impossible to confirm. How could anyone, including the wrongdoer, ever know what one could have or could not have done in circumstances which are, by definition, strictly nonrepeatable? Second, the circumstances that would make it literally true that someone couldn't help himself pertain to the unique individual. Even if one person couldn't help himself, it certainly doesn't follow that another person couldn't help himself either. The psychologically crushing burden for one person is a mere petty annoyance for another. Third, someone who says, "I couldn't help myself" in those circumstances in which moral responsibility is at issue naturally falls under the suspicion that if he was aware that he was doing wrong, he *could* indeed have helped himself. The plea of a Leontius, who acknowledges that he is doing what he ought not to do while he is doing it, somehow rings hollow. Leontius with his explicit self-disgust is not, at least, a dissembler. For many others, it is all too easy to make "I couldn't help myself" the emblem of exoneration, this despite not merely the absence of evidence but the impossibility of evidence.

In *Timaeus*, we find a passage which more than any other seems to address the explanation for (unwilling) wrongdoing in embodied souls.

> The diseases of the body come about in this way [that is, by disproportion of the elements, 81E–86A], whereas the diseases of the soul that come about through bodily constitution come about in this way. It should be granted that disease of the soul is folly, and that folly is of two kinds: the one is madness and the other is lack of understanding. Therefore, every state that one experiences that produces one of these should be called [psychical]

---

[34] An anonymous reader for Cambridge University Press queries the grounds for claiming that the madness of the lover is metaphorical madness. I would say that it is metaphorical because the loss of control of the lover is, unlike that of the clinically mad, in principle self-curable. The smitten lover, having discovered that his beloved is, in fact, the antithesis of the paragon of beauty and virtue that he imagines, could at least in principle cure himself of his madness.

disease, of which excessive pleasures and pains in the soul should be set down as among the greatest. When a person is experiencing excessive pleasure or excessive pain, in his rushing to seize the one precipitously or to flee the other, he is not able to see or hear rightly; he is in a frenzy and he is then least able to partake of rational calculation.

... when one's soul is made diseased and senseless by the body, it is thought that one is not diseased but that he is willingly bad. But the truth is that unbridledness in sexual matters is a disease of the soul which is for the most part owing to one kind of thing [marrow], which, owing to the porosity of the bones in the body, floods the body and makes it moist. And practically all that which is called incontinence of pleasures and is held to be blameworthy because it is the willing doing of bad things, is not rightly blamed. For no one does wrong willingly; rather, it is owing to some poor bodily habit or crude upbringing that the bad person becomes bad, things that are inimical to everyone and come to them unwillingly.

And in regard to pains, the soul gets much badness from the body in the same way ... [these pains] produce many different types of bad temper and despair, of rashness and cowardice, even of forgetfulness and stupidity.

In addition, when people variously bad live in bad commonwealths where bad discourse occurs both in private and in public, and where no remedial studies are pursued starting from youth, those who are bad become so unwillingly by means of [these] two things. The parents are always to be held responsible for this rather than the offspring, the educators rather than those being educated; nevertheless, one should strive in whatever way possible, to flee what is bad by means of education and fitting studies, and to pursue the opposite.[35]

---

[35] *Tim.* 86B1–87B8: Καὶ τὰ μὲν περὶ τὸ σῶμα νοσήματα ταύτῃ συμβαίνει γιγνόμενα, τὰ δὲ περὶ ψυχὴν διὰ σώματος ἕξιν τῇδε. νόσον μὲν δὴ ψυχῆς ἄνοιαν συγχωρητέον, δύο δ' ἀνοίας γένη, τὸ μὲν μανίαν, τὸ δὲ ἀμαθίαν. πᾶν οὖν ὅτι πάσχων τις πάθος ὁπότερον αὐτῶν ἴσχει, νόσον προσρητέον, ἡδονὰς δὲ καὶ λύπας ὑπερβαλλούσας τῶν νόσων μεγίστας θετέον τῇ ψυχῇ· περιχαρὴς γὰρ ἄνθρωπος ὢν ἢ καὶ τἀναντία ὑπὸ λύπης πάσχων, σπεύδων τὸ μὲν ἑλεῖν ἀκαίρως, τὸ δὲ φυγεῖν, οὔθ' ὁρᾶν οὔτε ἀκούειν ὀρθὸν οὐδὲν δύναται, λυττᾷ δὲ καὶ λογισμοῦ μετασχεῖν ἥκιστα τότε δὴ δυνατός .... καὶ λύπας, νοσοῦσαν καὶ ἄφρονα ἴσχων ὑπὸ τοῦ σώματος τὴν ψυχήν, οὐχ ὡς νοσῶν ἀλλ' ὡς ἑκὼν κακὸς δοξάζεται· τὸ δὲ ἀληθὲς ἡ περὶ τὰ ἀφροδίσια ἀκολασία κατὰ τὸ πολὺ μέρος διὰ τὴν ἑνὸς γένους ἕξιν ὑπὸ μανότητος ὀστῶν ἐν σώματι ῥυώδη καὶ ὑγραίνουσαν νόσος ψυχῆς γέγονεν. καὶ σχεδὸν δὴ πάντα ὁπόσα ἡδονῶν ἀκράτεια καὶ ὄνειδος ὡς ἑκόντων λέγεται τῶν κακῶν, οὐκ ὀρθῶς ὀνειδίζεται· κακὸς μὲν γὰρ ἑκὼν οὐδείς, διὰ δὲ πονηρὰν ἕξιν τινὰ τοῦ σώματος καὶ ἀπαίδευτον τροφὴν ὁ κακὸς γίγνεται κακός, παντὶ δὲ ταῦτα ἐχθρὰ καὶ ἄκοντι προσγίγνεται. καὶ πάλιν δὴ τὸ περὶ τὰς λύπας ἡ ψυχὴ κατὰ ταὐτὰ διὰ σῶμα πολλὴν ἴσχει κακίαν ... παντοδαπὰ νοσήματα ψυχῆς ἐμποιοῦσι μᾶλλον καὶ ἧττον καὶ ἐλάττω καὶ πλείω, πρός τε τοὺς τρεῖς τόπους ἐνεχθέντα τῆς ψυχῆς, πρὸς ὃν ἂν ἕκαστ' αὐτῶν προσπίπτῃ, ποικίλλει μὲν εἴδη δυσκολίας καὶ δυσθυμίας παντοδαπά, ποικίλλει δὲ θρασύτητός τε καὶ δειλίας, ἔτι δὲ λήθης ἅμα καὶ δυσμαθίας. πρὸς δὲ τούτοις, ὅταν οὕτως κακῶς παγέντων πολιτεῖαι κακαὶ καὶ λόγοι κατὰ πόλεις ἰδίᾳ τε καὶ δημοσίᾳ λεχθῶσιν, ἔτι δὲ μαθήματα μηδαμῇ τούτων ἰατικὰ ἐκ νέων μανθάνηται, ταύτῃ κακοὶ πάντες οἱ κακοὶ διὰ δύο ἀκουσιώτατα γιγνόμεθα· ὧν αἰτιατέον μὲν τοὺς φυτεύοντας ἀεὶ τῶν φυτευομένων μᾶλλον καὶ τοὺς τρέφοντας τῶν τρεφομένων, προθυμητέον μήν, ὅπῃ τις δύναται, καὶ διὰ τροφῆς καὶ δι' ἐπιτηδευμάτων μαθημάτων τε φυγεῖν μὲν κακίαν, τοὐναντίον δὲ ἑλεῖν. Cf. *Lg.* 5.734B–C.

5.2 How Does Embodiment Affect Moral Responsibility? 165

There are actually three explanations of wrongdoing in the soul given here. The first is some defect in the body; second, there is living under a bad constitution; third, is bad education. Regarding the bodily defects, they are divided into two, madness (μανία), and ignorance (ἀμαθία). The first pertains to the mortal part of the embodied soul; the second, to the immortal part of that soul. That is, the first is a defect in the appetitive and spirited parts of the soul, the second in the rational faculty.[36] Together, they seem to be the explanation for the claim that no one does wrong willingly, taking this claim as a denial of moral responsibility.[37] That this cannot be the full story is clear from the subsequent passage, in which Plato offers a typology of grades of culpable wrongdoing and the appropriate retributive punishment.[38]

Before we conclude that Plato has changed his mind about moral responsibility from *Republic* and, indeed, what will be said in *Laws*, let us consider what sort of cause moral responsibility assumes.[39] In *Phaedo*, in Socrates' "autobiography" we are given a critique of the sort of causal

---

[36] See *Lg.* 9.863B3–C1, 864B–C.
[37] Taylor 1928, 611–612, assumed that since Plato elsewhere affirms moral responsibility as well as the fact that no one does wrong willingly, the claim here must belong to Timaeus and not to Plato. By contrast, Cornford 1937, 343–349, takes the claim as indicating that *some*, but not all, moral errors are due to bodily constitution. Cornford is followed by Ilievski 2014, 103–106. Saunders 1991, 170, makes the valuable point that the disease of the immortal part of the soul cannot be owing to its own constitution; rather, it is owing to its embodied operation. It seems more difficult to exonerate operation if not dependent on constitution.
[38] See *Tim.* 90E–92C. Gill 2000, 69–70, ignores this passage in arguing for an unqualified interpretation of our passage according to which moral blame is inappropriate because all moral error is owing to the body or other external factors. The punishment for sexual wrongdoing in the male is reincarnation as a female (90E6–91A1). The wrongdoing consists in being "unpersuadable and self-willed like a creature disobedient to reason (ἀπειθές τε καὶ αὐτοκρατὲς γεγονός, οἷον ζῷον ἀνυπήκοον τοῦ λόγου)." Clearly, the rapist is not disobedient to nonnormative reasoning, but to normative reasoning, for which he is held to be morally blameworthy. By contrast, the account of the reincarnation of humans as birds, mammals, and fish does not indicate moral responsibility at all, but rather stupidity. Even in the case of those who had souls "impure from every kind of disorder (ὑπὸ πλημμελείας πάσης ἀκαθάρτως ἐχόντων, 92B3–4)" and who are reincarnated as fish, it is not clear that they are being held to be morally responsible for these disorders. See Carone 2005b, 60–62, who argues that bodily impediments are not completely exculpating. Campbell 2022, 124–126, follows Gill, arguing the first line of the passage should be translated "the diseases of the soul come about through the body in the following way." On this construal, there is no qualification. That is, all diseases of the soul come about through the body. Campbell does not address the seemingly inevitable abnegation of moral responsibility that this construal implies, although he recognizes that philosophy is somehow the antidote to vice.
[39] Cf. *Lg.* 10.896D5–8: Ἆρ'οὖν τὸ μετὰ τοῦτο ὁμολογεῖν ἀναγκαῖον τῶν τε ἀγαθῶν αἰτίαν εἶναι ψυχὴν καὶ τῶν κακῶν καὶ καλῶν καὶ αἰσχρῶν δικαίων τε καὶ ἀδίκων καὶ πάντων τῶν ἐναντίων, εἴπερ τῶν πάντων γε αὐτὴν θήσομεν αἰτίαν; (and shouldn't the next thing we agree on be, if we are going to posit soul as the cause of all things, that the soul is the cause of bad and good things, of beautiful and ugly ones, of just and unjust ones, and all such contraries?). Also, 10.904C6–7: Μεταβάλλει μὲν τοίνυν πάνθ' ὅσα μέτοχά ἐστι ψυχῆς, ἐν ἑαυτοῖς κεκτημένα τὴν τῆς μεταβολῆς αἰτίαν ... (So, then all things that have soul change, the explanation for their change they possess themselves).

explanations that Anaxagoras and others provide and the Platonic alternative.⁴⁰ Broadly speaking, Anaxagoras wants to give exclusively naturalistic explanations for things. The principal defect in such explanations is that they serve equally to explain contrary states of affairs or facts or things. Thus, the naturalistic or physicalistic explanation for Socrates sitting in prison, namely, that his body is disposed in a certain way, does not even begin to give the real explanation for his doing so, which is that he thinks it is the right thing to do. Similarly, the cardinality of a group of items should not be explained in terms of the material out of which they are composed but rather that they participate in the relevant Form. In fact, the sorts of explanations proposed by Anaxagoras can only provide necessary conditions for the operation of the true cause.⁴¹

In *Timaeus*, these necessary conditions are called "auxiliary causes (συναίτιαι)."⁴² Are we now to suppose that what in other contexts are merely conditions for the operation of the true cause are, in the case of moral disease, actually the true causes and not auxiliary causes? A passage earlier in the dialogue suggests strongly that we are not. Regarding the task the Demiurge set for the subordinate gods,

> He gave them the task of ruling and giving guidance to the mortal living being as far as possible as to what is beautiful and best so that they [i.e., the gods] not be responsible for any evils that it might bring upon itself.⁴³

This passage seems to separate clearly moral responsibility from the sense in which the gods contribute to human life by their creation of mortal bodies.

---

⁴⁰ See *Phd.* 95A4–102A9; *Phil.* 59A–B. See Gerson 2019, ch. 3, §2 for an extended analysis of the *Phaedo* passage.

⁴¹ See *Phd.* 99B3–4: ἐκεῖνο ἄνευ οὗ τὸ αἴτιον οὐκ ἄν ποτ' εἴη αἴτιον (that without which the explanation would not be an explanation).

⁴² See *Tim.* 46C7, D1, 76D6. At 46E3–6, Plato distinguishes between "two kinds of αἰτίαι," one which operates with νοῦς and one which does not. Cf. 68E4–7. The latter is identified with Necessity (ἀνάγκη). It is the "wandering cause (πλανωμένη αἰτία)" (47E3–48B2). See Johansen 2020, 109, on συναίτιαι as not merely conditions but also as instruments of the Demiurge. In the case of our embodiment by the subordinate gods, the body is the instrument required for the existence of the mortal animal called ἄνθρωπος. See Jorgenson 2021, 268.

⁴³ *Tim.* 41E1–4: ἄρχειν, καὶ κατὰ δύναμιν ὅτι κάλλιστα καὶ ἄριστα τὸ θνητὸν διακυβερνᾶν ζῷον, ὅτι μὴ κακῶν αὐτὸ ἑαυτῷ γίγνοιτο αἴτιον. I take it that this passage invites us to refer to *Rep.* 6.505E1–2, where every soul is said to "divine (ἀπομαντευομένη)" that the Good is "something (τι)." This permanent endowment in rational creatures along with embodiment as capable of providing only the necessary conditions for wrongdoing, ensures that moral responsibility cannot be altogether extinguished for anyone but the truly mad. We know, albeit vaguely, that the Good is "something." This knowledge "rescues" us from exoneration for wrongdoing on the basis of the impediments of embodiment. We are aware, albeit vaguely, that the true Good that we will is not alien to us even in our embodiment. Acting as if embodiment did this, we invite blame to at least *some* degree. See Renaut 2019, 79–81.

If a bad bodily constitution is really the cause for wrongdoing of, say, a sexual nature, why are the gods not to blame for this? Why didn't they prevent suppurating bone marrow from saturating the body? On the other hand, what would it mean to hold that the bodily condition is only an auxiliary cause of wrongdoing? What is the real cause?

If a certain bodily condition is a necessary condition for "unbridledness in sexual matters," it cannot be a sufficient condition; otherwise, there would be no difference between continence and incontinence in terms of moral responsibility. Continence and incontinence would be like having a normal temperature and having a fever. The real distinction between continence and incontinence fixes the further distinction between vice and virtue. The hierarchy – virtue, continence, incontinence, vice – presumes the possibility of moral responsibility if the bodily can be only an auxiliary cause and not the true cause of wrongdoing.

I suggest that we combine the notion of culpable ignorance with the bodily (and broadly speaking, cultural) necessary conditions for wrongdoing.[44] Thus, people can be more or less culpably ignorant of their own nature in their behavior owing to the bodily conditions which constitute their physical endowment and the social world within which they are raised. Every rational animal is able to control the ephemeral subjects of appetitive and emotional actions that it becomes owing to embodiment.[45] Moral responsibility is thus inseparable from the human

---

[44] At *Tim.* 87B4, the word αἰτιατέον, which I translate as "to be held responsible," should not be understood to mean "morally responsible" for the obvious reason that the parents, too, could then pass the blame onto their parents, ad infinitum. Within the context of this dialogue, it seems rather more likely that the upbringing provided by the parents and the *polis* is in reality more of an "auxiliary cause" of the moral responsibility of the wrongdoer. Cf. 44B8–C4, where one is held to account for neglecting (καταμελήσας) his own nurturing (τροφή). See Meyer 2014, 60–61. So, at 92B7, ignorance (ἀμαθία) is punished through reincarnation as a fish.

[45] The debate in recent scholarship regarding the question of whether the "parts" of the soul are subjects or not, exemplified for example in Price 1995; Bobonich 2002; Lorenz 2006, rests, I believe, on a false dichotomy which takes the only alternatives to be multiple *homunculi* or a unified subject variously operating with different cognitive, affective, and appetitive modalities. Price 2009, 10, reflecting on this debate, takes the central problem to be "co-consciousness," that is, how two putatively different selves are unified. The dichotomy and Price's characterization of it do not take into consideration that Plato has quite a bit to say about how two things can yet be one. In particular, he thinks, for example, that the Form of Beauty and Helen's beauty are one and yet asymmetrically different insofar as the latter is an image of the former. Helen's beauty is a manifestation of the Form of Beauty. Analogously, we might say, the subject of an appetite is a manifestation of the real self, clearly evident only upon separation from the body. Being the subject of an appetite is a sort of "role" that the real self takes on owing to embodiment. Our recognition of this as a role can be indexed to our acknowledgment of the authority of reason in action. The more clearly we acknowledge this, the fewer grounds we have for claiming that the body is the locus of our true self.

endowment. But moral responsibility can be diminished by physical exigencies.[46]

Let us return to the division between madness (μανία) and ignorance (ἀμαθία), the first pertaining to the mortal part of the soul and the second to the immortal part. Consider madness first. If someone who is mad in the way the passage envisions does wrong, he does so unwillingly. But this is also the case if there is nothing wrong with his marrow or if there is just a little excess of it since everyone does wrong unwillingly. What is the difference? Presumably, there is a gradation of possibilities, ranging from unbridledness (ἀκολασία) to incontinence (ἀκρασία) to continence (ἐγκράτεια) to the virtuous person who has no need to resist a nonexistent desire to do what is in fact wrong. One possible suggestion is that Plato has begun to see that his insistence on the claim that no one does wrong willingly makes the distinction between unbridledness and incontinence nugatory, which in turn makes the distinction between continence and virtue similarly nugatory. This is essentially the Stoic position. I am more inclined to the view that while this may pertain to those who practice or fail to practice popular or political virtue, it does not pertain to (successful) philosophers.

A quite different approach to this problem is suggested by the passage following our main passage in which Plato has Timaeus exhort people to exercise the "principal form of our soul (τοῦ κυριωτάτου παρ' ἡμῖν ψυχῆς εἴδους)" on behalf of living the best life.[47] If this part is properly exercised by doing philosophy, a person will "partake of immortality as much as is possible for human nature (καθ' ὅσον δ' αὖ μετασχεῖν ἀνθρωπίνῃ φύσει ἀθανασίας ἐνδέχεται)."[48] The significance of the curious phrasing is easy to miss. Plato believes that we have immortal souls. If this is so, what is the point of the qualification "as much as is possible for human nature?" The point is, as Plato insists elsewhere, that human beings are *not* immortal, although souls or rational souls or intellects are. Fortunately for us, we are really or primarily souls and not human beings, that is, composites of soul and body.[49] When Plato speaks about the "diseases" of the soul, he is perhaps not speaking about the immortal soul; rather, he is referring to the soul of the soul–body complex. The reason for thinking this is that a "disease" tends to destroy, whereas we learn from *Republic* that the immortal soul has no proper source of deterioration. That is why it is

---

[46] See *Lg.* 9.881A–B. Jorgenson 2021 thinks that embodiment *always* diminishes moral responsibility.
[47] *Tim.* 90A2–4.   [48] *Tim.* 90C2–3.   [49] See *Phdr.* 246C4–6.

5.2 How Does Embodiment Affect Moral Responsibility? 169

immortal.⁵⁰ So, the diseases of the soul, especially madness, are diseases on the psychical "side" of the soul–body complex, including the discursive reasoning that is impossible without a body.

As we have seen, however, the subject of appetites and emotions is not nonrational; it is a rational subject capable of conceptualizing a goal and planning how to achieve it. So, it would seem that the immortal part of the soul when embodied is not properly conceived of as being separated from the subjects of appetite and emotion. It is implicated in all human action. However, as we have seen, when one reasons, one makes appeal to the normative authority of rationality. The diseases of the soul which led one to do wrong unwillingly belong to the ensouled person. As much as is possible, one should strive to separate oneself from that and identify with the immortal subject. I think blameworthiness is meant by Plato to attach to a person who recognizes her true identity with the immortal subject and at the same time identifies with the subject of the appetites and emotions.⁵¹ To try to explain this blameworthiness according to the false dichotomy of Socratic intellectualism versus Platonic irrationalism is unhelpful. The blameworthiness is to be put at the doorstep of the embodied rational soul.⁵² This is a divided self, which is always the ἀρχή of action. Even though no one does wrong willingly, we can willingly act to achieve apparent goods at the same time as we acknowledge, implicitly or not, that they are not identical with the Good or instances of it.

Consider again the person in *Republic* Book 10 who is virtuous by habit "without philosophy."⁵³ Having realized his grievous error, he blames chance or daemons for his choice, anything "besides himself (ἀνθ' ἑαυτοῦ)." Presumably, we are supposed to think that he does this mistakenly; he himself is morally responsible for his bad choice. We cannot forget that he is a virtuous person, albeit not philosophically virtuous.

---

⁵⁰ *Rep.* 10.608E–611A. The argument is that the soul cannot be destroyed by an "external" evil, namely, the evils of the body. It could only conceivably be destroyed by its own evil. But its own evil is injustice and injustice does not destroy the soul, but only makes it apt for punishment, indeed, even everlasting punishment.

⁵¹ Proclus, *In Alc. I* 106.16–17 Segonds, puts the point succinctly and with precision: διὰ γὰρ τὴν πρὸς τὸ σῶμα ῥοπὴν καὶ τὸ αὑτῆς ἀγαθὸν κρίνει σωματικῶς (because of his [i.e., the one fallen into corruption] inclination to the body or because he judges his own good according to a bodily criterion). As Proclus goes on to explain, judging in this way means searching for one's own good among things that are alien to one's true self.

⁵² See Wolt 2019, 261–267, who distinguishes, rightly in my view, between the responsibility of the composite and the blamelessness of the intellectual soul. Wolt also suggests that the involuntariness of wrongdoing indicates that all punishments be tortious or meted out for the purpose of rehabilitation or the common good, meaning that moral responsibility is not a useful legal concept. Even if this is true for secular punishments, it can hardly be true for a putative afterlife.

⁵³ *Rep.* 10.619C8.

He could not have behaved virtuously in his embodied life if he did not have the ability to refrain from choosing to satisfy whatever desire he thought would be satisfied by living the life of a tyrant. Even a bodily constitution that provided the condition for his fecklessness would not be the cause or explanation for his choice. This is so because living the virtuous life he lived meant continually acknowledging the authority of reason in determining his own good.

Plato's adherence to the principle that no one does wrong willingly at the same time as he insists on the reality of moral responsibility – no matter whether it is attenuated or not – reveals the centrality of integrative unity to his moral realism. The awareness by someone that he is acting according to a desire that is opposed to his desire to instantiate the Good is, as in the obvious case of Leontius, the occasion for guilt. More generally, the awareness in oneself of the mere possibility of such acting, say, the temptation that is resisted, is constitutive of what is a moral agent or, in contemporary terms, a person.[54] Integrative unity is precisely what the remedy for guilt or the prophylactic for temptation is. The attainment of integrative unity, to the extent that that is possible for embodied human beings, is the release from what inhibits freedom. All of the above would be an arbitrary or fictional construct unless the inflexible standard of integrative unity were real. This standard, however, is not correctly conceived of if it is even intelligible to ask whether adherence to it is optional or desirable, that is, whether it is the Good that we will. To reject the standard while recognizing that what we will is the real good amounts to eschewing the only possible nonarbitrary standard for adjudicating among goods when they are in conflict. This is just as true for someone who embraces altruism as the standard as it is for someone who embraces egotism.

---

[54] See Frankfurt 1971.

CHAPTER 6

Philebus *and* Statesman

6.1 Moral Realism in the Later Dialogues

Plato's *Philebus* provides a crucial test case for the thesis that the criterion of integrative unity is at the heart of Plato's ethics. As difficult as is the argument of this dialogue and as contentious as its interpretation may be, its basic structure is passably clear.[1] The question that motivates the entire discussion is what is the good for human beings. Philebus maintains that the good for human beings is, broadly speaking, pleasure; Socrates and his companions maintain that the good for human beings lies in intellectual activity, again, broadly speaking.[2] As Socrates clarifies the matter a few lines later, both contestants are referring to a possession (ἕξις) or condition (διάθεσις) of the soul that is supposed to produce happiness (εὐδαιμονία).[3]

---

[1] See especially Hampton 1990, who demonstrates the unity of the dialogue by connecting its announced topic – the best life for a human being – and the ontological, methodological, and epistemological passages. Shorey 1888, 275–289, is a sustained attack on scholars, especially R. D. Archer-Hind and Henry Jackson, who suppose that metaphysics is the essential foundation for Plato's ethical writings, including *Philebus*. I have been arguing throughout this book that Shorey's approach has no more credibility than does the "metaphysics-free" approach to "Socratic" ethics in recent times.

[2] *Phil.* 11B4: Φίληβος μὲν τοίνυν ἀγαθὸν εἶναί τὸ χαίρειν πᾶσι ζῴοις (Philebus says that enjoyment, etc. is the good for all living things). In fact, the discussion will be limited to the good for human beings. This is not a trivial point since, as we have seen, we are not primarily human beings, but souls. The justification for taking ἀγαθόν without the definite article as "the good" rather than as "good" is, first, that "pleasure is good" is a trivial claim that almost no one denies and second, at 60A9 where the thesis is repeated and "the good (τἀγαθόν)" is supplied. Cf. also 13B7, 14B4, 20B8, 22C1–2, and 66D7–8. Also, see Shorey 1908, 343. Rudebusch 2020 disputes this on textual and grammatical grounds, though in my opinion unsuccessfully. He rightly points out that the use of comparatives and superlative adjectives for good (ἀμείνω, λῴω, ὠφελιμώτατον, 11B9–C2) need to be accounted for if we are to understand the hedonist's thesis as "pleasure is the good" and the antihedonist's thesis as "higher cognition is the good." My view is that the comparatives indicate the relative proximity of instantiations of the Good according to the metric of integrated unity according to kind. As the argument progresses, τὸ χαίρειν ("enjoyment") and τὸ φρονεῖν ("thinking") or νοῦς ("intellect") will generally serve as stand-ins for the array of affective and cognitive states here being considered. The question in *Philebus* evidently refers to the two basic views of the Good in *Republic* 6.505C5–6.

[3] *Phil.* 11D4–6. The word παρέχειν (produce) is ambiguous. It can indicate either the cause of which happiness is the effect or the constitutive identity of the possession or condition, that is, it is the kind

It will turn out – and not with a great many complications – that a life of either pleasure or intellectual activity alone will be inferior in its happiness-making capability to a "mixed" life containing both.[4] But as we eventually learn, not just any mixture will do. In order to produce the best life for a human being, the mixture (κρᾶσις) must not be a mere jumble (συμφόρησις); it will have to have measure (μέτρος) and symmetry (συμμετρία).[5] It is clear, I think, that the bulk of the dialogue is concerned with mixtures generally, and mixtures of pleasurable and intellectual states in a human life in particular, with a goal of determining the best possible one. In addition, the criterion according to which it will be possible to determine the best life is identical to the criterion according to which lives can be graded as better or worse.

Needless to say, Plato's passage from the posing of the initial question to its answer at the end of the dialogue raises numerous difficulties for the interpreter, but none so difficult, I believe, as Plato's assumption that there is a right answer to the question he poses. I assume that neither a life with no intellectual activity nor a life with no pleasure could be seriously embraced by anyone. Beyond that, the number of possible "mixtures" that people do endorse seem to be practically infinite. The challenge for Plato is to show the regulatory role of the Idea of the Good in determining the best life for a human being. As I have already argued, this task is only made intelligible, indeed, possible, if the Good is the One and proximity to the Good is understood as integrative unity according to kind. Thus, it must be shown that there is an optimal mixture comprised of the perfect integration of parts in the life of a human being.

From one perspective, it is hardly controversial to assert that Plato thinks that there must be an optimal mixture. He frequently urges the existence of a science (ἐπιστήμη) or craft (τέχνη) of good and evil which is the science or craft of how to achieve happiness.[6] But it is not so clear in what sense, if any, it aims to identify principles of integrative unity.

6.2 Integrative Unity and the Good Life

The theme of unity or oneness is introduced immediately after the formulation of the question that governs the entire dialogue. The determination of whether the best life is one of pleasure or intellectual activity runs up

---

of possession or condition which consists in being in a happy state. As we shall see, the resolution of this ambiguity is of some importance.

[4] See *Phil.* 11D11–E3, 20B7–9, 22A1–6.   [5] See *Phil.* 64E9–D3.
[6] See for example, *Charm.* 174B12–C3; *Gorg.* 472C6–D1.

6.2 Integrative Unity and the Good Life

against the problem of whether pleasures are sufficiently diverse so that no coherent conclusion could possibly be reached.[7] For if pleasure is good, and pleasure has a generic unity, then all pleasures are good. That is, there can be no bad pleasures. The identical difficulty attaches to Socrates' claim for the superiority of intellectual activity.[8] Thus, if all intellectual activities were good just insofar as they were intellectual activities, it would then not be possible to say that any intellectual activity was bad, that is, bad for oneself. For example, if a life were largely spent in the memorization of train schedules, and if memorization is good, then we are in no position to say that the activity of memorizing such trivia is bad.

Note that we have here another version of the Moorean problem. Both the hedonist and the intellectualist argue that their favored states – pleasure or thinking – are good. But even if it is true that these states are generically good, it does not follow that the Good we all seek is manifested in either or both in some combination or other. One who holds that pleasure is of course good just because it is pleasurable is stating a tautology masquerading as an ethical theory.[9] Another way of making the identical distinction is to point out that even if all pleasures are good, where "good" means that people desire to be in certain states, it does not follow that being in these states is desirable. Whether these states are desirable or not cannot be determined by a claim that they have a generic unity expressed by "good." If one replies that "desirable" means nothing other than "desired," then there is no basis for *any* ethical theory, including hedonism. Plato does in fact address this claim, as we shall see, but for now he assumes that his interlocutor is prepared to defend his own ethical theory as something other than a tautology.

The problem of the generic unity of pleasures or intellectual activities provides the entree to the metaphysical substructure needed before the original question can be answered. Socrates poses this as the problem of "the one and many (τὸ ἓν καὶ πολλά)."[10] He dismisses the sophistic version of the problem according to which there is a puzzle about how one thing can have many contraries such as tall and short, heavy and light, and the other sophistic version according to which it is puzzling how one individual can have many parts. Socrates dismisses these to concentrate on the

---

[7] See *Phil.* 12B–13D.   [8] See *Phil.* 14B1–7.
[9] I am supposing that the reader is meant to realize that such a claim puts one in company with the "many" of *Protagoras*, whose view entails the impossibility of *akrasia*, and also with Callicles in *Gorgias*, who wants to identify the good with pleasure.
[10] See *Phil.* 14D4–E4.

real one-and-many puzzle. This is the set of problems concerning "ones (μονάδες)" like "human being," "ox," "the beautiful, " and "the good." The problems are:

> First, should we suppose that such ones truly exist? Next, if they do exist, how should we suppose that each, while being one and neither susceptible to generation nor destruction, remains most securely the one that it is? After this, should we hypothesize that it [any one] is either dispersed among the infinity of things that become and thereby becomes many, or remains whole separate from itself, which of all things seems to be the most impossible, an identical thing which simultaneously comes to be in one and in many things.[11]

This famous and portentous passage has received considerable scholarly attention.[12] In particular, does this passage pose two questions or three? Delcomminette makes a strong case for there being three questions, all on grammatical grounds and concerning the important correspondence between this passage, assuming that there are three questions, and the three stages of dialectic described on the next page.[13] The three questions are: (1) Do Forms exist? (2) How can a Form, while being one, be divided definitionally in dialectic?[14] (3) How is the one Form to be multiply participated in while remaining one?

All three questions are obviously meant to recall the discussions in *Parmenides* and *Sophist*. The question of the existence of Forms is posed by Parmenides to the young Socrates.[15] The question of the unity of the Form underlies the very possibility of dialectic which seems to presuppose a *division* of Forms into their species.[16] And the question of participation is,

---

[11] *Phil.* 15B1–8: Πρῶτον μὲν εἴ τινας δεῖ τοιαύτας εἶναι μονάδας ὑπολαμβάνειν ἀληθῶς οὔσας· εἶτα πῶς αὖ ταύτας, μίαν ἑκάστην οὖσαν ἀεὶ τὴν αὐτὴν καὶ μήτε γένεσιν μήτε ὄλεθρον προσδεχομένην, ὅμως εἶναι βεβαιότατα μίαν ταύτην; μετὰ δὲ τοῦτ' ἐν τοῖς γιγνομένοις αὖ καὶ ἀπείροις εἴτε διεσπασμένην καὶ πολλὰ γεγονυῖαν θετέον, εἴθ' ὅλην αὐτὴν αὐτῆς χωρίς, ὃ δὴ πάντων ἀδυνατώτατον φαίνοιτ' ἄν, ταὐτὸν καὶ ἓν ἅμα ἐν ἑνί τε καὶ πολλοῖς γίγνεσθαι. Cf. *Soph.* 251A5–C7 on the various problems of the one and the many.
[12] See Delcomminette 2006, ch. 2, especially 56, for references to the literature.
[13] See Delcomminette 2006, 60–74, on the division into three questions. The three parts of dialectic: 1. 16C10–D2; 2. 16D3–7; 3. 16D7–E2 seem to correspond to three questions. Also, Hampton 1990, 16–21.
[14] We may recall that the absolute simplicity and uniqueness of the Good/One entails that any "one" Form cannot be absolutely one. That is, it has internal complexity. So, the problem is really how a "monad" can be one but not absolutely one.
[15] See *Parm.* 130B1–5. The use of the term "separate (χωρίς)" for the Forms and their participants is intended to heighten the problem of how a "one," while remaining one, can be "shared"; cf. 131A8–9.
[16] This is true in all the dialogues containing divisions, namely, *Phaedrus, Sophist, Statesman,* and *Philebus*. See especially *Phdr.* 266B3–7. At 16C2–3, Socrates says that dialectic is the source of every discovery of τέχνη. As *Gorg.* 506D7 explains, τέχνη requires the application of measure to produce integrated unities. This is why rhetoric is not a τέχνη; it is a mere knack (τριβή).

again, front and center in *Parmenides*.[17] What we learn from the logical exercise of the second part of *Parmenides* is that "one" is equivocal. When applied to a Form, the Form's oneness entails that it is not absolutely one.[18] The reason for this is that the existence of the Form and its essence or nature must be distinct.[19] If this were not the case, then the Form could not *have* an οὐσία. Nor could it just be an οὐσία if it is to be also an existent. Thus, participation in the οὐσία that the Form has, for example, Beauty or Justice, neither threatens the oneness of the Form nor its separation. Participation in the οὐσία of the Form entails that the participant has, in some way, the nature that the Form's name names; it does not entail that the participant has the properties of the Form qua eternal and immutable entity.[20]

All of this is particularly relevant to our main theme, which is the Good as the first principle of ethics. The Good is above οὐσία, and as Aristotle reports, is identical to the One.[21] If this is so, then the One that the Good is, is uniquely one or incomposite. Indeed, it cannot even be said to be one or to exist, where "exist" is taken to indicate something distinct from the kind of thing it is such that, for example, we can say, "*that* exists." Most important, though, is that on this view, something attains the Good, that is, instantiates the Good, by being one, an integrative unity. But for something to be one, it has to be one kind of thing; only the One or Good is not a kind. So, integrative unity is according to kind. It is not yet clear, though, how this relates to the question of the best life for a human being or the best mixture of pleasure and intellectual activity.

The transition to the solution is prompted by Protarchus, who challenges Socrates to describe a method whereby the problems of the one and many can be resolved.[22] The method – a gift of the gods – tells us that

---

[17] See *Parm.* 130E5ff.   [18] See *Parm.* 142B5–C2.
[19] See *Parm.* 142D1–5. For any "one" that has being, that one and its οὐσία cannot be identical.
[20] See Aristotle, *Meta.* A 9, 990b27–34, where Aristotle assumes that the distinction between a Form and its nature contradicts its oneness. So, if something is double by participating in the Form of Doubleness, the participant's doubleness must be eternal, as is the Doubleness of the Form. But a double here below is not eternal. So, it is not the case that something is double by participating in an eternal Form of Doubleness. It is clear enough, I think, that Plato believes that by distinguishing the Form from the nature that the Form's name names, he can avoid such objections. By contrast, Aristotle believes that he cannot; if the Form is a "one over many," then it does not possess the internal complexity that is required to avoid his objection. I believe the core dispute is whether or not absolute simplicity is found in primary οὐσία (Λ 7, 1072a31–32), as Aristotle holds, or whether absolute simplicity is found only in that which is "beyond οὐσία," as Plato holds. If the latter is the case, then it follows necessarily that the simplicity of everything else, including Forms, is qualified, principally by an internal real distinction between existence and essence.
[21] See above Chapter 2, §2.6.   [22] See *Phil.* 16A4–B3.

All things that are ever said to be are composed of one and many and also have by nature limit and unlimitedness in themselves.[23]

Two distinct but crucially related points are made here. The first is that the problems of one and many, both sophistical and real, arise from the fact that everything is, minimally, one in one way, and many in another. Nothing is unqualifiedly one (and not many) or unqualifiedly many (and not one). But in addition, everything has within it limit (πέρας) and unlimitedness (ἀπειρία). As is subsequently made abundantly clear, the connection between one and many, on the one hand, and unlimitedness and limit on the other is this.[24] The imposition of the principle of limit on the unlimited produces something with an οὐσία, something that is both one and many.[25] Leaving aside the multifarious ways in which both in reality and in language something can be one and many, it is enough for now simply to acknowledge that, as *Parmenides* has argued, whatever participates in οὐσία is one and many.[26]

Socrates' fourfold description of all things that now exist in the universe yields the unlimited, limit, the mixture (μεικτόν) of the two, and the cause (αἰτία) of the mixture.[27] It is not nearly so difficult as is sometimes thought to determine where Forms fit in this schema in the light of the previous paragraph.[28] It is the οὐσία that the Form's name names that provides limit to the unlimited, the result of which is the mixture.[29] The separate Form, apart from its οὐσία, is not itself the limit. Whereas the Forms are "ones,"

---

[23] *Phil.* 16C9–10: ὡς ἐξ ἑνὸς μὲν καὶ πολλῶν ὄντων τῶν ἀεὶ λεγομένων εἶναι, πέρας δὲ καὶ ἀπειρίαν ἐν αὑτοῖς σύμφυτον ἐχόντων. The placing of ἀεὶ in the line makes the reference ambiguous: Is it referring to eternal things, that is, to Forms, or to sensibles, or to both? Based on Aristotle's testimony, it will have to be both, but there is nothing against taking it, as does Delcomminette 2006, 99–100, as referring to expressions (τῶν λεγομένων) prior to ontological grading. At the beginning of dialectic, all the general terms in λόγοι are complex and will eventually need to be collected and divided in the correct manner. A general term will be collected from particular instances and so will have a "many" in it. But it will also have a "one" as a distinct general term.
[24] See *Phil.* 24A1–25B3.
[25] See *Phil.* 26D7–9, 27B8–9. The γένεσις εἰς οὐσίαν is the becoming of something with the being of sensibles. This is the mixture, that is, γεγενημένην οὐσίαν. The perfect being of intelligibles is a different kind of οὐσία. See *Phd.* 79A6: δύο εἴδη τῶν ὄντων. Limit and the unlimited are principles of being, analogous to the way that form, matter, and privation are principles of change for Aristotle.
[26] See *Parm.* 142B5–6, 143A5–6. See Delcomminette 2006, 245.
[27] See *Phil.* 23C4–D8. At 23C9–10, the words "in the universe (ἐν τῷ παντί)" perhaps refer to the sensible universe, thereby excluding Forms. But this is not clear. Cf. 29B10, C2, D2, D6, 30C3.
[28] See Delcomminette 2006, 212–214, for references to the literature and what is in my view essentially the right interpretation.
[29] This is the reason why the first principle must be beyond οὐσία, that is, because it must not be a limit as opposed to being the principle of limit. If it were a limit, it would be limited and so neither absolutely simple nor apt for explanatory ultimacy. At *Rep.* 6.504C1–4, it is implied that the Idea of the Good is the principle of measure (μέτρον). It is not measure itself – for example, in the way that one is a measure of number – but that which causes there to be measures, that is, the Forms. When at

the natures or οὐσίαι of Forms are not.³⁰ Things attain to unity or become things with natures via οὐσία, whose own oneness is just that of the Forms.³¹ Its "manyness" is that of all the participants in the Form. The natures of Forms are neither one nor many. When that nature is cognized, it is cognized universally, neither as one nor as many. Such oneness as the nature has in cognition is just the oneness of the cognitive act.³²

The governing question of *Philebus* is, given that some form of a life mixed with pleasure and intellectual activity is better than a life bereft of either, which "factor" in the best life ought to dominate. That is, what sort of unity is best.³³ Socrates contends that because the cause of the mixture of limit and unlimited in the universe is νοῦς, the element in the mixture of the good life – intellectual activity – is closer to the cause than pleasure, which is itself unlimited.³⁴ Most pertinent to the present investigation is that νοῦς, the cause, is the Demiurge of *Timaeus*, who is good precisely because of his proximity to the first principle of all.³⁵ A human life is good

---

Phil. 66A6–8 the best possession (κτῆμα) is said to be "somewhere (πῇ) in the region of" μέτρον, that is, the μέτριον (measured) and καίριον (appropriate), this is not a reference to the Good but to what is closest to it. The words "in the region of" are an expansion of the one word πῇ ("somewhere" or "somehow"), suggesting that Socrates is not talking about the Good which is uniquely and precisely "located" "above" οὐσία.

³⁰ See *Phil.* 26D4–5: Καὶ μὴν τό γε πέρας [οὔτε] <ὅτε> πολλὰ εἶχεν, οὔτ' ἐδυσκολαίνομεν ὡς οὐκ ἦν ἓν φύσει (and again, when the limit [turned out] to contain a many, we did not complain that it was not one by nature). To imply that the οὐσία is both one and many is equivalent to saying that it in itself is neither one nor many. I am here following the text of Apelt. It is important that the nature of a Form, its οὐσία, be neither one nor many. If this were not the case, the thinking about this nature would mean either being an example of it ("I am an elephant because I am thinking of an elephant") or else it would mean that what I am thinking about is not the nature but only a representation of it. The latter possibility is now the standard one, but it is not Plato's burden to explain how putative cognitional representations can possibly represent anything.

³¹ More precisely, as we learn from *Soph.* 244B–245E, the Forms belong to τὸ παντελῶς ὄν, which is one whole or many consisting of all the "monads" that are Forms. This follows immediately from the fact that the Good/One above Being is uniquely simple. The oneness or integrated unity of Being is indicated by the internal relatedness of all the "parts" of intelligible reality. *This* sort of oneness is not what participants in Forms have. See Gerson 2020, 135–147, for further details.

³² See *Rep.* 7.537C7: ὁ συνοπτικὸς διαλεκτικός (the dialectician is the one with a synoptic vision). That is, the dialectician aims to see intelligible reality as a complex unity. This complex unity is what the Good/One is virtually.

³³ See *Phil.* 22D7, which makes the criterion αἱρετὸς ἅμα καὶ ἀγαθός (simultaneously desirable and good). See Moore 2015, 214–215, who connects integrated unity and self-knowledge in *Philebus*.

³⁴ See *Phil.* 31A7–10, 54C6, D1. At 24A1–B2, hotter and colder, always admitting of more and less, are the example of intrinsic unlimitedness. The unlimitedness of pleasure must be distinguished from the nature that the Form's name names, which is neither one nor many. Because it is a nature, it is not unlimited. This would, of course, also be true for the nature of a Form of Pleasure. It is not true for the πάθος of pleasure in a human being, where unlimitedness is indicated in terms of intensity or magnitude. See 45D2–5. Pleasures that are able to be limited are mixed, not purely unlimited. See Delcomminette 2006, 498.

³⁵ See *Tim.* 29E1–3.

to the extent that its status as a one and many is dominated by intellect. The oneness comes from limit imposed on unlimitedness. So, we can grade lives according to their proximity to the first principle of all. In fact, this is the only way to determine the best life.

The cause of the mixture, νοῦς, always operates to produce the best possible mixture. A normatively neutral limit (πέρας) becomes good or measured (μέτριον) when it is produced or corrected by νοῦς. It is the dominance of the principle of unlimitedness – or what amounts to the same thing, the absence of νοῦς – that makes possible a deviation from the best.[36] It is clear from the text that νοῦς is the cause of mixtures that are necessarily good just because νοῦς causes them. And this is so because νοῦς is itself good, but not the Idea of the Good itself.[37] The Idea of the Good is the lynchpin of the entire theoretical framework within which this dialogue operates.[38] For without it, we could not advance beyond the anodyne agreement between Protarchus and Socrates that the best human life will be a mixture of pleasure and intellectual activity. The superordinate Good as One is the only criterion of judgment about the relative values of the lives proposed by the hedonist and the antihedonist. Thus, the life in which intellect dominates affective states will be the best mixture or "somewhere in the region" thereof.

An obvious Humean objection occurs. Why should we not suppose that a life in which reason serves appetite rather than dominates it is not the best? This will be a mixed life to be sure, but one in which reason serves as the cause of the dominance of pleasure. The unique way in which *Philebus* answers this objection is based upon a distinction that Plato makes elsewhere between two types of desire, that of the ensouled body and that of

---

[36] See *Phil.* 31D4–32B5. See 58B9–59B8, which evokes the failures of naturalists like Anaxagoras and perhaps Democritus to explain nature, since they do not employ νοῦς in their explanations. Their explanations lack accuracy (ἀκρίβεια) and security or stability (βεβαιότης). This is so because they do not appeal to the imposition of measure or good limit imposed by νοῦς in their explanations. Their explanations are inaccurate and unstable because they try to explain the sensible world in sensible terms, thereby excluding measure in principle.

[37] See *Phil.* 22D7–8, 65B7, C3, D3. Hampton 1990, 48–49 and n. 66 identifies divine νοῦς with the Idea of the Good. So, too, Benitez 1995, 135–137. As we have already seen, this would mean that the Demiurge is the Good which is textually unsupportable. Delcomminette 2006, 604, thinks that the Good is just the Form of οὐσία, that is, the Form of all the "formal" properties of Forms. It is obscure, to say the least, how properties of Forms can be the cause of the being of Forms, as the Good is explicitly said to be.

[38] Gosling 1975, 132–133, holds that "the good [at 61A4–5] is not the *Republic* Form of the Good, but the good for man." This is not just a distinction without a difference but a misunderstanding of the metaphysical foundation of Plato's moral realism. The "good for man" can only be instantiations of the Idea of the Good indexed to the integrated unity of the kind "human being."

6.2 Integrative Unity and the Good Life

the intellect.[39] The first is the desire for the satisfaction of ensouled bodily appetites; the second is the desire for the Good and its manifestations.[40] Let us call these "horizontal" desires and "vertical" desires, principally because these desires are orthogonal to each other, that is, they are not commensurable. So, on the Humean model, reason serving appetite is actually reason desiring the Good ("vertically") and deciding that the satisfaction of the appetite ("horizontally") is the means to this. As we have already seen, however, pleasure is not good in itself since there are bad pleasures. It cannot be, therefore, that a bad pleasure is constitutive of the good life, the satisfaction of the vertical desire for the Good. The way *Philebus* expresses this is to argue that pleasure in itself belongs to the class of unlimited since it is a "becoming (γένεσις)." It is limited only by its cessation or by its limitation. So, reason dominates pleasure in the best life since reason determines whether or to what extent pleasure is instrumental to the satisfaction of the desire for the Good.[41]

As we learn at the end of the dialogue, the Good is revealed in a triad of forms which need to be taken as a unity.

> So, if we are not able to capture the Good in one idea, let us get at it with three, with beauty and symmetry and truth, and say that we would be most correct to treat these as in a way one and responsible for what is in the mixture [of the elements in the good life], and that it is owing to this being good that it becomes so.[42]

The most remarkable feature of this passage is that Plato is here prepared to give the parameters of integrative unity. It is, of course, significant that these are to be treated as being in a way "one." It hardly seems fanciful to insist that here we have an implicit identification of the Good and the One: Goodness is achieved by the qualified oneness of (in the present case) a state of the soul in which beauty, symmetry, and truth are unified, that is, different aspects of a unity.[43]

---

[39] See *Phd.* 66B3ff; *Phdr.* 237D6–9; *Tim.* 88A8–B2.
[40] See *Phil.* 61A1–2: τὸ παντάπασιν ἀγαθόν.
[41] See the whole argument at *Phil.* 53C–55B. This argument is parallel to the argument in *Lysis* on the πρῶτον φίλον.
[42] *Phil.* 65A1–5: Οὐκοῦν εἰ μὴ μιᾷ δυνάμεθα ἰδέᾳ τὸ ἀγαθὸν θηρεῦσαι, σὺν τρισὶ λαβόντες, κάλλει καὶ συμμετρίᾳ καὶ ἀληθείᾳ, λέγωμεν ὡς τοῦτο οἷον ἓν ὀρθότατ' ἂν αἰτιασαίμεθ' ἂν τῶν ἐν τῇ συμμείξει, καὶ διὰ τοῦτο ὡς ἀγαθὸν ὂν τοιαύτην αὐτὴν γεγονέναι. Cf. *Tim.* 87C5–6, where beauty and symmetry are the criteria for the presence of goodness.
[43] Hampton 1990, 83–84, takes the triad as "parts" of the Good, inferring from this, 87, that the Good is complex and so not the absolutely simple One as per Aristotle's testimony. Since, however, the Good is above οὐσία, it can hardly have the triad as "parts." Chappell 2014, 318, reads the triad loosely as love, justice, and truth, where love is of the beautiful and justice is presumably symmetry

That there is difference between symmetry (συμμετρία) and measure (μετριότης) is clearer than the question of exactly what that difference is.[44] Philologically, we would expect that measure is simpler than *symmetry* (συμ . . .). And the loose identification of symmetry with beauty suggests that it is virtue that is correlated to measure.[45] Virtue is itself, of course, an ordering or complex of parts of the soul and so a sort of symmetry.[46] But the issue here is the mixed life of which pleasure has to be an irremovable part. If this is so, then the symmetry must refer to the virtuous embodied soul in connection with those pure or true pleasures that go to make up the best life. The incursion of false pleasures into a mixed life destroys the symmetry.[47] Proximity to the Good is achieved by separation from the body and thereby a simplification of life. The practice of virtue in the sensible world is "symmetrical" with the Form of the Virtue and the

---

in the human sphere. Chappell's constriction of Plato's cosmic comprehensiveness seems to spring from a certain discomfort in tying ethics as closely to metaphysics as Plato in fact does.

[44] See *Phil.* 64E5–7: Νῦν δὴ καταπέφευγεν ἡμῖν ἡ τοῦ ἀγαθοῦ δύναμις εἰς τὴν τοῦ καλοῦ φύσιν· μετριότης γὰρ καὶ συμμετρία κάλλος δήπου καὶ ἀρετὴ πανταχοῦ συμβαίνει γίγνεσθαι (So, now the nature of the Good has taken flight into the nature of the beautiful; for measure and symmetry, I suppose, happen everywhere to be beauty and virtue). As we saw, *Soph.* 235D6–E2 is helpful here. The division of τέχνη into εἰκαστική and φανταστική states that the former preserves τὰς συμμετρίας τοῦ παραδείγματος ("the symmetries of the paradigm"), while the latter says farewell to the truth. The association of truth and symmetry between images and their paradigms seems clear. The symmetrical image preserves the truth of the paradigm.

[45] See Delcomminette 2006, 577–581.

[46] See *Tim.* 89E3–90A2 where virtue is said to consist in the συμμετρία of the three εἴδη of the soul. This symmetry is equivalent to an integrated unity according to humankind. The exhortation in *Tht.* 176B1–2 to "assimilation to god (ὁμοίωσις θεῷ)" through virtue plus wisdom is, I take it, equivalent to an exhortation to achieve συμμετρία with the intelligible world. Perhaps there is an illuminating analogy between συμμετρία as used here and the Scholastic term *adaequatio* as in "veritas est adaequatio intellectus et rei."

[47] At *Phil.* 38A6–41A5, Socrates wants to argue that the falseness of some pleasures is the same as the falseness in false beliefs, or at least inseparable from a false belief. See 40E6–10: οὐδ' ἄλλον τινὰ τρόπον. See Dybikowski 1970 and Harte 2004 for discussions of the issues surrounding this claim and the various interpretations and criticisms of it. The falseness corresponds to what is produced by φανταστική τέχνη. The attribution of falseness to the pleasure is owing to its inseparability from belief or judgment. A state (πάθος) like pleasure or pain is not an intentional object. But at least for some pleasures, the pleasure is constitutive of an intentional object, for example, taking-pleasure-in-x where "x" refers to a proposition. If the proposition is false, then this falsity infects the pleasure, for if one comes to believe that x is false, then one would cease to be in a pleasurable state. See Thalberg 1962, 67–71, for a similar interpretation. Dybikowski, 158–162, suggests that such an account works only if the belief is the *cause* of the pleasure. If it is not, then the pleasure would not be false. The sophist who practices φανταστική τέχνη aims to produce false pleasures in his audience. See 40A9–12, where the false beliefs are φαντάσματα produced in the soul. In the previous lines, 39C4–5, Plato uses εἰκόνες for both true and false representations of true and false beliefs or λόγοι. I take it that a true representation of a false belief could still legitimately be called a φάντασμα. The sophist seems to be implicated in the production of the other types of false pleasure: error with respect to distance or closeness (40E–42C) and nonrecognition of a "neutral" condition (42C–44A). The falsity of a pleasure is an indication of its instability owing to its being without μέτρον.

Demiurge, and ultimately the Good. The soul of the just person, say, is one way the Form of Justice looks when it is instantiated here below. Socrates' virtue is "symmetrical" with the Form of Virtue analogous to the way a three-dimensional house is symmetrical with the blueprint for it. Philosophical virtue is superior to popular or political virtue, that is, closer to the One, because of the relative presence or lack of symmetry. Specifically, in the former, appetite is never in opposition to reason; in the latter it may be, although it is restrained. The discordance in the soul evidenced by continence has less unity than in the philosophical soul, where there is only philosophical virtue. But all types of virtue have more unity than that which is found in the acratic or in the vicious.

The association of beauty and truth is a well-established doctrine from *Symposium* and elsewhere. Beauty is the property of Being of attractiveness, and truth is the property of Being of intelligibility. These are in a way one, since it is Being that attracts the intellect. This attraction is satisfied by cognitive identity with Being. It is Plato's breathtaking speculative leap that all beauty and hence all attraction by animals is either an attraction to Being in the intelligible world or to images of it.[48] Plato does not say, but we may reasonably suppose, that with respect to attractiveness, the difference between something really beautiful and something merely apparently beautiful is that the former invites ascent to the intelligible world whereas the latter does not. This is because what we find attractive in the merely apparently beautiful is its material constitution; what we find attractive in the really beautiful is that it is a genuine manifestation of its paradigm.[49] In this lies its "symmetry." The superiority of the genuine manifestation to the merely apparent is that of an εἰκών to a φάντασμα.[50]

It might seem that the superordinate Idea of the Good is excludable from this analysis since beauty, virtue, truth, measure, and symmetry constitute the content of the good life. It would be more exact to say that the content of a good life will be the particular states or dispositions and actions of particular individuals and that the above four are really

---

[48] See Murdoch 1977, 37, "Eros is the desire for good which is somehow the same even when a degenerate 'good' is sought."
[49] At *Rep.* 6.508E4–5, the Good is said to be "more beautiful (κάλλιον)" than truth because it is the cause (αἰτία) of truth. Our ultimate attraction is to the Good which we attain only by cognitive identity with the truth, that is, with Being.
[50] See *Tim.* 92C7–9 on the sensible world as an εἰκών of the Living Animal. This is owing entirely to the handiwork of the divine Νοῦς and the other, subordinate gods.

criteria of the contents, not the contents themselves. But criteria of what? There is no doubt that Plato insists that they are criteria of the presence of the Good. But if this Good is not the superordinate Idea of the Good, then we are left with the question of whether the possession of beauty, and so on, is good. In other words, we are left with the original question of whether that good that is achieved by a life possessing the avatars of the Good is really good for oneself. The question still lingers if the Good has, like the Forms, an οὐσία; it is answerable only if the good that everyone agrees they will is an instantiation of the superordinate Idea of the Good. This Good has no specific content, but evidently the best simulacrum of it is for us is the unified triform beauty–symmetry–truth. After all, pleasure is admitted by all to be a good. Epicurus was a stellar example of a philosopher who both rejected false pleasures and, nevertheless, identified the Good with a life of pleasure. If Epicurus stood in for Protarchus, what would Socrates say to him? Presumably, he would say at least that a life in pursuit solely of pleasures – admittedly only true pleasures requiring intellect for their recognition – is not the good that Epicurus, like everyone else, wills. To claim that some pleasures are good but that they do not constitute the Good that one wills depends upon an argument that goods themselves can be graded according to a criterion.[51] The principle of that criterion is ultimately the Idea of the Good, only accessible to us via its representative, the triform criterion of integrative unity.

6.3 The *Statesman* as This-Worldly Demiurge

In *Statesman*, we find a continuation of the project begun in *Sophist*: to define the sophist, statesman, and philosopher. There is no record of Plato having written a *Philosopher*, nor is the proposed subject for that dialogue plausibly identified with any other work of his. Nevertheless, *Statesman* provides us with a mostly straightforward account of moral realism and its metaphysical foundation. At the conclusion of the dialogue, the final definition of the statesman is given:

> Let us say, then, that this is the completion of the weaving of the fabric of the work of the statesman: the felicitous weaving of the characters of courageous and self-controlled human beings, whenever the royal craft brings them

---

[51] See *Phd.* 83C5–8: Ὅτι ψυχὴ παντὸς ἀνθρώπου ἀναγκάζεται ἅμα τε ἡσθῆναι σφόδρα ἢ λυπηθῆναι ἐπί τῳ καὶ ἡγεῖσθαι περὶ ὃ ἂν μάλιστα τοῦτο πάσχῃ, τοῦτο ἐναργέστατόν τε εἶναι καὶ ἀληθέστατον, οὐχ οὕτως ἔχον (It is that the soul of every human being, when excessively pleased or pained, is compelled to think at the same time in regard to whatever it is that he is experiencing that it is clearest and most true, when in fact it is not so).

6.3 *The* Statesman *as This-Worldly Demiurge*

together into a common life marked by concord and friendship, completing the most magnificent and the best of all fabrics, covering with it all the others in the city including slaves and freemen; holding them together with this binding and rules and administers it to the extent that it belongs to a state to be happy, not falling short of this in any respect.[52]

The "weaving" practiced by the statesman is the production of an integrative unity for the *polis*. This is how the Idea of the Good is politically instantiated.[53] This may be doubted, since the weaving does not explicitly rest upon a universal normative standard. There may be, after all, many types of *poleis* that produce concord and friendship. What is the criterion of the best?

A previous passage, however, makes explicit the metaphysical foundation of goodness in the *polis*. This is the passage where the Eleatic Stranger distinguishes two types of measurement, the one relative and the other absolute. It is only if the latter exists that there can also exist a craft (τέχνη) of ruling.

> In our present discussion, must we not insist on the fact that excess and deficiency are measurable not only in relation to each other, but also in relation to the production of what has due measure. For if we do not attain agreement on this, it will not be possible for there indisputably to exist a statesman nor anyone else who is supposed to be knowledgeable about human actions . . . .
> Clearly, we should divide the craft of measurement, in the way we said, into two, one kind being that which measures number, length, depth,

---

[52] *Sts.* 311B7–C6: Τοῦτο δὴ τέλος ὑφάσματος εὐθυπλοκίᾳ συμπλακὲν γίγνεσθαι φῶμεν πολιτικῆς πράξεως τὸ τῶν ἀνδρείων καὶ σωφρόνων ἀνθρώπων ἦθος, ὁπόταν ὁμονοίᾳ καὶ φιλίᾳ κοινὸν συναγαγοῦσα αὐτῶν τὸν βίον ἡ βασιλικὴ τέχνη, πάντων μεγαλοπρεπέστατον ὑφασμάτων καὶ ἄριστον ἀποτελέσασα [ὥστ᾽ εἶναι κοινόν] τούς τ᾽ ἄλλους ἐν ταῖς πόλεσι πάντας δούλους καὶ ἐλευθέρους ἀμπίσχουσα, συνέχῃ τούτῳ τῷ πλέγματι, καὶ καθ᾽ ὅσον εὐδαίμονι προσήκει γίγνεσθαι πόλει τούτου μηδαμῇ μηδὲν ἐλλείπουσα ἄρχῃ τε καὶ ἐπιστατῇ.

[53] See Pradeau 2002, 90–99, 114–119, on the comparison of the statesman with the Demiurge. Since the Demiurge makes the elements that comprise the *polis*, the statesman, in producing order in the *polis*, is not just an analogue of the Demiurge but a kind of subordinate deity doing the Demiurge's work. So, political unity is not just an analogue of cosmic unity but constitutive of it. See *Sts.* 269C–D, 273B–D on the features of the Demiurge that are reflected in the statesman. White 2007, 95–96, expands upon the analogous status of the Demiurge and the statesman with his thesis of the centrality of the cosmic myth, 268D–274D, especially the contrasting "Age of Kronos" and "Age of Zeus." It is to be noticed that in the idyllic Age of Kronos, there is no politics. The statesman must confront circumstances in principle different from those that the Demiurge confronts when imposing order on the Receptacle. I do not share White's view that the dialogue is in part aporetic or that the Idea of the Good is essentially not present in it. Just as the Demiurge is good, even though that which makes him good, namely, the Good, is explicitly excluded from the discussion, so the statesman is good insofar as he does in the present age what the subordinate gods did under the direction of the Demiurge in the previous age.

breadth, and velocity relatively; the other being that which measures in relation to due measure, fittingness, right time, and what is required, and all such things as distance themselves from the extremes in the direction of the middle.⁵⁴

The objectivity and universality of the referents of the normative terms – due measure, fittingness, right time, what is required – stand or fall together with the possibility of there being a craft of statesmanship.⁵⁵ Moreover, in the last sentence, these are expressed mathematically, that is, as means between extremes. It is not, as we have seen, a co-ordinate Form of the Good, univocally predicable of all these various standards, but the superordinate Idea of the Good whose universality is undiminished by the fact that it is not univocally predicable of anything, since it has no οὐσία.⁵⁶

Not only does the latter kind of craft depend on norms, but the norms depend on the arts.⁵⁷ That is, this kind of craft (as opposed to the kind that just takes relative measures) is defined by its ability to instantiate the Good.⁵⁸ One is not a statesman if one does not produce the appropriate goods.⁵⁹ Statesmanship is separable from metaphysics only if statesmanship is merely a knack, and not an craft. This inseparability of

---

⁵⁴ *Sts.* 284B9–C4 … E2–8: οὕτω καὶ νῦν τὸ πλέον αὖ καὶ ἔλαττον μετρητὰ προσαναγκαστέον γίγνεσθαι μὴ πρὸς ἄλληλα μόνον ἀλλὰ καὶ πρὸς τὴν τοῦ μετρίου γένεσιν· οὐ γὰρ δὴ δυνατόν γε οὔτε πολιτικὸν οὔτ' ἄλλον τινὰ τῶν περὶ τὰς πράξεις ἐπιστήμονα ἀναμφισβητήτως γεγονέναι τούτου μὴ συνομολογηθέντος … Δῆλον ὅτι διαιροῖμεν ἂν τὴν μετρητικήν, καθάπερ ἐρρήθη, ταύτῃ δίχα τέμνοντες, ἓν μὲν τιθέντες αὐτῆς μόριον συμπάσας τέχνας ὁπόσαι τὸν ἀριθμὸν καὶ μήκη καὶ βάθη καὶ πλάτη καὶ ταχυτῆτας πρὸς τοὐναντίον μετροῦσιν, τὸ δὲ ἕτερον, ὁπόσαι πρὸς τὸ μέτριον καὶ τὸ πρέπον καὶ τὸν καιρὸν καὶ τὸ δέον καὶ πάνθ' ὁπόσα εἰς τὸ μέσον ἀπῳκίσθη τῶν ἐσχάτων. Cf. *Phil.* 56D–57A, 57D. See Krämer 1959, 148–171; Sayre 2006, ch. 9; Márquez 2012, 222–225.

⁵⁵ Statesmanship and other "productive" arts are distinguished from arts that only measure contraries without regard to normativity. In addition, sophistry is the counterpart of statesmanship. See 291B–C, 303C, where the sophists, C2, are said to be "experts in faction (στασιαστικούς)," the precise opposite of the unifying practical political science. Faction is, of course, a consequence of lack of integrated unity, a mere φάντασμα of an instance of a *polis*. The sophist's *métier* of purveying falsehoods is the principal cause of faction.

⁵⁶ Cf. Aristotle, *Meta.* E 1, 1026a30–31, where the primary referent of "being" is said to be universal because it is first, not because it is univocally expressed in everything that has being.

⁵⁷ See *Sts.* 284D6–8: τούτου τε γὰρ ὄντος ἐκεῖνα ἔστι, κἀκείνων οὐσῶν ἔστι καὶ τοῦτο, μὴ δὲ ὄντος ποτέρου τούτων οὐδέτερον αὐτῶν ἔσται ποτέ (for if this [the coming into existence of what has due measure] is so, then so is that [the arts of this] and if the arts exist, so does this [coming into existence of what has due measure]; but if one or other of these does not exist, then neither of them will ever exist).

⁵⁸ Cf. Aristotle's "the science of x and the science of good x are identical." In a Platonic context, the possibility of any distinct science or craft depends ultimately upon its having a Form that is produced by the Idea of the Good.

⁵⁹ Cf. *Gorg.* 447A–454B on rhetoric and craft. In *Rep.* 1.341–342, Thrasymachus makes the claim that only an expert in x is an "x-er." Socrates does not disagree with this; he only disagrees with

6.3 *The* Statesman *as This-Worldly Demiurge*

statesmanship and metaphysics rests entirely on the hierarchical metaphysics at the apex of which is the Idea of the Good, here understood as the principle of measure.[60] The criteria of the instantiation of that measure are what integrative unity is comprised of. It is only if the Good is the One and the One is the principle of measure that the normative appeal to measure makes any sense.[61] For example, the right time (ὁ καιρός) is both a norm and conforms to a principle of measure. There would be no good time to do something if it were not the right time and the right time is the application of measure across a temporal unlimited. The right time *is*, for example, the right time to plant crops, because it is conducive to integrative unity in whatever is active in a process.

There is a further connection made between normativity and the principle of measure in the lines leading up to the distinction between two types of measurement:

> One part will relate to the association of greatness and smallness to each other and the other part to the necessary being of becoming.[62]

The obscure phrase "necessary being of becoming" means at least the following. In the generation of any being in the sensible world, the generator, working with preexistent material ("necessity"), imposes order on the product.[63] The result is an image (εἰκών) of the paradigms of intelligibility. This is as true for the statesman as it is for the Demiurge and for any other producer here below. As we have already learned from *Republic*, the Good is the producer of the Forms or οὐσίαι. The Good is the principle of Forms as measures, successful recourse to which by the

---

Thrasymachus' assumption that the expertise is measured by achieving one's own interest. See Rudebusch 2003, 2007, on "agent-neutral" expertise.

[60] See *Rep.* 6.504C1–4, E2–3 on the Idea of the Good as principle of measure (μέτρον). See Lafrance 1995, 93–94, on the important distinction between Forms as measures and the Good as principle of measure.

[61] See *Sts.* 283E3–6 where good and bad people are distinguished from one another by the presence or absence in them of measure. Here "good" and "measured" are explicitly linked.

[62] *Sts.* 283D7–9: τὸ μὲν κατὰ τὴν πρὸς ἄλληλα μεγέθους καὶ σμικρότητος κοινωνίαν, τὸ δὲ κατὰ τὴν τῆς γενέσεως ἀναγκαίαν οὐσίαν. The preexistent necessity is indicated at *Tim.* 47E4–5, 68E1–3. Perhaps the word ἀναγκαίαν would be better translated as "necessitated" to indicate the constraint with which the producer must work. See LSJ s.v. ἀναγκαῖος II. Rodier 1957, 37–48, thinks that being in this passage refers to the logical generation of Forms, not to the sensible world. Lafrance 1995, 94–97, refutes Rodier. Miller 2004, 66, understands the phrase quite differently, as indicated in his translation: "the essential being necessary to coming-into-being." The "necessitated" or "constrained" being of becoming requires measure to achieve its good; without measure, ἀταξία (disorder) reigns.

[63] Cf. *Phil.* 26D7–9, 54C1–4; *Soph.* 219B4–6; *Tim.* 30A5, 46E5, 69B3.

producer makes good products.⁶⁴ The successful recourse results in an integrated unity in each case.

The instantiation of norms by the statesman is according to a mean between extremes. The extremes are termini along a continuum or of contraries, whatever admits of gradation. Such continua are presumably instantiations of the Indefinite Dyad. The only way the Good can be a principle of measure in relation to these continua is if it is the One whose manifestations or participants are integrative unities according to kind.⁶⁵ Most revealing is that the weaving of the statesman actually consists in a second-order imposition of measure on the state. The individuals, possessed of popular or political virtue, which manifest a first-order imposition of measure on the continua that comprise their affective states themselves become elements of symmetry in the body politic. So, the people who are disposed to courageous behavior most of all are "mixed" with the people who are disposed to self-controlled behavior.⁶⁶ Presumably, Plato is here referring not to philosophical virtue but to the "virtue by habit without philosophy" of *Republic* Book 10. For the ones in whom courage dominates and the ones in whom self-control or mildness dominates can be in conflict with each other precisely because it is with reference to their disposition to behave in a certain way that there is an issue.⁶⁷ Within the framework of political virtue, there can be no mutual implication among the virtues or reduction to a unity. This is why ordinary people need some kind of ruler or other to integrate, say, their courage, which comes without self-control, with the self-control of others, which comes without courage.⁶⁸

---

⁶⁴ See *Sts.* 284A5–B2.
⁶⁵ See Miller 2004, 141–161, for a thorough and convincing analysis of the two types of measurement and the dependence of measurement according to a norm on the doctrine of the principles of the One and Indefinite Dyad. The putative "craft of measurement" of pleasures in *Protag.* 356D4 presumably refers to the inferior craft of measurement of relatives along a continuum. Determining that one pleasure is greater than another, however, does not tell us whether or how it has a role in the best human life. Without identifying the Good with the One, it is indeed deeply puzzling how the superordinate Good is even relevant to ethics or politics or any other normative area of life.
⁶⁶ See *Sts.* 305E–306C. At *Lg.* 4.709E6–710A4, the ideal ruler of the *polis* has both courage and self-control, but of the "popular (δημώδη)" kind. See A5. Also, 3.696Bff, 12.963Eff. At 12.968A1–4, philosophers are said to have to rise above "popular virtues (δημοσίαις ἀρεταῖς)" if they are to rule.
⁶⁷ See *Sts.* 306Cff, especially 307C2–7. So, the mutual implication of the virtues pertains to philosophical virtue, not to popular virtue. Price 2011, 85–111, argues for the mutual implication of the virtues, but he assumes that the only virtue is philosophical virtue. Price takes the virtues in *Statesman* to be "tendencies" not virtues. I am not persuaded by his suggestion that a supposedly nonvirtuous "tendency" is different from a virtuous disposition, that is, a disposition to virtuous behavior. See White 2007, 120–123.
⁶⁸ See Bobonich 1995b, especially 314–315, on the absence of reciprocity in the popular or political virtues, though Bobonich's explanation for this differs from mine.

6.3 The Statesman as This-Worldly Demiurge

That political virtue is a "mean," and so an instantiation of the Good, does not suggest, then, that the "extremes" are vices. The "mixture" by the statesman of the elements of the *polis* is not a mixture of bad dispositions. On the contrary, the political virtues of the people who are the elements of the *polis* are clear, even though they do not possess philosophical virtue. And yet, Plato is perhaps supposing that since the *polis* is the natural locus of human happiness, any part of political virtue left to its own would in fact become evil. The courageous or the self-controlled persons left to their own devices could not but devolve into predator and prey.

If Hobbes is right and the state is an artifact, Plato would be mistaken to suppose that the statesman must look to the intelligible world to be able to understand integrative unity as a norm of the Good. But if Aristotle is right and the state exists by nature – which is no doubt what Plato believes – then the statesman can only practice his craft effectively if he looks to the Form of the *polis* and its relation to the Good.[69] The "happy" *polis* will be the one that attains to an integrative unity of politically virtuous people. The question that ought to trouble us is how this position amounts to anything more than rhetoric. What is the articulatable path from a vision of the Form and its relation to the Good leading to specific political practices and institutions and laws?

The particular *métier* of the statesman is variously identified as craft (τέχνη) and as science (ἐπιστήμη).[70] With the background of *Republic* (and *Gorgias*) in mind, we should inquire into why Plato practically treats τέχνη and ἐπιστήμη as identical since the latter is related to Forms and the former is related to sensible particulars. I suggest that Plato is here anticipating a logical distinction that Aristotle formalizes in his *Prior Analytics*. This is the distinction between an A proposition and an I proposition in the Square of Opposition. An A proposition is a universal positive claim, for example, all human beings are mortal. An I proposition is particular and refers to an instance of the universal subject of the A proposition. From the A proposition, one can make an immediate inference to its corresponding I proposition: If this is an A, then it is B. In a sense, if one has knowledge of the universal A proposition, then one can be said to have knowledge of what is immediately inferable from it. The qualification "in a sense" indicates that the putative knowledge of the I proposition is

---

[69] See Aristotle, *Pol.* A 2, 1253a18–29 on the *polis* existing by nature and its priority to the individual. Plato, *Rep.* 8.552A7–B2, refers to individual vocations or occupations – merchants, craftsmen, soldiers – as "parts (μέρη)" of the *polis*. I take it that these are essential parts, indicating that the *polis* is not an artifact.
[70] For τέχνη see 287D4, 296C5, 300E7, 311C1–2; for ἐπιστήμη see 258B3–5, 292B6–D5.

hypothetical: *If* this is an A, then it is B. There are, however, no hypotheticals in the sensible world. Either this is an A or it is not. That is why we can be said to know "in a sense" that if this a human being, then it is mortal.[71]

The relevance of this to the statesman is clear. Every attempt by the statesman to institute laws and practices that are virtuous will be irreducibly circumstantial. Take the example from Book 1 of *Republic*. *If* returning someone's rightful property is just, then there is a craft to determining whether returning someone's property when that person has lost his mind and intends to hurt someone with it is just or not. Again, in *Euthyphro* if piety is adhering to divine law, then there is a craft to determining whether prosecution of your father for negligent homicide is pious or not. In *Republic*, Plato seemed to assume that the philosopher, the practitioner of dialectic, would automatically have the relevant craft of ruling. He apparently eventually came to the entirely sensible conclusion in *Statesman* that the craft of applying knowledge, particularly of Virtue, to a *polis*, is not an inevitable result of successfully practicing dialectic.[72]

The specific types of measures belonging to the statesman's craft are all normative: due measure (τὸ μέτριον), fittingness (τὸ πρέπον), the right time (τὸ καιρόν), what is required (τὸ δέον).[73] The norm itself must be single if the craft of statesmanship is to be single. The unicity of the norm cannot be that of a virtue or even virtue in general. The "right time," for example, has nothing in particular to do with virtue. The statesman, Plato hopes, will know, for example, the right time to go to war. The unhypothetical first principle of all, the Idea of the Good, seems to be the obvious and ultimate truth-maker for the normative claims that a practitioner of the craft of statesmanship will make. As the One, it is the principle of integrative unity in the *polis* and in the individual.

The statesman's main business is producing symmetry among the parts of the *polis* by imposing good limits. The law, institutions, and practices she imposes on the populace are able to be judged as successful or not

---

[71] Whereas the statesman can "know" what constitutes an instantiation of the Good, the members of the *polis* can aspire only to true belief (ἀληθὴς δόξα) about these matters. See 309C5–8. They attain these beliefs with "security (βεβαιώσεως)" presumably because they trust their wise rulers. Cf. *Rep.* 4.429B8–C3, 430B6–9.

[72] See *Soph.* 253C6–D3, where ἡ διαλεκτική is the work of philosophy. As Márquez 2012, 184, notes, τέχνη is never used in association with διαλεκτική as it is with ἡ πολιτική. See for example, *Sts.* 267D7, 276E12, 280A1. See Rowe 2007, n. 29, for the apt observation that for Plato, the rule of reason in the soul does not automatically reveal the correct solutions to particular ethical problems. See also Márquez 2012, 346–350, for some astute remarks on the differences between the philosopher-king of *Republic* and the statesman.

[73] *Sts.* 284E6–8.

6.3 The Statesman *as This-Worldly Demiurge*

according to their achievement of political integrative unity. Stability is the most natural or obvious manifestation for a political order. But apparent stability is distinguishable from real stability according to whether the integrative unity of the members of the *polis* is or is not achieved. Stability in the associating of the virtuous is better than stability in the association of the oppressed with the oppressor. All of this may seem boringly obvious to a liberal-minded reader. Nevertheless, absent the metaphysical framework provided by Plato, there is no objective basis for preferring one form of stability over another. If Plato is wrong in thinking that we all desire the real Good and not any simulacrum of it, then philosophy, as Plato understands it, is altogether inapplicable to political questions. It would be as if the Good were like a fideist's conception of God, where the "subject" of the divine had strictly no relevance to other matters, scientific and political.

CHAPTER 7

Morality, Religion, and Politics

7.1 Introduction

Aristotle identifies theology with first philosophy or metaphysics.[1] Plato does not.[2] The study of the gods is for Plato of the utmost importance both for morality and for politics, even though this study does not dislodge the metaphysical foundation of moral realism as I have been describing it throughout this book. For Plato, theology is more like anthropology than like metaphysics. That is, it amounts to reflection on a race of extraordinary beings, principally gifted with immortality as well as some anthropomorphic characteristics but also, owing to their nature, able to have a purer access to the intelligible world than that which is available to mortal embodied creatures.[3] Because the gods have this access, they have the knowledge which guarantees their virtue.[4] All poetry which seeks to

---

[1] See *Meta*. E 1, 1026a29–32: εἰ δ' ἔστι τις οὐσία ἀκίνητος, αὕτη προτέρα καὶ φιλοσοφία πρώτη, καὶ καθόλου οὕτως ὅτι πρώτη· καὶ περὶ τοῦ ὄντος ᾗ ὂν ταύτης ἂν εἴη θεωρῆσαι, καὶ τί ἐστι καὶ τὰ ὑπάρχοντα ᾗ ὄν. (But if there is an immovable substance, this would be prior and the science of it would be first philosophy, and it would be universal in this way because it is first. And it would be the job of this science to investigate being qua being, both what it is and the properties of being.) The meaning of this passage is much contested, though it strains credulity to read it in any way other than that according to which the subject matter of metaphysics is identified with theology.
[2] See Van Riel 2016, esp. ch. 3. Bonazzi 2013 shows how later Platonists or "Neoplatonists" used Aristotle's conflation of first philosophy and theology in order to subordinate ethics to theology.
[3] See *Phdr.* 246C–D on the crucial distinction between gods and mortal beings: The latter have destructible bodies, the former do not. Perhaps *Tim.* 41A–B contradicts this in the address of the Demiurge to the gods, but not clearly so. See Van Riel 2013, 46–51. If the gods have bodies, these bodies must be made of indissoluble material. Presumably, that is why they are immune to pleasure and pain. See *Phil.* 33B8–9. Obviously, the celestial gods have bodies. Perhaps the safest conclusion is that gods without bodies are able to inhabit them at will but do not always need to do so. See *Lg.* 12.904A on the divine soul–body composite. Plato recognizes a hierarchy of gods: Olympians, gods of the underworld, daemons, heroes, ancestors, and living parents. See *Lg.* 4.717A6–B6. At *Tim.* 41A, the sun, the moon, and the planets are added to the list. These seem to be on the same level as the Olympians, differing only from the latter by being perpetually visible. A hint as to the criterion of hierarchy is breadth or area of influence. Cf. *Phil.* 30D. The description of the hierarchy, drawn from traditional Greek practices, reads very much like an anthropological report on an exotic, far-off society.
[4] See *Phdr.* 247C–E.

discredit the gods is to be resisted. Because the all-powerful gods are virtuous but not themselves the standards of morality, they are ideal enforcers of morality, both in this life and in the next.[5]

Plato distinguishes theology and religion, roughly, along the lines of the distinction between ἐπιστήμη and τέχνη.[6] His accounts of both of these provide important information about a variety of issues in moral philosophy, including evil, providence, rewards and punishments, and virtue. I shall first address a question which might seem too obvious even to raise: Why does Plato think that the gods are invariably good?

7.2 Why Are the Gods Good?

In Book 2 of *Republic*, Plato has Socrates excoriate the poets for representing the gods as having humanlike flaws or vices.[7] Socrates insists that the gods are in fact good.[8] This claim is often dismissed as disingenuous or unthinking. The political role of benign Olympians is certainly not irrelevant, neither here or in *Laws*. It is useful to rulers to convince the populace of the goodness of divinity. Within the context of Plato's moral realism, however, there is a good deal more that can be said about this.[9] In the myth in *Phaedrus*, the life of the souls of the gods is characterized as feasting on the sights "beyond heaven," that is, on intelligible reality.[10] A god is "nourished (τρεφομένη)" by "intellect

---

[5] See *Lg.* 4.716C4–6: ὁ δὴ θεὸς ἡμῖν πάντων χρημάτων μέτρον ἂν εἴη μάλιστα, καὶ πολὺ μᾶλλον ἤ πού τις, ὥς φασιν, ἄνθρωπος· (It is god who is especially the measure of all things, much more than some human being, as they say.) As the text goes on to explain, one adheres to this measure by assimilation to god, which requires virtue and wisdom (D1–2). It is fitting for someone who is assimilated to divinity to pray to the gods and to make divine offerings; it is unfitting for anyone else. Thus Plato undercuts the theory of petitionary prayer and sacrifice as an exchange of goods between gods and human beings.

[6] Bodéüs 1992 argues that Aristotle's remarks on the traditional deities as situated within a larger metaphysical/physical framework follow in some respects those of Plato. Bodéüs distinguishes Aristotle's traditional theology from the natural theology that is identified with first philosophy.

[7] *Rep.* 2.378B–380C. Cf. *Eu.* 7B. As Solmsen 1942, 40–43, points out, the condemnation of the Homeric representations of the gods cannot be said to fairly carry over to, for example, Aeschylus, who has a much more refined notion of the justice of Zeus. Nevertheless, Plato might well have been suspicious of an arbitrary (read: nonphilosophical) elevation of the moral standing of the gods.

[8] See *Rep.* 2.379B1: ἀγαθός ὅ γε θεὸς τῷ ὄντι (god is in fact really good). Cf. *Lg.* 10.900C8–D3; 12.941B2–C2. The singular θεός is, as many have shown, used by Plato frequently as a collective noun, referring to all the gods. See Van Camp and Canart 1956; Van Riel 2013, 25, 36–37; Bordt 2006, 55–95, with many examples from the dialogues.

[9] See Bordt 2006, 95–135, who argues for the claim that Plato's idea of god as essentially good is original and revolutionary in the history of Greek thought. But Bordt's central thesis – that the Demiurge is Plato's supreme god and so identical with the Idea of the Good – is, in my view, unsupportable.

[10] *Phdr.* 247C3–E6. Cf. *Tim.* 41E2–3, where the immortal part of our souls is shown "the nature of the universe (τὴν τοῦ παντὸς φύσιν)" by the Demiurge before being ensconced in a star. I take it that "the nature of the universe" refers to Forms or at least includes them. Cf. *Parm.* 132D2 in reference to Forms: παραδείγματα ἑστάναι ἐν τῇ φύσει (paradigms standing in nature).

(νῷ)" and by "undiluted knowledge (ἐπιστήμη ἀκηράτῳ)." The regular lives of the gods are like the life of the *successful* philosopher in the Greater Mysteries in *Symposium*. As a result of his vision of intelligible reality, he gives birth to and "cultivates (θρεψαμένῳ)" "true virtue (ἀρετὴν ἀληθῆ)."[11] And just as the philosopher naturally produces true virtue as the result of her knowledge, so, too, do the gods. The difference, of course, is that the gods, being gods and not humans, are not embodied in destructible bodies. As a result, knowledge is their natural endowment, not a problematic achievement.[12]

As we have already seen, Socrates regularly assumes that knowledge has a transformative effect in the direction of virtue. It is inadequate to suppose that this knowledge amounts to the ability to give an irrefutable definition of, say, the Form of Justice. As we have also seen, even if this definition includes the genus "Good" such that we define Justice as one kind of human good, this does not suffice to produce virtue in the knower on its own. In order to be motivated to be just or to do just deeds, one must recognize that justice is what one in fact desires, because one desires what is good for oneself. One must recognize that it is the Good that makes justice beneficial to oneself. As we further learn from *Republic*, one *cannot* know that justice is beneficial – or even what Justice is – unless one can see it in the light of the Good. So, it is reasonable to assume that Plato thinks of an (Olympian) god as a soul with the knowledge that produces true virtue.[13] These gods are like the Demiurge in that their goodness belongs to them as a result of their cognition of Forms.[14] If this is correct, then the gods can be

---

[11] See *Symp.* 212A5–6. The gods are "nourished" by knowledge of Forms, but the philosopher "cultivates" it in himself. The identical word is being used. The difference in meaning, I take it, is that knowledge has a direct and immediate effect on the souls that the gods are, whereas philosophers have the perpetual impediment of human embodiment that means that the cultivation of true virtue takes time and effort. For the philosopher, virtue is second nature; for the gods it is "first" nature. The "true virtue" produced by a vision of the Good is not contrasted with "false virtue," but with the popular or political virtue of ordinary people. See 209A5–8, where virtue as displayed in the Lower Mysteries, specifically self-control and justice, has its effects in "states and households." This point is quite important since some have argued that the true virtue here cannot be other-directed but is rather asocial. See, for example, Scott 2007, 149–151. On the contrary, cognizing the Good results in participating in its diffusion.

[12] See Alcinous, *Didask.* 10.164.13–18 Whittaker, where Alcinous takes it as obvious that our bodily endowment is an impediment to knowledge whereas the gods, owing in particular to freedom from sense perception, have knowledge εἰλικρινῶς τε καὶ ἀμιγῶς (purely and unmixed).

[13] See *Phdr.* 249C5–6; cf. 247D1–5. See Griswold 1986, 104, "The net result [of the divine circuit] is that the gods obtain an undistorted vision of Being." See Morrow 1960, 434–470, on the hierarchy of Olympian gods and their place in *Laws*.

[14] See *Sts.* 269D5–6 on the similarity of gods to immutable Forms. This accounts for their capacity for knowledge. Also, see *Phdr.* 249C6: πρὸς οἷσπερ θεὸς ὢν θεῖός ἐστιν (owing to proximity to [the Forms] a god is divine). This similarity is a specification of the unchanging nature of the gods. See *Rep.* 2.380D1–383C7.

confidently tasked by Plato with a great deal of honest labor, including the just imposition of rewards and punishment and, as we shall soon see, a benevolent approach to cosmic construction. The gods operate like successful philosophers, willingly participating in the "overflowing" of the Good.[15]

In addition, the ideal of assimilating oneself to god as much as possible by means of the cultivation of virtue, with the addition of wisdom, becomes clearer. To transcend popular or political virtue requires the knowledge that the gods possess. We can be sure that the knowledge that is the source of the transformation is what makes the gods good. The assurance is not circular; unencumbered and disembodied psychical existence is life in possession of the knowledge of intelligible reality. That is why, presumably, Plato is also confident that coming to possess knowledge here below is recollection of the contents of the pre-embodied life. Those who have suffered psychical impairment of one sort or another cannot automatically recover this life, and that is why they are destined to be reincarnated into a lower form of life.[16]

Given that Plato's view of theology in relation to metaphysics is different from Aristotle's, it is perhaps somewhat surprising that their accounts of assimilation to god are substantially the same. Aristotle says that the best life is the life of contemplation, the life in imitation of the Unmoved Mover.[17] In Plato's view, this life does not seem to be different in any important way from the life of the gods or the life of the successful philosopher. Yet it seems that for Aristotle, without the addition of a universal and superordinate Idea of the Good, the claim about the superiority of the contemplative life is subject to the same objection as any other substantive claim about the superiority of one activity or state to another. Thus, a contemplative life is desirable for whoever desires a contemplative life. For Plato, the superiority

---

[15] One might speculate in passing that the reluctance of successful philosophers in *Republic* to return to the cave is owing to the burden of embodiment that they bear. The gods have no such burden, even if they are embodied, because their bodies are not destructible or, more precisely, the Demiurge will not allow them to be destroyed. See *Tim.* 41A–B. Successful philosophers, as we have seen, produce true virtue, which may be but is not necessarily manifested in political life. Compelling philosophers to return to the cave is a purely political choice very much in line with other sorts of compulsion exercised by rulers. See below Sections 7.7–7.8. Sedley 2007, 272–279, thinks that the philosopher's reluctance to return to the cave is a reluctance to engage in altruistic behavior. But the returning philosopher will have recently come to understand that the presumed dichotomy between altruism and self-interest is a false one. All the same, one might well be reluctant to instantiate one good rather than another since the universality of Good certainly does not impel the instantiation of every possible good all the time. One thing we can be confident of: if the philosophical adept returns to the cave, it is not in defiance of his own true good.
[16] See *Phd.* 81Dff; *Tim.* 90E–91D.   [17] See *EN* K 7, 1177b30–1178a3; 8, 1178b21–23.

of the contemplative life is owing to its transformative effect, which results in our recognition that our good is identical with the knowledge at the apex of which is the Idea of the Good.

That Plato thought that the gods were exempt from immoral behavior is certainly not exceptional within the context of late-fifth- and early-fourth-century Athenian culture. Euripides' pronouncement, "if the gods do anything shameful, they are no gods," was not, to be sure, derived from philosophical principles.[18] What is unique to Plato is his philosophical explanation for the impossibility of a god acting viciously. For the purposes of the present work, the relevant conclusion to be drawn from this explanation is that ascent to the realm of the divine is coincident with the attainment of knowledge. Self-divinization and self-transformation through knowledge are virtually identical. Equally important is the fact that good gods, owing to their knowledge, that is, their knowledge of the Good, are naturally providential and just. Finally, a demonstration that the gods are good has an undoubtedly educational impact on a populace always in need of moral encouragement.[19]

7.3 The Theology of *Laws* Book 10

In *Laws* Book 10, the Athenian Stranger provides a reasoned preface to the laws regarding impiety.

> No one who believes in the gods according to the laws ever willingly committed an impious act or engages in lawless speech; if he does, it is owing to one of three things: as I said, either (1) he doesn't believe in the gods or (2) although he does believe in them, he doesn't think that they care for human beings or (3) that they can be easily won over and manipulated by prayers and sacrifices.[20]

---

[18] See Euripides fr. 292, 7 Nauck: εἰ θεοί τι δρῶσιν αἰσχρόν οὐκ εἰσιν. Of course, Euripides would add that since the Olympian deities are habitually represented as doing shameful things, they do not in fact exist.

[19] As Solmsen 1942, 73, notes, the good gods have the role for the general populace that the Forms, including the superordinate Good, have for philosophers. They embody the knowledge that philosophers seek. See Proclus, *In Alc.* 187, 5–8 Segonds, who points out that the gods do not need to discover or learn anything since they are always united to their objects of knowledge. This is, of course, self-knowledge.

[20] *Lg.* 10.885B4–9: Θεοὺς ἡγούμενος εἶναι κατὰ νόμους οὐδεὶς πώποτε οὔτε ἔργον ἀσεβὲς ἠργάσατο ἑκὼν οὔτε λόγον ἀφῆκεν ἄνομον, ἀλλὰ ἓν δή τι τῶν τριῶν πάσχων, ἢ τοῦτο, ὅπερ εἶπον, οὐχ ἡγούμενος, ἢ τὸ δεύτερον ὄντας οὐ φροντίζειν ἀνθρώπων, ἢ τρίτον εὐπαραμυθήτους εἶναι θυσίαις τε καὶ εὐχαῖς παραγομένους. The implication of this passage is not that one who denies the existence of gods does wrong willingly. It is that he willingly goes against the law, presumably because he believes that the gods do not exist and therefore that he can hope to escape punishment. Cf. *Rep.* 2.365D–E. He thinks the law is a bad law.

My main concern is with the arguments pertaining to (2) and (3), but I shall first say a few words about (1).

The proof of the existence of the gods, directed to incipient atheists or naturalists, rests upon the absolute priority of soul (ψυχή) over body (σῶμα).[21] Whatever belongs to soul necessarily, that is, its properties, are therefore also prior to body. The priority of soul to body does not mean the absolute priority of soul; it itself has a generation (γένεσις).[22] Atheists have supposed that bodies are prior to souls and that they exist by nature and chance and not by anything that pertains to soul, especially craft (τέχνη).[23] In addition, because they reject the reality of the gods, they also reject the reality or objectivity of beautiful and just things, claiming these to be artificial and culturally relative.[24] So, the substance of the debate between the theist lawgiver and the atheists is whether the undoubted order in nature is owing to a soul or souls that have applied craft to pre-existent material or whether this order can be accounted for solely by nature and chance. The proof proceeds by trying to establish that all the motions that constitute the dynamic order of nature are ultimately divisible into motions that are explained by other motions and motions that are self-explanatory, that is self-motions.[25] The former are posterior to the latter. The soul is exactly what a self-mover is.[26] So, self-explanatory psychical motion of some sort is prior to hetero-explicable bodily motion.

The proof belongs, along with a host of other versions, to the so-called argument from design. But there are some distinctive elements of Plato's version. First, there is no hint that the conclusion of the proof is that there is one soul only in charge of the order of the cosmos. A multitude of such souls are perfectly plausible given the trajectory of the argument: from any hetero-explicable motion we can infer the existence of a self-explicable motion, though it need not be the identical one in each case. Second, the bodily motions that constitute nature only need be supposed to have sufficient order to be characterized as contraries. If that which is hot comes from that which is cold and not from that which is bitter, say, that minimal orderliness is, according to the argument, ultimately explicable only by the self-motions of soul, including especially cognitive self-motions.[27] A fortiori, elaborate natural processes and events like generation

---

[21] *Lg.* 10.892Aff. See Carone 1994, 277–280.   [22] *Lg.* 10.892A4.   [23] *Lg.* 10.889B1–E1.
[24] *Lg.* 10.889E5–890A2. The atheists' claim is actually slightly more nuanced. They claim that there is a difference between what is beautiful by nature and what is conventionally beautiful; by contrast, they claim that justice is entirely conventional (νομῷ).
[25] *Lg.* 10.893Bff, 894B8–C1. Cf. *Tim.* 46D5–E2; *Phdr.* 245C5–9.
[26] *Lg.* 10.895E10–896A2. Cf. *Phdr.* 245C5–246A2.   [27] See *Lg.* 10.896E8–897B5.

and destruction will need soul to explain them. The reason for thinking this is not evident in this argument. We need to recur to Socrates' "autobiography" in *Phaedo*, where he argues that the naturalistic explanations of Anaxagoras are inadequate, only producing conditions and not real causes for natural changes or processes.[28] The real causes are the Forms, But what, we may ask, has the priority of Forms to bodies to do with the priority of soul to bodies?

The answer to this question is provided in *Timaeus*. There we learn of the eternal connectedness of the Demiurge and the Living Animal, that is, all the Forms. The connectedness is the contemplation by the one of the other. The Demiurge and the Living Animal are cognitively identical, that is, the Demiurge is the eternal active locus of all intelligible reality. So, there could be no explanation for the natural changes, events, and processes here below if there were not the Demiurge eternally contemplating the Living Animal. The Demiurge is the necessary supplement to the argument in *Phaedo* that aims to refute Anaxagoras and other naturalists.

The delicate further question is this. The Demiurge is an intellect (νοῦς) eternally contemplating the Living Animal. He makes the cosmos according to this model, installing a soul in its body, the soul of the universe.[29] The Demiurge thereby does two things: he makes the cosmos like himself and he makes it like the Living Animal.[30] What does the soul of the cosmos imitate? Does it imitate the intellect of the Demiurge or does it imitate the Living Animal, or do these possibilities amount to the same thing? I would say that the balance of probability is that the activity of the intellect that the Demiurge is the paradigm of embodied psychical activity; it is not psychical activity itself. That is, soul is subordinate to intellect. I have three reasons in support of this conclusion. First, Plato represents the activity of intellect as a motion, but he does not explicitly call it a motion of soul; he calls it "motion of intellect."[31] The self-moving gods imitate this intellectual activity.[32] So, it seems that intellectual motion is, as it were, the paradigm of the paradigm of motion, which is the self-motion of soul. Second, the activity of intellect is eternal whereas psychical motion is in time. There is a radical difference

---

[28] See *Phd.* 95A4–102A9 and Gerson 2020, 48–65. The conditions for true explanations become συναίτια in *Timaeus*.
[29] *Tim.* 34B3.   [30] *Tim.* 29E1–3, 30C2–D1.
[31] See *Lg.* 10.897D3: νοῦ κίνησις. See Perl 2014, 65–69.
[32] *Lg.* 10.897B1–2: νοῦν μὲν προσλαβοῦσα ἀεὶ θεὸν ὀρθῶς θεοῖς ([soul] attaching itself to intellect always rightly said to be a god among gods). The text here is uncertain but the overall meaning seems clear enough. See Proclus, *Platonic Theology* I 14, p.66.6 Saffrey-Westerink; Enders 1999, 164. Morrow 1960, 483–484, provides additional support for the identification of this intellect with the Demiurge, adding that the Demiurge must work through the souls of the gods.

between eternal motion and temporal motion. Aristotle will note the radical difference by introducing a new word, ἐνέργεια or "activity" to indicate a paradigm of motion that is complete at every moment and so never "in" time. And, adds Aristotle, this paradigm is not only life (ζωή) but the best life.[33] The third reason is that the souls of the gods have a very different relationship to the Forms from that of the Demiurge.[34]

We may assume that Plato thinks he has shown that one or more intellectual souls exist who follow the directives of the Demiurge in ordering the world. These souls possess perfect virtue.[35] A comforting assumption, one supposes. Because the gods are perfectly virtuous, they are providential and above and beyond reproach and corruption.[36] We have seen why the gods are perfectly virtuous. Why, though, does that mean that they should care for us?[37] After all, a perfectly virtuous human being does not necessarily care for lower creatures. The answer to this question takes us back to the central focus of Plato's moral realism, namely, the Idea of the Good. The Good is unlimited in its overflowing. The "channels," so to speak, for its flowing are provided by the articulated structure of the intelligible world. Anything – not just the gods – that is apt for reception of the Good according to its own kind acts on its natural achievement. For example, when the human soul is appropriately disposed, it receives the virtue of justice which is not only made good or beneficial by the Good but is also a purveyor of the Good to whoever possesses it. And the overflowing of the Good – its diffusiveness – is passed on according to the powers or abilities of whoever has it. Doing just deeds is just instantiating the Good anew.

Because the gods are perfectly good, they are perfectly virtuous.[38] Because they are perfectly virtuous, they act accordingly. Like the Demiurge himself,

---

[33] *Meta.* Λ 7, 1072b26–30.
[34] See *Phdr.* 247A–E. The souls of the gods are intellectual souls, but they are not reducible to eternal intellect; rather, they are derived by generation. See *Lg.* 10.892A4–5, C3–4, 896C1–2; 12.967D4–E1, where νοῦς is clearly superior to ψυχή, which, though separate from and superior to body, is generated. See Hackforth 1965 [1936] who provides a convincing argument to this effect. Also, Menn 1995, 19. As in *Timaeus*, the soul of the universe is subordinate to a divine intellect. Bordt 2006, 214–237, recognizes the subordination of the souls of the gods to eternal intellect, but he identifies the divinity of eternal intellect with the Good.
[35] *Lg.* 10.898C6–8, 899B5, 906A7–B3. Cf. *Rep.* 2.379C4–5.
[36] *Lg.* 10.899D4–905D1, 905E5–907B7.
[37] The term that Plato uses for "care" is ἐπιμέλεια, not "providence (πρόνοια)." The latter term appears at *Tim.* 30C1 in relation to the Demiurge's work. The gods *could* care for us without being provident, for example, in rendering justice in the afterlife. Perhaps Plato reserves πρόνοια for the Demiurge and ἐπιμέλεια for the subordinate gods because of the relative proximity of the gods to us. They can be "hands on" care-givers and enforcers. In addition, providence is associated with eternity; care with temporality.
[38] See *Lg.* 10.899B5–8; *Phdr.* 249C5–6.

practical reasoning is the natural overflowing of theoretical knowledge. The fulfilled desire for the Good produces an *external* realization of virtue. When the Demiurge puts the gods in charge of human beings, this is ultimately the externalization of the Good.[39] The virtuous human being, in whom reason rules, externalizes her dominant or ruling rational faculty in the rest of her soul analogous to the way the gods externalize their virtue in the generation of human beings and the Demiurge does in the gods and the Good does in the Demiurge, who is eternally contemplating the Living Animal. Reason in human beings is divine precisely because it is what the gods and the Demiurge are. But human beings are more and less than divine and their achievement of integrative unity is dependent on the proper use of the equipment provided to them by the Demiurge and the gods.[40]

The providence of the gods must be set within the context of (1) our innate desire for the Good and (2) the endowment by the Demiurge of reason in human beings. Their attention to detail does not mean that they are in any sense collaborators in the pursuit of apparent goods or in the satisfaction of unlawful appetites.[41] That is why they are not responsible for wrongdoing.[42] And it is why they are the perfect cosmic enforcers, ensuring that all human beings get the fate they deserve.[43]

---

[39] See *Tim.* 41D1–3; *Lg.* 10.902B8–9. We are possessions (κτήματα) of the gods, but not personal possessions. We are more like the gods' "charges." They are a species through which the Good is communicated to us. The gods' care for this cosmos is characterized as a sort of amusement for them, not because they do not take their job seriously, but because it is so easy for them to do what they do, like a trained mathematician teaching long division.

[40] See *Tim.* 89E3–90D7 where the emphasis is on the proper use of the three εἴδη of soul in the person with the goal of divinization or achieving immortality. This is the "reversion (ἐπιστροφή)" spoken of earlier.

[41] See *Lg.* 10.902A1–4, 903B4–C5 on the gods' attention to the detailed construction and management of the universe, including us as parts of a whole. See Plotinus, *Enn.* III.2 [47], 9.10–16 Henry-Schwyzer, who recognizes universal providence over the entire cosmos without attention to particular details. See Solmsen 1942, 151–155, where the absence of personal providence flows from the universality of the Good. If my good is never achieved at your expense, then personal providence melds with a commitment to universal order. See Jorgenson 2021, 267–268, on providence in *Timaeus* operating at the specific, not personal, level.

[42] *Rep.* 10.617E4–5: αἰτία ἑλομένου· θεὸς ἀναίτιος (the one who has chosen is responsible; god is without responsibility). Cf. *Lg.* 10.904B8–C2 where the αἰτία is identified with the acts of βούλησις of each person. Presumably, this is not the βούλησις for the real Good but a desire for the apparent good.

[43] *Lg.* 10.903D3–E1. See Carone 1994, 292, on divine rewards and punishments as part of a framework of universal cosmic and spiritual order. The universal principle "like goes with like" is operating here. It is a sort of cosmological affront for the wicked ultimately to prosper. This is an idea, of course, with deep roots in Hellenic culture. Plato's moral realism is, among other things, an attempt to provide an intellectual basis for this idea.

The gods are unimpeachable and infallible enforcers of cosmic order.[44] The punishments and rewards they visit on human beings do not have to entail the discovery of *mens rea* in he who is judged. They operate more along the lines of civil judges who assign civil responsibilities. Like a judge who exacts compensatory damages from a defender and assigns them to a complainant, so the gods help restore the order of the cosmos threatened by vice. It might seem as if the gods are acting more like criminal judges than like civil judges, because their judgments concern the person whereas the judgments of civil judges concern the property of persons. But all the cosmos is the property of the gods, and the demotion or promotion of the human being is not, after all, personal.[45]

7.4 Religious Experience

Throughout this book, I have had a number of occasions to point out the difficulties faced by Plato in positing a first principle that is "above οὐσία" and is yet at the same time an object of the "greatest study." In a passage in *Republic* whose significance has already been touched on in Chapter 2, Plato makes an important and subtle distinction between the perception of the Good and the reasoning about it that occurs as a result of this perception.

> having seen it, it ought to be concluded, then, that it is the cause of all that is right and beautiful in all things, as generator of light in the visible realm and of its source, and as authoritative over truth and intellect in the intelligible realm, and that it is necessary to see it for anyone who intends to do anything intelligent in private or in public.[46]

This passage seems to make a distinction between the "perceptual" experience of the Good and the reasoning process that goes on as a result of this perception. This distinction is in line with that which Plato makes frequently between sense perception and reasoning about that.[47] The problem, of course,

---

[44] See *Phd.* 113Dff where in the afterlife the gods render judgments on the embodied lives of the newly arrived souls. Because the gods are infallible knowers, they can evidently "see" into the souls of those who are judged and render to them their just deserts. Cf. *Phdr.* 249A–C. See Saunders 1991, ch. 6, esp. 202–207.

[45] See *Lg.* 1.644D7–645E6 for the famous image of humans as "puppets" of the gods. Cf. 7.804B3.

[46] *Rep.* 7.517B7–C9: ὀφθεῖσα δὲ συλλογιστέα εἶναι ὡς ἄρα πᾶσι πάντων αὕτη ὀρθῶν τε καὶ καλῶν αἰτία, ἔν τε ὁρατῷ φῶς καὶ τὸν τούτου κύριον τεκοῦσα, ἔν τε νοητῷ αὐτὴ κυρία ἀλήθειαν καὶ νοῦν παρασχομένη, καὶ ὅτι δεῖ ταύτην ἰδεῖν τὸν μέλλοντα ἐμφρόνως πράξειν ἢ ἰδίᾳ ἢ δημοσίᾳ.

[47] The most obvious example is the second definition of ἐπιστήμη in *Tht.* 187Aff which is that ἐπιστήμη is not sense perception (αἴσθησις), but on our judgments made about our sense perceptions. The fact that the argument shows that true belief (ἀληθὴς δόξα) is not knowledge, does not change the fact that δόξα is derived from sense perception.

is whether there is a form of perception which is not sense perception and which has as an object not what is strictly intelligible, but what is beyond intelligibility. We have already seen that Plato assumes that everyone – not only philosophers – "divines (ἀπομαντευομένη)" that the Good is something, even though they do not know exactly what that is.[48] Presumably, what philosophers aim for and what they will have to spend decades in attaining is something more than this. Between the modest intuition that the Good is something and the "synoptic" vision of the accomplished philosopher, there are presumably a wide range of possibilities for experience, perceptual or otherwise.[49] And, again, given the ancillary role of the gods, there are numerous ways to explain the facilitating of these experiences, for example, dreams, waking visions, trances, rapturous feelings, signs, and the like. Socrates, repeatedly and without irony, has recourse to these, the meaning of which he always tries to articulate.[50]

I shall assume that a religious experience differs from any other experience (πάθος) by its source. The former is exclusively derived from the gods. Two features of these experiences stand out. The first is shared with all other experiences, namely, that they are passive. Even if we are the source of our experience in some sense, the experience itself is what happens to us, not something we do. Even being in a cognitive state implies passivity. The second feature – and this is what makes religious experience so important for Plato's moral realism – is that it is facilitated for us by gods who are not the ultimate source of the experiences but the mediators of the Demiurge and, ultimately, the Good. Just as the philosopher in the Greater Mysteries in *Symposium* spontaneously produces true virtue as a result of his vision of the Forms, so the gods reveal to us in various unpredictable ways the goodness that they possess as a result of their knowledge.

As Socrates says in *Phaedrus*, no living thing could be incarnated as a human being if it did not have, prior to incarnation, knowledge of Forms.[51] This fact in a way makes the gods' work easier; but in another way, it makes it impossible, which is to say that they become philosophically

---

[48] *Rep.* 6.505E1–2.
[49] See *Rep.* 7.537C7 on the "synoptic vision" of the successful dialectician. See Broadie 2021, 191–193, on how this vision evidently encompasses both the intelligible world and the intelligible aspect of the sensible world.
[50] For example, at *Phd.* 60D8–E7, Socrates tells Cebes that he hears in a dream an exhortation to "make art and practice it." Socrates interprets this as an exhortation to engage in philosophical discussions. After his condemnation, he reinterprets the dream as an exhortation to make more conventional art, namely, poetry.
[51] *Phdr.* 249B5–6: οὐ γὰρ ἥ γε μήποτε ἰδοῦσα τὴν ἀλήθειαν εἰς τόδε ἥξει τὸ σχῆμα ([a soul] that has never seen the truth will never take this [human] shape).

7.4 Religious Experience

exiguous. A god can give to Er a vision of the afterlife, the meaning of which is his to contemplate. Or a god can give a bit of wisdom to an oracle who can pass it on to the petitioner. But in both cases, the resulting experience does not guarantee that anyone will make sense out of it or be able to articulate to themselves the truth of what they experienced. If philosophy is necessary to make sense of the universal intuition that the Good is something, then the role of the gods is inevitably diminished.

The paradigm of this range of experiences is the madness (μανία) of the philosophical lover bestowed on some by the gods.[52] This form of madness is expressed in unmistakably religious language, especially the language of the Eleusinian cult.[53] It is this form of madness that is associated with the recollection (ἀνάμνησις) of the Forms.[54] The collocation of the concepts of madness and recollection is, I think, illuminated by placing them within the framework of moral realism. The salient feature of madness is loss of self-control.[55] The difference between bad madness and good madness is that the loss of self-control in the latter is really a loss of the self-control exhibited by ordinary people, those who at best practice political or popular virtue. As we have seen, this is virtue in practice without the inner self-transformation that alone can produce true virtue. The loss of self-control of the philosopher is actually the liberation from the control exercised over one by one's own appetites and emotions. This occurs by means of recollection of the intelligible world. So, the recollection is a self-transformation or, as Charles Griswold carefully shows, the achievement of self-knowledge.[56] The recollection of Forms is self-knowledge because the true self is really cognitively identical with intelligible reality. And the reason the good we all seek is identical with the Idea of the Good is that the Good is virtually all intelligible reality. The beneficent madness that takes one outside of oneself is the madness when in the grips of which one finds one's own good in the Good.[57]

---

[52] *Phdr.* 244A4–10, 249D4ff.
[53] See *Phdr.* 250C4: μυούμενοι ("initiates"), ἐποπτεύοντες ("those having a revelation"), καθαροί ("purified").
[54] *Phdr.* 249B5–D3.   [55] See, for example, *Phdr.* 244A8–B3.
[56] See Griswold 1986, 111–137, esp. 121–123. See 113, where Griswold identifies self-knowledge and "existential completeness or satisfaction" which I understand as the achievement of one's own good. See Renz 2017 for a contemporary version of "Socratic" self-knowledge as natural achievement.
[57] See *Lg.* 9.863C1–D4 for disastrous double ignorance (τὸ διπλοῦν ἀμαθία) which is the burden of someone who is not just ignorant of what the good is (see 864A1–2: τὴν δὲ τοῦ ἀρίστου δόξαν) but also thinks that he knows what it is. At *Phil.* 48C7–E11, the ignorance that is the polar opposite of self-knowledge is in fact this double ignorance, not just of knowing what the good is, but thinking that one is wise with regard to it. Cf. *Alc.* I 129C4–130A1; *Lys.* 218A–B. See Layne 2019 who nicely draws the connection between double ignorance and the excessive self-love in *Laws* discussed above.

Socrates announces at his trial that he has been instructed by the gods, through oracles and dreams, to practice philosophy.[58] There is no indication by Socrates of how exactly this instruction was delivered. Even if we should choose to suppose that the instruction was as straightforward as a voice saying, "philosophize!," Socrates would still need to decide whether this was a delusion on his part or not. It seems more likely that Socrates woke up one day with the belief – an experiential state – that philosophical activity was his divine destiny. To attribute this awareness to a directive by the gods perhaps amounts just to the conscious experience of disassociation from one's endowed self and affinity for the ideal subject of thinking. There is nothing especially remarkable about one experiencing a vocation or calling. The role of the gods in this respect seems to ensure that such an experience is interpreted within the correct metaphysical framework.

In the *Timaeus* passage to which I have alluded on several occasions, Timaeus declaims on the choices available for humans, adding the important point that the intellect is a daemon given to us by god.[59] Access to our daemon means access to our intellect. But this access is not just thinking, which is, after all, an activity with which we are endowed. The access is identification with the intellect, which is to say, desiring only what the intellect wills, namely, the Good. Socrates' own daemon holds him back from doing things that are inconsistent with achieving the Good. This amounts to, as the *Laws* passage discussed earlier in this section states, acting out of excessive self-love, privileging the idiosyncratic apparent good. A daemon is guaranteed to each rational animal, no one of whom would have been incarnated if had not already experienced intelligible reality. Soul care is, after all, god care.

7.5 Evil

Let us begin with an important distinction Plato makes but which is not always observed in the literature. The opposite of virtue (ἡ ἀρετή) is vice (ἡ κακία, pl. κακίαι).[60] The opposite of the adjective or noun good (ἀγαθόν, pl. ἀγαθά) is evil (κακόν, pl. κακά). As I have been arguing throughout this

---

[58] *Ap.* 33C4–7.
[59] *Tim.* 90A2–4: τὸ δὲ δὴ περὶ τοῦ κυριωτάτου παρ' ἡμῖν ψυχῆς εἴδους διανοεῖσθαι δεῖ τῇδε, ὡς ἄρα αὐτὸ δαίμονα θεὸς ἑκάστῳ δέδωκεν ... (we should consider that the principal type of our soul is a daemon that god has given to each of us); cf. C5. There is no doubt that this "principal part" is intellect. See D4.
[60] See for example, *Me.* 72A2–5; *Rep.* 1.353E7–8; *Lg.* 10.904B2–5.

book, Plato holds that the Form(s) of Virtue is good or beneficial because it partakes of the Idea of the Good. So, a virtuous person or deed is good and her practice of virtue beneficial insofar as she partakes of the Form of Virtue. In addition, as we have seen, an index of virtue is integrative unity according to kind. From this it should follow rather straightforwardly that an index of vice is *dis*integration according to kind. The theoretical terminus of disintegration is just what evil is. Therefore, "evil" has no meaning apart from the Good and apart from a potential trajectory away from it. This does not imply, however, that a vicious person or deed is evil insofar as she partakes of a Form of Vice. Since *all* Forms are good owing to the Good, we do not need to try to figure out how a Form of Vice can be good. The unique determinant of value is the Good and failure to partake of the Good may be properly termed evil, but not because of participation in the intelligible world. And yet, as we learn in *Theaetetus*,

> It is not possible for evils to be destroyed, Theodorus, for it is necessary that there always be something set over against the Good, nor is it possible for them to be ensconced among the gods; rather, they necessarily lurk in mortal nature and here below. For this reason, we should try to flee from here to there as quickly as possible.[61]

We have already learned why there is no evil among the gods.[62] What, though, beyond the fact that there are vicious persons, is usefully added if we say that there are evils in this world? And why do they exist of necessity?

It seemed obvious to everyone in antiquity that the Good against which evils are set is in fact the Idea of the Good. But this has been frequently denied in more recent times.[63] On this more recent view, good and evil are held to be contraries so that the necessity of evil or evils follows from the existence of good or goods. Thus, the absence of any good would be evil. In the ever-changing sensible world, we could be confident that the generation of any good would eventually be followed by an evil, that is, the

---

[61] *Tht.* 176A5–9: Ἀλλ' οὔτ' ἀπολέσθαι τὰ κακὰ δυνατόν, ὦ Θεόδωρε – ὑπεναντίον γάρ τι τῷ ἀγαθῷ ἀεὶ εἶναι ἀνάγκη – οὔτ' ἐν θεοῖς αὐτὰ ἱδρῦσθαι, τὴν δὲ θνητὴν φύσιν καὶ τόνδε τὸν τόπον περιπολεῖ ἐξ ἀνάγκης. Διὸ καὶ πειρᾶσθαι χρὴ ἐνθένδε ἐκεῖσε φεύγειν ὅτι τάχιστα. Cf. *Tim.* 86B7–8. See Ilievski 2014, 143–164; 2016, 221–222.

[62] See *Rep.* 2.379C2–7.

[63] See for example Sedley 2014, 74, who translates "something opposite to good," omitting the definite article before "good" and thereby treating evils as a contrary to good. Sedley's thesis is that *Theaetetus* represents Socrates as the "midwife of Platonism." What this means, among other things, is that the Idea of the Good in *Republic* should not be read into a dialogue which is actually representing a Socratic rather than a Platonic position. This "Socratic" position is to put "god" as a paradigm at the apex of moral philosophy. It is the "Platonic" position to posit a "higher entity," the Idea of the Good. See 76–77.

absence or disappearance of that good. The reference to good, taken in the context of the entire passage, does not in fact indicate contraries (ἐναντίαι), but rather an opposition between the sensible world in which evils dwell, and the intelligible world, in which there is no evil at all. So, if "the good" in this passage refers to a co-ordinate Form of the Good and not to the superordinate Idea of the Good, we still do not have grounds for saying that evil is contrary to it; although we *could* say that evil is contrary to an instance of it. So, suppose that pleasure is a good, and the absence of pleasure, call it "pain," is evil. It is, I would suggest, a singularly inept reading of this passage to suppose that the evils "lurking in mortal nature" include, among other things, the removal of a pleasure, either causing a real pain or a "neutral" state mistaken as a pain, as in *Philebus*. The exhortation to flee from here is surely not an Epicurean exhortation to avoid all painful states. Insisting on the restoration of the definite article for "good," we have every reason to take this passage as central to the moral realism being examined in this book.

The necessity of evils is owing to the necessity of there being something set over against the Good. This is not a trivial or insignificant claim. What is "set over against" or "opposite (ὑπεντάντίον)" the Good can be neither without οὐσία (since it would then *be* the Good), nor with οὐσία (since it would then participate in a Form, which participates in the Good and so would be in itself good). Stated otherwise, it cannot be beyond the productive power of the Good (since then the Good would be limited in its productive ability, which is impossible for that which is beyond οὐσία), nor can it be within the productive power of the Good insofar as that power utilizes the array of οὐσίαι that is the intelligible world. What is opposite the Good is produced by the Good *without* the instrumentality of the Forms and Demiurge. This strange pseudo-product, called "evil," is a sort of residue or side-effect of the Good's productive activity. It is the unqualified condition for the possibility of the instantiation of the Forms. But it is also a terminus of the trajectory in the direction opposite to that of the Good and opposite to the direction of integrative unity. Within this framework, *evils* are the multiple results of failed attempts to instantiate Good; they are "instantiations" of the principle of unlimitedness conceived of as evil insofar as that is a terminus of action.[64]

The Indefinite Dyad is the principle of unlimitedness, as the Good or One is the principle of limit. As such, the Indefinite Dyad is outside the

---

[64] See Ilievski 2014, 148–150, for a similar interpretation.

scope of the causal activity of the Forms and Demiurge. Its manifestation in the sensible world is the Receptacle or necessity, which, too, is outside the scope of the Demiurge's activity. The necessary condition for the possibility of the variegated cosmos is also a principle of evil, but only in the sense of being the terminus of the trajectory of the activity of embodied souls. What cannot be destroyed is the permanent possibility of disintegration of the embodied self.[65] I suggest that Plato is not maintaining that it is impossible for there to be a world in which there is no vice; he is maintaining that it is impossible for there to be a world in which embodied selves are not constantly apt for or tempted to self-disintegration.[66]

If evil or evils are necessarily "here" and not "there," it seems reasonable enough to infer that this is at least in part owing to whatever differentiates the sensible world from the intelligible world. The principal features of the sensible world that separate *us* from the intelligible world are embodiment and changeability.[67] It is the bodily and changeable element (σωματοειδές) that is the source of all of our woes. It would be highly misleading to identify this bodily element with, say, parts of our bodies or even our entire anatomies. After all, the parts of human bodies themselves participate in intelligible natures according to their functions and structures, and so on. It is an unalloyed good for a human being to have lungs and a heart since without these we could not exist as human beings. The bodily element responsible for evils is that which necessitates that the unified soul be dispersed or "scattered (σκεδαστή)."[68] In order to successfully inhabit a body, the unified self must be divided among the ephemeral subjects of embodied activities and powers. As a result of this dispersal, human beings are prone to incontinence and vice. This is because – for whatever reason – they identify themselves as the adventitious subjects of those bodily states. And since every subject desires its own good, that subject seeks a good

---

[65] See *Crit.* 121A7–B7 where this disintegration is vividly described. It occurs when "human nature" takes the ascendancy over the "divine nature" within us. This occurs when πλεονεξία (greed for physical possessions) and a desire for δύναμις (power) appears to humans as the source of their happiness.
[66] See *Tim.* 48A6–7: ... τὸ τῆς πλανωμένης εἶδος αἰτίας, ᾗ φέρειν πέφυκεν (the form of the wandering cause [i.e., necessity] whose nature it is to carry things off). See Archer-Hind 1888, 167, *ad loc.*, "The πλανωμένη αἰτία is the source of instability and uncertainty (relative to us) in the order of things; whence Plato terms it the moving influence." Archer-Hind is followed by Cornford 1937, 160, n.2.
[67] See *Phd.* 81B1–C6. Cf. *Sts.* 269D5–7, 273A1–E5. Whatever is embodied is susceptible to change, including disintegration unless, like a god, it has an indestructible body.
[68] See *Tim.* 37A5.

within corporeal parameters. Presumably, the principal evils that inhabit this world are the consequences of incontinence and vice for embodied subjects themselves and for other persons. The practitioner of vicious behavior is the one who suffers evil. So, evil is the necessary result of vice, impossible to escape.[69]

As a result of our predicament, the elimination of ignorance (ἀμαθία) is, of course, of paramount importance.[70] I would urge that the most perspicuous way to describe this ignorance is as the ignorance of the fact that one's own good and the instantiation of the Idea of the Good are identical.[71] With the abolition of the ignorance of *this*, one could be confident that one will never be inclined to identify oneself as other than the subject of thinking. This is so because the ephemeral subjects of appetite and emotion aim for goods that are private and nonshareable, and as likely as not to require for their acquisition what is bad for someone else.

The cosmic foundation for the bodily element that represents the permanent possibility of evil is found in *Timaeus*. All of the intelligibility that there is in the sensible world was inserted there by the Demiurge, who imposed shapes and numbers on the pre-cosmic chaos.[72] Since the Demiurge is good, nothing that comes from him is evil.[73] The cosmic foundation for the bodily element is the Receptacle, the nurse of becoming.[74] It is the principle that is the condition for the possibility of there being living animals, who imitate the Living Animal eternally contemplated by the Demiurge. Aristotle claims that the Receptacle is matter, that is, prime matter.[75] We need not dwell on the enormous body of literature questioning or defending this interpretation.[76] For our purposes,

---

[69] Thus, there is no need to posit an evil world-soul opposed to the world-soul made by the Demiurge. See *Lg.* 10.903D-904C. 906B. See Ilievski 2014, 193–202.

[70] See, for example, *Protag.* 353Aff, 355Aff; *Me.* 77A–78B; *Lg.* 3.688C–D. The study of the Good would be the crowning achievement of any effort to remove all morally relevant ignorance.

[71] See *Lg.* 10.903C4–5: ... οὐχ ἕνεκα σοῦ [the universe] γιγνομένη, σὺ δ' ἕνεκα ἐκείνου (... the generation of the cosmos is not on account of your benefit, but your generation is on account of its). Cosmically speaking, one's own good can never be separated from the good of the universe because Good is one.

[72] *Tim.* 53C5, 54D4–5. Even if it is true that all cosmic motion originates in soul (see *Phdr.* 245C9; *Lg.* 10.896A5–B1), this fact tells us nothing about precosmic motion. Or, if we do not take the generation of the cosmos literally, it tells us nothing about the disorderly or chaotic motion that is owing to the Receptacle. See Vlastos 1965, 397; Hager 1962, 73–74.

[73] See *Tim.* 29E1–2; *Phdr.* 247A7 on the absence of φθόνος (grudging) from the divine generally; *Rep.* 2.379B1–C7 on the goodness of the divine and its incapacity for evil. Also, *Lg.* 10.900E1–8, 906A7–B3.

[74] *Tim.* 48E7.   [75] *Phys* Δ 2, 209b11–17.

[76] See Hager 1962; Happ 1971, 95–130, with nn. 64ff, for a comprehensive survey of the previous literature. Although there has, of course, been a great deal of additional work done on the Receptacle since then, these have mainly been repetitions and defenses of older positions all ably catalogued by Happ.

it suffices to point out that it is the Receptacle that enables embodiment and hence the possibility of the disintegration that is vice. We should note, however, that being a principle of this possibility does not thereby make the Receptacle evil or a principle of evil.[77] Only insofar as a person succumbs to vice and turns away from the Good can the "terminus" of disintegration be described as a principle of evil.[78] But of course this terminus is unattainable by anything that retains sufficient intelligibility and unity to be called "this" rather than "that" or "something" rather than "nothing."

As the principle of embodiment, the Receptacle is the manifestation of the Indefinite Dyad or the unlimited as described in *Philebus*.[79] The imposition of limit on the unlimited by an intellect, divine or otherwise, is what makes possible identity (ταυτότης), difference (ἑτερότης), and sameness (ὁμοιότης) here below. In our case, the imposition of one kind of soul onto a body is what makes one kind of animal rather than another. And the imposition of the *right* measure of limit is what makes a good version of that animal. Virtue is, in general, the imposition of the right limit or measure on the embodied soul. The particular virtues are named by the particular limits imposed on particular psychical dispositions of the embodied soul. The evils in this world arise from excess or defect in the appropriate limits.[80] Evils are the result of vice either in oneself or in others. What are called "physical" or "natural evils" are in fact necessary concomitants of the administration of the universe by the gods.[81] The result of excess or defect is just disintegration according to kind. So, the principle of evil is that which is manifested variously as a result of vice or as the result of embodiment. In both cases, matter is the underlying necessary condition.

This account provides us with a further insight into the connection between vice and apparent goods. That which is merely apparently good but not really so is such because of our reliance on sense perception and

---

[77] See Robin 1908, 574–580, who argues, correctly in my view, that matter is the condition for the possibility of evil, but not evil itself. See also Ilievski 2014, 166–192.
[78] See *Sts.* 270A1–2 where it is denied that evil is to be attributed to gods with contrary attributes. The alternatives are good governance and no governance, the latter of which merely makes vice possible.
[79] See Aristotle, *Meta.* A 6, 988a14–15, where he says that Plato assigned evil to the principle of the unlimited. Also, *M* 10, 1075a32–36; *N* 4, 1091b30–35; *Phys.* A 9, 192a4–17.
[80] See *Lg.* 10.906C2–6: φαμὲν δ' εἶναί που τὸ νῦν ὀνομαζόμενον ἁμάρτημα, τὴν πλεονεξίαν, ἐν μὲν σαρκίνοις σώμασι νόσημα καλούμενον, ἐν δὲ ὥραις ἐτῶν καὶ ἐνιαυτοῖς λοιμόν, ἐν δὲ πόλεσι καὶ πολιτείαις τοῦτο αὐτό, ῥήματι μετεσχηματισμένον, ἀδικίαν (We say that the error now named "having more than is appropriate" is in organic bodies called "sickness," in the seasons and years called "plague," in states and governments the identical thing, with a change of names, "injustice").
[81] See *Rep.* 8.546A–B on the necessary decay of all that is generated. See Broadie 2001, 6.

belief (δόξα). The belief is inextricably bound up with having a body.[82] So, one believes that satisfying the appetite which appears to be good for oneself really is so. And so it may be. But it is the role of an intellect to make that determination. If the intellect knows that the Good is instantiated in this way, then what appeared to be good really is so. If it does not know this, then all manner of confusion is practically guaranteed. For most people, most of the time, what appears to be good is far removed from an instance of the universal Good itself for the obvious reason that this good will appear as idiosyncratic, that is, indexed to a particular appetite or emotion. One may, like the paradigmatic tyrant, concede that what one thinks is good for oneself is at odds with the Good. It is hard to see how these can be identical. This inability to discern the merely apparent good is the burden of embodiment and the reason for identifying matter with the permanent possibility of evil.

In *Laws* Book 9, there is an important passage, already discussed in Chapter 5, in which the Athenian Stranger is asked by Cleinias to give a clear account of the difference between injustice and injury and the difference between the voluntary and the involuntary.[83] It turns out that pleasure, anger, and ignorance are virtually identical in diverting persons from what they really will for themselves.[84] As we know, what people will is their own good. And as we have also learned, what is good for the individual is just what is universally good. The reason why pleasure, anger, and ignorance produce injustice, whether voluntarily or involuntarily, is that these are apt to lead to the disintegration of the individual. What prevents this is when "belief in the best (τὴν δὲ ἀρίστου δόξαν)" rules in the soul.[85]

As we learn explicitly in *Timaeus*, the Receptacle exists independently of the Demiurge.[86] But it does not exist independently of the Good, if indeed the Good is the unhypothetical first principle of all. I suspect that at least one reason for resisting the idea that embodiment leads to evil because of

---

[82] See *Tim.* 51D5–7: ὡς τισιν φαίνεται, δόξα ἀληθής νοῦ διαφέρει τὸ μηδέν, πάνθ' ὁπόσ' αὖ διὰ τοῦ σώματος αἰσθανόμεθα θετέον βεβαιότατα (if as it appears to some, true belief does not differ from intellect, all such things as are perceived through the body should be taken as the most secure).
[83] *Lg.* 9.863A3–864C1.   [84] *Lg.* 9.863E2.
[85] *Lg.* 9.864A1–2. The line is ambiguous, suggesting either that δόξα is equivalent to knowledge of the Good or that it is not, in which case it amounts to a belief in the rule of reason in the individual. The latter seems more appropriate given that the passage goes on to make the qualification, "even if some mistake is made (κἂν σφάλληται τι)." It is possible that one with knowledge of the Good might err in applying this knowledge, but it seems more likely that the *Laws* passage is picking up the notion of popular or political virtue from *Republic*. Cf. *Lg.* 3.689A5–C3.
[86] *Tim.* 51E6–52D1.

matter is that *Timaeus* is being read in isolation from the larger context which includes the Good whose causal powers extend beyond those of the Demiurge. What the Good produces is the condition for the possibility of maximally manifesting goodness. Without the Receptacle there could be no living things because there could be no elements with which to compose them. Evils become a reality when, owing to embodiment, human beings misidentify themselves and act in a manner that is contrary to what promotes their integrative unity. Everyone does indeed desire only the Good. But in addition, everyone can only pursue what appears to be an instance of Good. If what appears to be so is not so, then the ultimate terminus of action is evil and not the Good.

Embodiment constitutes a permanent invitation to evil since the soul of an embodied creature must be "dispersed" into the multiple subjects of affective, conative, and cognitive states. To be born into this world is to be set on a trajectory to *dis*integration. The pervasive practical dimension of Plato's moral realism should be evident when we consider the enormous space Plato devotes in the dialogues to education, love, politics, religion, and to the essentially aristocratic activity of philosophy. All of these belong to strategies for mounting resistance to the disintegration of the self. The natural trajectory of the will (βούλησις) is in permanent conflict with the natural trajectory of the embodied soul.

7.6 Politics and Metaphysics

Aristotle has an entirely perspicuous way of separating politics from metaphysics. He distinguishes between the practical sciences and the theoretical sciences, with politics belonging to the former and metaphysics to the latter. The sciences are generically different since they have different starting points or principles. And because ethics is a part of political science, it, too, is separate from metaphysics.[87] By contrast, for Plato, the scientific nature of ethics and politics is the same because both are

---

[87] See *EN* A 1, 1094b11 and throughout the work, where the political nature of ethics is emphasized. It is worth reflecting on the fact that *Eudemian Ethics* expresses no such political context. See, however, A 6, 1216b35–39, where the absence of direct political contextualization may indicate that this treatise is focusing more on the theoretical foundation of a practical science. Aristotle, *Meta.* α 1, 993b19–21, says that theoretical sciences aim at truth, while practical sciences aim at action. But from this it does not follow, of course, that there are no theoretical foundations for a practical science. The very fact that ethics and politics are sciences indicates that they have their own theoretical knowledge. Baracchi 2008 goes beyond an argument for the existence of a theoretical foundation for practical science in holding that theory, or at least wisdom (σοφία), is an integral part of the practical sciences as such. Her provocative thesis that for Aristotle, ethics *is* first philosophy, cannot be addressed here.

applications of metaphysical principles.[88] In particular, bringing about virtue in the family and in the *polis* is the task of one practiced in philosophical science or dialectic.[89] And even if we insist that the statesman is different from the philosopher, nevertheless, she needs to access the results of dialectic in order to instantiate the Good. She needs to acquire the craft that rests upon the science or knowledge that is the grasp of intelligible reality in the light of the Idea of the Good.[90] Because Aristotle has a principled way to establish the autonomy of politics, he need not trouble himself with a whole host of questions that for Plato are unavoidable. These are questions regarding the very possibility of a connection between metaphysics and politics and especially regarding the *bona fides* of the statesman. The second question is especially vexing.

As we have seen, everyone acts according to how the Good appears to them, including even those who think that one's own good and the Good may diverge. The virtuous person for whom the apparent good is identical with the real good is no exception. This is just a fact about the psychology of embodied moral agents. There is, however, an interpersonal consequence of this fact which is, politically speaking, unavoidable. Since I can only judge as good what appears to me to be good (and the opposite), I can only judge what you claim to be good according to whether or not it appears to me to be good, too. If you claim to know what is good for me and for you together, I must suppose that it appears to you that so and so is good for us and if I agree, then it appears to me that what appears to you to be good for us is in fact so. But if what appears to you to be good for us does not appear to me to be so, then we have a problem, indeed. For my acknowledgment of your authority over me would seem to depend on it appearing to me that what appears to you to be good for us is in fact so.[91]

---

[88] Both Aristotle, *Pol.* B 3, 1265a2–4 and Cicero, *De leg.* 2.6.14, assume the continuity of *Republic* and *Laws*, with the former work providing the ultimate metaphysical foundation for the latter. This continuity only suggests a common metaphysical framework, not an agreement even about legislation much less constitutional matters.

[89] I am doubtful of the claim of Cartledge 2000, 17–18, that the Greek πόλις was essentially a "stateless community" meaning that it did not possess any of the characteristics of the modern state. It seems to me, however, that the principal characteristic of any state – that it have a monopoly of force on a defined population – was true of the ancient πόλις.

[90] See Márquez 2012, 223–225, on the Good as the ultimate measure of political τέχνη.

[91] Lane 1998, 201, concludes her study of *Statesman* thus, "The knowledge of the good in time, which makes it possible to determine the particularities of timing, is in this Platonic dialogue the sole basis for genuine political authority." I think that Lane's use of the word "authority" is slippery. As a reason for acting, knowledge is certainly a good authority; in fact, it is logically unimpeachable. But as a justification for the exercise of political power, there is a serious problem when the one over whom the putative authority is being exercised denies the claim to knowledge, *even if the denial is mistaken*. My argument is that the *interpersonal* authority of knowledge is illusory.

At the moment it no longer seems to me to be that what appears to you to be good for us is so, you must lose in my eyes authority to direct my actions. For *all* my actions are directed to what appears to me to be good. But if I believe that what appears to you to be good for me is not in fact so, then I have absolutely no motive for acting to achieve a result that I believe is not good for me.

Of course, I might defer to your claimed expertise in determining what is good for us because I am in doubt or because I recognize your intellectual acuity and moral virtue. But then again, I might not. And even if I were to defer, that would be because it appeared to me that what appears to you (the expert) to be good for me is in fact so or perhaps more likely to be so than how it appears to me. Actually, I have no special access to the potential benefit of your expertise if I do not possess that expertise myself. Readers will recognize here a political analogue of the epistemological problem posed by Plato of how to transmit knowledge. Plato, as we know, urges the superiority of oral transmission via conversation to written transmission. But whereas my inability to grasp, say, a metaphysical distinction that you orally present to me merely leaves me ignorant of the distinction, within a political context, my inability to grasp the correctness of your political directive – whether orally transmitted or not – has significant consequences. It forces me to act or to be acted upon over and against what, *ex hypothesi*, appears to me to be good.

It will not do, of course, to appeal to democratic values to solve this problem. Plato heaps scorn on the notion of a majority possessing the expertise that is thought to follow from knowledge of the Good just because it is a majority.[92] Even if somehow it did, that would not solve the problem. For someone in the minority can run through the same dialectical steps regarding appearances in regard to the majority that one person can do in regard to another. It has to appear to me to be good for me to want to do it even if it may be the case that it appears to me to be so upon reflection on the fact that it so appears to a majority. When in *Apology*, Socrates expresses his view that it would be absurd for him to do something that he believes would hurt him – in this case, corrupting the youth – the generalization of his sensible point is actually quite devastating. Why would or should anyone do anything or accede to anything that they regard as detrimental to themselves? It is not a satisfactory answer to this question to say that I might accede to

---

[92] See, for example, *Rep.* 8.544B–C; *Sts.* 303A-B. But see *Sts.* 300B3–4 where laws are instituted upon the consent of τὸ πλῆθος (the majority). So, too, *Lg.* 3.690C1–3. What is supposed to happen when the subjects are no longer willing is not stated.

what is detrimental to me because I think it will serve the greater good. For in that case, my desire to serve the greater good turns the accession into something that is *not* detrimental to me. All things considered, I would rather serve the greater good than myself. But then of course, I *could* decide that I serve the greater good only when I look after my own good and not the good of another. The apparent promotion of the "greater good" certainly *can* be, if it is not always, a vehicle for the imposition of perpetual mischief on a population.

It is worth noting that Aristotle does not avoid this problem entirely by cutting politics off from metaphysics. For though the person who is the best political leader does not, according to Aristotle, make decisions based upon the results of Platonic dialectic, he still relies on there being a science of human action and a skill of instituting laws and practices that promote the best actions for everyone. When a member of the political community or *polis* demurs in the ruler's assessment of the actions to be undertaken, there is no real pathway to legitimate authority; there is only a fallback to force.[93]

This problem has nothing to do with relativism. Acknowledging that my good and the Good are identical still leaves me with this inevitable result: it appears to me that this is how my good (= an instance of the Good itself) is achieved here and now.[94] To say this is *not* to agree that if it appears to be good for you, then it really is good for you, which is what the relativist wants to maintain. The defeat of the relativist only results in the recognition that something is not good for someone just because it appears to that person to be good for him. It does not free us from the bondage of appearance and, in regard to the present problem, from the fact that what appears to me to be the path to what is really good for me might well not coincide with what appears to you to be the path to what is really good for me.

If we stipulate that the authentic Platonic ruler is one who knows what is good for the *polis*, and therefore what is good for each and every member of it, this ideal perspective is in fact infinitely removed from the practical perspective of those who deny or doubt the rulers' claims to knowledge.

---

[93] The problem is no less acute in the case in which one appeals to divine authority. It makes perfectly good sense to rely on divine authority if you believe that you have access to divine commands. If you do not, then you have nothing else to fall back upon than how things appears to you even when they appear as diametrically opposed to how it appears to those who recognize divine authority.

[94] In *Lg.* 1.645A1f; 4.714A2; 12.957C6f, Plato associates law (νόμος) with intellect (νοῦς) or, better, the deliverances of intellect. The latter is transmuted into the former. One may or may not be persuaded that a law is in one's own interest even if we stipulate that if it is not, then it is no law.

To say that, in this circumstance, one can safely ignore the latter perspective since it is, by definition, self-defeating, is to abstract from the real-world problem of conflicting claims to knowledge. Because Plato thinks that politics as well as ethics has a metaphysical foundation, he can proceed quite a long way without confronting the problem of legitimacy, which is not at all a theoretical problem. When he does confront this problem, not directly, but indirectly by considering what to do with citizens who reject the legitimacy of the rule of the *soi-disants* knowers, he proposes some exceedingly harsh and repellent solutions.

7.7 The Common Good

Perhaps Plato is not in fact badly placed to solve this problem. For if good is good just in the way that 3+4 = 7, then whenever good is done, it is a common good. If I act justly, it is good for you that I act justly even if that involves my punishing you.[95] So, substitute "ruler of the *polis*" for "me." If the ruler makes a just law with a sanction and the law is disobeyed because obedience does not appear to some to be in their own interest, then no matter. The one who resists just punishment is actually worse off if he avoids it; he is better off if he endures it.[96] How is it different for one who denies the legitimate authority of the ruler? *Res ipsa loquitur.* Whether the law is just or not is logically independent of how the law appears both to the one who institutes it and to the one who suffers under its yoke. If I were to acknowledge the justice of my punishment, then it would appear to me that suffering it is in my interest, so long of course as it appears to me that justice is good for me.

It is entirely understandable that one might assume that whoever postulates a universal Good as first principle of all is doing nothing different from postulating a common good. After all, could there be anything more "common" than that which is universal? A moment's reflection, though, should lead us to conclude that "universal" does not necessarily imply "common," at least in the sense in which it is relevant to political theory.

---

[95] Mackenzie 1981, 191, argues that Plato's advocacy of an "individualist account" of punishment is in direct opposition to a Protagorean emphasis on the public good of punishment. But the universality of Good supersedes this false dichotomy.

[96] See *Sts.* 293C5–E6, where it is clear that the only thing that differentiates a good constitution from a bad one is the results of its implementation: βελτίω ποιῶσι κατὰ δύναμιν (making it [the *polis*] better so far as possible, E1). It is blithely mentioned, 293C7, that legitimacy is reserved to those whom the ruled "discover (εὑρίσκοι)" to have the requisite knowledge. If they discover this, would they not already have the knowledge themselves? The skepticism of the ruled in regard to the knowledge claims of the ruler will carry over to the claims about successful rule made by the ruler. In real life, what people actually discover is the subtle power of sophistry, as Plato so well knew.

For as we have already seen, the universality of the Good makes it impossible that the very thing that is an instantiation of it in my case could not be an instantiation of it in yours. And yet any but the most attenuated sense of the common good in political theory at least allows for the possibility that the achievement of the common good is not going to be good for *someone*. The more one is committed to the common good, the more one is going to acquiesce in its attenuation in meaning so, finally, no sincere protest by someone who feels unjustly treated is going to be taken seriously – so long as the common good is advanced.[97]

The idea of the common good has always thrived in a profoundly un-Platonic context wherein utilitarianism and democracy are positively valued. And yet without some idea of the common good, it is far from clear how any of Plato's centralizing political ideals in *Republic*, *Statesman*, and *Laws* could be defended.[98] There are two problems here. The first is whether there actually is such a thing as a common good and the second is whether there is any legitimacy for someone imposing his determination of the common good on someone to whom things appear otherwise.

If good for something is indexed according to integrative unity of a natural kind, then the first step is to establish that the *polis* exists by nature.[99] It is not unreasonable to assume that Plato supposed that if human beings form a natural kind, then their agency is natural, too. And of course the integrative unity of a person is produced through activity, including social activity. And, to continue this line of thinking, if virtue is that which produces integrative unity, then it is not so far-fetched at all to think that the associations of persons, including especially the political association (κοινωνία) that is a *polis*, can achieve an integrative unity, or at

---

[97] See *Lg.* 9.875A1–B1, where the Athenian speculates on a corrupt ruler who places his own (ἴδιον) good above that of the common (κοινόν) good. This might suggest that Plato countenances a common good that might actually conflict with a private good. But the contrast here need only indicate that to the corrupt ruler his own good appears to be in conflict with the common good; in reality, it cannot be. The same reasoning applies in the case of someone who thinks that a conflict between a putative common good and a private or personal good should necessarily be resolved in favor of the former.

[98] See esp. *Rep.* 4.420B3–421C6; *Lg.* 5.739B8–E7; and the passage cited in the note above, 9.875A1–B1, on the priority of the common good over that of individuals. Also, *Sts.* 296B5–D4, D8–E4.

[99] See *Rep.* 2.369B7–9, where Socrates asserts that the *polis* comes about because no one is self-sufficient. This claim perhaps seems more anodyne than it is. If a *polis* is one kind of κοινωνία ("association") (C1–4) it is, generically speaking, unquestionably true that most people cannot live or at least live happily without some human associations. But a *polis* is a specific type of association, the existence of which entails a great deal more than voluntary human interaction. At *Lg.* 10.889D6–E5, the Athenian Stranger describes the position of atheists as holding that "political (πολιτικήν)" affairs have very little to do with nature. This is the position that is opposed in Bk. 10. So, we may safely assume that Plato wants to maintain that the *polis*, a political association, exists by nature.

least something analogous to this.¹⁰⁰ So, we get the analogy between the individual and the *polis* and their virtues in Book 4 of *Republic*. I take it that the univocity of the virtues when applied to the understanding of integrative unity in the individual and in the *polis* is going to have to be a key premise in any argument that Plato constructs for a common good.¹⁰¹

So, we need to ask next about the legitimacy of the imposition of someone's determination of the common good on someone to whom things appear otherwise. Plato evidently sees this as a fundamental problem since the understanding of the universality of the Good is explicitly limited to philosophers. For the rest of the members of the *polis*, what appears to be in one's own interest is more likely than not often seen as being in conflict with the interests of others. The problem leads Plato to have Socrates articulate and defend one of the more notorious ideas in the entire corpus, that of the noble falsehood (γενναῖον ψεῦδος).¹⁰² The falsehood is in the form of a myth consisting of two parts. The first part is a myth about the origins of the members of a *polis*. In this myth, people are not born and raised in the ordinary way but are "sown" in the earth and disgorged by their earth mother at the appropriate time. The purpose of the myth is to impel people to regard each other as siblings and the earth, that is, the land comprising their *polis*, as their mother and to act accordingly. That is, they are to treat other citizens and the *polis* itself as family, with the implication that they will regard their good as identical to their own.¹⁰³ The second part of the myth, the myth of metals, is of a very different sort. It imagines people as having "mixtures" of gold, silver, bronze, or iron in their souls, these corresponding to their capacity for work as guardians or auxiliaries or as those who produce the goods and services that are the *raison d'être* of the *polis*. If, for example, parents with silver souls bear a child with iron in his

---

¹⁰⁰ See Pradeau 1997, 2002, esp. ch. 5, who provides an illuminating analysis of the various grades of unity that Plato attaches to different types of *poleis*. The achievement of political unity understood as the dissolution of στάσις (discord) is the fundamental theme of *Laws*, and identified with its greatest good. See *Rep.* 4.422E4–423B1; *Lg.* 1.624A1–628E1. See also the insightful remarks of Wilburn 2021, 193–201; 240–248.

¹⁰¹ See 2.368E2–3: δικαιοσύνη, φαμέν, ἔστι μὲν ἀνδρὸς ἑνός, ἔστι δέ που καὶ ὅλης πόλεως; (We say, don't we, that there is justice in a single man, and there is somehow justice in the whole state?) The cautious qualification που ("somehow") indicates at least that it is not obvious that the justice discovered in an individual will be identical to that which is found in the state.

¹⁰² See *Rep.* 3.414B–415D; cf. 5.459E6–460A6 on the rigged mating lottery. See for a good summary of the argument and its attendant problems Schofield 2006, ch. 7. Schofield, 316, calls the noble falsehood "a Socratic form of paternalism." By calling it "Socratic," Schofield means that it encapsulates Plato's response to the life and death of Socrates. I suppose that "Socratic" is also intended by Schofield to mitigate the bad associations of the word "paternalism."

¹⁰³ See Schofield 2006, 286.

soul or with gold, then their demotion or promotion to another class will not be resisted but rather celebrated.

The two myths are very different. The first is a preposterous story, perhaps only slightly less preposterous than other myths of national and ethnic origins.[104] But the second myth has a rather straightforward and benign, even sensible, interpretation, which is that it promotes meritocracy. It tells a story in which *Beruf* or vocation is distinguishable from biology. But the meritocracy is still here tied to biology because though the golden child of bronze parents is not destined to be a farmer rather than a guardian, she is nevertheless destined by her biology to one position in the *polis* rather than another. The biological destiny is severable from parenthood on behalf of support for the first myth. If people are persuaded that their own good is identical with that of the whole *polis*, then they will acquiesce in having their children do the opposite of following in their own footsteps.

What makes the falsehood "noble" instead of ignoble? The distinction between the two depends on a deeper distinction between a falsehood in the soul and a falsehood in words.[105] A falsehood in the soul is a false belief and no one wants to have false beliefs in their soul.[106] Indeed, it does not even seem possible to have, knowingly, a false belief in one's soul. Plato has a sweeping account to give of our propensity for true beliefs rather than false ones, including especially our desire for the Good. But we may set that aside for the moment. The falsehood in the soul is contrasted with a falsehood in words, which is a sort of "imitation (μίμημα)" or "image (εἴδωλον)" of the former.[107] As an expression of a falsehood in the soul, or as a device for instilling falsehoods in the soul, designating it as an imitation or image hardly seems to make it any better. It is like the pathogen that travels between hosts. But then Socrates adds a crucial qualification. The falsehood in words, unlike the falsehood in the soul, can be "useful (χρήσιμον)," especially if it approximates the truth as much as possible.[108] As the examples adduced by Socrates show, usefulness overcomes falsity, strictly conceived. So, a falsehood spoken to an enemy or a falsehood spoken to a friend who has gone insane and is

---

[104] In *Menex.* 239A1–5, the myth is vaguer: we are all born of one mother (ἰσογονία) for which reason we have ἰσονομία (equality before the law). Aristotle, *Pol.* B 1–6, makes a sustained criticism of Plato's efforts to achieve political unity, although he does not refer to the myths which are supposed to facilitate this. Rowett 2016 offers an interesting interpretation of the first myth according to which it actually refers to a common educational system. If this is true, then there is no falsehood here, only a myth for the many who are incapable of understanding the deep basis for political unity. If Rowett is correct, then it would seem that no one would need persuasion to tell them that they were products of the same educational system as all other citizens.

[105] See *Rep.* 2.382A4–D4.   [106] *Rep.* 2.382B1–4.   [107] *Rep.* 2.382B8–9.   [108] *Rep.* 2.382C7–D4.

7.7 *The Common Good*

attempting to harm himself or others is justified by its good goal. This is a goal that is, presumably, not achievable with the truth.[109]

So, the noble falsehood is supposed to be a falsehood in words that approximates the truth and is useful because it achieves a goal that is otherwise not achievable.[110] In the present case, political solidarity is the useful goal where this solidarity amounts to the (true) belief that the good of the *polis* and the good of the individual member are identical.[111] Viewed from this perspective and with this background, the story behind the noble falsehood may seem entirely benign on the assumption that it does indeed approximate the truth and on the further crucial assumption that it is in fact useful for producing political solidarity in those for whom there is no other way of achieving this result.[112]

There is, however, a deeper problem here. The agreement by all that goodness is one thing and that my good is never achievable at your expense is still disconnected from the common good viewed as the aim of a political program or policy. For it may appear to one person, who accepts completely the basic premise, that the baseline for pursuing her own good is a renunciation of aggression against anyone else. So long as she does not aggress, the basic principle has not been violated. Whatever she decides to do beyond that is below the threshold for political action. Yet it may well appear to another person, again accepting completely the basic premise, that all sorts of laws and institutional practices intended to promote the good of all are possible and even necessary. In other words, having established a *polis* in which everyone is – whether through philosophy or by swallowing a myth – in agreement about the unity of goodness, we are again thrown back on the problem of appearances.[113] It may well appear to one that the Good is not instantiated in a way or by means that to another appear correct. What then? Plato has a number of answers to this question, including corporeal punishment, banishment, and execution. He does not offer an answer or even conceive of an answer that privileges something like

---

[109] See Rist 1998, 69–70, who points out that "bourgeois" virtue – which is the only virtue that the nonphilosophers in the *polis* are capable of – has to be cultivated with deception and self-deception.

[110] Joyce 2001 proposes a pragmatically convenient "fictionalism" as a substitute for moral discourse, which he regards as fundamentally misguided because, roughly, there exists nothing real for such discourse to refer to. Plato's noble falsehood seems to be a bit of fictionalism *within* a vast realm of truth claims resting on metaphysical foundations. Joyce 238–239 suggests that the noble falsehood should be justified under the rubric of fictionalism.

[111] Note that the word χρήσιμος is the word used to indicate that it is the Idea of the Good that makes the Virtues useful.

[112] As Schofield 2006, 287, notes, this helps especially to explain the pervasive role of religion in *Laws*.

[113] Here I disagree with Schofield 2006, 304–309, who thinks that the noble falsehoods are indispensable and that philosophy does not offer an alternative source of motivation for devotion to the state.

inviolable individual autonomy in this regard.[114] Nor does he countenance the possibility that few if any institutions or laws are even likely to avoid disregarding the claim that one person's good is not achievable at the expense of another. It is difficult to see how a utilitarian calculus of some sort would not have to operate in the institution of laws and practices with even minimal content. So, the common good is not problematic if at the most general level it is just equivalent to the instantiation of the Good in a *polis*. But as soon as that instantiation begins to bite, one can hardly go even a single step without its violation. Beyond the foreswearing of aggression against others, it is implausible in the extreme to suppose that enforced decisions about the common good can avoid devolving into utilitarian calculations that undercut the universality of the Good and its being identical to the good of every single individual.[115]

In *Statesman*, we get an inkling of Plato's awareness of the problem when he insists that what differentiates the statesman from the tyrant is that the former rules willing subjects (ἑκουσίῳ) whereas the tyrant rules by force (βιαίῳ).[116] Superficially, the distinction seems benign, but it will seem less so if we realize that the "willing" subject has it in his power at any moment to turn the statesman into a tyrant by becoming an "unwilling" subject, in which case force will be needed. In addition, it is not unreasonable to expect that even in a small population of "subjects" there will be some who resist the authority of the statesman even if they are in the minority. The problem is not that one calling himself a statesman is really a sophist because his claimed knowledge is unreal, but that even if it is real, its political relevance depends upon whether it appears to be so to those who are forced to endure its application. The appeal to knowledge is made later in the dialogue, when the distinction between consent and force is explicitly rejected and it is said that the only difference between the statesman and the tyrant is knowledge (ἐπιστήμη).[117] But the supposition that one can without difficulty move from "knowledge is sufficient for virtue" to "knowledge is sufficient for political legitimacy" is an illusion. Plato certainly knew that transmitting knowledge from person to person is more than problematic; it is practically impossible. So, the putative knowing statesman has to transmit

---

[114] See for example *Lg.* 11.923A6–B2, where individual autonomy of person or property is peremptorily rejected in favor of clans, ancestors, and descendants, which themselves belong ultimately to the *polis*. Cf. 11.925D5–E5; 12.942A–C.

[115] See Duffy 2020, 1067–1068. As Duffy points out, the analogy between political rule and medicine used at *Sts.* 291B1–C3 and 293D4–E2 strongly suggests that just as the doctor will sacrifice one part of the body for the good of the whole, so the ruler will sacrifice some citizens, or at least their wellbeing, for the good of the whole.

[116] *Sts.* 276E6–8. [117] *Sts.* 291E1–292D1, 300A4–7.

true beliefs. Perhaps this is somewhat easier, but it is far from inevitably accomplished. Even if we concede that the tyrant in all of us, who does what seems best but not what he really wills, would be benefited by being led to see things truly and clearly, we are only pretending that the mere logical possibility of universal agreement is realizable in practice.

The inevitable paternalism of Plato's conception of politics or rule in the *polis* is, one might suppose, mitigated or excused by the hypothetical scientific character of the rule. As we saw in the last chapter, the statesman is not a philosopher, although the statesman is presumed to have knowledge and to have the craft of insinuating that knowledge into the fabric of the political community.[118] And we should add that the knowledge is ultimately of the fundamental norm of all reality, the Good. The statesman is in this regard not just like the trained physician but like a physician who is also a scientist. She knows *why* this treatment or that is the best.[119] The analogy, though, cuts more than one way. For the patient may decide that a particular treatment will cure the disease but only at a cost that she does not wish to bear. Unflinching paternalism insists that she does not have the right to refuse treatment. If we recoil from this conclusion, the supposed power of political expertise vanishes, too. For the *ex hypothesi* good institution or practice or law that the statesman imposes may be rejected by someone not because she has renounced her pursuit of the real good, but because what exactly that is appears to her to be other than what the statesman says it is.

7.8 Legitimacy in the *Polis*

Plato maintains that the legitimacy of rule in the *polis* is derived from the knowledge of the rulers.[120] This knowledge is how to instantiate the Good, which is necessarily a common good. He is also clearly aware that there is a fundamental problem of the acceptance of legitimacy by those who are ruled but do not have knowledge.[121] Plato seems to think that knowledge trumps ignorance absolutely. No one, Plato thinks, would prefer to be treated by an ignorant physician as opposed to a knowledgeable one. In this regard,

---

[118] See Márquez 2012, 111, on knowledge as the only difference between tyrant and statesman.
[119] Mackenzie 1981, 222, proposes as a justification of the suppression of autonomy by the ruler that her success in instantiating the Good in the ruled entails no infringement of rights. Is this not another noble falsehood?
[120] See *Rep.* 5.473C11–D6; *Sts.* 292B–293C; *Lg.* 3.690B8–C1; 9.875C3–D2. It has rarely been noticed in the literature that what Glaucon calls the "city of pigs" is an ἀληθινὴ πόλις ("true *polis*"), even though it has no guardians. It seems that only with the "luxurious *polis*" is the need for guardians introduced, and the concomitant problem of compulsion by the rulers of the ruled.
[121] See *Rep.* 7.516E7–517A2.

he seems to have no difficulty with the analogy between τέχνη in medicine and τέχνη in politics.[122] It is far from clear, however, that the legitimacy flows from the knowledge, or rather from the acceptance by the ruled of the claims to knowledge, by the rulers. If the former, then "legitimacy" becomes entirely a theoretical term; if the latter, then lack of acceptance entails *illegitimacy*.

Plato's recognition of this problem is evident in the multifarious devices he deploys to maximize acceptance of the legitimacy of a ruler by a potentially obstreperous public. Principal among these are education and persuasion, and constitutional arrangements, the presumed acceptance of which by a founding people will tend to minimize dissent further down the line.[123] For example, an original egalitarian distribution of property is to be sought.[124] All of these devices are aimed at producing the greatest possible unity within the *polis*.[125] But just because it is sometimes extremely difficult to persuade someone that you have knowledge – above all the knowledge of what is good for them – resting legitimacy on knowledge is a far more demanding proposal than resting it on something else, including democracy. The democratically chosen rulers do not have to rest their claim to legitimacy on knowledge, but only on the majority beliefs about what is in the common interest.

There is perhaps one potential solution to this problem to be found in the gap between ideal and reality, as explained in *Republic*. As Socrates says to Glaucon,

> Is it possible for something to be put into practice as described, or is it natural for practice to have less contact with the truth than speech, even if it doesn't seem so to someone? Do you agree or not? – I agree, he said – Then don't force me to demonstrate that what we have described in theory must in every way come about in practice. Rather, if we are able to discover a *polis* that most closely approximates what we have described can be founded, you have to allow that all that you have mandated we show has been discovered to be possible.[126]

---

[122] See, for example, *Gorg.* 521E6–522A7; *Rep.*3.389B–C; *Sts.* 296A–297B.
[123] See, for example, *Lg.* 4.722B5–C2, 9.857C2–E5.   [124] See *Lg.* 5.737A–738B.
[125] See *Lg.* 5.739D3–4: καὶ κατὰ δύναμιν οἵτινες νόμοι μίαν ὅτι μάλιστα πόλιν ἀπεργάζονται (whatever laws that make the *polis* as unified as is possible). These are the laws for a *polis* of human beings, as opposed to *Republic* which is a *polis* for "gods or the children of gods." See Laks 1990, 214. At 4.716E7ff, the arriving colonists of Magnesia are addressed in a way that is intended to produce maximal acceptance of the constitution of the *polis*. An appeal to god as "measure of all things" is an integral part of the address.
[126] *Rep.* 5.473A1–B1: Ἆρ' οἷόν τέ τι πραχθῆναι ὡς λέγεται, ἢ φύσιν ἔχει πρᾶξιν λέξεως ἧττον ἀληθείας ἐφάπτεσθαι, κἂν εἰ μή τῳ δοκεῖ; ἀλλὰ σὺ πότερον ὁμολογεῖς οὕτως ἢ οὔ; – Ὁμολογῶ, ἔφη—Τοῦτο μὲν δὴ μὴ ἀνάγκαζέ με, οἷα τῷ λόγῳ διήλθομεν, τοιαῦτα παντάπασι καὶ τῷ ἔργῳ δεῖν γιγνόμενα <ἂν> ἀποφαίνειν· ἀλλ', ἐὰν οἷοί τε γενώμεθα εὑρεῖν ὡς ἂν ἐγγύτατα τῶν εἰρημένων πόλις οἰκήσειεν, φάναι ἡμᾶς ἐξηυρηκέναι ὡς δυνατὰ ταῦτα γίγνεσθαι ἃ σὺ ἐπιτάττεις.

7.8 *Legitimacy in the* Polis

In the ideal *polis*, there will be complete agreement among all the participants about constitutional and legal matters. After all, since everyone is virtuous by definition, one can expect universal agreement that the good of each person is identical with the good of all. This would presumably be the case, even for the producers who, in contrast to the guardians, do not have property and families in common. Anything short of the complete consent of the governed would constitute a falling away from the ideal, however the absence of consent was addressed.[127]

Plato can grant that dissenters do not undermine the ideal; their existence only speaks to the degree to which the ideal is approached by any actual *polis*.

Plato seems right to suppose that most people will be content to put their future happiness into the hands of those who can persuade them that they have the knowledge necessary for putting into practice the laws that will most likely facilitate this. He seems to be on less solid ground in supposing that the political unity thus achieved is more stable than it actually is. Even more important, I think, is that if the *polis* does exist by nature, and integrative unity is its ideal achievement, then the real alternatives are not between a *polis* and anarchy, but among a hierarchy of *poleis*, in which the criterion of ranking is approximation to the ideal.

The above analysis suggests, perhaps surprisingly, that there is no obvious political application for Plato's moral realism. For a commitment to the universality of Good is not undermined by the recognition of the fallibility of appearances. The moral realism plus this recognition do not easily cohere with the exercise of political authority. At least they do not when political authority directly conflicts with the appearances, albeit fallible, of those upon whom the authority is exercised. The most sincere and wholehearted commitment to the common good is not betrayed by someone who concludes that the ways that putative manifestations of the Good appear to the rulers are not just fallible, but false.

In conclusion, it is perhaps worth pointing out that the infirmity of Plato's moral realism in the face of the challenge of political authority does not necessarily indicate a defect in that moral realism. Nor does it suggest that an alternative ethical theory is going to have an easier time in establishing the legitimacy of political authority. Nor, again, does it follow that Aristotle's separation of politics and ethics from metaphysics opens up a plausible approach to the problem. Plato does not accept the autonomy

---

[127] See *Lg.* 8.832C2–5 on the requirement of consent of the governed. See *Rep.* 9.590C7–D6 which assumes "external (ἔξωθεν)" control absent consent.

of politics, basing it ultimately on metaphysics. Aristotle's approach would seem to be more promising insofar as he separates politics from metaphysics. But though he insists on the authoritative status of politics in relation to ethics, he nevertheless conceives of politics along the lines of the ethical question "how should people live?" So, he does not really separate politics from his own version of moral realism. Insofar as Plato's political philosophy follows upon metaphysics and ethics, its failure does not substantially affect the first two. Insofar as Aristotle's politics has "architectonic" superiority in relation to ethics, the failure of a solution to the legitimacy problem leaves his moral realism without support, metaphysical or otherwise.

CHAPTER 8

Concluding Remarks

Aristotle made a sharp distinction between the practical sciences and the theoretical sciences, with ethics belonging to the former and metaphysics belonging to the latter. The end of a practical science is action; the end of a theoretical science is truth. Of course, the knowledge sought in theoretical science is not irrelevant to action. Still, knowledge in metaphysics or mathematics or physics does not belong to the starting points or principles of a science of action. By contrast, for Plato ethics is inseparable from metaphysics because the fundamental principles of ethics are metaphysical principles. The Platonic position, however, is more radical than an insistence on rooting ethics in fundamental truths about the world. Plato agrees with Aristotle that ethics is about action and so about particulars. But all particulars belong to the sensible world and as such they are merely images of eternal reality. So, it is not just the case that ethical claims must be deduced from metaphysical truths, but that nothing about the sensible world, including human action and norms, can be grasped or explained unless the images are accurately represented as such.

Plato's moral realism is both breathtakingly ambitious in its scope and, at the same time, surprisingly modest in its defensible conclusions. To maintain that there is an absolutely simple first principle of all that is both metaphysical and axiological is to be committed to extreme systematic unity. Yet for this very reason, the steps from "the Good is universally one and the same everywhere" to "the Good is manifested here and now in this specific action of mine" are perilous, to say the least. It is not, I think, inapposite to combine an insistence on the reality of the metaphysical-cum-axiological first principle with a relatively high degree of skepticism in regard to the beneficial effects of one's behavior, especially with regard to other people. This claim does not amount to a counsel of inaction. As Socrates would no doubt point out, often to refrain from acting is perforce to act. To be guided by the principle that one's own good cannot be purchased at the expense of another, to reflect continually on whether one's self-love is so "excessive" as to constitute a violation of this principle, and to adhere to the trifold criteria of integrative unity consisting in beauty, truth, and symmetry, seems to describe a robust moral realism without grandiose illusions about one's success at casuistry. The philosopher is, according to Plato, better off than everyone else insofar as he knows or even just believes that the sensible world is only an image of the intelligible world, and that morality is embedded in metaphysics. But he is no miracle worker, since he is embodied and living in the sensible world. His incapacities multiply exponentially the more widely he casts his net in practical affairs.

The principal feature of the sensible world that is relevant to Plato's moral realism is that human beings, though they desire the Good and manifestations of it are, owing to embodiment, destined to act to achieve what appears to them to be good. They do this always with the hope and even expectation that what appears to them to be good is in fact so, though there is no necessity of this. The principal attraction of the acquisition of virtue is that the virtuous person can forge a more reliable connection between what appears to her to be good and what is in fact so.

Plato uses the word "good (ἀγαθόν)" in a popular sense and also in a technical sense. According to the popular sense, it is evident to all that there are many human goods, that is, many things or states that human beings typically aim to obtain. According to the technical sense, the superordinate Idea of the Good is the source of the real goodness in anything properly so called. To deny that physical health or pleasure or friendship or thinking or virtue are goods in the popular sense would be to put oneself outside the scope of normal rational discourse, and not in a good way. Nevertheless, we are not truly human beings and the Good we desire is not the goods or aims of human beings. It is always open at any critical juncture in life to question whether one or more of the goods that human beings typically pursue are in fact manifestations of the Good that we all will. It is also open to question whether among the human goods one or another prioritization of these will actually achieve the Good. It is not too much of an exaggeration to say that Plato's moral realism is focused on strategies for bringing popular goods in line with real manifestations of the Good in the technical sense.

The contrast between apparent goods and real goods is not identical to the contrast between human goods and manifestations of the Idea of the Good. For one thing, while apparent goods are in fact really good when we are referring to the appearances of a virtuous person, human goods are always defeasible as manifestations of the Good. As Plato has Socrates say, wisdom turns human goods into manifestations of the Good. A human good such as pleasure does not stop being a human good for a virtuous person to whom it appears that some pleasures are bad.

The distinction between veridical and nonveridical appearance turns up dramatically throughout the dialogues, especially among Socrates' interlocutors who, conceding that they will the Good, identify their pursuit of manifestations of it in ways that betray their misunderstanding of the imagistic nature of the sensible world. For example, Socrates' multifaceted argument against Callicles to the effect that pleasure is not the Good is not intended to deny that pleasure is good. It is intended to show the mistake in thinking that pleasure is the Good because it is pleasure, and so obviously desirable or a good. The closer one gets to realizing that the way to instantiate the Good is not to identify it with the material out of which instantiations are formed, the closer one gets to a healthy assessment of images of the real and our interaction with them. So, a human good like pleasure may appear veridically or nonveridically to manifest the Good. The former, like the true pleasures in *Philebus*, are true even though they are images of disembodied cognitive states. The latter, like the false pleasures of anticipation in *Philebus*, are false, not because they are not pleasures, but because they nonveridically appear to manifest the Good.

The putative metaphysical foundation of moral realism for Plato, the Idea of the Good, is saved from irrelevance by its identification with the One such that integrative unity according to kind is an index of our attainment of the Good. The One is not, as we have repeatedly seen, the number one or a unity. It is a principle of measure and, therefore, a principle of number, which is only one type of measure. It is a principle the manifestations of which are necessarily complex unities. Anything other than the first principle of all is complex. Anything that is complex has a unity of some sort; otherwise, it would not be one complex, but many complexes, which themselves would have to be unities, too. Integrative unity according to kind is the ideal unity for anything. It represents the achievement or fulfillment of the nature or kind that is an endowment. Ideal and nonideal types of integration are precisely gradable according to proximity to the Good that everything seeks. Perfect or absolute integration is not possible for that which is complex. "Union" with the Good is a misconceived idea. Nevertheless, a watershed in the process of achieving integrative unity is separation from the body, which is a permanent source of disunity. Psychical separation involves the identification of the self with the subject of thinking. Physical separation at death presumably leaves the achieved self, whether ideal or not, to its own fate.

Within this framework, it is easy to see the importance of gradations of virtue. There are indefinitely many ways of achieving unity in a life, even if there is only one way of achieving the ideal. Plato's taxonomy of *poleis* and of individual souls is only the barest sketch of the major possibilities indexed to the tripartite soul. But within that general schema, every personal narrative – especially in retrospect – will present a unique version.

For Plato, the resources of ancient Greek high culture are adequate for bringing about popular or political virtue in individuals and the *polis*. But it is philosophy, and philosophy alone, that is able to advance integrative unity both in the individual and the state and to the achievement of the ideal. Many misunderstandings of Plato's moral realism, as I have tried to show throughout this book, arise from not taking sufficiently seriously the distinction between the two principal grades of virtue. Popular or political virtue *is* virtue just as false pleasure is pleasure. But the integrative unity that it achieves is unstable and unreliable. Socrates' ringing declaration in *Apology* that the unexamined life is not livable for a human being is but a gesture in the direction of the articulated and exhaustive philosophical educational program in *Republic*. Again in *Apology*, the valorization of "soul-care" does not rise much above the level of a banal slogan until it is clear that the soul is the self, and that this self has taken on the travails of embodiment and so lost its way. When these truths are clear, philosophy understood as transformative self-discovery comes into its own. At that point, one begins to see that the Good that we all desire is definitely not to be identified with any human good, even when it is manifested in one or another human good. The successful philosopher, who does not mistake the image for the real thing, is able to attain a healthier perspective on these human goods than is one who looks to one or another, or to all, as the locus of the Good. I take it that this is what Plato is getting at when in Book 9 of *Republic* he makes the astonishing claim that the philosopher will enjoy physical pleasure more than one who is addicted to it.

I have argued that the moral realism exposed in this book does not translate smoothly into a political context. The self-limiting rule never to attempt to achieve the good for oneself at the expense of anyone else is not, I believe, a rule that can legitimate the exercise of political power. It is difficult – for me at any rate – to conceive of any form of state that does not have recourse to some form of utilitarianism in the imposition of its laws. But Plato's moral realism is unalterably opposed to utilitarianism. I suppose that there have been political regimes that were, broadly speaking, non-utilitarian. But they are one and all totalitarian, wherein not some but all are apt for sacrifice to some ideal or other. Plato himself evidently saw the problem of legitimacy for his ideal and quasi-ideal *poleis*. I do not think, however, he saw clearly enough that, while my knowledge is a firm basis for my actions, political legitimacy requires more, or from another perspective, less than this. Plato does indeed recognize the need to persuade citizens of a new *polis* of the desirability of its laws, institutions, and practices. But successful persuasion does not require knowledge, and some are not persuadable, even by those who, *ex hypothesi*, know.

I conclude with the following comparison from the dialogues and from Plato's central methodological strategy. In *Parmenides*, Plato sets up a radical dilemma: either nominalism or Platonism. And then he goes further. If you opt for nominalism, then you cannot even say legitimately that there are two things in the world since then each would be one and they would share "oneness" even though they are two. So, the only alternative to the radical and preposterous extreme nominalism that is Eleaticism is Platonism. With regard to Plato's moral realism, there is a similar dilemma: either a moral realism rooted in the superordinate Idea of the Good or there is no basis whatsoever for any universal propositional claims about good or bad, right or wrong. Plato supposed, I imagine, that if you recoil from the latter, sooner or later you will embrace the former.

Bibliography

Primary Sources

All citations from Plato are from the five-volume Oxford Classical Texts Plato (OCT), edited by John Burnet, *Platonis opera, Oxford, 1900–1907 with the Addition of Platonis Rempublicam*, edited by S. R. Slings (Oxford, 2003) and *Platonis opera*, Tetralogias I–II, edited by E. A. Duke, W. F. Hicke, W. S. M. Nicoll, D. B. Robinson, and J. C. G. Strachan (Oxford, 1995).
All citations from Aristotle are from the *OCT* editions of Aristotle.
Alcinous. *Enseignement des doctrines de Platon (Didaskalilos)*, edited by J. Whittaker. Paris, 2002.
Atticus. *Fragments*, edited by É. des Places. Paris, 1977.
Iamblichus. *Les mystères d'Égypt*, edited by É. des Places. Paris, 1966.
Jaeger, W. (ed.). *Aristotelis Metaphysica*. Oxford, 1957.
Plotinus. *Plotini opera*, 3 volumes, edited by P. Henry and R. Schwyzer. Oxford, 1964–1983.
Proclus. *Elements of Theology*, 2nd ed., edited by E. R. Dodds. Oxford, 1963.
   In Platonis rem publicam, 2 volumes, edited by W. Kroll. Leipzig, 1899–1901.
   In Platonis Parmenidem commentaria, 3 volumes, edited by C. Steel. Oxford, 2007–2009.
   In Platonis Timaeum commentaria, 3 volumes, edited by E. Diehl. Leipzig, 1903–1906.
   Sur le premier Alcibiade de Platon, 2 volumes, edited by A.-P. Segonds. Paris, 1985–1986.
   Théologie platonicienne, 6 volumes, edited by H. D. Saffrey and L. G. Westerink. Paris, 1968–1997.
Ross, W. D. (ed.) *Aristotle's Metaphysics*, 2 vols. Oxford, 1924.

Secondary Sources

Adam, J. A. 1921. *The* Republic *of Plato*, with critical notes, commentary, and appendices. 2 vols. Cambridge, UK.
Adams, R. 1983. "Divine Necessity." *The Journal of Philosophy* 80: 741–752.
   1999. *Finite and Infinite Goods: A Framework for Ethics*. Oxford.

Ademollo, F. 2018. "On Plato's Conception of Change." *Oxford Studies in Ancient Philosophy* 55: 35–83.
Allan, D. J. 1955. "Plato's Moral Philosophy." *Classical Review* 5(1): 53–56.
Anderson, A. 1969. "Socratic Reasoning in the *Euthyphro*." *Review of Metaphysics* 22: 61–76.
Anderson, M. 2020. "What Are the Wages of Justice? Rethinking the *Republic*'s Division of Goods." *Phronesis* 65: 1–26.
Annas, J. 1981. *An Introduction to Plato's* Republic. Oxford.
    1993. "Virtue as the Use of Other Goods." In *Virtue, Love and Form: Essays in Memory of Gregory Vlastos*, edited by T. Irwin and M. Nussbaum (= *Apeiron* 25, 3/4). Edmonton, AL: 53–66.
    1997. "Understanding the Good: Sun, Line, and Cave." In *Plato's* Republic: *Critical Essays*, edited by R. Kraut. Lanham, MD: 143–168.
    1999. *Platonic Ethics: Old and New*. Ithaca, NY.
    2008. "Virtue Ethics and the Charge of Egoism." In *Morality and Self-Interest*, edited by P. Bloomfield. Oxford: 205–221.
    2011. "Plato's Ethics." In *The Oxford Handbook of Plato*, edited by G. Fine. Oxford: 267–285.
    2015. "Plato's Defense of Justice: The Wrong Kind of Reason?" In *The Quest for the Good Life: Ancient Philosophers on Happiness*, edited by O. Rabbas, E. Emilsson, H. Fossheim, and M. Tuominen. Oxford: 49–65.
Anscombe, E. 1958. "Modern Moral Philosophy." *Philosophy* 33: 1–19.
    2000. *Intention*, 2nd ed. Cambridge, MA.
Apelt, O. 1912. "Das Prinzip der platonischen Ethik." *In Platonische Aufsätze*. Leipzig: 109–120.
Archer-Hind, R. D. (ed.) 1888. *The* Timaeus *of Plato*. With introduction and notes. London.
Ayers, M. (ed.) 2007. *Rationalism, Platonism, and God*. Oxford.
Baker, S. 2017. "The Metaphysics of Goodness in the Ethics of Aristotle." *Philosophical Studies* 174: 1839–1856.
    2021. "A Monistic Conclusion to Aristotle's *Ergon* Argument: The Human Good as the Best Achievement of a Human." *Archiv für Geschichte der Philosophie* 103(3): 373–403.
Baracchi, C. 2008. *Aristotle's Ethics as First Philosophy*. Cambridge, UK.
    2014. "One Good: The Mathematics of Ethics." *Graduate Faculty Philosophy Journal* 25(2): 19–49.
Baras, D. 2017. "A Reliability Challenge to Theistic Platonism." *Analysis* 77: 479–487.
Barney, R. 1998. "Commentary on Rist: Is Plato Interested in Meta-Ethics?" *Proceedings of the Boston Area Colloquium in Ancient Philosophy* 14: 73–81.
    2010a. "Notes on Plato on the Kalon and the Good." *Classical Philology* 105: 363–377.
    2010b. "Plato on the Desire for the Good." In *Desire, Practical Reason, and the Good: Classical and Contemporary Perspectives*, edited by S. Tenenbaum. Oxford: 34–64.

Becker, L. 1998. *A New Stoicism*. Princeton, NJ.
Bedke, M. 2009. "Intuitive Non-Naturalism Meets Cosmic Coincidence." *Pacific Philosophical Quarterly* 90: 188–209.
Beere, J. 2011. "Philosophy, Virtue, and Immortality in Plato's *Phaedo*." *Proceedings of the Boston Area Colloquium in Ancient Philosophy* 26: 253–288.
Beierwaltes, W. 2002. "Das Eine als Norm des Lebens. Zum metaphysischen Grund Neuplatonischer Lebensform." In *Metaphysik und Religion: Zur Signatur des Spätantiken Denkens*, edited by T. Kobusch and M. Erler. Leipzig: 121–151.
Benitez, E. E. 1995. "The Good or the Demiurge: Causation and the Unity of the Good in Plato." *Apeiron* 28: 113–140.
Benson, H. J. 2000. *Socratic Wisdom*. Oxford.
  (ed.). 2006. *A Companion to Plato*. Malden, MA.
Berman, S. 2003. "A Defense of Psychological Egoism." In *Desire, Identity and Existence*, edited by N. Reshotko. Kelowna, BC: 143–157.
Berti, E. 1983. "Il Platone di Krämer e la metafisica classica." *Rivista di filosofia neoscolastica* 75: 313–326.
  2004. "Is There an Ethics in Plato's 'Unwritten Doctrines'?" In *Plato Ethicus: Philosophy Is Life. Proceedings of the International Colloquium Piacenza*, edited by M. Migliori and L. Napolitano. Sankt Augustin: 35–48.
  2017. *Aristotele: Metafisica*. Bari.
Blackson, T. 2015. "Two Interpretations of Socratic Intellectualism." *Ancient Philosophy* 35(1): 23–39.
Blanshard, B. 1961. *Reason and Goodness*. London.
Bobonich, C. 1991. "Persuasion, Compulsion, and Freedom in Plato's *Laws*." *Classical Quarterly* 41: 365–388.
  1995a. "Plato's Theory of Goods in the *Laws* and *Philebus*." *Proceedings of the Boston Area Colloquium in Ancient Philosophy* 11: 101–139.
  1995b. "The Virtues of Ordinary People in Plato's *Statesman*." In *Reading the Statesman: Proceedings of the III Symposium Platonicum*, edited by C. Rowe. Sankt Augustin: 313–329.
  2002. *Plato's Utopia Recast: His Later Ethics and Politics*. Oxford.
  (ed.) 2017. *The Cambridge Companion to Ancient Ethics*. Cambridge, UK.
Bodéüs, R. 1992. *Aristote et la théologie des vivants immortels*. St-Laurent, PQ.
Bonazzi, M. 2013. "Il posto dell' etica nel sistema del platonismo." In *Ethik des antiken Platonismus*, edited by C. Pietsch. Stuttgart: 25–33.
Bordt, M. 2006. *Platons Theologie*. Munich.
Boyd, R. 1988. "How to Be a Moral Realist." In *Essays on Moral Realism*, edited by G. Sayre-McCord. Ithaca, NY: 181–228.
  2003a. "Finite Beings, Finite Goods: The Semantics, Metaphysics and Ethics of Naturalist Consequentialism, Part 1." *Philosophy and Phenomenological Research* 66: 505–553.
  2003b. "Finite Beings, Finite Goods: The Semantics, Metaphysics and Ethics of Naturalist Consequentialism, Part 2." *Philosophy and Phenomenological Research* 67: 24–47.

Boys-Stones, G. 2014. "Unity and the Good: Platonists Against οἰκείωσις." In *Unité et origine des vertus dans la philosophie ancienne*, edited by B. Collette-Dučić and S. Delcomminette. Brussels: 297–320.
　2018. *Platonist Philosophy 80BC to AD 250: An Introduction and Collection of Sources in Translation*. Cambridge, UK.
Bradley, F. H. 1876 [1927]. "Why Should I Be Moral?" In *Ethical Studies*. London: 58–84.
Brenner, A. 2018. "Theism and Explanationist Defenses of Moral Realism." *Faith and Philosophy* 35(4): 447–463.
Brickhouse, T. 1979. "Plato's Moral Theory." *New Scholasticism* 53(3): 529–535.
Brickhouse, T. and Smith, N. D. 1987. "Socrates on Goods, Virtue, and Happiness." *Oxford Studies in Ancient Philosophy* 5: 1–27.
　1994. *Plato's Socrates*. Oxford.
　2000. *The Philosophy of Socrates*. Boulder, CO.
　2002. "Incurable Souls in Socratic Psychology." *Ancient Philosophy* 22: 21–36.
　2006. "The Socratic Paradoxes." In *A Companion to Plato*, edited by H. Benson. Malden, MA: 263–277.
　2007. "Socrates on Akrasia, Knowledge, and the Power of Appearance." In *Akrasia in Greek Philosophy*, edited by P. Destrée and C. Bobonich. Leiden: 1–17.
　2010. *Socratic Moral Psychology*. Cambridge, UK.
Brink, D. 1989. *Moral Realism and the Foundation of Ethics*. Cambridge, UK.
Brisson, L. 2018. "Sur le Bien: Métamorphose d'une anecdote." Χώρα 16: 167–180.
Broad, C. D. 1959. *Five Types of Ethical Theory*. Paterson, NJ.
Broadie, S. 2001. "Theodicy and Pseudo-History in the *Timaeus*." *Oxford Studies in Ancient Philosophy* 21: 1–28.
　2021. *Plato's Sun-Like Good: Dialectic in the* Republic. Cambridge, UK.
Brown, E. 2012. "The Unity of the Soul in Plato's *Republic*." In *Plato and the Divided Self*, edited by R. Barney, T. Brennan, and C. Brittain. Cambridge, UK: 53–73.
Brown, L. 2007. "Glaucon's Challenge, Rational Egoism and Ordinary Morality." In *Pursuing the Good: Ethics and Metaphysics in Plato's* Republic, edited by D. Cairns, F. G. Hermann, and T. Penner. Edinburgh: 42–60.
Brunschwig, J. 1971. "*EE* 18, 1218a15-31 et le περὶ τἀγαθοῦ." In *Untersuchungen zur Eudemischen Ethik*, edited by P. Moraux. Berlin: 197–222.
Burkert, W. 1972. *Lore and Science in Ancient Pythagoreanism*. Cambridge, MA. (Translation of 1962, *Weisheit und Wissenschaft: Studien zu Pythagoras, Philoloaus und Platon*, Nuremberg.)
Burnyeat, M. 1999. "Culture and Society in Plato's *Republic*." *The Tanner Lectures on Human Values* 22: 215–324.
　2000. "Plato on Why Mathematics Is Good for the Soul." In *Mathematics and Necessity: Essays in the History of Philosophy*, edited by T. Smiley. Oxford: 1–81.
　2006. "The Truth of Tripartition." *Proceedings of the Aristotelian Society* 106: 1–23.
Bury, R. G. 1910. "The Ethics of Plato." *The International Journal of Ethics* 20(3): 271–281.

Butchvarov, P. 1989. *Skepticism in Ethics*. Bloomington, IN.
Butler, T. 2019. "Refining Motivational Intellectualism: Plato's *Protagoras* and *Phaedo*." *Archiv für Geschichte der Philosophie* 101(2): 153–176.
Cairns, D., Hermann, F.-G., and Penner, T. (eds.). 2007. *Pursuing the Good: Ethics and Metaphysics in Plato's* Republic. Edinburgh.
Callard, A. 2014. "Ignorance and Akrasia-Denial in the *Protagoras*." *Oxford Studies in Ancient Philosophy* 47: 31–80.
    2016. "Acratics as Hedonists: *Protagoras* 352B-355A." *Ancient Philosophy* 36(1): 47–64.
    2017. "Everyone Desires the Good: Socrates' Protreptic Theory." *Review of Metaphysics* 70: 617–644.
Campbell, D. 2022 "The Soul's Tomb: Plato on the Body as the Cause of Psychic Disorders." *Apeiron* 55(1): 119–139.
Carone, G. 1994. "Teleology and Evil in *Laws* 10." *Review of Metaphysics* 48(2): 275–298.
    2001. "*Akrasia* in the *Republic:* Does Plato Change His Mind?" *Oxford Studies in Ancient Philosophy* 20: 107–148.
    2004. "Calculating Machines or Leaky Jars? The Moral Psychology of Plato's *Gorgias*." *Oxford Studies in Ancient Philosophy* 23: 55–96.
    2005a. "Mind and Body in Late Plato." *Archiv für Geschichte der Philosophie* 87: 227–269.
    2005b. *Plato's Cosmology and Its Ethical Dimensions*. Cambridge, UK.
Cartledge, P. 2000. *The Greeks: Crucible of Civilization*. Oxford.
Catana, L. 2019. *Late Ancient Platonism in Eighteenth-Century Thought*. Cham.
Centrone, B. 2003. "Platonic Virtue as a *Holon*: From the *Laws* to the *Protagoras*." In *Plato Ethicus: Philosophy Is Life. Proceedings of the International Colloquium Piacenza*, edited by M. Migliori and L. Napolitano. Sankt Augustin: 93–106.
    2021. *La seconda polis: Introduzione alle Leggi di Platone*. Rome.
Chambers, L. P. 1936. "Plato's Objective Standard of Value." *Journal of Philosophy* 33(22): 596–605.
Chan, B. 2021. "A Platonic Kind-Based Account of Goodness." *Philosophia* 49(4): 1369–1389.
Chappell, T. 1993. "The Virtues of Thrasymachus." *Phronesis* 38: 1–17.
    2008. "Moral Perception." *Philosophy* 83, 4: 421–437.
    2010. "Euthyphro's 'Dilemma,' Socrates' Daimonion, and Plato's God." *European Journal of Philosophy* 1: 39–64.
    2014. *Knowing What to Do: Imagination, Virtue, and Platonism in Ethics*. Oxford.
Cheney, D. R. 1971. *Broad's Critical Essays in Moral Philosophy*. London.
Cherniss, H. 1971 [1954]. "The Sources of Evil According to Plato." In *Plato II*, edited by G. Vlastos. Garden City, NJ: 244–258.
Chilcott, C. M. 1923. "The Platonic Theory of Evil." *Classical Quarterly* 17(1): 27–34.
Chlup, R. 2012. *Proclus: An Introduction*. Cambridge, UK.
Clark, J. 2012. "The Strength of Knowledge in Plato's *Protagoras*." *Ancient Philosophy* 32(2): 237–255.

Clark-Doane, J. 2012. "Morality and Mathematics: The Evolutionary Challenge." *Ethics* 122: 313–340.
Cook, A. B. 1896. *The Metaphysical Basis of Plato's Ethics*. Cambridge, UK.
Cooper, J. 1977. "The Psychology of Justice in Plato." *American Philosophical Quarterly* 14: 151–157. (Reprinted in 1999, *Reason and Emotion*. Princeton, NJ: 138–149.)
    1984. "Plato's Theory of Human Motivation." *History of Philosophy Quarterly* 1: 3–21. (Reprinted in 1999, *Reason and Emotion*. Princeton, NJ: 118–137.)
    1999 [1984]. *Reason and Emotion*. Princeton, NJ.
Cornford, F. M. 1923. *Greek Religious Thought*. London.
    1937. *Plato's Cosmology*. London.
Crisp, R. 2006. *Reason and the Good*. Oxford.
Crisp, R. (ed.) 2013. *The Oxford Handbook of the History of Ethics*. Oxford.
Crombie, I. M. 1962. *An Examination of Plato's Doctrines*, Vol. I. New York.
Cross, R. C. and Woozley, A .D. 1964. *Plato's* Republic: *A Philosophical Commentary*. London.
Dancy, J. 2004. *Ethics without Principles*. Oxford.
Dasgupta, S. 2017. "Non-naturalism and Normative Authority." *Proceedings of the Aristotelian Society* 117(3): 297–313.
Davidson, D. 1993. "Plato's Philosopher." In *Virtue, Love and Form: Essays in Memory of Gregory Vlastos*, edited by T. Irwin and M. Nussbaum (= *Apeiron* 25, 3/4). Edmonton, AL: 175–194.
De Sousa, R. 1974. "The Good and the True." *Mind* 83: 534–551.
De Strycker, E. 1970. "L'Idée du Bien dans la *République* de Platon: Données philologiques et signification philosophique." *L'antiquité classique* 39: 450–467.
De Vogel, C. 1986. *Rethinking Plato and Platonism*. Leiden.
Deigh, J. 2018. *From Psychology to Morality: Essays in Ethical Naturalism*. Oxford.
Delcominette, S. 2006. *Le* Philèbe *de Platon: Introduction à l'Agathologie platonicienne*. Leiden.
Demos, R. 1967. "Plato on Moral Principles." *Mind* 76(301): 125–126.
Denyer, N. 2007. "Sun and Line: The Role of the Good." In *The Cambridge Companion to Plato's* Republic, edited by G. Ferrari. Cambridge, UK: 284–309.
Desjardins, R. 2004. *Plato on the Good*. Leiden.
Despland, M. 1985. *The Education of Desire: Plato and the Philosophy of Religion*. Toronto.
Destrée, P. 2017. "How Does Contemplation Make You Happy?" In *Plato:* Symposium. *A Critical Guide*, edited by P. Destrée and Z. Giannopolou. Cambridge, UK: 216–234.
Devereux, D. 1992. "The Unity of the Virtues in Plato's *Protagoras* and *Laches*." *Philosophical Review* 101: 765–789.
    1995. "Socrates' Kantian Conception of Virtue." *Journal of the History of Philosophy* 33: 381–408.
    2008. "Socratic Ethics and Moral Psychology." In *The Oxford Handbook of Plato*, edited by G. Fine. Oxford: 139–164.

2017. "Virtue and Happiness in Plato." In *The Cambridge Companion to Ancient Ethics*, edited by C. Bobonich. Cambridge, UK: 52–71.
Diès, A. 1927. *Autour de Platon*. 2 vols. Paris.
Dillon, J. 2003. *The Heirs of Plato*. Oxford.
  2013. "The Hierarchy of Being as Framework for Platonic Ethical Theory." In *Ethik des Antiken Platonismus*, edited by C. Pietsch. Stuttgart: 91–98.
Dodds, E. R. 1959. *Plato: Gorgias. A Revised Text with Introduction and Commentary*. Oxford.
Dorter, K. 1994. *Form and Good in Plato's Eleatic Dialogues*. Berkeley.
  2006. *The Transformation of Plato's Republic*. Lanham, MD.
Drefcinski, S. 2014. "What Does It Mean to Become Like God? *Theaetetus* 176A–177B." *International Philosophical Quarterly* 54(4): 411–427.
Dreier, J. 1992. "The Supervenience Argument against Moral Realism." *The Southern Journal of Philosophy* 30: 13–38.
  1993. "The Structure of Normative Theories." *Monist* 76(1): 22–40.
Duffy, H. 2020. "Rules for Rulers: Plato's Criticism of Law in the *Politicus*." *British Journal of the History of Philosophy* 28(6): 1053–1070.
Dybikowski, J. 1970. "False Pleasure and the *Philebus*." *Phronesis* 15: 147–165.
Eklund, M. 2017. *Choosing Normative Concepts*. Oxford.
El Murr, D. 2019. "Pourquoi le Bien? Apparence, realité et le désir du Bien (*République* VI, 504B–506D)." *Journal of Ancient Philosophy*, supplementary vol. I: 26–41.
Enders, M. 1999. "Platons Theologie: Der Gott, die Götter, und das Gute." *Perspektiven der Philosophie, Neues Jahrbuch* 25: 131–185.
Enoch, D. 2011. *Taking Morality Seriously: A Defense of Robust Realism*. Oxford.
  2021. "Thanks, We're Good: Why Moral Realism Is Not Morally Objectionable." *Philosophical Studies* 178: 1689–1699.
Erler, M. 2007. *Die Philosophie der Antike*. Vol. II, *Platon*. Basel.
Evans, M. 2010. "A Partisan Guide to Socratic Intellectualism." In *Desire, Practical Reason, and the Good: Classical and Contemporary Perspectives*, edited by S. Tenenbaum. Oxford: 6–25.
Ewing, A. C. 1947. *The Definition of Good*. London.
  1973. *Value and Reality*. London.
Ferber, R. 1989. *Platons Idee des Guten*. 2nd ed. Sankt Augustin.
  2002. "The Absolute Good and the Human Goods." In *New Images of Plato: Dialogues on the Good*, edited by G. Reale and S. Scolnicov. Sankt Augustin: 187–196.
  2020 [1991]. "Sokrates: Tugend ist Wissen." In *Platonische Aufsätze*. Berlin/Boston: 8–28.
  2020 [2013]. "Was jede Seele sucht und worumwillen sie alles tut." In *Platonischen Aufsätze*. Berlin/Boston: 93–113.
Ferber, R. and Damschen, G. 2015. "Is the Idea of the Good Beyond Being? Plato's *epekeina tēs ousias* Revisited (*Republic* 6, 509b8–10)." In *Second Sailing: Alternative Perspectives on Plato*, edited by D. Nails and H. Tarrant. Helsinki: 197–203.

Ferrari, F. 2001. "La causalità del Bene nella 'Repubblia' di Platone." *Elenchos* 1: 5–37.
  2003. "L'idea del bene: collocazione ontologicaa e funzione causale." In *La Repubblica: Traduzione e commento*, Vol V, edited by M. Vegetti. Naples: 287–325.
  2020. "Il Bene e il demiurgo: identità o gerarchia? Il conflitto delle interpretazioni nel medioplatonismo." In *Interpretare Platone*, edited by M. Gatti and P. De Simone. Milan: 239–261.
Ferrari, G. R. F. 1992. "Platonic Love." In *The Cambridge Companion to Plato*, edited by R. Kraut. Cambridge, UK: 248–276.
Fine, G. (ed.). 2011. *The Oxford Handbook of Plato*. Oxford.
Foot, P. 2001. *Natural Goodness*. Oxford.
Forest, P. 1996. *God without the Supernatural*. Ithaca, NY.
Frankfurt, H. 1969. "Alternate Possibilities and Moral Responsibility." *Journal of Philosophy* 66: 829–839.
  1971. "Freedom of the Will and the Concept of a Person." *Journal of Philosophy* 68: 5–20.
Frede, M. 1992. "Introduction." *Plato:* Protagoras, translated with notes by S. Lombardo and K. Bell. Indianapolis, IN: vii–xxxiii.
  1996. "Introduction." In *Rationality in Greek Thought*, edited by M. Frede and G. Striker. Oxford: 1–28.
Freeland, C. 2017. "The Science of Measuring Pleasure and Pain." In *Plato's Protagoras: Essays on the Confrontation of Philosophy and Sophistry*, edited by O. Pettersson and V. Songe-Møller. Dordrecht: 123–136.
Gadamer, H.G. 1986. *The Idea of the Good in Platonic-Aristotelian Philosophy*, translated by P. C. Smith. New Haven, CT.
Gaiser, K. 1963. *Platons ungeschriebene Lehre: Studien zur systematischen und geschichtlichen Begründung der Wissenschaften in der Platonischen Schule.* Stuttgart.
Gaita, R. 2004. *Good and Evil: An Absolute Conception*. 2nd ed. London.
Ganson, T. 2009. "The Rational/Non-Rational Distinction in Plato's *Republic*." *Oxford Studies in Ancient Philosophy* 36: 179–197.
Gauthier, R. A. and Jolif, J. Y 1970 [1958–1959]. *L'Ethique à Nicomaque*, 2nd ed. 2 vols. Paris.
Gerson, L. 1997. "Socrates' Absolutist Prohibition of Wrongdoing." In *Wisdom, Ignorance, and Virtue: New Essays in Socratic Studies*, edited by M. McPherran. Edmonton, AL: 1–11.
  2003. *Knowing Persons: A Study in Plato*. Oxford.
  2006. "A Platonic Reading of Plato's *Symposium*." In *Plato's* Symposium*: Issues in Interpretation and Reception*, edited by J. Lesher, D. Nails, and F. Sheffield. Cambridge, MA: 47–67.
  2013. *From Plato to Platonism*. Ithaca, NY.
  2014a. "The Myth of Plato's Socratic Period." *Archiv für Geschichte der Philosophie* 96: 403–430.
  2014b. "Plato's Rational Souls." *Review of Metaphysics* 67: 37–59.

2015. "Ideas of Good?" In *Second Sailing: Alternative Perspectives on Plato*, edited by D. Nails and H. Tarrant. Helsinki: 225–242.

2018. "Socrates' Autobiography: An Epitome of Platonism." In *Plato's Phaedo: Selected Papers from the Eleventh Symposium Platonicum*, edited by G. Cornelli, T. Robinson, and F. Bravo. Baden-Baden: 323–327.

2019. "Virtue with and without Philosophy in Plato and Plotinus." In *Passionate Mind: Essays in Honor of John Rist*, edited by B. David. Sankt Augustin: 191–208.

2020. *Platonism and Naturalism: The Possibility of Philosophy*. Ithaca, NY.

Gill, C. 2000. "The Body's Fault? Plato's *Timaeus* on Psychic Illness." In *Reason and Necessity: Essays on Plato's Timaeus*, edited by R. Wright. London: 59–84.

Gersh, S. 1973. ΚΙΝΗΣΙΣ ΑΚΙΝΗΤΟΣ: *A Study in Spiritual Motion*. Leiden.

Goetz, S. 2005. "Frankfurt-Style Counterexamples and Begging the Question." *Midwest Studies in Philosophy* 29: 83–105.

Gosling, J. 1973. *Plato: The Arguments of the Philosophers*. London.

1975. *Plato: Philebus*. Oxford.

1978. "Plato's Moral Theory." *Philosophical Books* 19(3): 97–102.

Gosling, J. and Taylor, C. C. W. 1982. *The Greeks on Pleasure*. Oxford.

Gould, J. 1955. *The Development of Plato's Ethics*. Cambridge, UK.

Griswold, C. 1986. *Self-Knowledge in Plato's Phaedrus*. New Haven, CT.

Grube, G. M. A. 1935. *Plato's Thought*. London.

Guthrie, W. K. C. 1975. *A History of Greek Philosophy: IV. Plato: The Man and His Dialogues. Earlier Period*. Cambridge, UK.

1978. *A History of Greek Philosophy: V. The Later Plato and the Academy*. Cambridge, UK.

Hacker-Wright, J. 2009. "Human Nature, Virtue, and Rationality." *Philosophy* 84: 413–427.

Hackforth, R. 1946. "Moral Evil and Ignorance in Plato's Ethics." *The Classical Quarterly* 40(3/4): 118–120.

1965 [1936]. "Plato's Theism." In *Studies in Plato's Metaphysics*, edited by R. E. Allen. London: 439–447.

Hager, F. P. 1962. "Die Materie und das Böse im antiken Platonismus." *Museum Helveticum* 19(2): 73–103

1970. *Die Vernunft und das Problem des Bösen im Rahmen der platonischen Ethik und Metaphysik*. Bern.

1987. *Gott und das Böse im antiken Platonismus*. Würzburg.

Halfwassen, J. 1997. "Monismus und Dualismus in Platons Prinzipienlehre." *Bochumer Philosophisches Jahrbuch für Antike und Mittelalter* 2: 1–21.

2015. *Auf den Spuren des Einen*. Tübingen.

Hall, R. W. 1963. *Plato and the Individual*. The Hague.

Hampton, C. 1987. "Pleasure, Truth, and Being in Plato's *Philebus*: A Reply to Professor Frede." *Phronesis* 32: 253–262.

1990. *Pleasure, Knowledge, and Being: An Analysis of Plato's Philebus*. Albany, NY.

Hanann, N. 2020. "Knowledge and Voluntary Injustice in the *Hippias Minor*." *Apeiron*. DOI: http:// doi.org/10.1515/apeiron-2020-0031: 1–25.

Happ, H. 1971. *Hyle: Studien zum aristotelischen Materie-Begriff*. Berlin.
Haraldsen, V. 2017. "Is Pleasure Any Good? Weakness of Will and the Art of Measurement in Plato's *Protagoras*." In *Plato's Protagoras: Essays on the Confrontation of Philosophy and Sophistry*, edited by O. Pettersson and V. Songe-Møller. Dordrecht: 99–121.
Hardy, J. 2014. "Is Virtue Knowledge? Socratic Intellectualism Reconsidered." In *Ancient Ethics*, edited by J. Hardy and G. Rudebusch. Göttingen: 141–170.
Hardy, J. and Rudebusch. G. (eds.). 2014. *Ancient Ethics*. Göttingen.
Harman, G. 1977. *The Nature of Morality*. Oxford.
Harman, G. and Thompson, J. 1996. *Moral Relativism and Moral Objectivity*. Oxford.
Harte, V. 2004. "The *Philebus* on Pleasure: The Good, the Bad, and the False." *Proceedings of the Aristotelian Society* 104: 113–130.
Hayward, M. 2019. "Immoral Realism." *Philosophical Studies* 176: 897–914.
Herrmann, F.-G. 2007. "The Idea of the Good and the Other Forms in Plato's *Republic*." In *Pursuing the Good: Ethics and Metaphysics in Plato's* Republic, edited by D. Cairns, F. G. Hermann, and T. Penner. Edinburgh: 202–230.
Herzberg, S. 2017. "Aristoteles Metaphysik des Guten." *Theologie und Philosophie* 92: 532–559.
Hitchcock, D. 1982. "The Good in Plato's *Republic*." *Apeiron* 19(2): 65–92.
Höffe, O. 1996. *Praktische Philosophie – Das Modell des Aristoteles*. 2nd ed. Berlin.
Hoffmann, M. 1996. *Die Entstehung von Ordnung: Zur Bestimmung von Sein, Erkennen und Handeln in der späteren Philosophie Platons*. Stuttgart.
Horn, C. 1998. *Antike Lebenskunst: Glück und Moral von Sokrates bis zu den Neuplatonikern*. Munich.
  2016. "The Unity of the World-Order According to *Metaphysics* Λ 10." In *Aristotle's Metaphysics Lambda – New Essays*, edited by C. Horn. Boston: 269–293.
Huemer, M. 2013. "An Ontological Proof of Moral Realism." *Social Philosophy and Policy* 30(1–2): 259–279.
Huffman, C. 2005. *Archytas of Tarentum: Pythagorean, Philosopher, and Mathematical King*. Cambridge, UK.
Hurka, T. 1987. "'Good' and 'Good For.'" *Mind* 86: 71–73.
  2020. "Against 'Good For'/'Well-Being', For 'Simply Good.'" *Philosophical Quarterly* 71(4): 803–822.
Ilievski, V. 2014. *Platonic Theodicy and the Platonic Cause of Evil* (Ph.D. dissertation, Central European University).
  2016. "Plato's Theodicy in the *Timaeus*." *Rhizomata* 4(2): 201–224.
Irani, T. 2021. "Socrates's Great Speech: The Defense of Philosophy in Plato's *Gorgias*." *Journal of the History of Philosophy* 59(3): 349–369.
Irwin, T. 1977. *Plato's Moral Theory*. Oxford.
  1992 [1986]. "Socrates the Epicurean?" In *Essays on the Philosophy of Socrates*, edited by H. Benson. Oxford: 198–219.
  1995. *Plato's Ethics*. Oxford.
  2007. *The Development of Ethics*, Vol. I. Oxford.

Jaeger, W. 1943 [1936]. *Paideia: The Ideals of Greek Culture*. 3 vols. Translated by G. Highet. New York.
Johansen, T. K. 2020. "From Craft to Nature: The Emergence of Natural Teleology." In *The Cambridge Companion to Greek and Roman Science*, edited by L. Taub. Cambridge, UK: 102–120.
Jonas, M. 2018. "The Role of Practice and Habituation in Socrates' Theory of Ethical Development." *British Journal of the History of Philosophy* 26(6): 987–1005.
Jones, R. 2012. "Rational and Nonrational Desires in *Meno* and *Protagoras*." *Analytic Philosophy* 53: 224–233.
Jordan, J. 2019. "Natural Normativity and the Authority-of-Nature Challenge." *International Philosophical Quarterly* 59(1): 23–36.
Jordan, M. 2013. "Theism, Naturalism, and Meta-Ethics." *Philosophy Compass* 8: 373–380.
Jorgenson, C. 2016. "Becoming Immortal in the *Symposium* and the *Timaeus*." In *Plato in Symposium: Selected Papers from the Tenth Symposium Platonicum*, edited by M. Tulli and M.Erler. Sankt Augustin: 243–248.
  2018. *The Embodied Soul in Plato's Later Thought*. Cambridge, UK.
  2021. "Responsibility, Causality, and Will in the *Timaeus*." In *Plato's* Timaeus: *Proceedings of the 10th Symposium Platonicum Pragense*, edited by C. Jorgenson, F. Karfik, and F. Špinka. Leiden and Boston: 259–273.
Joyce, R. 2001. *The Myth of Morality*. Cambridge, UK.
  2006. *The Evolution of Morality*. Boston, MA.
Kahn, C. 1992 [1981]. "Did Plato Write Socratic Dialogues?" In *Essays on the Philosophy of Socrates*, edited by H. Benson. Oxford: 35–52.
  1987. "Plato's Theory of Desire." *Review of Metaphysics* 41: 77–103.
  1996. *Plato and the Socratic Dialogue*. Cambridge, UK.
  2002. "On Platonic Chronology." In *New Perspectives on Plato, Modern and Ancient*, edited by J. Annas and C. Rowe. Cambridge, MA: 93–127.
Kamtekar, R. 1998. "Imperfect Virtue." *Ancient Philosophy* 18: 315–339.
  2006. "Plato on the Attribution of Cognitive Attitudes." *Archiv für Geschichte der Philosophie* 88: 127–162.
  2017a. *Plato's Moral Psychology*. Oxford.
  2017b. "Plato's Ethical Psychology." In *The Cambridge Companion to Ancient Ethics*, edited by C. Bobonich. Cambridge, UK: 72–85.
Kane, R. 2019. "Dimensions of Responsibility: Freedom of Action and Freedom of Will." *Social Philosophy and Policy* 36(1): 114–131.
Karamanolis, G. 2004. "Transformations of Plato's Ethics: Platonist Interpretations of Plato's Ethics from Antiochus to Porphyry." *Rhizai* 1: 73–105.
Karfik, F. 2004. *Die Beseelung des Kosmos: Untersuchungen zur Kosmologie, Seelenlehre und Theologie in Platons* Phaidon *und* Timaios. Leipzig.
Katsimanis, K. S. 1977. *Étude sur le rapport entre le beau et le bien chez Platon*. Lille.
Kauppinen, A. 2019. "Rationality as the Rule of Reason." *Nous* 53: 1–22.
Kolodny, N. 2005. "Why Be Rational?" *Mind* 114: 509–563.
Korsgaard, C. 1983. "Two Distinctions in Goodness." *Philosophical Review* 92, 2: 169–195.

1996. *The Sources of Normativity*. Cambridge, UK.
2009. *Self-Constitution: Agency, Identity, and Integrity*. Oxford.
2018. "Prospects for a Naturalistic Explanation of the Good." *Proceedings of the Aristotelian Society*, supplementary vol. 92: 111–131.
Kosman, L. A. 1976. "Platonic Love." In *Facets of Plato's Philosophy*, edited by W. H. Werkmeister. Assen: 53–69.
2007. "Justice and Virtue: The *Republic's* Inquiry into Proper Difference." In *The Cambridge Companion to Plato's* Republic, edited by G. R. F. Ferrari. Cambridge, UK: 116–137.
Krämer, H. J. 1959. *Arete bei Platon und Aristoteles*. Heidelberg.
1967 [1964]. *Der Ursprung der Geistmetaphysik: Untersuchungen zur Geschichte des Platonismus zwischen Platon und Plotin*. Amsterdam.
2014 [1969]. "Nochmals: Für die Frühdatierung des platonischen Vortrags 'Über das Gute' bei Aristoxenus." In *Gesammelte Aufsätze zu Platon*, edited by D. Mirbach. Berlin: 241–270.
Kraut, R. (ed.) 1992. *The Cambridge Companion to Plato*. Cambridge, UK.
2011. *Against Absolute Goodness*. Oxford.
Kronqvist, C. 2019. "A Personal Love of the Good." *Philosophia* 47: 977–994.
Krüger, G. 1948. *Einsicht und Leidenschaft: Das Wesen des platonischen Denkens*. Frankfurt.
Lafrance, Y. 1995. "Métrétique, mathématiques et dialectique en *Politique* 283 C-285 C." In *Reading the* Statesman: *Proceedings of the III Symposium Platonicum*, edited by C. Rowe. Sankt Augustin: 89–101.
Laks, A. 1990. "Legislation and Demiurgy: On the Relationship Between Plato's *Republic* and *Laws*." *Classical Antiquity* 9(2): 209–229.
Lane, M. 1998. *Method and Politics in Plato's* Statesman. Cambridge, UK.
Lang, P. M. 2010. "The Ranking of Goods at *Philebus* 66A–67B." *Phronesis* 55: 153–169.
Lavecchia. S. 2006. *Una via che conduce al divino: La "homoiosis theo" nella filosofia di Platone*. Milan.
2010. *Oltre l'uno ed i molti: Bene ed essere nella filosofia di Platone*. Milan.
Layne, D. 2019. "Double Ignorance and the Perversion of Self-Knowledge." In *Knowledge and Ignorance of Self in Platonic Philosophy*, edited by J. Ambury and A. German. Cambridge, UK: 206–222.
Lear, J. 1983. "Ethics, Mathematics, and Relativism." *Mind* 92(365): 38–60.
Ledger, G. R. 1989. *Re-counting Plato: A Computer Analysis of Plato's Style*. Oxford.
Leiter, B. 2015. "Normativity for Naturalists." *Philosophical Issues* 25(1): 64–79.
2019. "The Death of God and the Death of Morality." *Monist* 102: 386–402.
Leslie, J. 1979. *Value and Existence*. London.
2019. "What God Might Be." *International Journal for Philosophy of Religion* 85: 63–75.
Liske, M. T. 1987. "Ist Platons Ethik deontologisch oder teleologisch?" *Salzburger Jahrbücher für Philosophie* 32: 65–77.
Lodge, R. 1928. *Plato's Theory of Ethics*. London.

Long, A. A. 2021. "Politics and Divinity in Plato's *Republic*: The Form of the Good." In *Themes in Plato, Aristotle and Hellenistic Philosophy*, edited by F. Leigh. London: 63–82.
Lorenz, H. 2006. *The Brute Within: Appetitive Desire in Plato and Aristotle*. Oxford.
Lott, M. 2014. "Why Be a Good Human Being? Natural Goodness, Reason, and the Authority of Human Nature." *Philosophia* 42: 761–777.
Louden. R. 1996. "Towards a Genealogy of 'Deontology.'" *Journal of the History of Philosophy* 34: 571–592.
Mabbott, J. D. 1971. "Is Plato's *Republic* Utilitarian?" In *Plato. Ethics, Politics, and Philosophy of Art and Religion*, edited by G. Vlastos. Garden City, NJ: 57–65.
MacDonald, S. (ed.). 1991. *Being and Goodness: The Concept of Good in Metaphysical and Philosophical Theology*. Ithaca, NY.
Mackenzie, M. M. 1981. *Plato on Punishment*. Berkeley, CA.
Mackie, J. L. 1977. *Ethics: Inventing Right and Wrong*. Harmondsworth.
  1982. *The Miracle of Theism*. Oxford.
Männlein-Robert, I. 2013. "Tugend, Flucht und Ekstase: zur ὁμοίωσις θεῷ in Kaiserzeit und Spätantike." In C. Pietsch (ed.), *Ethik des antiken Platonismus: der platonische Weg zum Glück in Systematik Entstehung und historischem Kontext*. Stuttgart: 99–111.
Márquez, X. 2012. *A Stranger's Knowledge: Statesmanship, Philosophy, and Law in Plato's Statesman*. Las Vegas.
Marshall, C. 2018. *Compassionate Moral Realism*. Oxford.
McCabe, M. M. 2005. "Out of the Labyrinth: Plato's Attack on Consequentialism." In *Virtue, Norms, and Objectivity: Issues in Ancient and Modern Ethics*, edited by C. Gill. Oxford: 191–214.
McGinley, J. 1977. "The Doctrine of Good in *Philebus*." *Apeiron* 11: 27–57.
McTighe, K. 1983. "Nine Notes on Plato's *Lysis*." *American Journal of Philology* 104 (1): 67–82.
  1984. "Socrates on Desire for the Good and the Unwillingness of Wrongdoing: *Gorgias* 466A–468E." *Phronesis* 29: 193–236.
Meldrum, M. 1950. "Plato on the ἀρχὴ κακῶν." *Journal of Hellenic Studies* 70: 65–74.
Mele, A. 1987. *Irrationality*. Oxford.
Menn. S. 1992. "Aristotle and Plato on God as Nous and as the Good." *Review of Metaphysics* 45(3): 543–573.
  1995. *Plato on God as Nous*. Carbondale, IL.
Merker, A. 2011. *Une Morale pour les mortels: L'éthique de Platon et Aristote*. Paris.
Merlan, P. 1953. *From Platonism to Neoplatonism*. The Hague.
Meyer, S. 2014. "God Is Not to Blame: Divine Creation and Human Responsibility in Plato's *Timaeus*." *Proceedings of the Boston Area Colloquium in Ancient Philosophy* 29: 55–69.
Migliori, M. and Napolitano, L. (eds.) 2003. *Plato Ethicus: Philosophy Is Life*. Sankt Augustin.

Miller, M. 1985. "Platonic Provocations: Reflections on the Soul and the Good in the *Republic*." In *Platonic Investigations*, edited by D. O'Meara. Washington, DC: 163–193.

　1990. "The God-Given Way." *Proceedings of the Boston Area Colloquium on Ancient Philosophy* 6: 323–359.

　2004 [1980]. *The Philosopher in Plato's* Statesman *with "Dialectical Education and Unwritten Teachings in Plato's* Statesman*"*. Las Vegas.

　2007. "Beginning the 'Longer Way.'" In *The Cambridge Companion to Plato's* Republic, edited by G. R. F. Ferrari. Cambridge, UK: 310–344.

Mirus, C. 2012. "Order and the Determinate: Good as a Metaphysical Concept in Aristotle." *The Review of Metaphysics* 65(3): 499–523.

Mitsis, P. 1988. *Epicurus' Ethical Theory: The Pleasures of Invulnerability*. Ithaca, NY.

Mohr, R. 1989. "Plato's Theology Reconsidered: What the Demiurge Does." In *Essays in Ancient Greek Philosophy*, Vol. III, *Plato*, edited by J. Anton and A. Preus. Albany, NY: 293–307.

Monteils-Laeng, L. 2014. *Agir sans vouloir*. Paris.

Moore, C. 2015. *Socrates and Self-Knowledge*. Cambridge, UK.

Moore, G. E. 1971 [1903]. *Principia Ethica*. Cambridge, UK.

Moran. R. 2001. *Authority and Estrangement: An Essay on Self-Knowledge*. Princeton, NJ.

Morris, M. 2006. "Akrasia in the *Protagoras* and the *Republic*." *Phronesis* 51: 195–229.

Morrow, G. 1960. *Plato's Cretan City*. Princeton, NJ.

Morton, J. 2019. "Can Theists Avoid Epistemological Objections to Moral (and Normative) Realism." *Faith and Philosophy* 36(3): 291–312.

Moss, J. 2008. "Appearances and Calculations: Plato's Division of the Soul." *Oxford Studies in Ancient Philosophy* 34: 35–68.

　2012. *Aristotle on the Apparent Good*. Oxford.

　2014. "Hedonism and the Divided Soul in Plato's *Protagoras*." *Archiv für Geschichte der Philosophie* 96: 285–319.

Mulgan, T. 2015. *Purpose in the Universe*. Oxford.

Murdoch, I. 1970. *The Sovereignty of Good*. London.

　1977. *The Fire and the Sun*. Oxford.

　1992. *Metaphysics as a Guide to Morals*. London.

Nagel, T. 1986. *The View From Nowhere*. Oxford.

　2005. "The Problem of Global Justice." *Philosophy and Public Affairs* 33(2): 113–147.

Nehamas, A. 1999. "Socratic Intellectualism." In *Virtues of Authenticity*. Princeton: 27–58. (Reprinted from *Proceedings of the Boston Area Colloquium in Ancient Philosophy* 2, edited by J. Cleary. Langham, MD, 1987: 275–316.)

Nettleship, R. L. 1961 [1897]. *Lectures on the* Republic *of Plato*. London. (Reprinted in 1901 as "Plato's Conception of Goodness and the Good." In *Philosophical Remains*, edited by A. C. Bradley, 2nd ed. London: 237–398.)

Nightingale, A. 1996. "Plato on the Origins of Evil: The *Statesman* Myth Reconsidered." *Ancient Philosophy* 16: 65–91.

Nill, M. 1985. *Morality and Self-Interest in Protagoras, Antiphon, and Democritus.* Leiden.
O'Brien, D. 2003. "Socrates and Protagoras on Virtue." *Oxford Studies in Ancient Philosophy* 24: 59–131.
O'Brien, M. 1958. "Modern Philosophy and Platonic Ethics." *Journal of the History of Ideas* 19: 451–472.
  1967. *The Socratic Paradoxes and the Greek Mind.* Chapel Hill, NC.
Oddie, G. 2005. *Value, Reality, and Desire.* Oxford.
Orsi, F. 2015. "The Guise of the Good." *Philosophy Compass* 10: 714–724.
Parfit, D. 2006. "Normativity." *Oxford Studies in Metaethics* 1: 325–380.
  2011. *On What Matters.* Volumes 1 and 2. Oxford.
Pasnau, R. 2021. "Where Socratic Akrasia Meets the Platonic Good." *Journal of the History of Philosophy* 59(1): 1–21.
Patzig, G. 1971. *Ethik ohne Metaphysik.* Göttingen.
Pears, D. 1984. *Motivated Irrationality.* Oxford.
Penner, T. 1971. "Thought and Desire in Plato." In *Plato II*, edited by G. Vlastos. New York: 96–118.
  1973a. "Socrates on Virtue and Motivation." In *Exegesis and Argument: Studies in Greek Philosophy Presented to Gregory Vlastos,* edited by E. Lee, A. Mourelatos, and R. Rorty. *Phronesis* supplementary Vol. 1: 133–151.
  1973b. "The Unity of Virtue." *Philosophical Review* 82(1): 35–68.
  1991. "Desire and Power in Socrates: The Argument of *Gorgias* 466A–468E that Orators and Tyrants have no Power in the City." *Apeiron* 24: 147–202.
  1992. "Socrates and the Early Dialogues." In *The Cambridge Companion to Plato*, edited by R. Kraut. Cambridge, UK: 121–169.
  1996. "Knowledge vs. True Belief in the Socratic Psychology of Action." *Apeiron* 19: 199–230.
  1997. "Socrates on the Strength of Knowledge: *Protagoras* 351B–357E." *Archiv für Geschichte der Philosophie* 79: 117–149.
  2002. "The Historical Socrates and Plato's Early Dialogues: Some Philosophical Questions." In *New Perspectives on Plato, Modern and Ancient*, edited by J. Annas and C. Rowe. Washington, DC: 189–212.
  2003. "The Forms, the Form of the Good, and the Desire for the Good in Plato's *Republic.*" *Modern Schoolman* 80: 191–233.
  2005. "Socratic Ethics, Ultra Realism, Determinism, and Ethical Truth." In *Virtue, Norms, and Objectivity: Issues in Ancient and Modern Ethics*, edited by C. Gill. Oxford: 157–187.
  2007a. "The Good, Advantage, Happiness, and the Form of the Good: How Continuous is Socratic Ethics with Platonic Ethics?" In *Pursuing the Good: Ethics and Metaphysics in Plato's* Republic, edited by D. Cairns, F.-G. Herrmann, and T. Penner, Edinburgh: 93–123.
  2007b. "What Is the Form of the Good the Form of? A Question About the Plot of the *Republic.*" In *Pursuing the Good: Ethics and Metaphysics in Plato's Republic*, edited by D. Cairns, F.-G. Herrmann, and T. Penner, Edinburgh: 15–41.

2011. "Socratic Ethics and the Socratic Psychology of Action." In *The Cambridge Companion to Socrates*, edited by D. Morrison. New York: 260–292.
Penner, T. and Rowe, C. 2005. *Plato's* Lysis. Cambridge, UK.
Perl, E. 2014. *Thinking Being: Introduction to Metaphysics in the Classical Tradition.* Leiden.
Petrucci, F. 2017. "Plato on Virtue in the *Menexenus*." *Classical Quarterly* 67(1): 49–70.
Pietsch, C. (ed.) 2013. *Ethik des antiken Platonismus: Der platonische Weg zum Glück in Systematik, Entstehung und historischem Kontext.* Stuttgart.
Pölzler T. 2019. "How to Determine Whether Evolution Debunks Moral Realism." *Jahrbuch für Wissenschaft und Ethik* 23(1): 35–60.
Pradeau, J.-F. 1997. *Platon et la cité.* Paris.
  2002. *Plato and the City.* Translated by Janet Lloyd. Exeter.
Prauscello, L. 2014. *Performing Citizenship in Plato's* Laws. Cambridge, UK.
Price, A. W. 1989. *Love and Friendship in Plato and Aristotle.* Oxford.
  1995. *Mental Conflict.* London and New York.
  1996. "Plato's Ethics." *Ancient Philosophy* 16(1): 189–194.
  2009. "Are Plato's Soul-Parts Psychological Subjects." *Ancient Philosophy* 29 (1): 1–15.
  2011. *Virtue and Reason in Plato and Aristotle.* New York.
Prichard, H. A. 1968. *Moral Obligation and Duty and Interest.* Oxford.
  2003 [1928]. *Moral Writings*, edited by J. MacAdams. Oxford.
Primavesi, O. 2012. "Aristotle's *Metaphysics* A: A New Critical Edition with Introduction." In C. Steel, *Aristotle's* Metaphysics *Alpha*, edited by C. Steel. Oxford: 385–516.
Putnam, H. 2005. *Ethics without Ontology.* Cambridge, MA.
  2015. "Naturalism, Realism, and Normativity." *Journal of the American Philosophical Association* 1(2): 312–328.
Railton, P. 1995. "Moral Realism." *The Philosophical Review* 95: 163–207.
  2003. *Facts, Values, and Norms: Towards a Morality of Consequence.* Cambridge, UK.
Rawson, G. 1996. "Knowledge and Desire for the Good in Plato's *Republic*." *Southwest Philosophy Review* 12(1): 103–115.
Rea, M. 2006. "Naturalism and Moral Realism." In *Knowledge and Reality*, edited by M. Davidson. T. Crisp, and D. Vander Laan. Dordrecht: 215–242.
Reale, G. 1997 [1984]. *Toward a New Interpretation of Plato.* Translated by J. Catan. Washington, DC. (10th edition 1991, *Per una nuova interpretazione di Platone: Rilettura della metafisica dei grandi dialoghi alla luce "Doctrine non scritte."*)
  2003. "'Henological' Basis of Plato's Ethics." In *Plato Ethicus: Philosophy Is Life. Proceedings of the International Colloquium Piacenza*, edited by M. Migliori and L. Napolitano. Sankt Augustin: 255–264.
Reed, D. 2020. "Deficient Virtue in the *Phaedo*." *Classical Quarterly* 70(1): 119–130.
Reeve, C. D. C. 1988. *Philosopher-Kings: The Argument of Plato's* Republic. Princeton, NJ.

1989. *Socrates in the* Apology. Indianapolis, IN.
Renaud, F. 1999. *Die Resokratisierung Platons: Die platonische Hermeneutik Hans-Georg Gadamers*. Sankt Augustin.
Renaut, O. 2019. "The Analogy Between Vice and Disease from the *Republic* and the *Timaeus*." In *Psychology and Ontology in Plato*, edited by L. Pitteloud and E. Keeling. Cham: 67–83.
Renz, U. 2017. "Self-Knowledge as a Personal Achievement." *Proceedings of the Aristotelian Society* 117(3): 253–272.
Rescher, N. 2010. *Axiogenesis: An Essay in Metaphysical Optimalism*. Lanham, MD.
Rice, H. 2000. *God and Goodness*. Oxford.
Richard, M.-D. 2005. *L'enseignement oral de Platon*. Paris.
Rist, J. 1998. "The Possibility of Morality in Plato's *Republic*." *Boston Area Colloquium in Ancient Philosophy* 14: 53–72.
  2002. *Real Ethics: Rethinking the Foundations of Morality*. Cambridge, UK.
  2012. *Plato's Moral Realism*. Washington, DC.
Ritter, C. 1933. *The Essence of Plato's Philosophy*. Translated by A. Alles. London.
Roberts, J. 1987. "Plato on the Causes of Wrongdoing in the *Laws*." *Ancient Philosophy* 7: 23–37.
Robin, L. 1908. *La theorie platonicienne de l'amour*. Paris.
Rodier, G. 1957 [1924]. *Études de philosophie grecque*. Paris.
Ross, W. D. 1930. *The Right and the Good*. Oxford.
  1939. *The Foundations of Ethics*. Oxford.
  1951. *Plato's Theory of Ideas*. Oxford.
Rowe, C. 1976. *An Introduction to Greek Ethics*. London.
  2005. "What Difference Do Forms Make to Platonic Epistemology." In *Virtue, Norms, and Objectivity: Issues in Ancient and Modern Ethics*, edited by C. Gill. Oxford: 215–232.
  2007. "The Form of the Good and the Good in Plato's *Republic*." In *Pursuing the Good. Ethics and Metaphysics in Plato's Republic*, edited by D. Cairns, F. G. Hermann, and T. Penner. Edinburgh: 124–153.
Rowe, C. and M. Schofield (eds.). 2000. *The Cambridge History of Greek and Roman Political Thought*. Cambridge, UK.
Rowett, C. 2016. "Why the Philosopher Kings Will Believe the Noble Lie." *Oxford Studies in Ancient Philosophy* 50: 67–100.
Rowlands, M. 2018. "Self-Awareness and Korsgaard's Naturalistic Explanation of the Good." *Proceedings of the Aristotelian Society*, supplementary Vol. 92: 133–149.
Rudebusch, G. 2003. "Socratic Perfectionism." In *Plato and Socrates: Desire, Identity, and Existence*, edited by N. Reshotko. Edmonton: 127–141.
  2007. "Socratic Neutralism." In *The Good and the Form of the Good*, edited by D. Cairns, F.-G. Herrmann, and T. Penner. Edinburgh: 76–92.
  2017. "The Unity of Virtue, Ambiguity, and Socrates' Higher Purpose." *Apeiron* 37: 1014.
  2020. "*Philebus* 11B: Good or the Good." *Apeiron* 53(2): 161–185.
Ruse, M. 1989. *The Darwinian Paradigm*. London.
Russell, D. 2005. *Plato on Pleasure and the Good Life*. Oxford.

Sachs, D. 1963. "A Fallacy in Plato's *Republic*." *Philosophical Review* 72: 141–158.
Santas, G. 1966. "Plato's *Protagoras* and Explanations of Weakness." *Philosophical Review* 75: 3–33.
  1979. *Socrates: Philosophy in Plato's Early Dialogues*. London.
  1985. "Two Theories of Good in Plato's *Republic*." *Archiv für Geschichte der Philosophie* 67: 223–245.
  2002. "The Form of the Good as Paradigm and Its Essence." In *New Images of Plato*, edited by G. Reale and S. Scolnicov. Sankt Augustin: 359–378.
  2010. *Understanding Plato's Republic*. Malden, MA.
Sartre, J.-P. 1989. "Existentialism Is a Humanism." In *Existentialism from Dostoyevsky to Sartre*, edited by W. Kaufmann. New York.
Sassi, M. 2008. "The Self, the Soul, and the Individual in the City of the *Laws*." *Oxford Studies in Ancient Philosophy* 35: 127–148.
Saunders, T. 1968. "The Socratic Paradoxes in Plato's *Laws*. A Commentary on 859 C-864B." *Hermes* 96: 421–434.
  1991. *Plato's Penal Code*. Oxford.
Sayre, K. 1995. *Plato's Literary Garden: How to Read a Platonic Dialogue*. Notre Dame, IN.
  2006. *Metaphysics and Method in Plato's* Statesman. Cambridge.
Sayre-McCord, G. 1988. "The Many Moral Realisms." In *Essays on Moral Realism*, edited by G. Sayre-McCord. Ithaca, NY: 1–26.
Schofield, M. 2006. *Plato: Political Philosophy*. Oxford.
  2011. "Plato in His Time and Place." In *The Oxford Handbook of Plato*, edited by G. Fine. Oxford: 36–62.
Schöpsdau, K. 1984. "Zum Strafrechtsexkurs in Platons *Nomoi*." *Rheinisches Museum für Philologie* 127(2): 97–132.
Scott, D. 2007. "Erōs, Philosophy, and Tyranny." In *Maieusis: Essays in Ancient Philosophy in Honour of Myles Burnyeat*, edited by D. Scott. Oxford: 136–153.
  2015. *Levels of Argument: A Comparative Study of Plato's* Republic *and Aristotle's* Nicomachean Ethics. Oxford.
  2020. *Listening to Reason in Plato and Aristotle*. Oxford.
Sedley, D. 2000. "The Ideal of Godlikeness." In *Plato*, edited by G. Fine. Oxford: 791–810.
  2007. "Philosophy, the Forms, and the Art of Ruling." In *The Cambridge Companion to Plato's* Republic, edited by G. R. F. Ferrari. Cambridge: 256–283.
  2009. "Three Kinds of Platonic Immortality." In *Body and Soul in Ancient Philosophy*, edited by D. Frede and B. Reis. Berlin: 145–161.
  2013. "Socratic Intellectualism in the *Republic's* Central Digression." In *The Platonic Art of Philosophy*, edited by G. Boys-Stones, D. El Murr, and C. Gill. Cambridge, UK: 70–89.
  2014. *The Midwife of Platonism*. Oxford.
  2019. "The *Timaeus* as Vehicle for Platonic Doctrine." *Oxford Studies in Ancient Philosophy* 56: 45–71.

Šegvić, H. 2000. "No One Errs Willingly: The Meaning of Socratic Intellectualism." *Oxford Studies in Ancient Philosophy* 19: 1–45.
Seifert, J. 2002. "The Idea of the Good as the Sum-Total of Pure Perfections." In *New Images of Plato: Dialogues on the Idea of the Good*, edited by G. Reale and S. Scolnicov. Sankt Augustin: 407–424.
Senn, S. J. 2005. "Virtue as the Sole Intrinsic Good in Plato's Early Dialogues." *Oxford Studies in Ancient Philosophy* 28: 1–21.
Shafer-Landau, R. 2003. *Moral Realism: A Defense*. Oxford.
Sheffield, F. 2017. "Plato on Love and Friendship." In *The Cambridge Companion to Ancient Ethics*, edited by C. Bobonich. Cambridge, UK: 86–102.
Shields, C. 2007. "Unified Agency and *Akrasia* in Plato's *Republic*." In *Akrasia in Greek Philosophy*, edited by C. Bobonich and P. Destrée. Leiden: 61–86.
    2015. "The *summum bonum* in Aristotle's Ethics: Fractured Goodness." In *The Highest Good in Aristotle and Kant*, edited by J. Aufderheide and R. Bader. Oxford: 83–111.
Shorey, P. 1888. "Recent Platonism in England." *American Journal of Philology* 9 (3): 274–309.
    1895. "The Idea of Good in Plato's *Republic*." *University of Chicago Studies in Classical Philology* 2: 188–239.
    1903. *The Unity of Plato's Thought*. Chicago.
    1908. "A Note on *Philebus* B, C." *Classical Quarterly* 3(3): 343–345.
    1933. *What Plato Said*. Chicago.
Sidgwick. H. 1902 [1886]. *Outline of the History of Ethics*. London.
    1907 [1874]. *The Methods of Ethics*. 7th ed. London.
Singpurwalla, R. 2006a. "Reasoning with the Irrational: Moral Psychology in the *Protagoras*." *Ancient Philosophy* 26(1): 244–258.
    2006b. "Plato's Defense of Justice." In *The Blackwell Guide to Plato's* Republic, edited by G. Santas. Malden, MA: 263–282.
Smith, M. 2004. "Moral Realism." *In Ethics and the A Priori*. Cambridge, UK: 181–207.
Smith, N. 2004. "Did Plato Write *Alcibiades I*?" *Apeiron* 37: 93–108.
    2014. "Socratic Metaphysics?" *Apeiron* 47(4): 419–434.
    2018. "A Problem in Plato's Hagiography of Socrates." *Athens Journal of Humanities and Arts* 5(1): 81–103.
Sobel, D. 2016. *From Valuing to Value: Towards a Defense of Subjectivism*. Oxford.
Solmsen, F. 1942. *Plato's Theology*. Ithaca.
Sprigge, T. L. S. 1988. *The Rational Foundation of Ethics*. London.
Stalley, R. F. 1982. "Mental Health and Individual Responsibility in Plato's *Republic*." *The Journal of Value Inquiry* 15(2): 109–124.
    1996. "Punishment and the Physiology of the *Timaeus*." *Classical Quarterly* 46 (2): 357–370.
    2000. "*Sōphrosunē* in the *Charmides*." In *Plato: Euthydemus, Lysis, Charmides. Proceedings of the V Symposium Platonicum*, edited by T. M. Robinson and L. Brisson. Sankt Augustin: 265–277.

Steel, C. 2012. "Plato as Seen by Aristotle (*Metaphysics* A 6)." In *Aristotle's Metaphysics Alpha*, edited by C. Steel. Oxford: 167–200.

Stemmer, P. 1988. "Der Grundriss der platonischen Ethik." *Zeitschrift für philosophische Forschung* 42: 529–569.

Stocker, M. 1979. "Desiring the Bad: An Essay in Moral Psychology." *The Journal of Philosophy* 76: 738–753.

Storey, D. 2014. "Appearance, Perception, and Non-Rational Belief: *Republic* 602 C-603A." *Oxford Studies in Ancient Philosophy* 47: 81–118.

Street, S. 2008. "Reply to Copp: Naturalism, Normativity, and the Varieties of Realism Worth Worrying About." *Philosophical Issues* 18: 207–228.

Sturgeon, N. 1988. "Moral Explanations." In *Essays on Moral Realism*, edited by G. Sayre-McCord. Ithaca, NY: 229–255.

  2006. "Moral Explanations Defended." In *Contemporary Debates in Moral Theory*, edited by J. Dreiser. London: 241–255.

Szlezák, T. 1985. *Platon und die Schriftlichkeit der Philosophie*. Berlin.

  1997. "Über die Art und Weise der Erörterung der Prinzipien im *Timaios*." In *Interpreting the Timaeus-Critias*, edited by T. Calvo and L. Brisson. Sankt Augustin: 195–203.

  2003. *Die Idee des Guten in Platons* Politeia. Sankt Augustin.

Taylor, A. E. 1924. *Platonism and Its Influence*. Boston, MA.

  1928. *A Commentary on Plato's* Timaeus. Oxford.

Taylor, C. C. W. 1976. *Plato's* Protagoras. Translation with notes. Oxford.

  1998. "Platonic Ethics." In *Ethics: Companions to Ancient Thought 4*, edited by S. Everson. Cambridge, UK: 49–76.

Thalberg, I. 1962. "False Pleasures." *Journal of Philosophy* 59(3): 65–74.

Thesleff, H. 2009. *Platonic Patterns: A Collection of Studies*. Las Vegas.

Timmermann, F. 2019. *Der Magnetismus des Guten*. Berlin.

Trabattoni, F. 2000. "Sull' Etica di Platone in Margine a un Novo Commento allo 'Republica.'" *Rivista di Storia della Filosofia* 55(4): 607–618.

  2020. *La filosofia di Platone: Verità e ragione umana*. Rome.

  2022. "Antiochus of Aascalon's 'Platonic' Ethics." *Elenchos* 43(1): 85–103.

Van Ackeren, M. 2003. *Das Wissen vom Guten: Bedeutung und Kontinuität des Tugendwissens in den Dialogen Platons*. Amsterdam.

Van Camp, J. and Canart. P. 1956. *Le sens du mot θεῖος chez Platon*. Leuven.

van Inwagen P. 1986. "Ability and Responsibility." In *Moral Responsibility*, edited by J.M. Fischer. Ithaca, NY: 153–173.

Van Riel, G. 1999. "Beauté, proportion et verité comme 'vestibule du bien' dans le *Philèbe*." *Revue philosophique de Louvain* 97: 253–267.

  2016. *Plato's Gods*. London.

Vasiliou, I. 2008. *Aiming at Virtue in Plato*. Cambridge, UK.

  2015. "Plato, Forms, and Moral Motivation." *Oxford Studies in Ancient Philosophy* 49: 37–70.

  2021. "Psychological Eudaimonism and the Natural Desire for the Good: Comments on Rachana Kamtekar's *Plato's Moral Psychology*." *Philosophy and Phenomenological Research* 103: 234–239.

Vegetti, M. 2003. "Megiston Mathema: L'idea del 'buono' e le sue funzioni." In *La Repubblica: Traduzione e commento*, Vol. V, Books VI and VII, edited by M. Vegetti. Naples: 253–286.
Velleman, D. 1992. "The Guise of the Good." *Noûs* 26: 3–26.
Verdenius, W. J. 1954. "Platons Gottesbegriff." In *La Notion du divin depuis Homère jusqu'à Platon*. Entretien Hardt I. Vandoeuvres-Geneva: 241–283.
Vlastos, G. 1969. "Reasons and Causes in the *Phaedo*." *Philosophical Review* 78: 291–325.
  1971a. "Introduction: The Paradox of Socrates." In *The Philosophy of Socrates*, edited by G. Vlastos. Garden City, NY: 1–21.
  1971b. "Justice and Happiness in the *Republic*." In *Plato: A Collection of Critical Essays. II: Ethics, Politics, and Philosophy of Art and Religion*, edited by G. Vlastos. Garden City, NY: 66–95.
  1973 [1972]. *Platonic Studies*. Princeton, NJ.
  1991. *Socrates: Ironist and Moral Philosopher*. Ithaca, NY.
  1994. *Socratic Studies*. Cambridge, UK.
Vogler, C. 2002. *Reasonably Vicious*. Cambridge, MA.
Vogt, K. 2017. *Desiring the Good*. Oxford.
Warren, J. 2017. "Plato." In *Cambridge History of Moral Philosophy*, edited by S. Golob and J. Timmermann. Cambridge, UK: 28–41.
Watson, G. 2003. "The Work of the Will." In *Weakness of Will and Practical Irrationality*, edited by S. Stround and C. Tappolet. Oxford: 172–200.
  2004 [1975]. "Free Agency." In *Agency and Answerability: Selected Essays*. Oxford: 13–32.
Weiss, R. 2007. "Thirst as Desire for Good." In *Akrasia in Greek Philosophy from Socrates to Plotinus*, edited by C. Bobonich and P. Destrée. Leiden: 87–100.
White, D. 2007. *Myth, Metaphysics, and Dialectic in Plato's* Statesman. Burlington, VT.
White, N. 1985. "Rational Prudence in Plato's *Gorgias*." In *Platonic Investigations*, edited by D. O'Meara. Washington, DC: 139–162.
  2006. "Plato's Conception of Goodness." In *A Companion to Plato*, edited by H. Benson. Malden, MA: 356–372.
  2013. "Plato's Ethics." In *The Oxford Handbook of the History of Ethics*, edited by R. Crisp. Oxford: 21–43.
Widerker, D. 2005. "Blameworthiness, Non-robust Alternatives and the Principle of Alternative Expectations." *Midwest Studies in Philosophy* 29: 292–306.
Williams, B. 1985. *Ethics and the Limits of Philosophy*. Cambridge, MA.
Williams, J. (ed.). 2007. *Moore's Paradox: New Essays on Belief, Rationality, and the First Person*. Oxford.
Wilberding, J. 2009. "Plato's Two Forms of Second-Best Morality." *Philosophical Review* 118: 351–374.
Wilburn, J. 2012. "Akrasia and Self-Rule in Plato's *Laws*." *Oxford Studies in Ancient Philosophy* 43: 23–53.
  2013. "Tripartition and the Causes of Criminal Behavior in *Laws* IX." *Ancient Philosophy* 33(1): 111–134.

2021. *The Political Soul: Plato on Thumos, Spirited Motivation, and the City*. Oxford.
Wolf, S. 1986. "Asymmetrical Freedom." In *Moral Responsibility*, edited by J. M. Fischer, Ithaca, NY: 225–240.
Wolfsdorf, D. 2006. "The Ridiculousness of Being Overcome by Pleasure." *Oxford Studies in Ancient Philosophy* 31: 113–136.
Wolt, D. 2019. "The Involuntary in the *Timaeus* and the *Eudemian Ethics*." *Apeiron* 52(3): 245–272.
Woodruff, P. 2000. "Socrates and the Irrational." In *Reason and Religion in Socratic Philosophy*, edited by N. Smith and P. Woodruff. Oxford: 86–106.
Wreen, M. 2018. "What Is Moral Relativism?" *Philosophy* 93: 337–354.
Zeyl, D. 1989. "Socrates and Hedonism: *Protagoras* 351b-358d." In *Essays in Ancient Greek Philosophy*, Vol. III, *Plato*, edited by J. Anton and A. Preus. Albany, NY: 5–25.
Zhao, M. 2020. "Meaning, Moral Realism, and the Importance of Morality." *Philosophical Studies* 177: 653–666.

Index Locorum

Alcinous
  Didaskalikos
    10.164.13–18: 192n.12
    10.164.22: 50n.68
    10.164.36: 50n.68
    10.179.41–2: 50n.68
Alexander of Aphrodisias
  De fato
    164.19: 148n.4
    169.13–15: 148n.4
    181.12–14: 148n.4
    199.8–9: 148n.4
    211.31–33: 148n.4
  Mantissa
    172.30–31: 148n.4
Aristotle
  De Anima
    Γ 10, 433a28-29: 123n.24
  De Caelo
    Γ 2, 301a5-12: 107n.96
  Eudemian Ethics
    A 5, 1216b3-10: 131n.42
    A 6, 1216b35-39: 209n.87
    A 8, 1218a15-32: 69n.136
    Γ 1, 1229a15: 131n.42
    Γ 1, 1230a8: 131n.42
    H 13, 1246b33-35: 131n.42
    Θ 3, 1248b40-1249a5: 89n.49
  Metaphysics
    A 6, 987a29-988a17: 20n.56
    A 6, 987a14-18: 68n.132
    A 6, 987a29-b9: 119n.11
    A 6, 987b18-25: 68n.133
    A 6, 987b25-6: 69n.138
    A 6, 988a8-14: 69n.135
    A 6, 988a14-15: 207n.79
    A 8, 990a29-32: 68n.134
    A 9, 990b27-34: 175n.20
    A 9, 992a20-22: 72n. 147
    A 1, 993b19-21: 209n.87
    B 1, 995b15ff.: 68n.132
    Δ 1, 1013a7-8: 69n.137
    Δ 3, 1014a26-27: 69n.137
    E 1, 1026a29-32: 190n.1
    E 1, 1026a30-31: 184n.56
    Z 2, 1028b19-21: 68n.132
    Z 7, 11.103b13-25: 68n.134
    K 1, 1059b2: 68n.132
    Λ 1, 1069a33ff.: 68n.132
    Λ 7, 1072a27-b3: 2n.6
    Λ 7, 1072a31-31: 175n.20
    Λ 7, 1072a32-34: 83n.26
    Λ 7, 1072b26-30: 197n.33
    Λ 7, 1072b31-34: 14n.41, 45n.49
    Λ 7, 1076a26-28: 33n.12
    Λ 8, 1073a18-19: 68n.133
    Λ 10, 1075b18-20: 72n.145
    M 1, 1076a19ff.: 68n.132
    M 4, 1078b9-12: 68n.134
    M 6, 1080a12-30: 20n.56
    M 6, 1080b4-33: 20n.56
    M 7, 1081a12-17: 20n.56
    M 7, 1081a21-25: 20n.56
    M 7, 1081b17-22: 20n.56
    M 8, 1083a18: 68n.134
    M 8, 1083a20-b19: 20n.56
    M 8, 1084a7-8: 68n.134
    M 8, 1084a32-34: 73n.149
    M 8, 1084a37-b2: 72n.147
    M 8, 1084b13-1085a2: 83n.26
    M 9, 1086a11-13: 68n.132,134
    M 10, 1075a32-36: 207n.79
    N 1, 1087b9-12: 72n.144
    N 2, 1089a31-b15: 20n.56
    N 2, 1090a4-6: 68n.134
    N 3, 1090a16: 68n.134
    N 3, 1090b35-36: 68n.132
    N 4, 1091b13-15: 69n.136
    N 4, 1091b30-35: 207n.79
    N 7, 1081a22: 69n.138
  Nicomachean Ethics
    A 1, 1094a2-3: 33n.12

Index Locorum 251

A 1, 1094b11: 209n.87
A 6: 36n.21
B 3, 1104b31: 60n.107
Γ 1, 1110b9ff.: 161n.31
Γ 2, 1110b24-30: 150n.9
Γ 4, 1136b6-7: 148n.4
Γ 5, 1112b11-12: 62n.116
Γ 5, 1112b32-34: 62n.116
Γ 7, 1113b3-4: 62n.116
Γ 7, 1114a11ff.: 161n.31
Γ 8, 1116b5: 131n.42
Z 13, 1144b1ff.: 103n.88
Z 13, 1144b18-20: 131n.42
Z 13, 1144b28-30: 101n.82
H 2-3: 131n.42
H 2, 1145b8-11: 104n.91
H 7, 1152a33: 104n.91
I 4, 1166b2-29: 145n.81
K 7-8: 143n.78
K 7, 1177b30-1178a3: 110n.103, 193n.17
K 7, 1178b21-23: 193n.17
Physics
A 9, 192a4-17: 207n.79
Δ 2, 209b11-17: 206n.75
Θ 1, 252a11-16: 107n.96
Politics
A 2, 1253a18-29: 187n.69
B 1-6: 216n.104
B 3, 1265a2-4: 210n.88
Statesman
Fr. 2: 134n.56
[Aristotle]
Magna Moralia
A 1, 1182a15-17: 131n.42
A 1, 1182a27-30: 71n.141
A 1, 1183b9: 131n.42
A 1, 1183b20: 131n.42
A 9, 1187a5-12: 131n.42
A 20, 1190b28: 131n.42
A 20, 1190b34: 131n.42
A 34, 1198a10-13: 131n.42
B 6, 1200b25-30: 131n.42
Aristoxenus
Elementa harmonica
2.30-31: 70n.141
Atticus
fr.12: 52n.78

Cicero
Academica
I 19: 3n.7
De legibus
2.6.14: 210n.88

Diogenes Laertius
Lives of Eminent Philosophers
II 106: 74n.151
III 6: 74n.151
VII 101-103: 88n.42

Epicurus
Principal Doctrines
V: 33n.13
XXXI-XL: 33n.13
Euripides
Bellerophon
fr. 286 f: 79n.10
fr. 292, 7: 194n.18
Trojans
886: 76n.5

Iamblichus
De mysteriis
I 5, 15.5-11: 36n.22

Plato
Alcibiades I
113D1-8: 1n.2
116D3: 1n.2
129C4-130A1: 201n.57
130C1-3: 90n.50
Apology
20C1-3: 151n.14
21D2-7: 151n.14
22B9-D4: 82n.21
23B2-4: 151n.14
28D6-10: 129n.39
29B6-7: 129n.39
29E5-30A2: 139n.70
30A8-B4: 139n.70, 140n.73
30A10-B4: 87n.40
30B2-4: 16n.44
30C5-D5: 139n.70
31C4-D6: 39n.32
33C4-7: 202n.58
37A5: 75n.1, 149n.6
37C7: 123n.21
38A5-6: 121n.16
41C8-D2: 139n.70
Charmides
156E-157E: 89n.48
160E7-11: 18n.49
165B4-C2: 151n.14
166C7-D6: 151n.14
167E1-5: 123n.24
173A7-D5: 87n.40
174B12-C3: 172n.6

Plato (cont.)
Cratylus
  386E1: 32n.11
Critias
  121A7-B7: 205n.65
Crito
  40A6-7: 129n.39
  47D-E: 89n.48
  48B4-10: 139n.70
  48C6-D5: 129n.39
  48C6-49B6: 40n.33
  49A4-5: 76n.4
  49B-C: 78n.8
  49B8: 129n.39
  50 C-51 C: 114n.109
Euthydemus
  278E3-6: 32n.11, 57n.92
  279A-C: 31n.9
  279A8-B3: 87n.38
  279B4-C4: 87n.38
  281B-D: 18n.49
  282A1-7: 57n.92
  282D2-E5: 87n.39
Euthyphro
  5A7-C5: 151n.14
  7B: 191n.7
  10A2-3: 54n.83
  11A7: 35n.20
  12C3: 24n.70
  15C12: 151n.14
  15E5-16A4: 151n.14
Gorgias
  447A-454B: 184n.59
  452B1: 16n.44
  452C1-2: 16n.44
  452C5: 16n.44
  452D3-4: 16n.44
  455B8: 42n.38
  459C8-D3: 10n.28
  460B10-13: 86n.36
  465A: 82n.21
  466A-468E: 134n.55
  466A4-467C4: 77n.7
  466B1-468E5: 129n.36
  467 C-468E: 62n.116
  467E4-6: 88n.46
  468A-B: 31n.9
  468B1-4: 32n.11, 124n.29
  468B2-6: 129n.38
  469B12: 129n.39
  470E4-11: 139n.70
  472C6-D1: 172n.6
  473A2-475E6: 78n.8
  474D4: 60n.107
  474D4-E7: 29n.1
  476A2-D4: 78n.8
  477B-480E: 89n.48
  477B3-4: 80n.14
  482Cff.: 107n.98
  483E3: 77n.6
  488A3: 75n.1, 149n.6
  491E8: 97n.70
  495E2-499B3: 135n.57
  499B4-500A6: 156n.22
  499E: 31n.9
  500A4-6: 141n.74
  500C3-4: 105n.92
  500D6-10: 105n.93
  501A: 82n.21
  502B1-3: 82n.22
  503D5ff.: 105n.94
  503E4ff.: 42n.38
  504B-505B: 89n.48
  506C9-E5: 106n.95
  506D7: 174n.16
  506E1-4: 42n.38
  507A5-C7: 55n.87
  507B8-C7: 139n.70
  507C2-3: 87n.38
  507E6-508A8: 107n.96
  508E: 129n.39
  509A4-6: 151n.14
  512A-B: 78n.8
  521E6-522A7: 220n.122
  522E2: 123n.21
  527C1-2: 78n.8
  527C5-6: 78n.8
Hippias Major
  286C8-E2: 151n.14
  295C2-3: 60n.107
  304D4-E5: 151n.14
Laches
  184E11-185E6: 82n.21
  186B8-C5: 151n.14
  186D8-E3: 151n.14
  191C8-E1: 123n.24
  192B9-D9: 18n.49
  192 C-D: 60n.107
  194C7-D9: 82n.21
  199C4-D1: 82n.22
  200E2-5: 151n.14
Laws
  1.624A1-628E1: 215n.100
  1.631B-D: 16n.44
  1.631 C: 103n.87
  1.631C5-D1: 100n.78
  1.644C8-9: 153n.17
  1.644D7-645B1: 154n.21
  1.644D7-645E6: 199n.45
  1.645A1 f.: 212n.94

Index Locorum
253

2.659D4: 24n.70
3.688 C-D: 206n.70
3.689A1-B4: 15n.42
3.689A5-C3: 208n.85
3.690B8-C1: 219n.120
3.690C1-3: 211n.92
3.696B: 103n.87
3.696Bff.: 186n.66
4.709E: 103n.87
4.709E6-710A4: 186n.66
4.710A5: 100n.79
4.714A2: 211n.92
4.716C4-5: 111n.104
4.716C4-6: 191n.5
4.716D1-2: 191n.5
4.716Eff.: 220n.125
4.717A6-B6: 190n.3
4.722B5-C2: 220n.123
4.731B: 149n.6
5.731 C-D: 75n.1
5.731D6-732B4: 63n.119, 157n.24
5.732A: 153n.17
5.734B-C: 164n.35
5.737A-738B: 220n.124
5.739B8-E7: 214n.98
5.739D3-4: 220n.125
6.757B-C: 107n.97
7.798D3-5: 147n.2
7.804B3: 199n.45
8.832C2: 221n.127
9.860D1-3: 149n.6
9.861E1-4: 150n.10
9.862A2-B1: 150n.12
8.862A7: 150n.8
9.862B5-C4: 150n.8
8.862B7-8: 150n.8
8.862C1: 150n.8
9.857C2-E5: 220n.123
9.863A3-864C1: 208n.83
9.863A7-B9: 151n.14
9.863B3-C1: 165n.36
9.863C1-D4: 151n.13, 201n.57
9.863E2: 208n.84
9.863E3: 154n.21
9.864A1-2: 201n.57, 208n.85
9.864B-C: 165n.36
9.864B6-7: 153n.17, 159n.27
9.870A-B: 153n.17
9.875A1-B1: 214n.97,98
9.875B7-8: 123n.21
9.875 C-D2: 219n.120
9.881A-B: 168n.46
10.885B4-9: 194n.20
10.886B: 153n.17
10.889B1-E1: 195n.23
10.889D6-E5: 214n.99
10.889E5-890A2: 195n.24
10.892Aff.: 195n.21
10.892A4: 195n.22
10.892A4-5: 197n.34
10.892C3-4: 197n.34
10.893Bff.: 195n.25
10.894B8-C1: 195n.25
10.895E10-896A2: 195n.26
10.896A5-B1: 206n.72
10.896C1-2: 197n.34
10.896D5-8: 165n.39
10.896E8-897B5: 195n.27
10.897B1-2: 196n.32
10.897D3: 196n.31
10.898C6-8: 194n.18
10.899B5: 197n.35
10.899B5-8: 197n.38
10.899D4-905D1: 197n.36
10.900C8-D3: 191n.8
10.900E1-8: 206n.73
10.902A: 153n.17
10.902A1-4: 198n.41
10.902B8-9: 198n.39
10.903B4-C5: 198n.41
10.903C4-5: 206n.71
10.903D-904 C: 206n.69
10.903D1: 153n.17
10.903D3-E1: 150n.8, 198n.43
10.904A: 190n.3
10.904B2-5: 202n.60
10.904B8-C2: 198n.42
10.904B8-D3: 150n.8
10.904C6-7: 165n.39
10.905B7: 153n.17
10.905C2: 153n.17
10.905E5-907B7: 197n.33
10.906A7-B3: 197n.35, 206n.73
10.906B: 206n.69
10.906C2-6: 207n.80
11.923A6-B2: 218n.114
11.925D5-E5: 218n.114
12.941B: 153n.17
12.941B2-C2: 191n.8
12.942A-C: 218n.114
12.957C6 f.: 212n.94
12.960Dff.: 153n.17
12.963E: 103n.87
12.963Eff.: 186n.66
12.967D4-E1: 197n.34
12.968A1-4: 186n.66
12.968A2: 100n.79

Lysis
212A4-7: 151n.14
216D2: 64n.124

Plato (cont.)
   217B4: 61n.112
   218A-B: 201n.57
   219C1-D5: 62n.116
   219D7: 61n.112
   220B7: 64n.121
   221B7: 61n.112
   221D3: 64n.122
   221E3-6: 36n.24, 48n.59, 61n.112
   222C3: 64n.123
   222C3-5: 32n.11
   222D2: 61n.112
   223B4-8: 151n.14
Menexenus
   239A1-5: 216n.104
Meno
   72A2-5: 202n.60
   77A-78 C: 134n.55
   77A-78B: 206n.70
   77B2-78B2: 84n.30
   77C1-2: 75n.1
   78A6: 32n.11
   81 C-D11: 107n.96
   87C5-89A6: 90n.51
   87D-88 C: 18n.49
   88C3: 18n.49, 57n.92
   97B1-7: 86n.37
   97E-98B: 102n.84, 142n.76
Parmenides
   130B1-5: 174n.15
   130B7-9: 35n.19
   130E5ff.: 175n.17
   131A8-9: 174n.15
   132B2: 72n.146
   132B3-C11: 4n.14
   132D2: 46n.54, 191n.10
   133C4: 35n.20
   140A1-3: 71n.143
   142B5-6: 19n.53, 70n.139, 176n.26
   142B5-C2: 175n.18
   142D1-5: 175n.19
   143A5-6: 176n.26
   144A6: 72n.146
   149C5: 72n.146
   150B8: 72n.146
   151D3: 72n.146
   158C4: 72n.146
Phaedo
   60D8-E7: 200n.50
   62E2: 123n.21
   65D4-7: 35n.19
   65D13: 35n.20
   66B3ff.: 79n.13, 179n.39
   68C5-69A3: 100n.78
   69B6-7: 100n.77

   75C10-D2: 35n.19
   75E6-11: 125n.31
   76B9-12: 85n.33
   76D7-9: 35n.19
   77A2: 35n.20
   78D1: 35n.20
   81B1-C6: 205n.67
   81Dff.: 193n.16
   82A10-B3: 55n.87, 93n.59, 100n.78, 141n.75
   82Eff.: 36n.24
   83C5-8: 182n.51
   87A11-B3: 100n.77, 141n.75
   92A4-102A9: 47n.58
   94C9-D6: 95n.66
   95A4-102A9: 166n.40, 196n.28
   99B3-4: 166n.41
   99B5-6: 41n.36
   99C5-6: 58n.96
   113Dff.: 199n.44
Phaedrus
   237D6-9: 79n.13, 159n.27, 179n.39
   244A4-10: 201n.52
   244A8-B3: 201n.55
   245C5-9: 195n.25
   245C5-246A2: 195n.26
   245C9: 206n.72
   246A6-7: 41n.36
   246 C-D: 190n.3
   246C4-6: 168n.49
   247A-E: 197n.34
   247A7: 206n.73
   247 C-E: 190n.4
   247C3-E6: 191n.10
   247D1-5: 192n.13
   249A-C: 199n.44
   249B5-6: 200n.51
   249B5-D3: 201n.54
   249C5-6: 192n.13, 197n.38
   249C6: 192n.14
   249D4ff.: 201n.52
   250C4: 201n.53
   252C3-253C6: 55n.85
   256A5-B3: 104n.90
   260E5-6: 82n.24
   266B3-7: 174n.16
   270B-C: 89n.48
Philebus
   11B4: 171n.2
   11B9-C2: 171n.2
   11D4-6: 171n.3
   11D11-E3: 172n.4
   12B-13D: 173n.7
   12D3: 153n.17
   13B7: 171n.2
   14B1-7: 173n.8

Index Locorum 255

14B4: 171n.2
14D4-E4: 173n.10
15B1-8: 174n.11
15D4: 58n.97
16A4-B3: 175n.22
16C1-17A5: 69n.138
16C2-3: 174n.16
16C7-D8: 109n.99
16C9-10: 176n.23
16C10-D2: 174n.13
16D3-7: 174n.13
16D7: 72n.146
16D7-E2: 174n.13
20B7-9: 172n.4
20B8: 171n.2
20 C-21A: 57n.92
20D: 31n.9
20D4-6: 53n.80
20D7-10: 134n.55, 13n.37
22A1-6: 172n.4
22C1-2: 171n.2
22D7: 177n.33
22D7-8: 52n.76, 178n.37
23 C-26D: 20n.57
23 C-27 C: 69n.138
23C4-D1: 109n.99
23C4-D8: 176n.27
24A1-B2: 177n.34
24A1-25B3: 176n.24
26D4-5: 177n.30
26D7-9: 176n.25, 185n.63
26E1-31A10: 109n.101
27B8-9: 176n.25
29B10: 176n.27
29C2: 72n.146, 176n.27
29D2: 176n.27
29D6: 176n.27
30C3: 176n.27
30D: 190n.3
31A7-10: 177n.34
31D4-32B5: 178n.36
33B8-9: 190n.3
35B3-4: 123n.25
35C6-D3: 109n.100
38A6-41A5: 180n.47
39C4-5: 180n.47
40A9-12: 180n.47
40E-42 C: 180n.47
40E6-10: 180n.47
41C4-7: 123n.25
42 C-44A: 180n.47
45D2-5: 177n.34
48C7-E11: 201n.57
53 C-55B: 179n.41
54C1-4: 185n.63

54C6: 177n.34
54D1: 177n.34
56D-57A: 184n.54
57D: 184n.54
58B9-59B8: 178n.36
59A-B: 166n.40
60A9: 171n.2
61A1-2: 179n.40
63E8: 123n.21
64A2-3: 40n.32
64E9-D3: 172n.5
65A-B: 23n.66
65A1-5: 60n.108, 42n.40, 110n.102, 179n.42
64E5-7: 180n.44
65B7: 178n.37
65C3: 178n.37
65D3: 178n.37
66A6: 21n.58
66A6-7: 111n.104
66A6-8: 176n.29
66D7-8: 171n.2
67A5-8: 53n.80
Protagoras
319: 82n.22
333D9-10: 16n.44, 29n.1
339E5ff.: 56n.88
345D8: 75n.1
345D9-E6: 75n.2
349E: 60n.107
352A8-C7: 137n.65
352C2-7: 75n.1
352D-358D: 131
352E5-353A2: 132n.49
353D5-354E5: 134n.54
354B5-7: 132n.48
354D8: 134n.54
355A5ff.: 152n.16
356D4: 186n.65
358C7: 149n.6
354E6-7: 135n.59
354E8-355A2: 132n.49
355Aff.: 206n.70
355A1-2: 132n.47
355A1-6: 132n.48
355B1: 135n.60
357B5-6: 103n.88, 133n.53
358B6-C1: 75n.1, 132n.47, 134n.55
358C1-3: 135n.58
358C6-D2: 32n.11, 132n.47, 134n.55
359E5-7: 18n.49
361B5-7: 90n.51
Republic
1.331 C-D: 66n.127
1.335C1-7: 139n.70
1.335E5-6: 26n.74

Plato (cont.)
1.337E4-5: 151n.14
1.338C2ff.: 40n.34
1.338E3-4: 41n.35
1.340Cff.: 14in.74
1.341–342: 184n.59
1.340D2-341A4: 31n.8
1.344A3-6: 97n.70
1.344B1-C2: 97n.70
1.344C5-9: 31n.8
1.347E2-4: 97n.70
1.348D2: 31n.8
1.352D2-4: 97n.70
1.353E7-8: 202n.60
1.354A-B: 1n.2
2.357C2-3: 89n.48
2.365D-E: 194n.20
2.367Aff.: 92n.56
2.367C6-D3: 89n.48
2.367C8-9: 79n.12, 92n.57
2.368E2-3: 215n.101
2.369B7-9: 214n.99
2.369C1-4: 214n.99
2.378B-380 C: 191n.7
2.379B-C: 54n.83, 206n.73
2.379B1: 191n.8
2.379B11: 1n.2
2.379C2-7: 203n.62
2.379C4-5: 197n.35
2.380 C: 54n.83
2.380D1-383C7: 192n.14
2.382A4-D4: 216n.105
2.382B1-4: 216n.106
2.382B8-9: 216n.107
2.382C7-D4: 216n.108
3.389B-C: 220n.122
3.391C4: 84n.32
3.412D4-7: 95n.63
3.414B-415D: 215n.102
4.420B3-421C6: 214n.98
4.422E4-423B1: 215n.100
4.423B9-10: 97n.72
4.423D3-6: 83n.28, 97n.72
4.429B8-C3: 188n.71
4.430A3-B2: 104n.90
4.430B6-9: 188n.71
4.430E7-431A6: 98n.73, 158n.25
4.435B1-2: 84n.32
4.436A8-B4: 124n.27
4.436B8-C1: 112n.107
4.437D8-E6: 122n.18
4.437D9-438A2: 123n.25
4.439A4-7: 122n.18
4.439D2: 84n.32
4.439D7: 122n.20

4.441A8-B2: 158n.26
4.441E3: 98n.73
4.442C10-D1: 123n.22
4.442D2: 98n.73
4.443B-444E: 89n.48
4.443C9-D1: 100n.78
4.443C9-A2: 160n.28
4.443D4: 98n.73
4.443E1: 15n.42, 41n.36, 83n.28, 97n.72
4.444D12-E1: 80n.14
4.444E6-445A4: 78n.8, 94n.61
5.459E6-460A6: 215n.102
5.462A2-B3: 83n.28, 97n.72
5.462B1-2: 41n.36
5.470C5-10: 84n.32
5.473A1-B1: 220n.126
5.473C11-D6: 219n.120
5.476A9-480A13: 86n.35
5.476A10-D5: 65n.126
5.477C6-D2: 103n.87
6.485A-487A: 103n.87
6.496B-C: 44n.46
6.500B8-C8: 55n.85
6.503B-D: 103n.87
6.504C1-4: 176n.29, 185n.60
6.504D2-505A4: 96n.68
6.504E2-3: 185n.60
6.505A2-4: 1n.2, 29n.1, 94n.61
6.505B5-6: 132n.47
6.505C5-6: 171n.2
6.505C6: 132n.47
6.505D5-9: 162n.32
6.505D5-E5: 13n.37, 32n.11
6.505E1-2: 40n.32, 124n.29, 134n.55, 166n.43, 200n.48
6.506D7-E1: 68n.130
6.507B4-6: 35n.19
6.508A9-B7: 34n.14, 81n.16
6.508B6-7: 12n.36
6.508D10-E2: 43n.42, 49n.61
6.508E1-4: 34n.14, 81n.16
6.508E4-5: 43n.43, 181n.49
6.509A3: 49n.61, 81n.20
6.509A6: 30n.6
6.509B1-3: 45n.47
6.509B5-9: 23n.67, 30n.6, 46n.56, 81n.19
6.509B6-7: 34n.14, 45n.48, 81n.16
6.509B8-9: 49n.62
6.509B9-10: 3n.8
6.509E6-510A3: 81n.20
6.510B6-7: 1n.1
6.511B2-C2: 30n.4
6.511B5-6: 1n.1, 48n.60
6.511B6-7: 81n.17,18
6.511B8: 73n.149

Index Locorum 257

6.511B8-C2: 81n.16
7.516C1-2: 13n.38, 45n.47
7.516E7-517A2: 219n.121
7.517B7-C4: 34n.14, 199n.46
7.517C1: 1n.2, 24n.70, 114n.110
7.517C2-3: 81n.16
7.517C3-4: 1n.4, 87n.40
7.518C9: 30n.6
7.528D9-10: 100n.79
7.518D9-519A5: 93n.59
7.523A8: 40n.32
7.526E4-5: 30n.6, 53n.79
7.531D5: 40n.32
7.532C6-7: 48n.60
7.533C3-6: 30n.4
7.533C8-D4: 1n.1
7.533C9: 48n.60
7.534B8: 48n.60
7.534B8-10: 1n.1
7.534B8-C1: 44n.45
7.534.B8-D1: 29n.3
7.534C4-5: 37n.26
7.537C7: 177n.32, 200n.49
7.540A9: 43n.44
8.544C7: 84n.32
8.543C4-6: 55n.85
8.544B-C: 211n.92
8.546A-B: 207n.81
8.550B1-7: 159n.27
8.551D5-7: 97n.72
8.552A7-B2: 187n.69
8.554D9-10: 15n.42, 41n.36
8.560Cff.: 103n.87
9.575E2-576A6: 96n.67
9.577D13-E1: 77n.7
9.577E1-2: 129n.36
9.580D6-7: 127n.34
9.580E2-581A1: 124n.28
9.588B-590A: 83n.28
8.589A7-B1: 90n.50
9.589C6: 75n.1, 149n.6
9.590C7-D6: 221n.127
9.591A10-B7: 78n.8
10.602 C-605 C: 112n.107
10.602D6-E2: 136n.64
10.604D9: 123n.23
10.608E-611A: 169n.50
10.608C1-E6: 35n.19
10.611B1: 124n.27
10.611D8-612A6: 36n.24
10.617E: 54n.83
10.617E4-5: 198n.42
10.619B7-D1: 100n.78
10.619C8: 55n.87, 93n.59, 169n.53

Sophist
219B4-6: 185n.63
228A4-B4: 15n.42
235D6-E2: 43n.41, 60n.106, 180n.44
236A4: 43n.41
236C3-4: 60n.106
236C4: 43n.41
244B-245E: 84n.29, 177n.31
247E5: 49n.62
251A5-C7: 174n.11
253C6-D3: 188n.72
263A2: 58n.97
263E12-264A2: 160n.29

Statesman
258B3-5: 187n.70
267A8-C3: 82n.23
267D7: 188n.72
268D-274D: 183n.53
269 C-D: 183n.53
269D5-7: 192n.14, 205n.67
270A1-2: 207n.78
273A1-E5: 205n.67
273B-D: 183n.53
276E6-8: 218n.116
276E12: 188n.72
280A1: 188n.72
283D7-9: 185n.62
283E3-6: 185n.61
283E8: 35n.20
284A5-B2: 186n.64
284B9-E8: 268–270, 184n.54
284D1-2: 134n.56
284D6-8: 184n.57
284E6-8: 188n.73
287D4: 187n.70
291B-C: 184n.55
291B1-C3: 218n.115
291E1-292D1: 218n.117
292B-293 C: 219n.120
292B6-D5: 187n.70
293C5-E6: 213n.96
293D4-E2: 218n.115
294B1-2: 153n.18
296A-297B: 220n.122
296B5-D4: 214n.98
296C5: 187n.70
296D8-E4: 214n.98
300A4-7: 218n.117
300B3-4: 211n.92
300E7: 187n.70
303A-B: 211n.92
303 C: 184n.55
305A12-B11: 103n.87
305E-306 C: 186n.66
306B9-10: 104n.91

Plato (cont.)
   306Cff.: 186n.67
   309C5-8: 188n.71
   311B7-C6: 183n.52
   311C1-2: 187n.70
Symposium
   186B-C: 60n.110
   189D2-193C5: 60n.110
   201E5: 57n.90
   202A9: 100n.79
   202E6-7: 58n.96
   204A1-B5: 58n.98
   204D4: 57n.90
   204D7: 57n.91
   204E: 34n.15
   204E1-2: 64n.124
   204E6-205A3: 57n.92
   205A6-7: 32n.11
   205D1-3: 57n.93
   205E6-7: 64n.123
   205E7-206A4: 57n.92, 134n.55
   206B1-8: 58n.99
   206E2: 57n.90
   207D-208B: 126n.32
   207D1-3: 64n.122
   207E1-5: 125n.31
   207E1-208A7: 126n.32
   209A5-8: 192n.11
   210A-212B: 22n.62
   211D1-3: 59n.104, 121n.16
   211E4-212A7: 59n.102
   212A1-3: 81n.17
   212A5-6: 100n.77, 145n.81, 192n.11
Theaetetus
   176A5-9: 203n.61
   176A5-C2: 55n.85
   176B1-2: 9n.25, 180n.46
   186A8: 35n.19
   186A9: 1n.3
   187Aff.: 199n.47
Timaeus
   28C3-4: 50n.63
   29A2: 50n.64
   29E1-2: 206n.73
   29E2: 50n.64,65
   29E2-3: 50n.66
   29E1-3: 177n.35, 196n.30
   30A1-2: 50n.67
   30A5: 185n.63
   30C1: 197n.37
   30C2-D1: 196n.30
   30C2-31A: 52n.74
   31B8-C4: 15n.42
   32A5-7: 15n.42
   32B3-C4: 15n.42
   34B3: 196n.29
   34B8: 52n.72
   37A5: 205n.68
   39E7-8: 52n.73
   40E3-4: 52n.77
   41A: 190n.3
   41A-B: 190n.3, 193n.15
   41D1-3: 198n.39
   41E1-4: 166n.43
   41E2-3: 40n.32, 191n.10
   42E5-6: 100n.76
   44B8-C4: 167n.44
   46C7: 166n.42
   46D1: 166n.42
   46D5-E2: 195n.25
   46E3-6: 166n.42
   46E5: 185n.63
   47E4: 52n.73
   47E4-5: 185n.62
   48A6-7: 205n.66
   48C2-6: 51n.70
   48E7: 206n.74
   51D5-7: 208n.82
   51E6-52D1: 208n.86
   53C5: 206n.72
   53D4-7: 51n.70
   54D4-5: 206n.72
   68E1-3: 185n.62
   68E4-7: 166n.42
   69B3: 185n.63
   75E5-48A5: 52n.75
   76D6: 166n.42
   77B1-6: 122n.18
   86B1-87B9: 151n.14, 164n.35
   86D7-E1: 75n.1
   86D7-8: 149n.6
   87B4: 167n.44
   87C5-6: 42n.40, 110n.102, 179n.42
   88A8-B2: 79n.13, 179n.39
   89E3-90A2: 180n.46
   89E3-90D7: 198n.40
   90A-D: 110n.103
   90A2-4: 168n.47, 202n.59
   90C2-3: 168n.48
   90C5: 202n.59
   90D4: 202n.59
   90E-92 C: 165n.38
   90E-91D: 193n.16
   92B7: 167n.44
   92C7-9: 181n.50
[Plato]
  Epinomis
   978B3-4: 35n.20
Plotinus
  Enneads
   III.2 [47], 9.10–16: 198n.41
   V.1 [10], 1.1ff.: 46n.51
   V.5 [32], 4.13: 34n.17
   V.8 [31], 4.4–11: 84n.29

VI.7 [38], 2: 84n.29
VI.7 [38], 25.12–14: 36n.22
VI.8 [39], 10.34: 35n.17
Proclus
Elements of Theology
Props. 25–39: 99n.75
In Alc. I
106.16–17: 169n.51
187, 5–8: 194n.19
In Parm.
III.811.6–7: 36n.21
In Rep.
Essay 10, 1.269.4–287.17: 36n.21
1.269.19–270.20: 36n.23
1.270.19–2701.25: 36n.22
1.278.22–279.2: 36n.22
In Tim.
I 304.5: 52n.72
I 305.8: 52n.72
I 359.20–360.4: 52n.72
Platonic Theology
I 14, p. 66.6: 196n.32

Sextus Empiricus
Adversus Mathematicos
VII, 16: 3n.7
X, 261: 72n.144
X, 281–283: 72n.147
XI, 64–67: 88n.44
Simplicius
In Phys.
151, 6–19: 71n.141
453, 22–30: 71n.141
454, 8–9: 72n.144
545, 23–25: 71n.141
Stobaeus
Eclogues
2.84.18–85.11: 88n.43
Syrianus
In Meta.
168.33–35: 134n.56

Theophrastus
Metaphysics
6b11-16: 12n.34, 73n.149

General Index

absolute simplicity, 20, 41, 49, 53, 71, 83, 109
absolutism, 37, 40, 129–131, 142–145
Adam, J. A., 29, 51, 97, 112
Adams, R., 10
Ademollo, F., 126
Alcinous, 3, 50, 192
Alexander of Aphrodisias, 148
altruism vs egotism, 63, 170
Anaxagoras, 23, 47, 166, 178
Anderson, M., 92
Annas, J., 3, 4, 6, 9, 32, 35, 38, 82, 86, 87, 88, 89, 90, 123
Anscombe, E., 11
Antiphon, 6
Apelt, O., 24
appetite, 95, 109, 125–127, 136
Archer-Hind, R.D., 171, 205
argument from design, 195
Aristotle
  on division of sciences, 2, 209
  on ethics, 161
  on politics, 187, 212
  on theology, 190, 193
Aristotle's testimony, 20, 51, 67–73
Aristoxenus, 70
assimilation to god, 55, 193
Atticus, 52
auxiliary causes (συναίτιαι), 166

Baker, S., 2, 33, 36
Baracchi, C., 209
Barney, R., 5, 13, 34, 134
beauty, 23, 43, 60, 110, 179–182
  apparent vs real, 59–60
becoming one out of many, 41, 83, 96, 98
Beere, J., 95
Beierwaltes, W., 42
belief (δόξα), 85, 102–103, 142, 208
Benitez, E.E., 50, 51, 178
Benson, H.J., 4, 79, 116, 152
Berman, S., 4

Berti, E., 45, 71
Blackson, T., 9, 132
Blanshard, B., 18
Bobonich, C., 112, 167, 186
Bodéüs, R., 191
Bonazzi, M., 190
Bordt, M., 50, 191, 197
Boyd, R., 21
Boys-Stones, G., 9, 50, 91, 100
Bradley, F. H., 112
Brenner, A., 10
Brickhouse, T. and Smith, N. D., 4, 9, 78, 82, 116
Brink, D., 16, 17, 21
Brisson, L., 70
Broadie, S., 1, 36, 43, 44, 48, 67, 200, 207
Brown, L., 32
Brunschwig, J., 69
Burkert, W., 107
Burnyeat, M., 5, 14, 32, 67, 112
Bury, R. G., 45
Butchvarov, P., 18, 25
Butler, T., 9

Callard, A., 9, 116, 131, 133, 136
Campbell, D., 165
Carone, G., 165, 195, 198
Cartledge, P., 210
Catana, L., 11
Centrone, B., 100, 103
Chan, B., 97
Chappell, T., 11, 31, 114, 138, 179
Chlup, R., 99
Clark, J., 137, 152
Clarke-Doane, J., 21
consequentialism, 25–27
continence (*enkrateia*), 136–137, 167, 181
Cook, A. B., 51
Cooper, J., 2, 58, 103, 121, 123, 124, 154
Cornford, F. M., 79, 160, 165, 205
Cradle Argument, 108
craft (τέχνη), 10, 44, 82, 91, 141

260

General Index

Crombie, I. M., 38
Cross, R. C. and Woozley, A. D., 4
culpable ignorance, 150–160, 167

Davidson, D., 2
De Strycker, E., 73
De Vogel, C., 51
Delcomminette, S., 29, 46, 174, 176, 177, 178, 180
Demiurge, 50–57, 72, 110, 177, 181, 185, 192–198, 204–209
Democritus, 33, 81, 130
Denyer, N., 45
deontology, 25
desire, 13, 113, 120
   apparent vs real, 57, 114, 124
   first-order vs second-order, 127
   horizontal vs vertical, 179
Desjardins, R., 15
Destrée, P., 59
Devereux, D., 9, 103, 116, 123
Diès, A., 53
Dillon, J., 3
Dodds, E.R., 107
Dorter, K., 30, 37
Drefcinski, S., 55
Dreier, J., 18
Duffy, H., 218
duty. See right
Dybikowski, J., 180

early dialogues, 119
Eklund, M., 4
El Murr, D., 2
elenctic knowledge, 119, 141
Enders, M., 51, 196
Enoch, D., 11, 14
Epicurus, 33, 81, 130, 182
Erler, M., 2
Euripides, 76, 79, 194
Evans, M., 9, 131, 135
evil, 202–209

Ferber, R., 123, 128, 132
Ferber, R. and Damschen, G., 30
Ferrari, F., 45, 50, 52, 81
Ferrari, G. R. F., 60
first principle, 4, 14–17, 223
Foot, P., 95
Form of the Good, 15, 35–37, 44, 80, 90, 102, 184, 204
Forms, 30, 39, 46, 54, 56, 69, 82, 119, 174, 177, 197
Frankfurt, H., 125, 148, 170
Frede, M., 56, 123, 131
Freeland, C., 133

Gaiser, K., 71
Gauthier, R. A. and Jolif, J. Y., 101
Gersh, S., 99
Gerson, L., 1, 4, 12, 22, 30, 35, 47, 59, 68, 83, 86, 93, 117, 118, 129, 166, 177, 196
Gill, C., 165
goal (τέλος), 31, 35, 58
gods, 190–199, 207
Goetz, S., 148
good, 1–5, 15, 224
   common good, 213–219
   object of will vs object of desire, 88
   real vs apparent, 17, 26, 34, 37, 111–114, 124
Gosling, J., 46, 86, 178
Gosling, J. and Taylor, C. C. W., 133
Gould, J., 30, 118
Great and Small. See Indefinite Dyad
Griswold, C., 192, 201
Grube, G. M. A., 80
Guthrie, W. K. C., 50, 131

Hackforth, R., 197
Hager, F. P., 206
Halfwassen, J., 67, 71, 72
Hall, R. W., 15
Hampton, C., 15, 171, 174, 178, 179
Hanann, N., 76
Happ, H., 206
happiness, 34, 57, 94, 138–146
Haraldsen, V., 131, 133
Hardy, J., 9, 86
Hardy, J. and Rudebusch, G., 9
Harman, G., 21
Harte, V., 180
Hayward, M., 3, 21
hedonism, 131–134, 173
Hermann, F.-G., 73
Herzberg, S., 2, 36
Hitchcock, D., 34, 97
Höffe, O., 2
Hoffmann, M., 42
Horn, C., 2
Huemer, M., 157
Huffmann, C., 107
Hume, D., 33
Hurka, T., 19
hylomorphism, 20, 70

Iamblichus, 36
Idea of the Good, 1–5, 12–28, 29–74, 90, 105–115, 119–121, 125–128, 141–146, 148, 161, 172, 178–187, 192–194, 202–209, 223
   as beyond οὐσία, 3, 12, 18, 25, 33–35, 37, 45, 46, 49, 52, 64, 70, 83, 92, 95–96, 111, 175, 199
   as cause/explanation, 46–49, 102

Idea of the Good (cont.)
  identical with the One, 17, 19, 43, 56, 67–74, 97, 99, 102, 109, 146, 172, 175, 179, 184–189
  as "overflowing," 12, 45, 49, 100, 197
  as principle/source, 41–45, 50, 130, 134, 185
  as superordinate, 8, 17, 18, 28, 36, 38, 44, 81, 114
  as unique, 48, 71
Ilievski, V., 52, 165, 203, 204, 206, 207
incommensurability, 89
incontinence (*akrasia*), 122, 128–138, 151, 159, 167, 181, 205
Indefinite Dyad, 20, 51, 69–73, 110, 186, 204, 207
integrative unity, 15–20, 42, 49, 83, 97, 98–111, 146, 170, 171–175, 182–187, 198, 214
intellect (νοῦς), 53, 109, 177, 196
intellectualism, 9, 120–122, 127, 131, 134, 141, 169, 173
intelligible realm, 30
Irani, T., 34
irrationalism, 121, 131, 169
Irwin, T., 4, 9, 64, 79, 82, 86, 101, 116, 123, 124, 126, 133, 138

Jaeger, W., 53
Johansen, T. K., 166
Jordan, J., 46
Jorgenson, C., 42, 166, 168, 198
Joyce, R., 7, 33, 217
justice, 29, 33, 92, 93, 98, 109, 114
  Form of, 24, 33, 84, 95

Kahn, C., 9, 46, 58, 62, 86, 116, 119, 121, 123, 126, 132, 143
Kamtekar, R., 9, 101, 124, 133
Kane, R., 162
Kant, I., 25–27, 113–115
Karamanolis, G., 55
Kauppinen, A., 154, 160
knowledge (ἐπιστήμη), 54–57, 80–87, 96, 137, 194
  is virtue, 101, 109, 120, 138
  of Forms, 82, 85, 95, 142
Korsgaard, C., 3, 46, 88, 95
Kosman, L. A., 63, 94
Krämer, H. J., 14, 42, 50, 62, 67, 68, 69, 70, 73, 184
Kraut, R., 8, 19, 60
Kronqvist, C., 60
Krüger, G., 57, 58

Lafrance, Y., 185
Laks, A., 220
Lane, M., 210
Lavecchia, S., 51, 53, 55, 67, 71
law of nature, 77
Layne, D., 201

Ledger, G. R., 118
legitimacy, 212–214, 219
Leiter, B., 23
Leslie, J., 14, 45
limit and unlimited, 20, 70, 109, 176–178, 207
Living Animal, 56, 110, 196–197, 206
Lodge, R., 15
Long, A. A., 50
Lorenz, H., 125, 167
Lott, M., 95
love (ἔρως), 57–61

Mabbott, J. D., 6
Mackenzie, M. M., 120, 121, 147, 151, 213, 219
Mackie, J. L., 58
madness (μανία), 163–168, 201
Männlein-Robert, I., 55
Márquez, X., 184, 188, 210, 219
matter, 69, 206–209
McCabe, M. M., 60, 91
McTighe, K., 62, 77
measure, 109–111, 134, 172, 180, 188
Menn, S., 36, 197
Merlan, P., 73
Meyer, S., 167
Miller, M., 15, 37, 45, 68, 185, 186
Mirus, C., 107
Mitsis, P., 33
Mohr, R., 53
Monteils-Laeng, L., 9, 102, 124
Moore, C., 123, 177
Moore, G. E., 11, 18
moral agency, 148, 155, 162
moral realism, 9–14, 21, 23–28, 29, 35, 49, 54, 61, 63, 74, 90, 92, 108, 110, 170, 182, 223
moral responsibility, 147–170
Morris, M., 131
Morrow, G., 192, 196
Moss, J., 123
Murdoch, I., 5, 11, 18, 56, 60, 67, 181

Nagel, T., 76
naturalism, 21, 47, 92, 166
nature (φύσις), 15, 46–47, 105–108, 110
necessity, 52, 205
Nehemas, A., 9, 116
Nettleship, R. L., 51
Nill, M., 6, 33
no one does wrong willingly, 75–77, 149–153, 159–160
noble falsehood, 215–217
nonnormative vs normative rationality, 124–128
normativity, 46, 54, 106, 128, 149, 161, 185
Numenius, 91

General Index

O'Brien, D., 103
O'Brien, M., 8, 9, 78, 151
objectivity, 5–8, 37, 78, 184
Oddie, G., 10
One, 15, 20, 23, 51, 69, 71–74, 106, 181
   as principle of limit/measure, 21, 110–111, 185
   as principle of unity, 17, 70, 97, 188
order. *See* structure
οὐσία, 27, 175

Pasnau, R., 131, 133
Penner, T., 3, 4, 9, 33, 34, 35, 37, 58, 67, 77, 79, 84, 103, 116, 118, 120, 121, 122, 123, 127, 128, 129, 130, 137, 144, 149
Penner, T. and Rowe, C., 30, 64, 120
Perl, E., 51, 53, 196
Petrucci, F., 100
philosopher, 95, 104
pleasure, 105, 173, 180
πλεονεξία, 107
Plotinus, 34, 36, 45, 84, 198
polis, 182–189, 190–222
Pradeau, J.-F., 183, 215
Prauscello, L., 103
Price, A.W., 59, 62, 112, 126, 167, 186
Prichard, H., 6, 24, 115
Proclus, 36, 52, 99, 169, 194, 196
πρῶτον φίλον, 61–67
prudentialism, 4–6, 25, 34, 37–40, 67, 77–81, 88–94, 102, 111, 120, 129, 144
Putnam, H., 5, 22, 94
Pythagoreanism, 74, 107

Railton, P., 10, 21, 26
Rawson, G., 35
Rea, M., 10, 21
Reale, G., 62
reason, 95, 108, 125, 156
Receptacle, 52, 204–209
recollection, 142, 201
Reed, D., 100
Reeve, C. D. C., 131
relativism, 38, 44, 48
remaining – procession – reversion, 99
Renaut, O., 166
Renz, U., 201
Rescher, N., 14
Rice, H., 50
Richard, M.-D., 68, 72
right, 24–26, 112–115
Rist, J., 4, 8, 21, 31, 33, 50, 217
Roberts, J., 150
Robin, L., 59, 207
Rodier, G., 185
Ross, W. D., 24, 73

Rowe, C., 2, 4, 9, 14, 32, 33, 38, 73, 116, 118, 121, 131, 188
Rowett, C., 216
Rudebusch, G., 4, 171, 185
Ruse, M., 22
Russell, D., 131

Sachs, D., 104
Santas, G., 46, 78, 94, 116, 131
Sartre, J.-P., 12
Saunders, T., 150, 153, 165, 199
Sayre, K., 46, 184
Schofield, M., 107, 215, 217
Schöpsdau, K., 152
Scott, D., 192
Sedley, D., 12, 42, 73, 83, 96, 120, 193, 203
Šegvić, H., 9, 75, 77, 131
Seifert, J., 46, 51
self
   as divided, 126, 154
   real or ideal, 127, 155, 159
self-knowledge, 201
self-love, 158
self-sufficiency, 53, 58
Senn, S. J., 87
Sheffield, F., 9
Shields, C., 36, 97
Shorey, P., 2, 4, 13, 33, 171
Sidgwick, H., 4, 33, 116
Singpurwalla, R., 58, 135
Smith, M., 10
Smith, N., 116, 118, 119, 145, 151
Socratic ethics, 4, 116–122, 128, 131, 138, 143
Socratic paradoxes, 8, 39, 78, 119, 144
Solmsen, F., 50, 191, 194, 198
soul
   of the cosmos, 196
   as embodied, 126, 163, 169
   immortal part, 110, 169
Speusippus, 14, 45, 69
Stalley, R. F., 91
statesman, 182–189, 210, 218
Stemmer, P., 4, 11, 95, 120
Stocker, M., 47
Stoic ethics, 87, 91, 148, 168
structure, 105, 108, 199
Sturgeon, N., 21
symmetry, 23, 43, 60, 110, 172, 179–182, 186, 188
Szlezák, T., 51, 62, 67, 81

Taylor, A.E., 47, 165
Taylor, C. C. W., 4, 8, 132
Thalberg, I., 180
Theophrastus, 12
Thesleff, H., 61

Timmermann, F., 4, 10, 30, 39
truth, 23, 34, 43, 60, 110, 179–182
truth-makers, 9, 10, 26, 27
tyrant, 30–35, 77–78, 88, 89, 95, 96, 114, 129, 144, 155, 218

unhypothetical first principle of all, 1, 11, 23, 35, 36, 41, 48, 67, 188, 208
unity, 111, 172, 176–178
  of action, 111
  of Form, 174
  generic vs specific, 36
universality, 5–8, 17, 22, 34–41, 56, 63, 78–80, 113, 145, 152, 184, 213
utilitarianism, 7, 40, 44, 214

values, 26, 27
Van Camp, J. and Canart, P., 191
van Inwagen, P., 147
Van Riel, G., 50, 150, 190, 191
Vasiliou, I., 59, 97, 133
Verdenius, W. J., 45, 50
vice, 103, 167, 181, 202–208
virtue, 29–32, 56, 80–91, 95–97, 105, 130, 138, 139, 141–143, 167, 180
  Form(s) of, 30, 59, 180
  gradations of, 100–105

philosophical or true virtue, 59, 64, 86, 93–105, 110, 141–143, 145, 181, 191–193
political or popular virtue, 60, 94, 96–105, 110, 141–143, 168, 181, 187
Vlastos, G., 3, 4, 62, 63, 64, 65, 79, 85, 87, 94, 101, 103, 116, 117, 118, 119, 121, 130, 139, 141, 206
Vogt, K., 5

Warren, J., 9
Watson, G., 17, 124
Weiss, R., 122
White, D., 183, 186
White, N., 4, 9, 29
Widerker, D., 148
Wilburn, J., 151, 154, 215
will (βούλησις), 114, 161
wisdom (σοφία), 90, 93, 100
Wolf, S., 161
Wolfsdorf, D., 131
Wolt, D., 169
Wreen, M., 38

Xenocrates, 3

Zeyl, D., 131
Zhao, M., 17

For EU product safety concerns, contact us at Calle de José Abascal, 56–1°, 28003 Madrid, Spain or eugpsr@cambridge.org.

www.ingramcontent.com/pod-product-compliance
Ingram Content Group UK Ltd.
Pitfield, Milton Keynes, MK11 3LW, UK
UKHW020238140226
468021UK00022B/713